Shojo Beat

Skip·Beat!

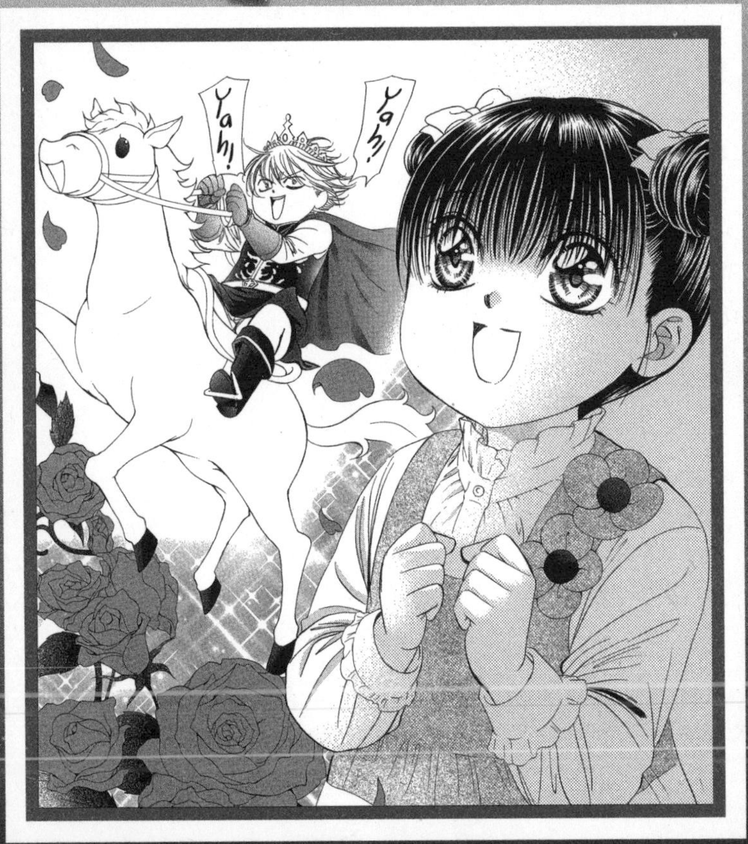
Yah!
Yah!

39

Skip·Beat!

Volume 39

CONTENTS

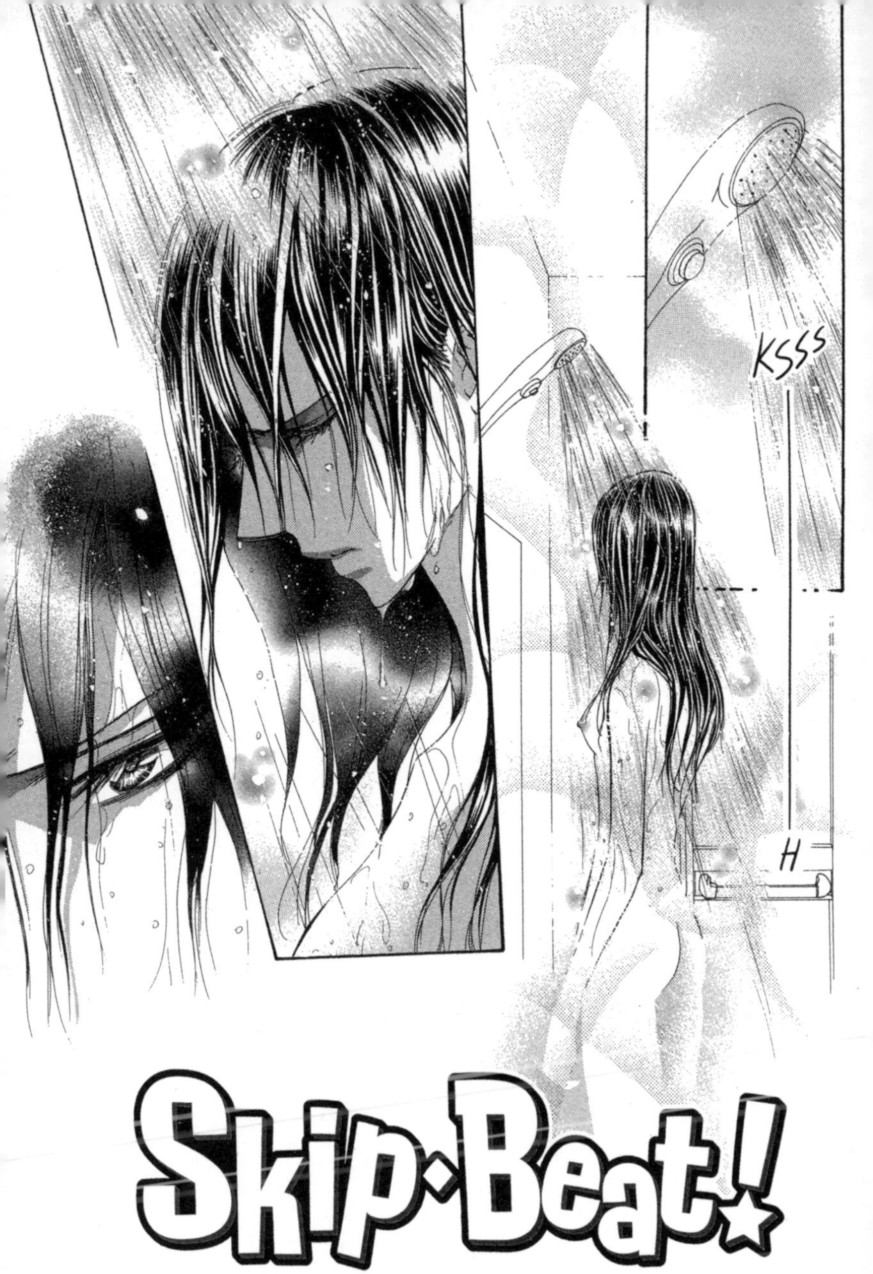
KSSS
H

Skip·Beat!

Act 231: Ground Call

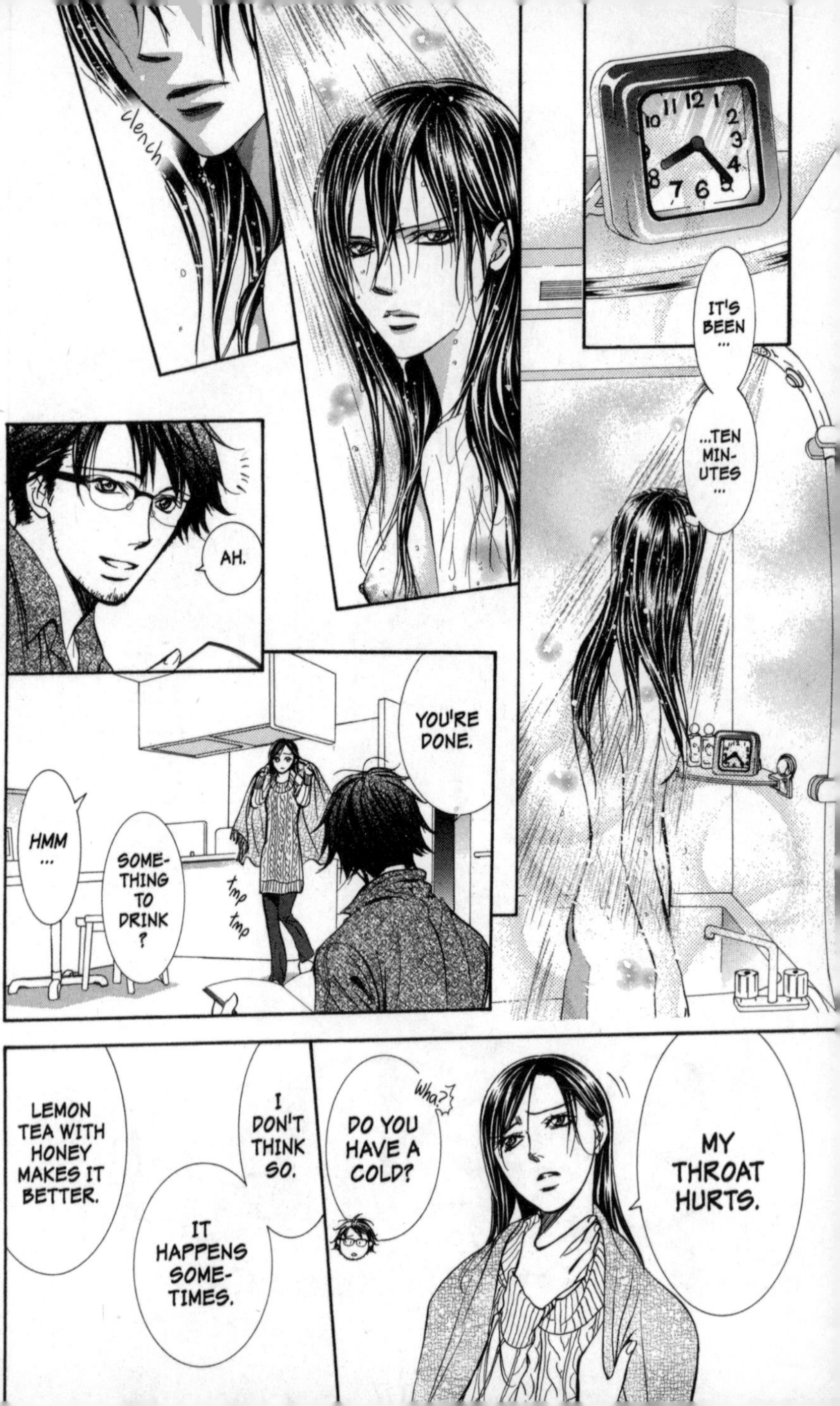
IT'S BEEN ...
...TEN MIN-UTES ...
clench
AH.
YOU'RE DONE.
tmp tmp
SOME-THING TO DRINK?
HMM ...
MY THROAT HURTS.
Wha?
DO YOU HAVE A COLD?
I DON'T THINK SO.
IT HAPPENS SOME-TIMES.
LEMON TEA WITH HONEY MAKES IT BETTER.

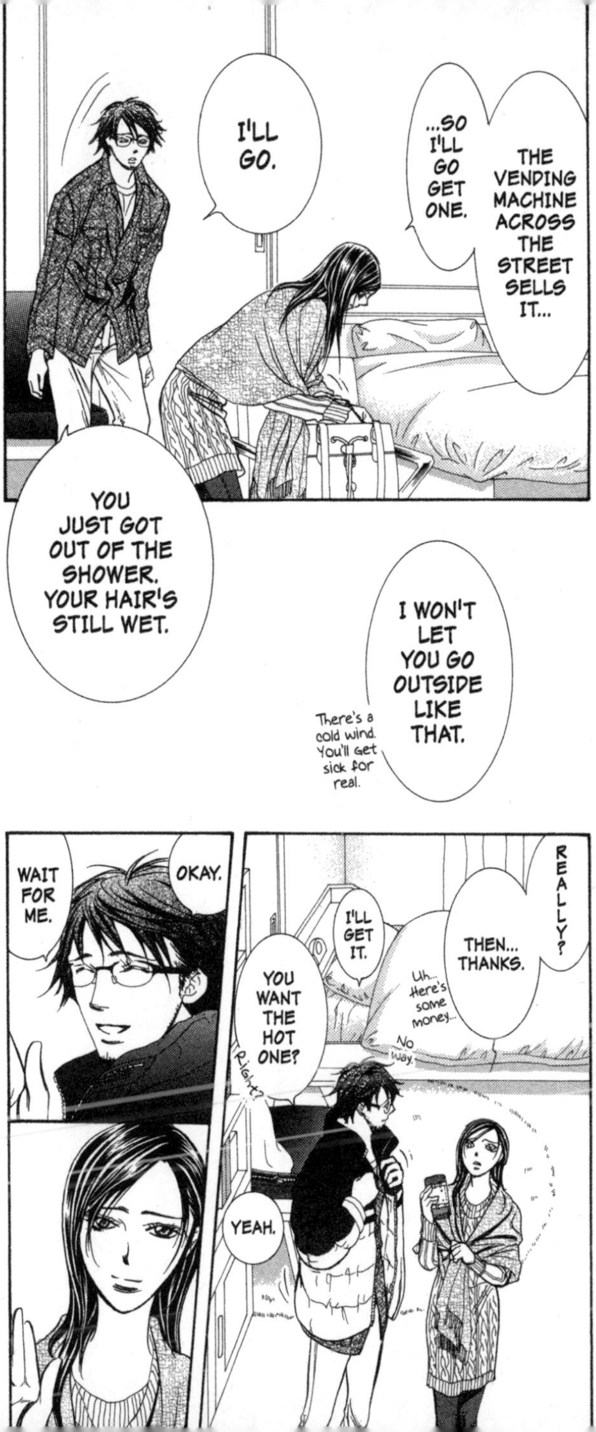
THE VENDING MACHINE ACROSS THE STREET SELLS IT...
...SO I'LL GO GET ONE.
I'LL GO.
YOU JUST GOT OUT OF THE SHOWER. YOUR HAIR'S STILL WET.
I WON'T LET YOU GO OUTSIDE LIKE THAT.
There's a cold wind. You'll get sick for real.
REALLY?
THEN... THANKS.
Uh... Here's some money...
I'LL GET IT.
No way.
YOU WANT THE HOT ONE?
Right?
YEAH.
OKAY.
WAIT FOR ME.
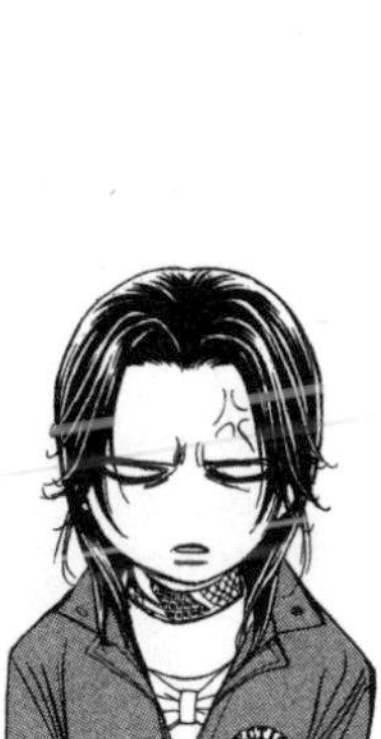

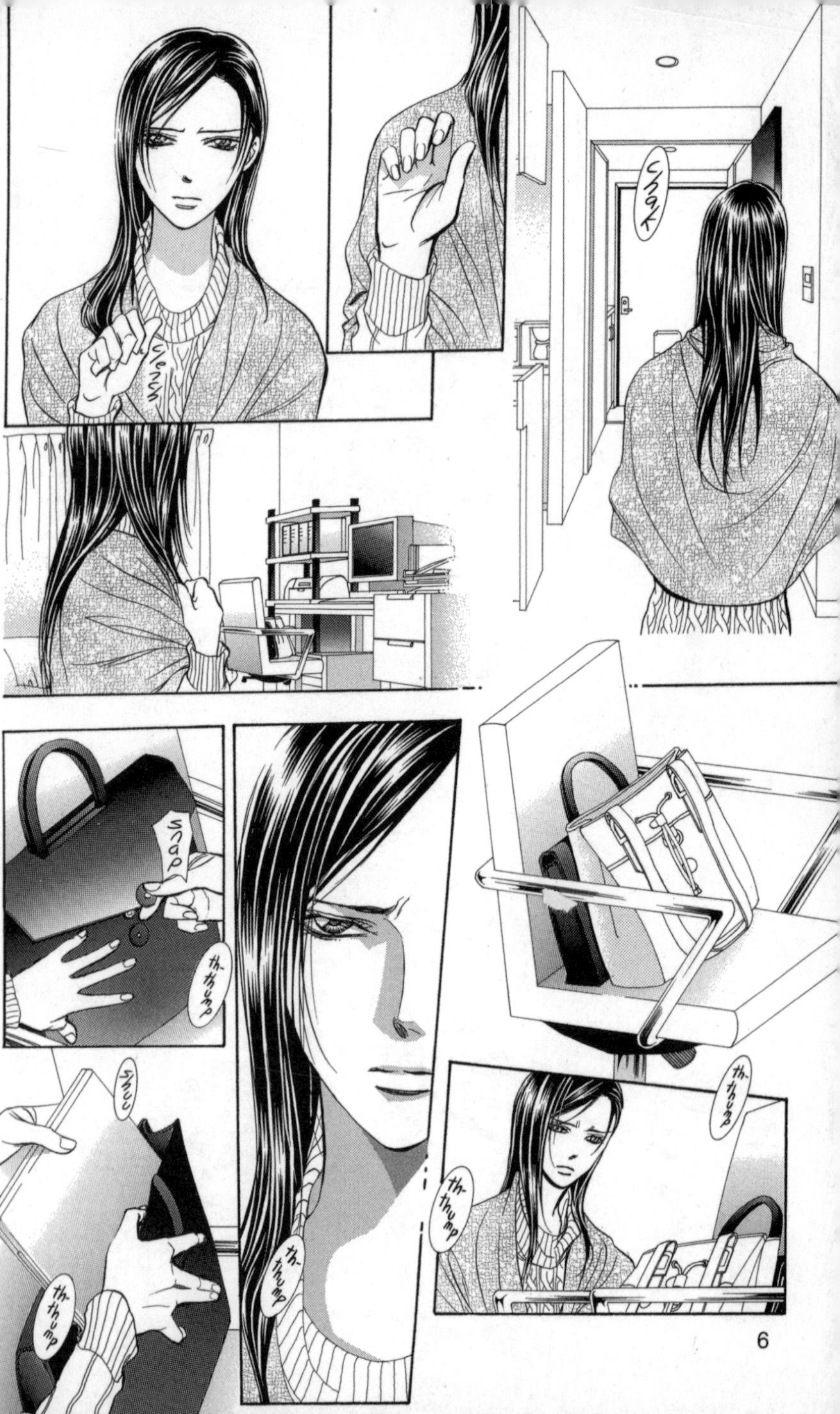
chak
clench
th-thump
th-thump
th-thump
snap
th-thump
shuu
th-thump

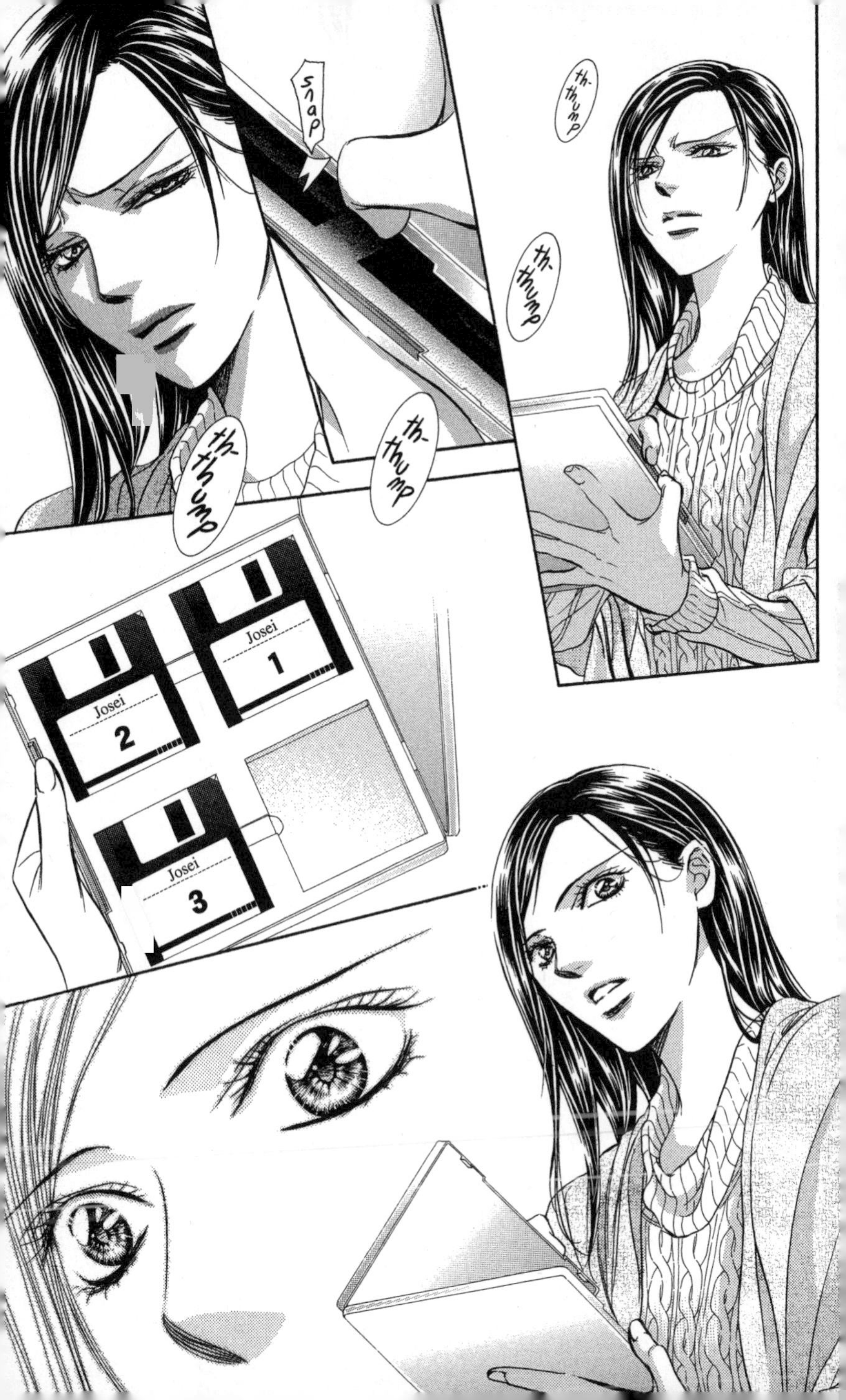
th-thump
th-thump
snap
th-thump
th-thump
Josei 1
Josei 2
Josei 3

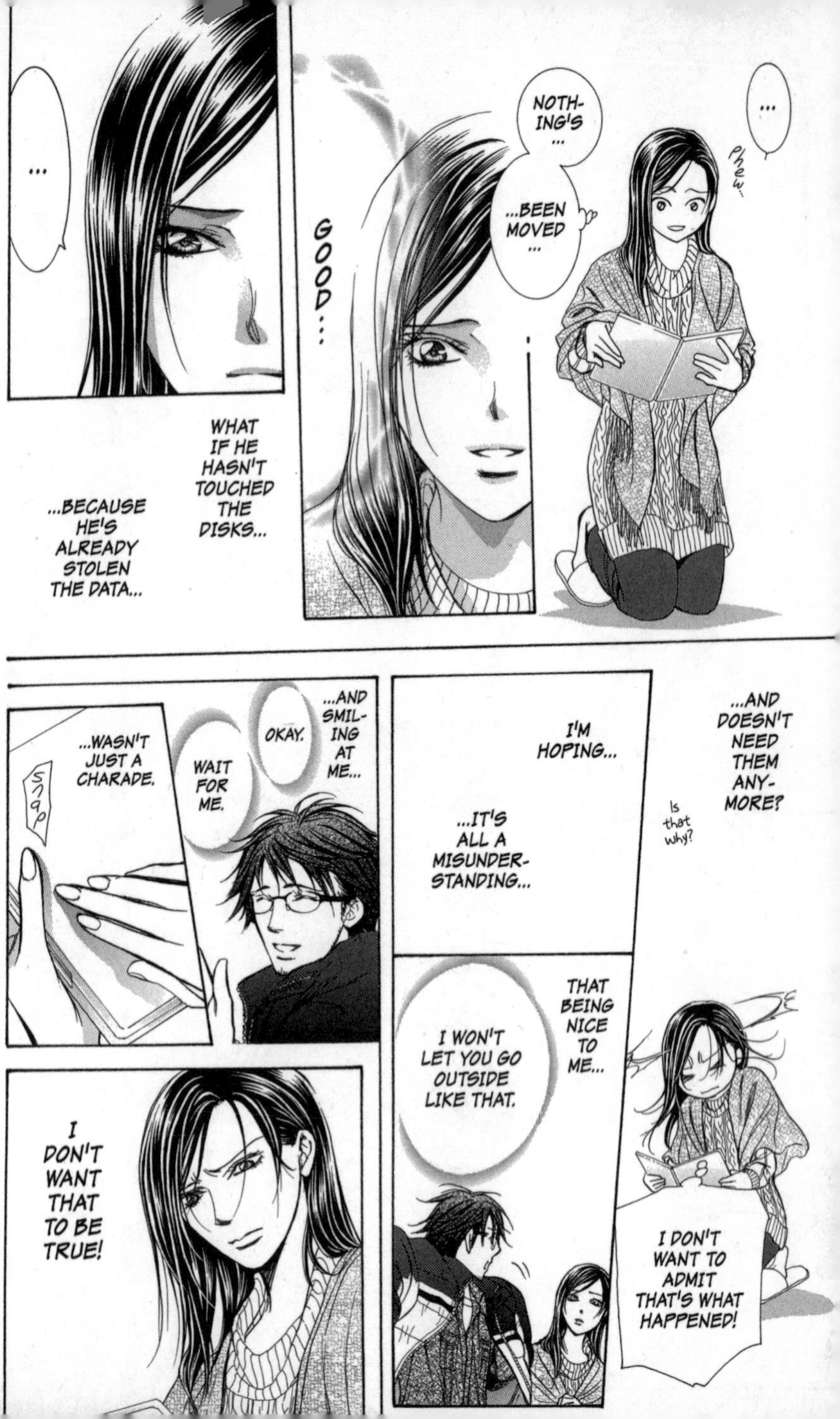
...
Phew...
NOTH-ING'S...
...BEEN MOVED...
GOOD...
...
WHAT IF HE HASN'T TOUCHED THE DISKS...
...BECAUSE HE'S ALREADY STOLEN THE DATA...
...AND DOESN'T NEED THEM ANY-MORE?
Is that why?
I'M HOPING...
...IT'S ALL A MISUNDER-STANDING...
THAT BEING NICE TO ME...
I WON'T LET YOU GO OUTSIDE LIKE THAT.
...AND SMIL-ING AT ME...
OKAY.
WAIT FOR ME.
...WASN'T JUST A CHARADE.
Snap
I DON'T WANT TO ADMIT THAT'S WHAT HAPPENED!
I DON'T WANT THAT TO BE TRUE!

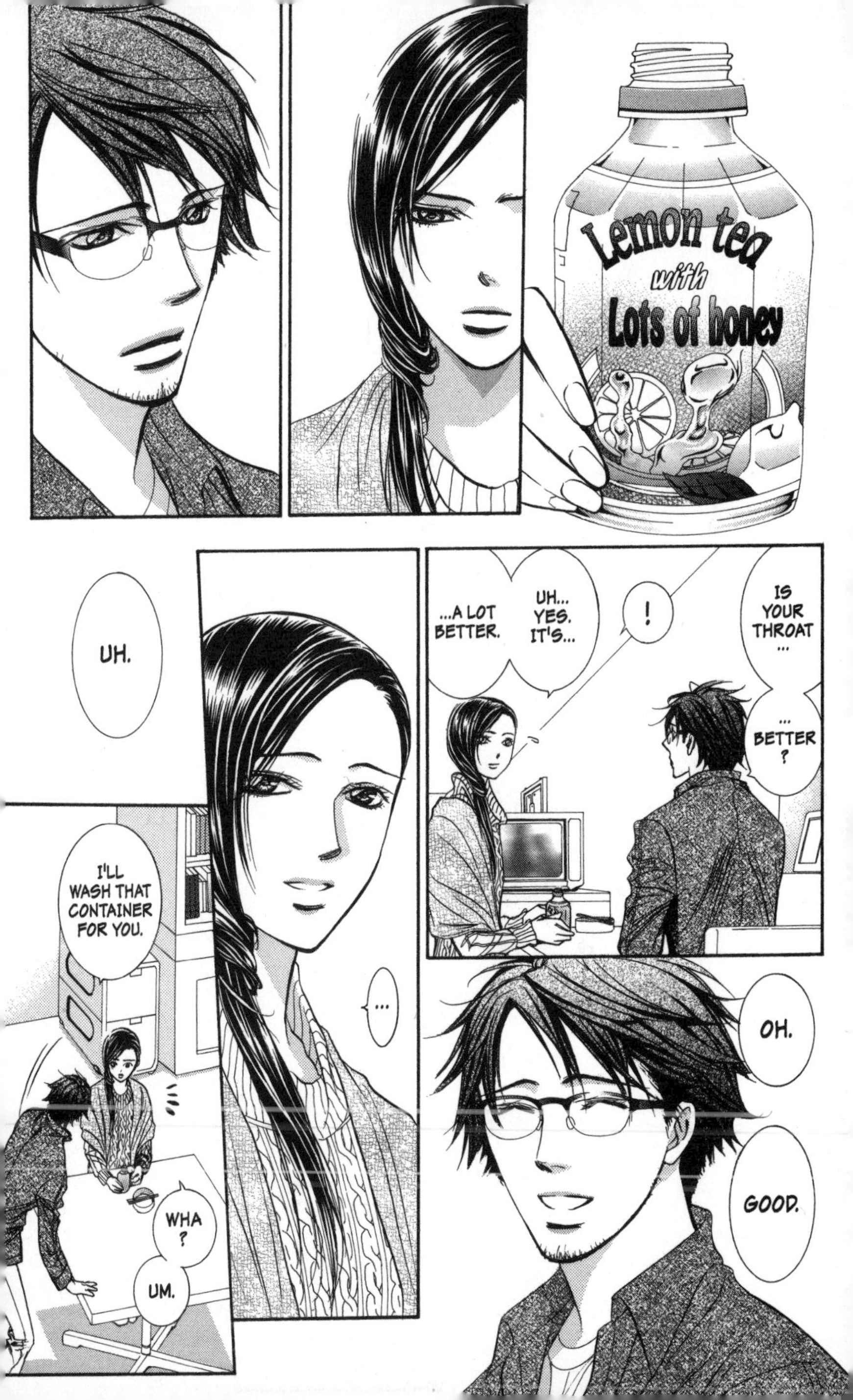
Lemon tea
with
Lots of honey
IS YOUR THROAT ...
... BETTER ?
!
UH... YES. IT'S...
...A LOT BETTER.
OH.
GOOD.
...
UH.
I'LL WASH THAT CONTAINER FOR YOU.
WHA ?
UM.

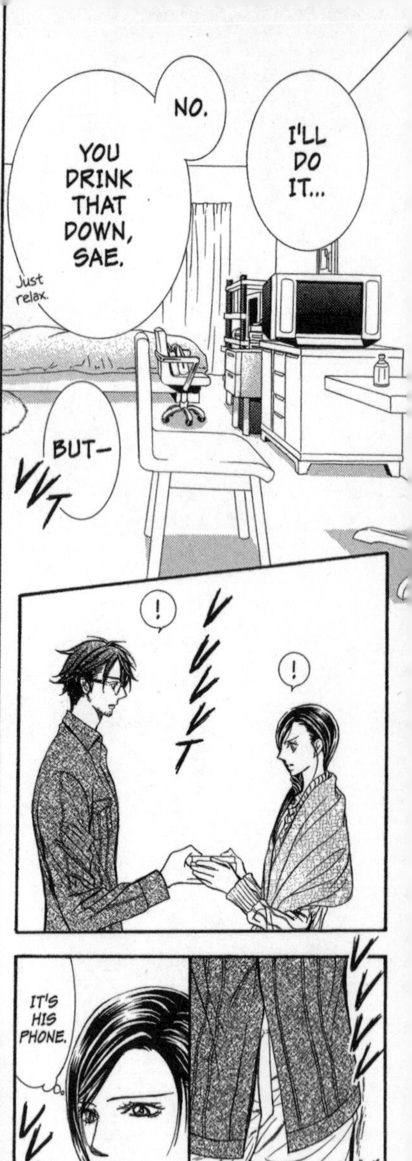
I'LL DO IT...
NO.
YOU DRINK THAT DOWN, SAE.
Just relax.
BUT—
VVT
!
!
VVVVVT
VVVVVVT
IT'S HIS PHONE.
ISN'T ...
VVVVVT
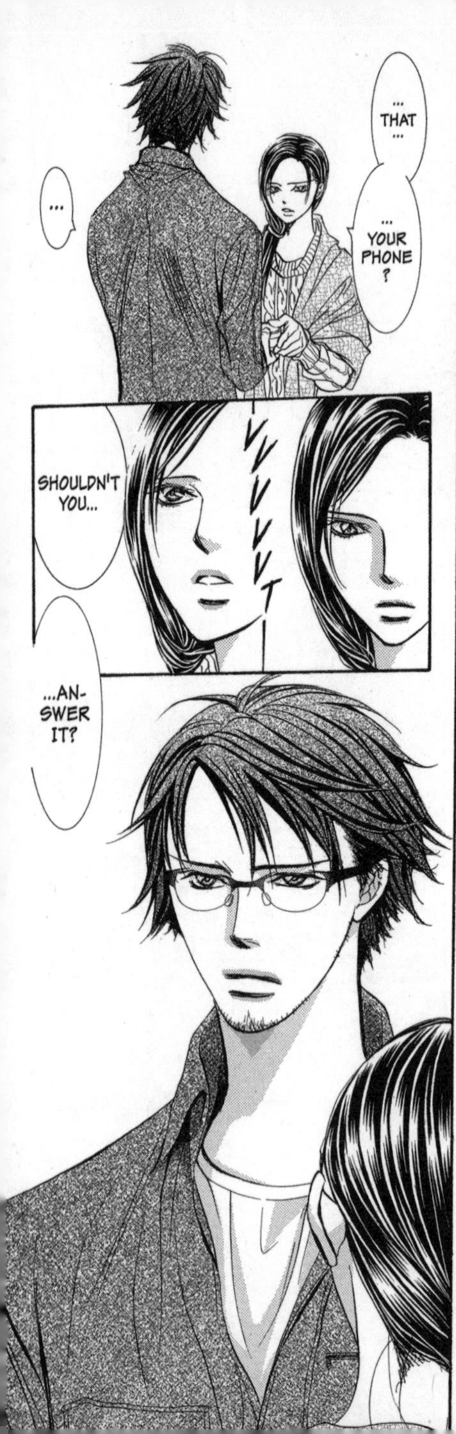
... THAT ...
... YOUR PHONE?
...
VVVVVT
SHOULDN'T YOU...
...AN-SWER IT?

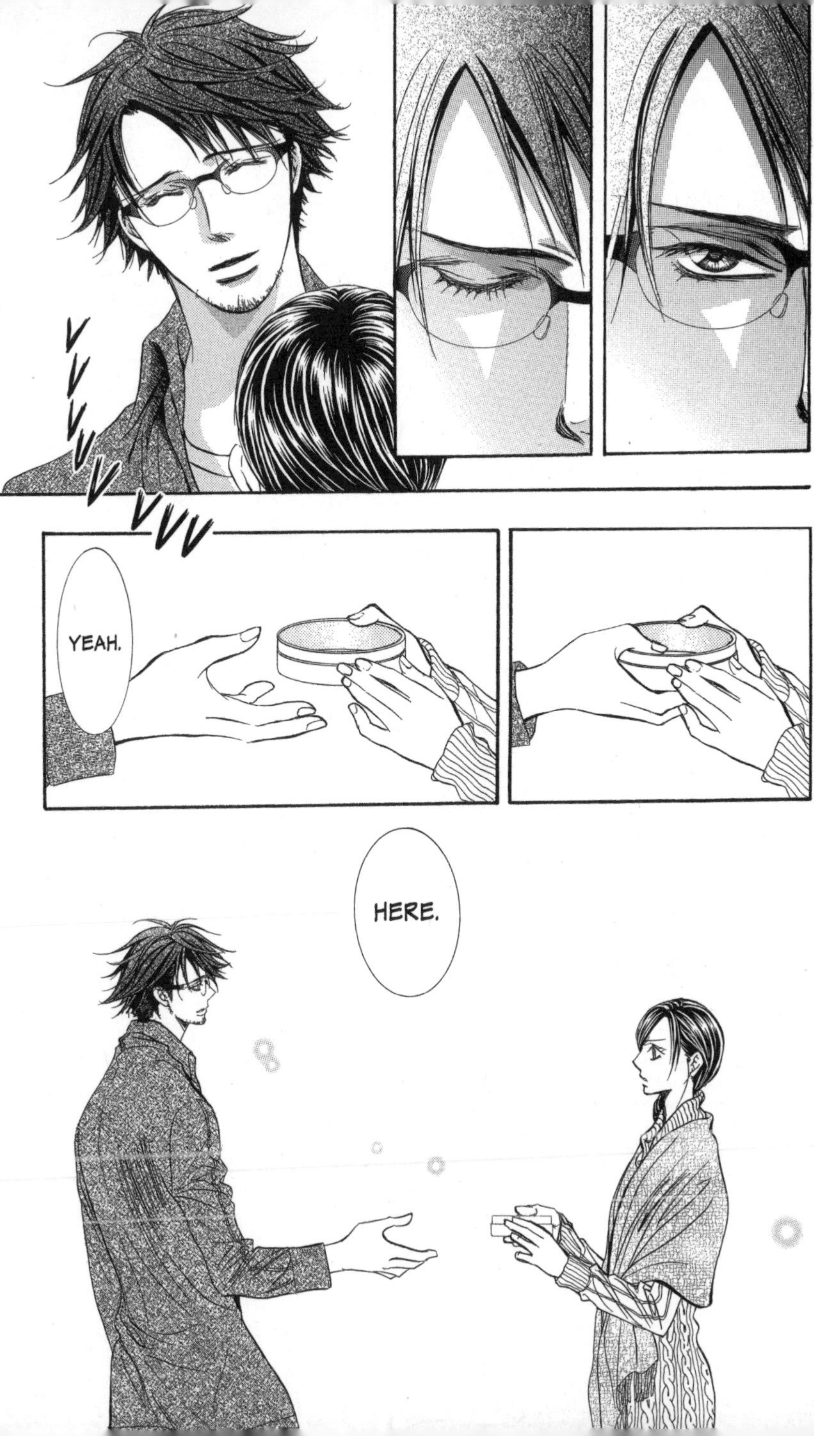
YEAH.
HERE.

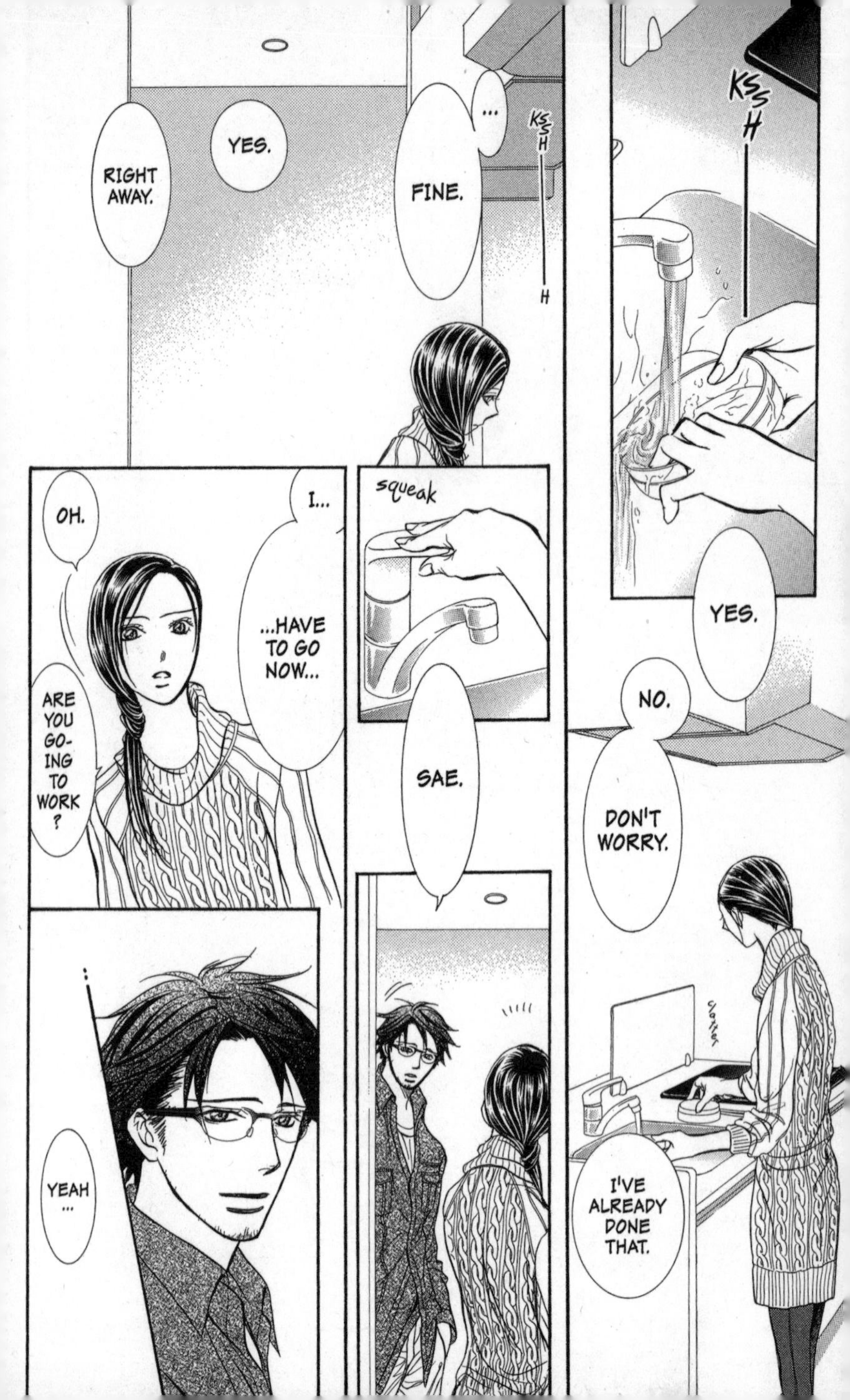
KSSH
...
FINE.
KSSH
H
YES.
RIGHT AWAY.
YES.
NO.
DON'T WORRY.
clatter
I'VE ALREADY DONE THAT.
squeak
I...
...HAVE TO GO NOW...
OH.
ARE YOU GOING TO WORK?
SAE.
...
YEAH ...

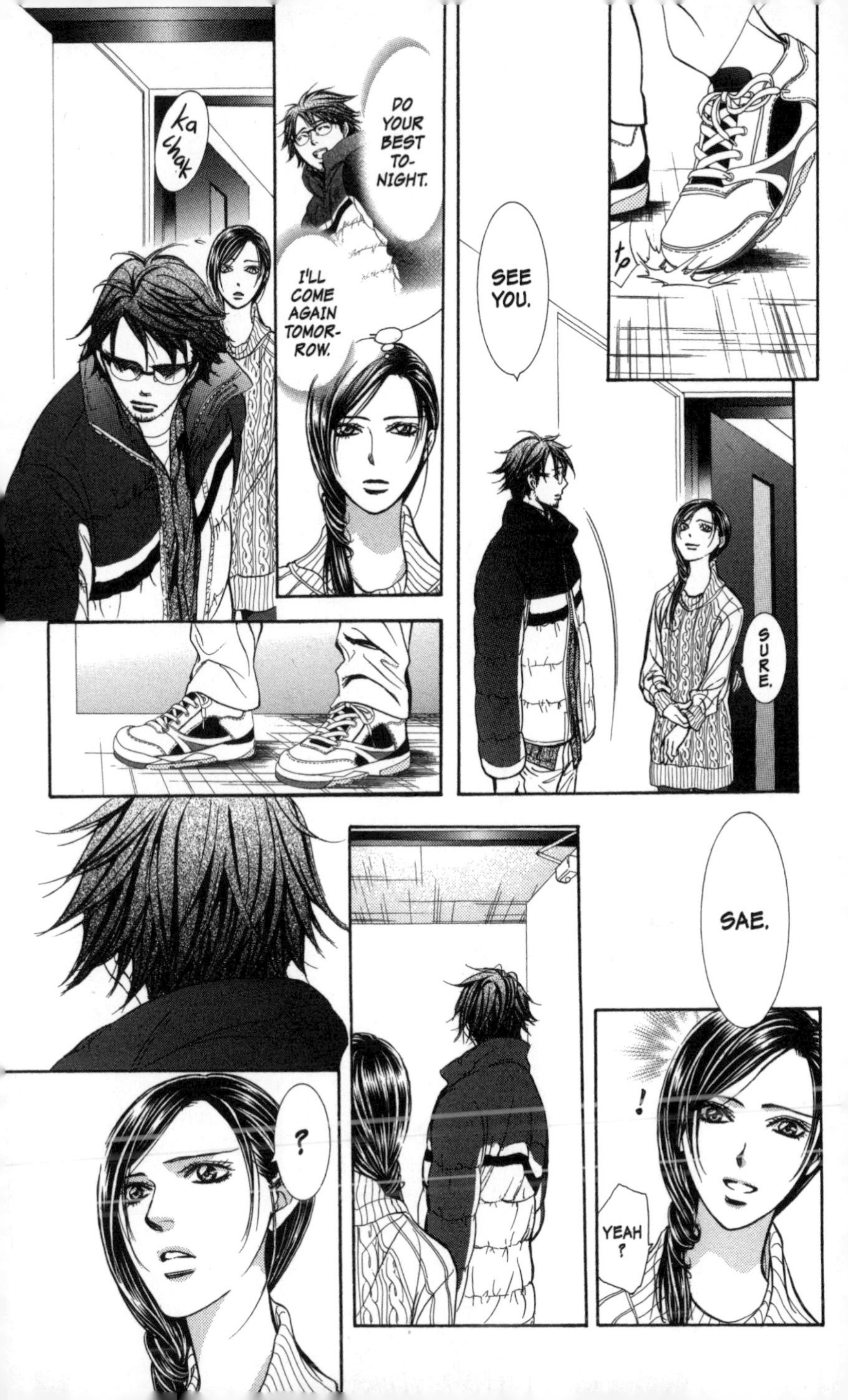
tp
SEE YOU.
SURE.
DO YOUR BEST TO-NIGHT.
I'LL COME AGAIN TOMOR-ROW.
ka chak
SAE.
!
YEAH?
?

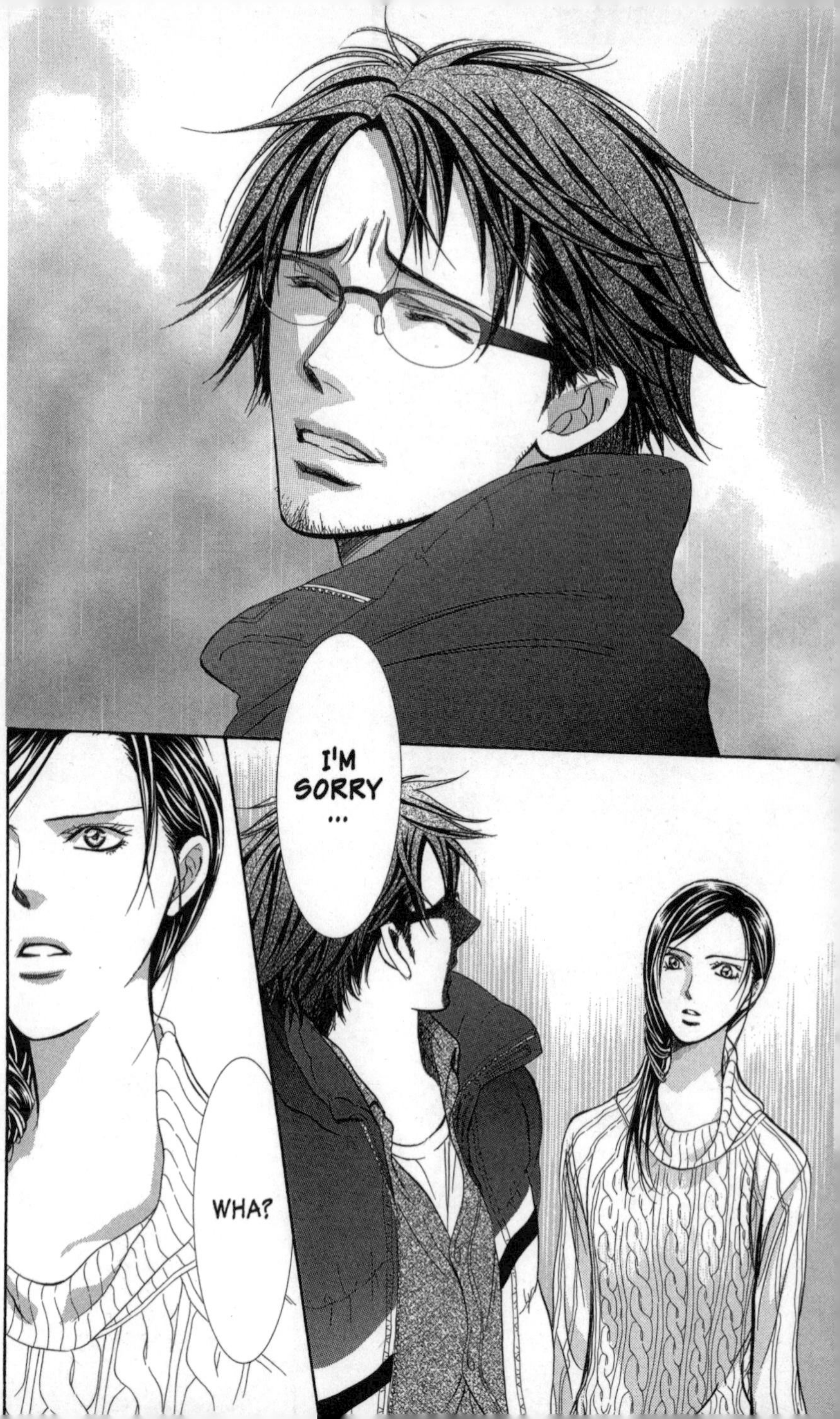
I'M SORRY ...
WHA?

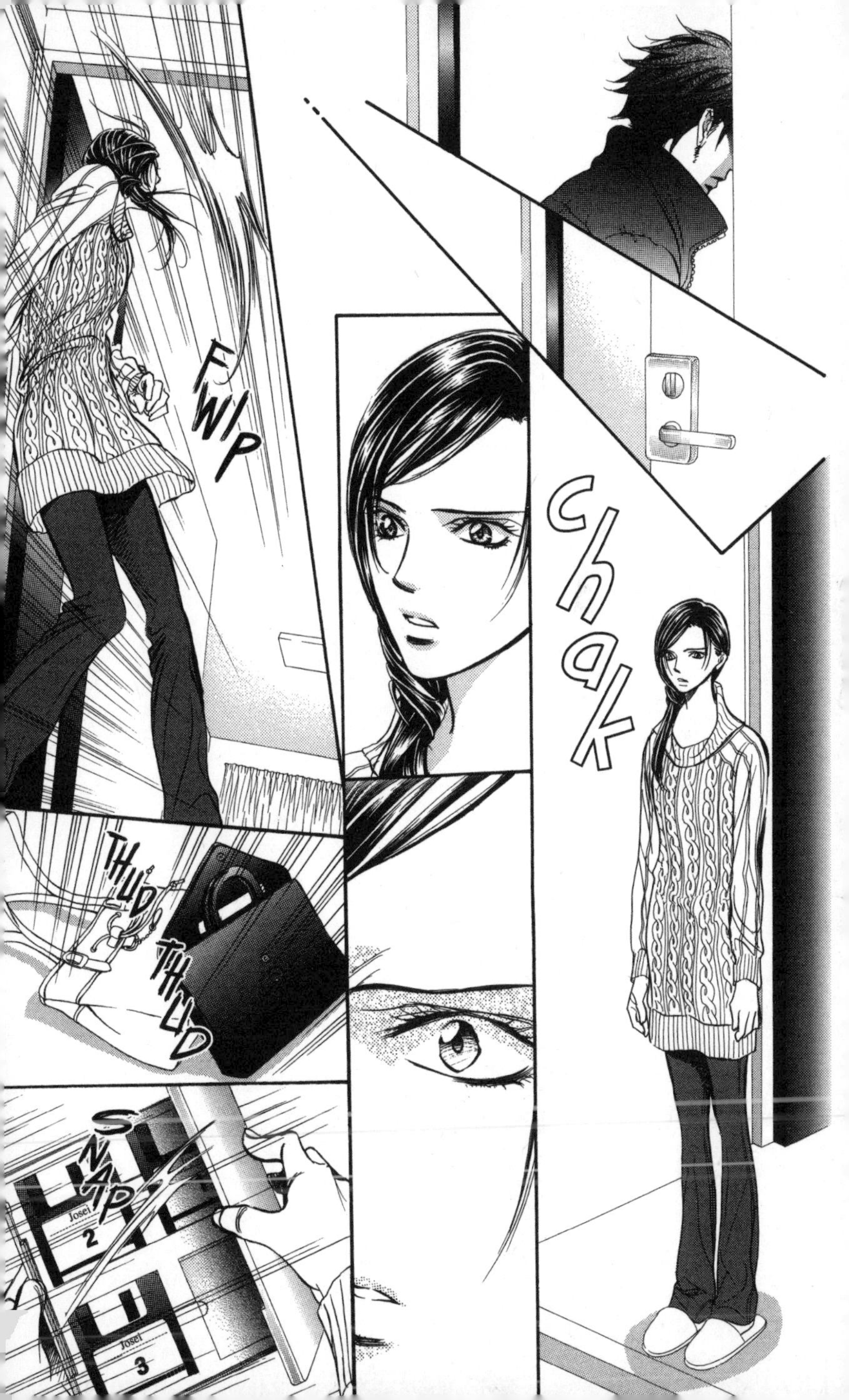

chak
FWIP
THUD THUD
SNAP
Josei
2
Josei
3

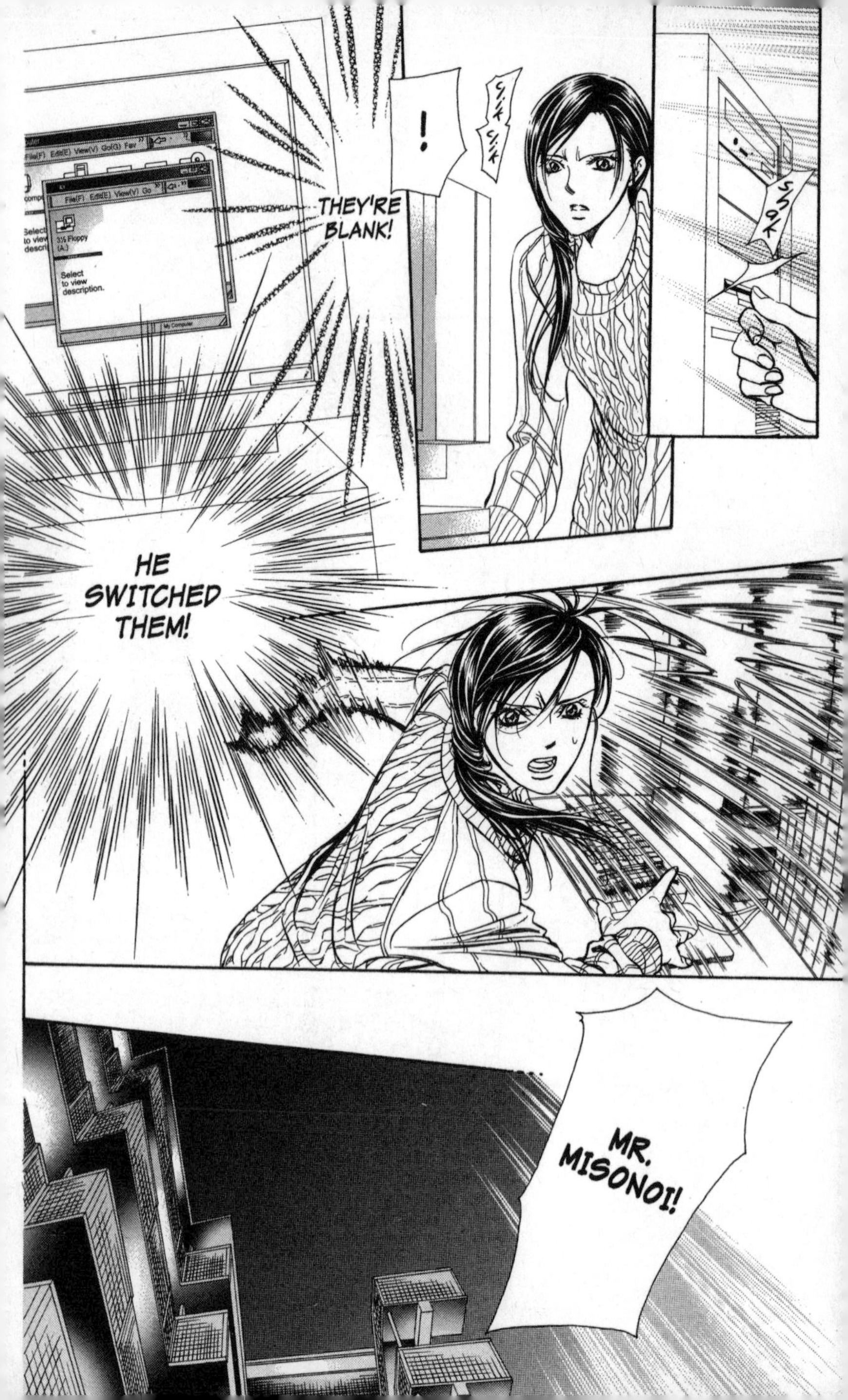
clik clik
!
File(F) Edit(E) View(V) Go(G) Fav
3½ Floppy (A:)
Select to view description.
THEY'RE BLANK!
HE SWITCHED THEM!
MR. MISONOI!

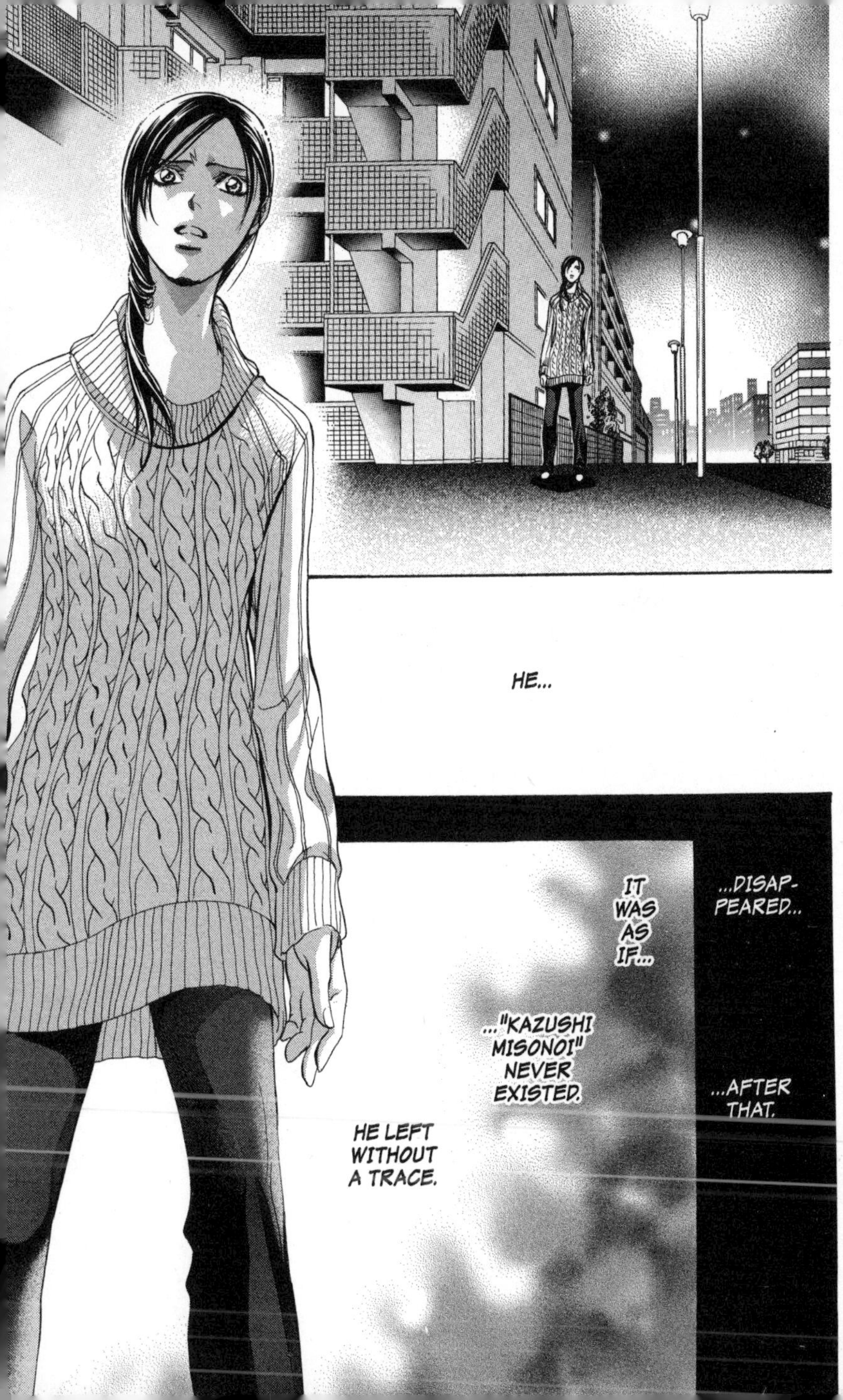
HE...
...DISAP-PEARED...
...AFTER THAT.
IT WAS AS IF...
..."KAZUSHI MISONOI" NEVER EXISTED.
HE LEFT WITHOUT A TRACE.

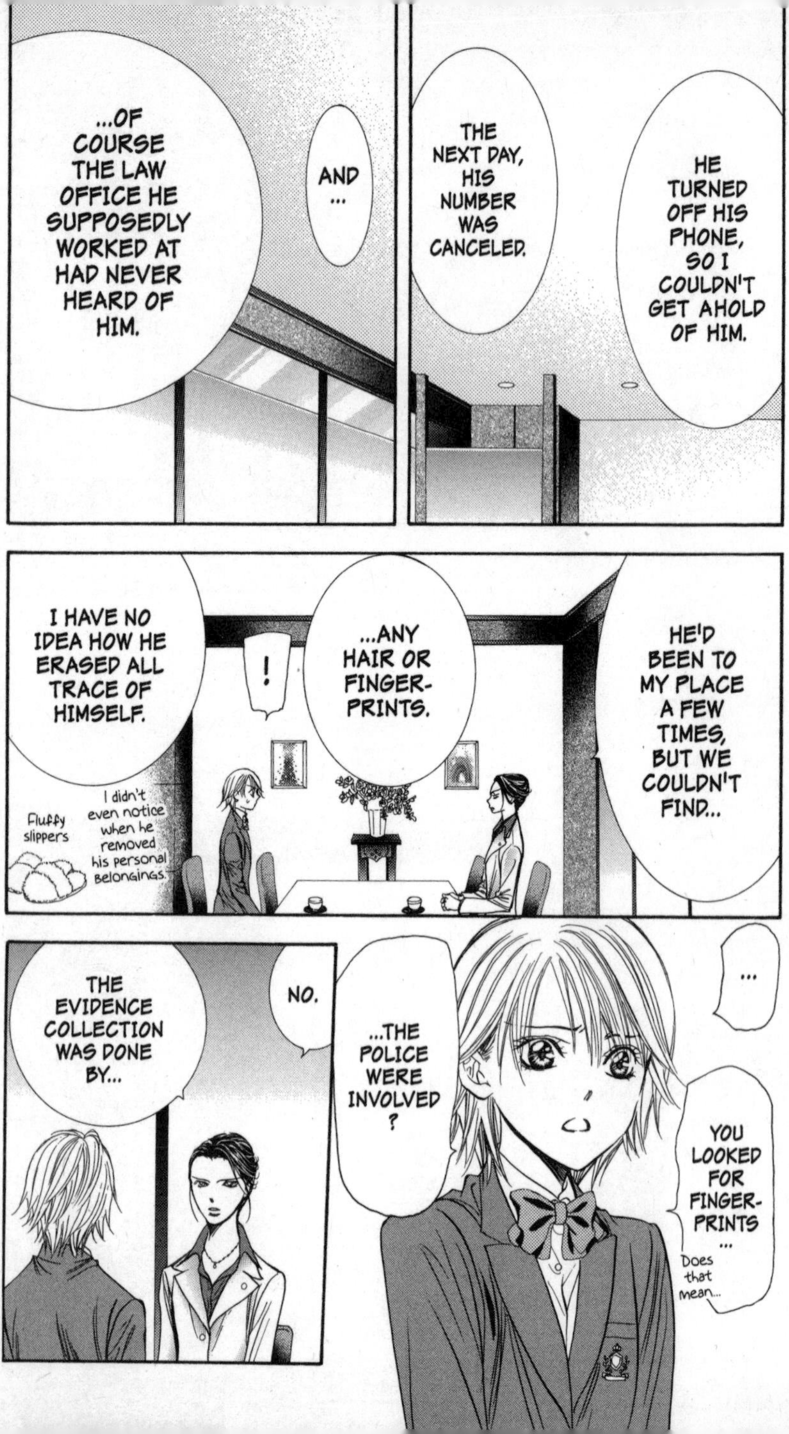
HE TURNED OFF HIS PHONE, SO I COULDN'T GET AHOLD OF HIM.
THE NEXT DAY, HIS NUMBER WAS CANCELED.
AND ...
...OF COURSE THE LAW OFFICE HE SUPPOSEDLY WORKED AT HAD NEVER HEARD OF HIM.
HE'D BEEN TO MY PLACE A FEW TIMES, BUT WE COULDN'T FIND...
...ANY HAIR OR FINGER-PRINTS.
!
I HAVE NO IDEA HOW HE ERASED ALL TRACE OF HIMSELF.
I didn't even notice when he removed his personal belongings.
Fluffy slippers
...
YOU LOOKED FOR FINGER-PRINTS ...
Does that mean...
...THE POLICE WERE INVOLVED ?
NO.
THE EVIDENCE COLLECTION WAS DONE BY...

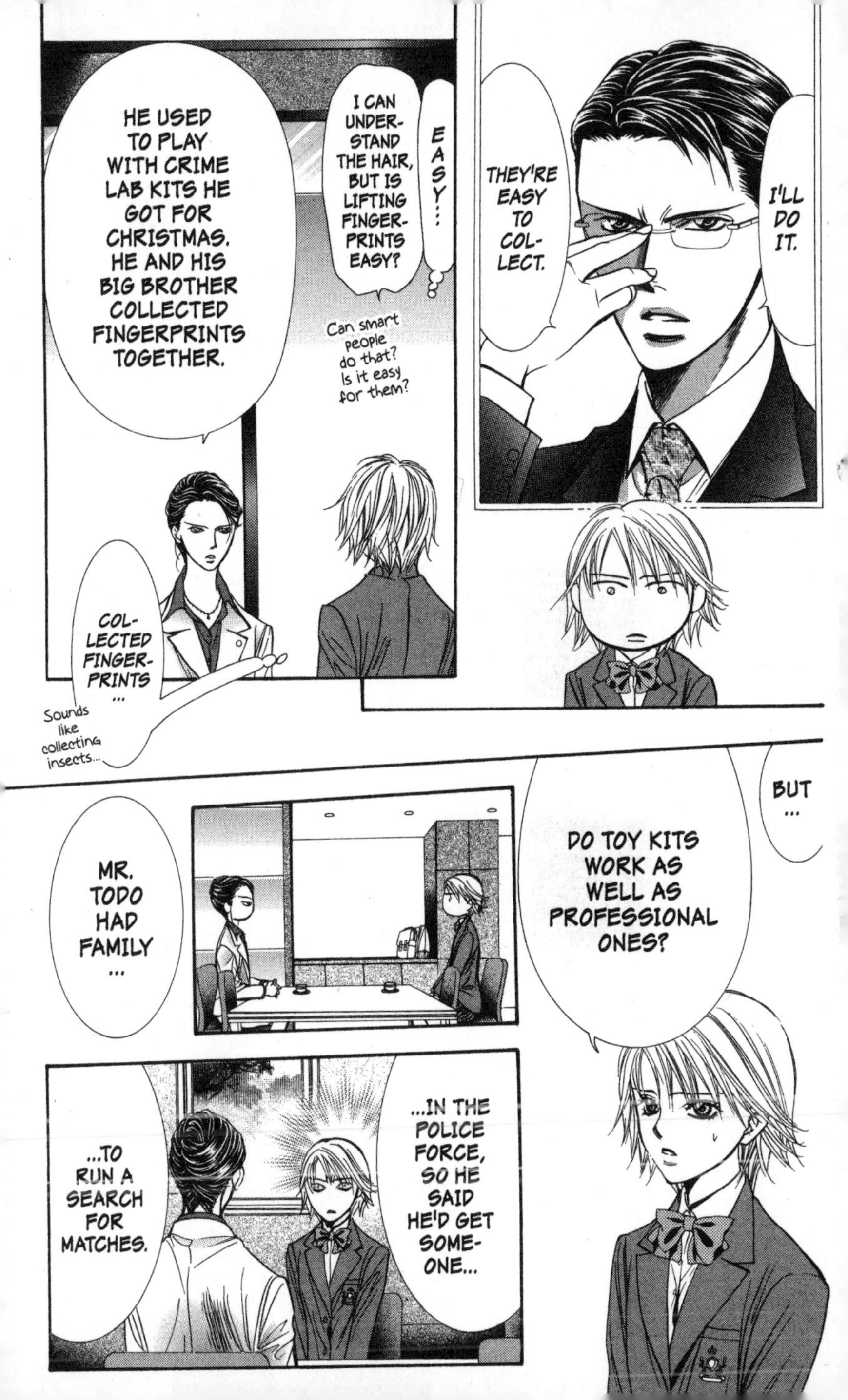
I'LL DO IT.
THEY'RE EASY TO COLLECT.
EASY...
I CAN UNDERSTAND THE HAIR, BUT IS LIFTING FINGERPRINTS EASY?
Can smart people do that? Is it easy for them?
HE USED TO PLAY WITH CRIME LAB KITS HE GOT FOR CHRISTMAS. HE AND HIS BIG BROTHER COLLECTED FINGERPRINTS TOGETHER.
COLLECTED FINGERPRINTS...
Sounds like collecting insects...
BUT...
DO TOY KITS WORK AS WELL AS PROFESSIONAL ONES?
MR. TODO HAD FAMILY...
...IN THE POLICE FORCE, SO HE SAID HE'D GET SOMEONE...
...TO RUN A SEARCH FOR MATCHES.

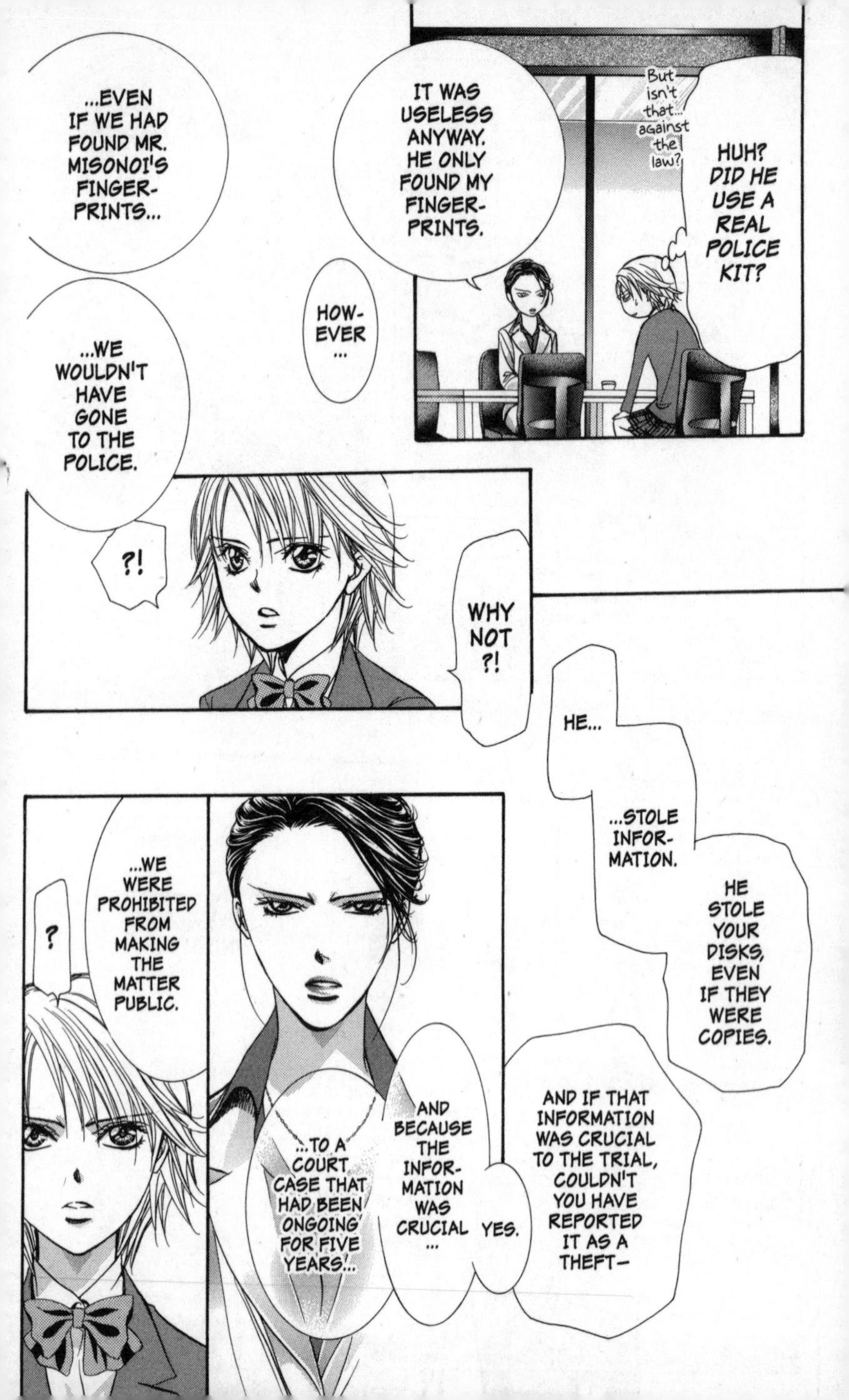
HUH? DID HE USE A REAL POLICE KIT?
But isn't that... against the law?
IT WAS USELESS ANYWAY. HE ONLY FOUND MY FINGER-PRINTS.
HOW-EVER...
...EVEN IF WE HAD FOUND MR. MISONOI'S FINGER-PRINTS...
...WE WOULDN'T HAVE GONE TO THE POLICE.
?!
WHY NOT?!
HE...
...STOLE INFOR-MATION.
HE STOLE YOUR DISKS, EVEN IF THEY WERE COPIES.
AND IF THAT INFORMATION WAS CRUCIAL TO THE TRIAL, COULDN'T YOU HAVE REPORTED IT AS A THEFT—
YES.
AND BECAUSE THE INFOR-MATION WAS CRUCIAL...
...TO A COURT CASE THAT HAD BEEN ONGOING FOR FIVE YEARS!...
...WE WERE PROHIBITED FROM MAKING THE MATTER PUBLIC.
?

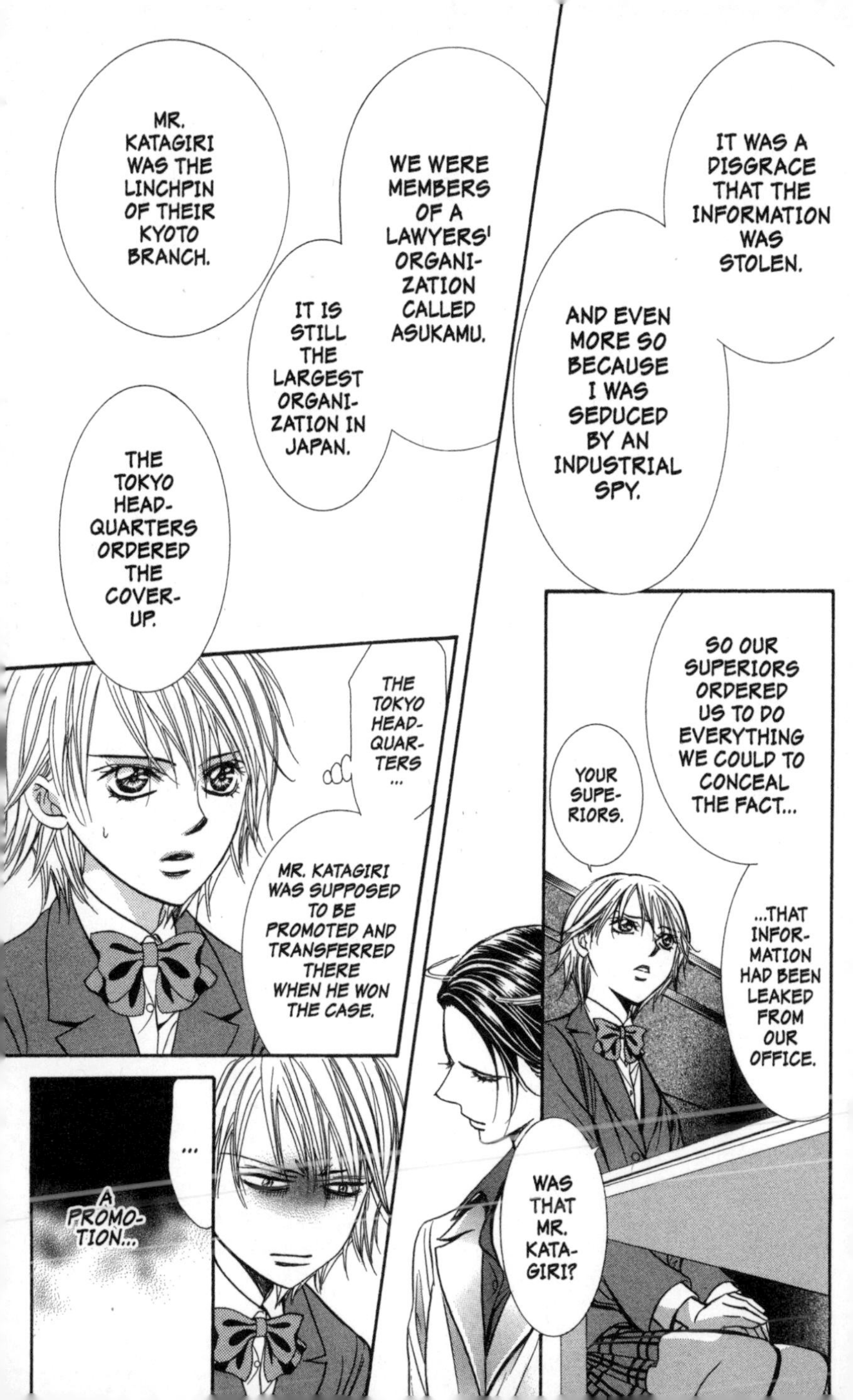
IT WAS A DISGRACE THAT THE INFORMATION WAS STOLEN.
AND EVEN MORE SO BECAUSE I WAS SEDUCED BY AN INDUSTRIAL SPY.
WE WERE MEMBERS OF A LAWYERS' ORGANIZATION CALLED ASUKAMU.
MR. KATAGIRI WAS THE LINCHPIN OF THEIR KYOTO BRANCH.
IT IS STILL THE LARGEST ORGANIZATION IN JAPAN.
THE TOKYO HEADQUARTERS ORDERED THE COVER-UP.
SO OUR SUPERIORS ORDERED US TO DO EVERYTHING WE COULD TO CONCEAL THE FACT...
YOUR SUPERIORS.
...THAT INFORMATION HAD BEEN LEAKED FROM OUR OFFICE.
WAS THAT MR. KATAGIRI?
THE TOKYO HEADQUARTERS...
MR. KATAGIRI WAS SUPPOSED TO BE PROMOTED AND TRANSFERRED THERE WHEN HE WON THE CASE.
...
A PROMOTION...

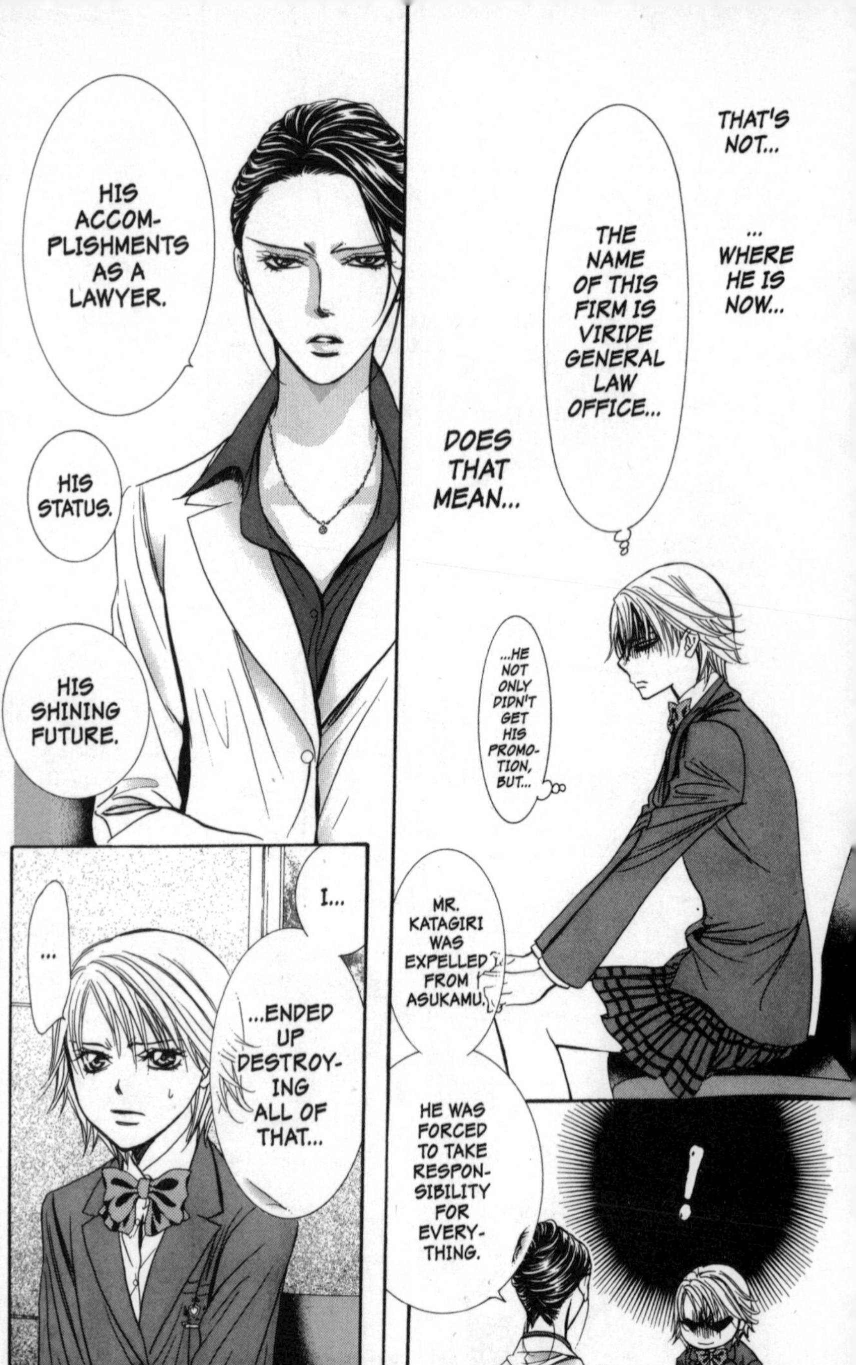
THAT'S NOT...
...WHERE HE IS NOW...
THE NAME OF THIS FIRM IS VIRIDE GENERAL LAW OFFICE...
DOES THAT MEAN...
...HE NOT ONLY DIDN'T GET HIS PROMOTION, BUT...
MR. KATAGIRI WAS EXPELLED FROM ASUKAMU.
HE WAS FORCED TO TAKE RESPONSIBILITY FOR EVERYTHING.
!
HIS ACCOMPLISHMENTS AS A LAWYER.
HIS STATUS.
HIS SHINING FUTURE.
I...
...ENDED UP DESTROYING ALL OF THAT...
...

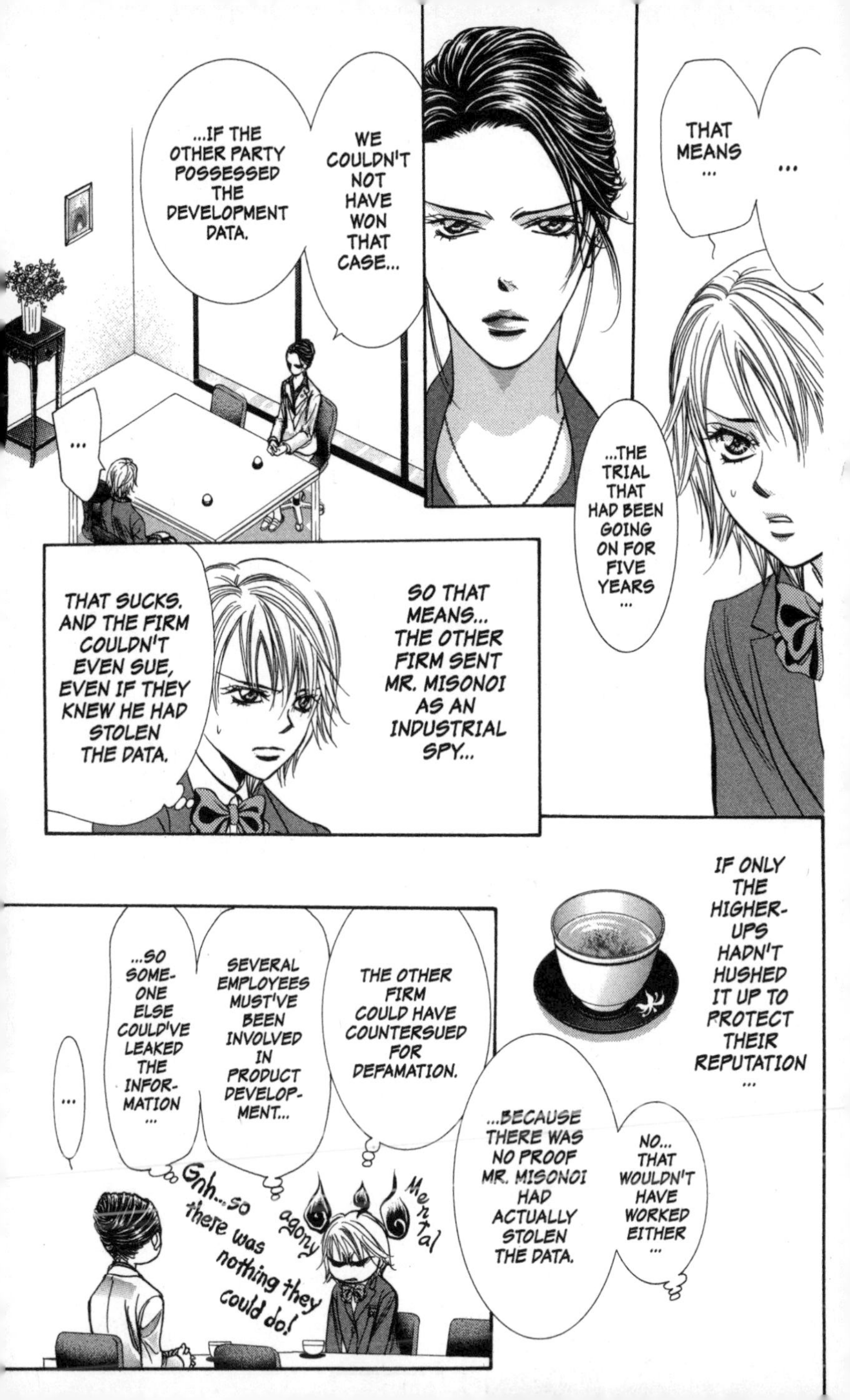
THAT MEANS ...
...
...THE TRIAL THAT HAD BEEN GOING ON FOR FIVE YEARS ...
WE COULDN'T NOT HAVE WON THAT CASE...
...IF THE OTHER PARTY POSSESSED THE DEVELOPMENT DATA.
...
SO THAT MEANS... THE OTHER FIRM SENT MR. MISONOI AS AN INDUSTRIAL SPY...
THAT SUCKS. AND THE FIRM COULDN'T EVEN SUE, EVEN IF THEY KNEW HE HAD STOLEN THE DATA.
IF ONLY THE HIGHER-UPS HADN'T HUSHED IT UP TO PROTECT THEIR REPUTATION ...
NO... THAT WOULDN'T HAVE WORKED EITHER ...
...BECAUSE THERE WAS NO PROOF MR. MISONOI HAD ACTUALLY STOLEN THE DATA.
THE OTHER FIRM COULD HAVE COUNTERSUED FOR DEFAMATION.
SEVERAL EMPLOYEES MUST'VE BEEN INVOLVED IN PRODUCT DEVELOPMENT...
...SO SOMEONE ELSE COULD'VE LEAKED THE INFORMATION ...
...
Mental agony
Gnh...so there was nothing they could do!

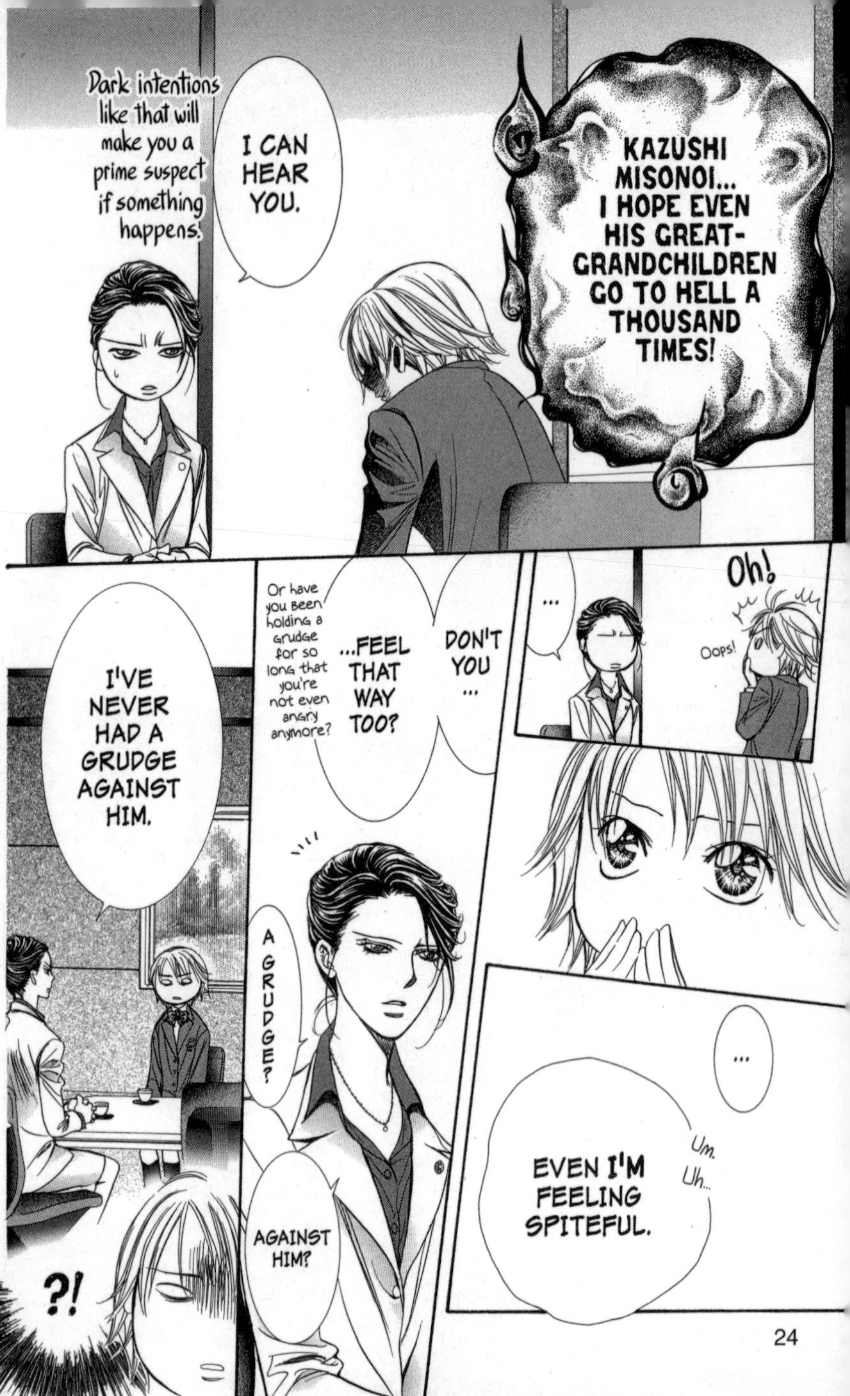
KAZUSHI MISONOI... I HOPE EVEN HIS GREAT-GRANDCHILDREN GO TO HELL A THOUSAND TIMES!
I CAN HEAR YOU.
Dark intentions like that will make you a prime suspect if something happens!
Oh!
Oops!
...
...
Um. Uh...
EVEN I'M FEELING SPITEFUL.
DON'T YOU ...
...FEEL THAT WAY TOO?
Or have you been holding a grudge for so long that you're not even angry anymore?
A GRUDGE?
AGAINST HIM?
I'VE NEVER HAD A GRUDGE AGAINST HIM.
?!

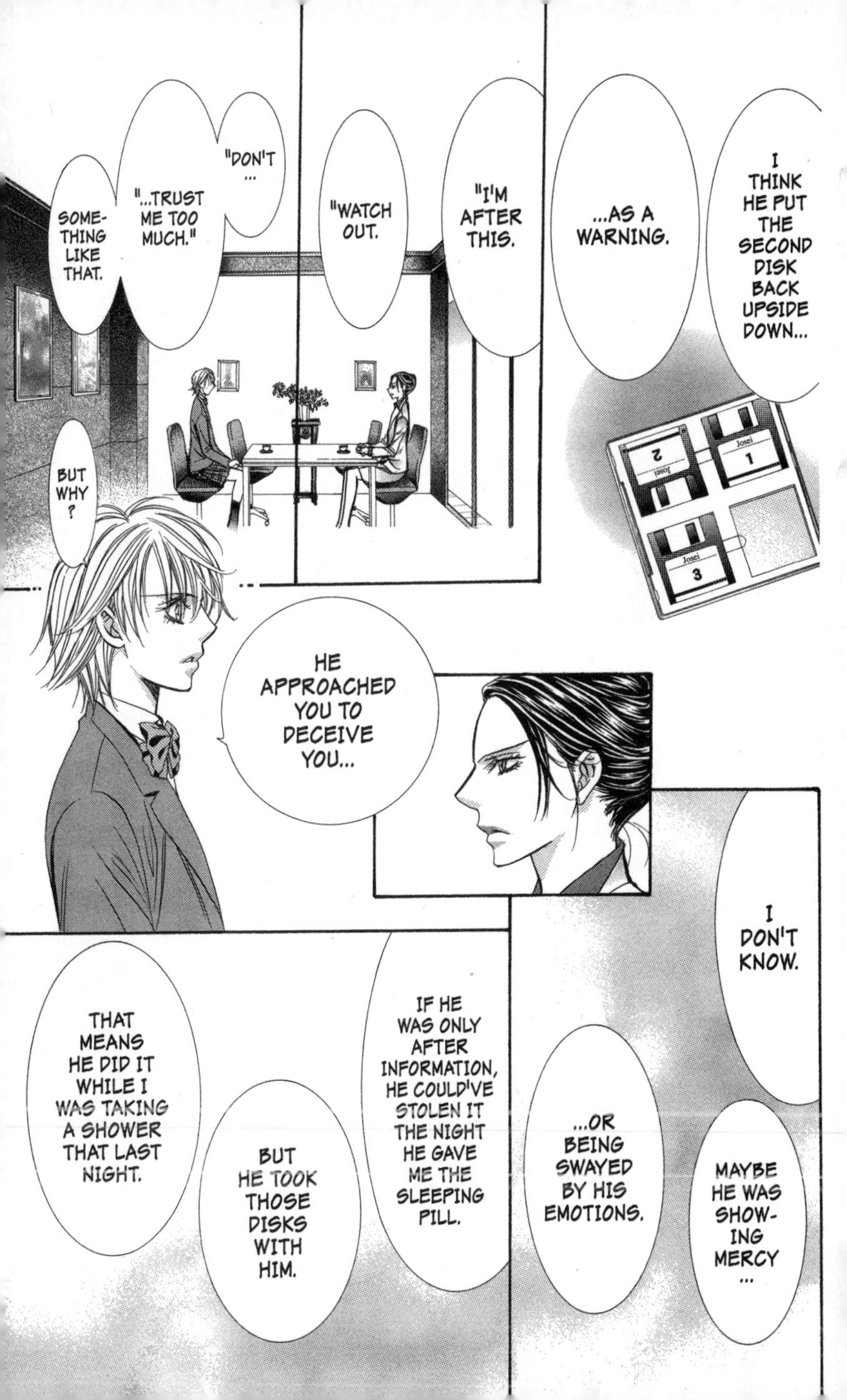
I THINK HE PUT THE SECOND DISK BACK UPSIDE DOWN...
...AS A WARNING.
Josei 1
Josei 2
Josei 3
"I'M AFTER THIS.
"WATCH OUT.
"DON'T ...
"...TRUST ME TOO MUCH."
SOME-THING LIKE THAT.
BUT WHY?
HE APPROACHED YOU TO DECEIVE YOU...
I DON'T KNOW.
MAYBE HE WAS SHOW-ING MERCY ...
...OR BEING SWAYED BY HIS EMOTIONS.
IF HE WAS ONLY AFTER INFORMATION, HE COULD'VE STOLEN IT THE NIGHT HE GAVE ME THE SLEEPING PILL.
BUT HE TOOK THOSE DISKS WITH HIM.
THAT MEANS HE DID IT WHILE I WAS TAKING A SHOWER THAT LAST NIGHT.

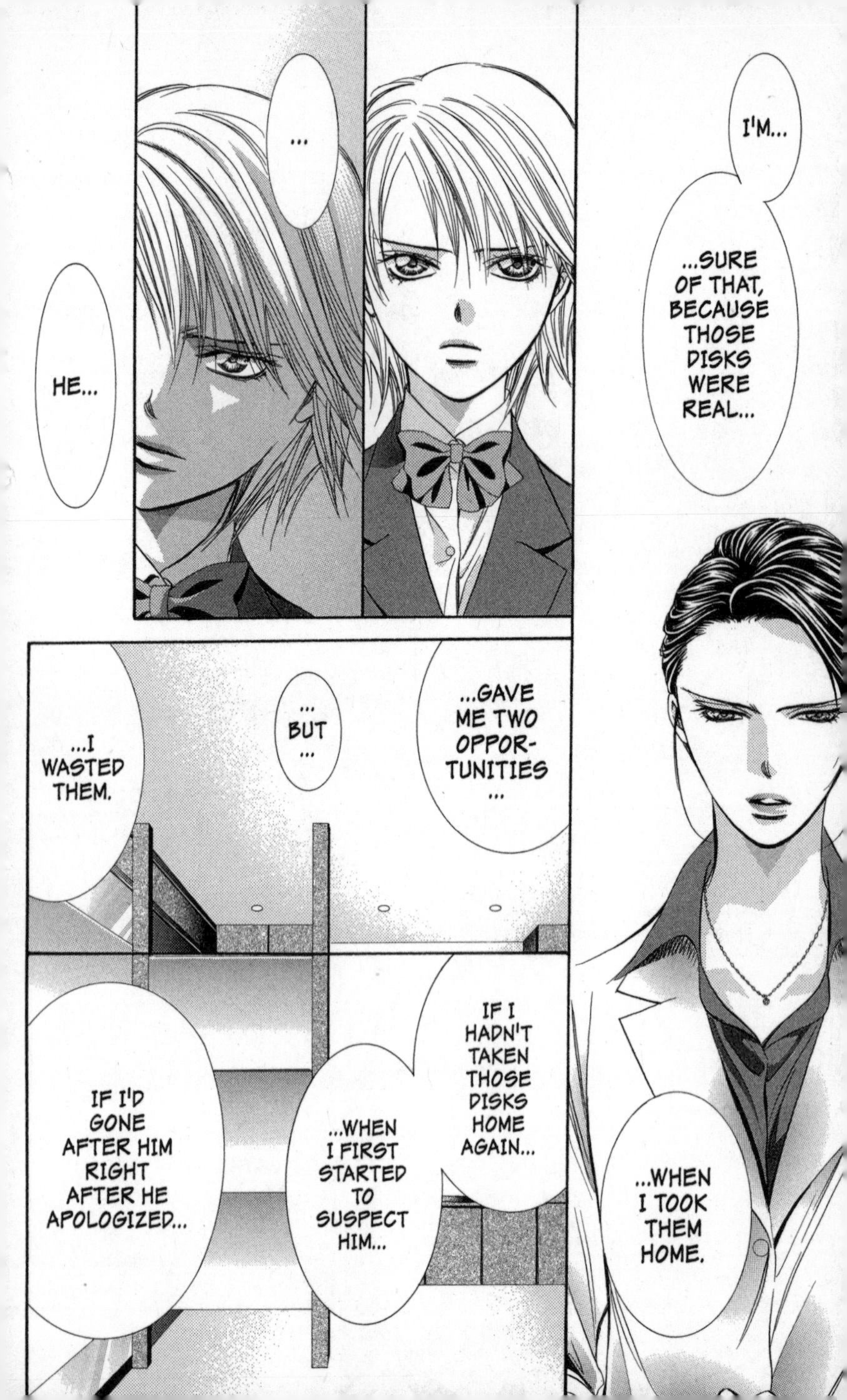
I'M...
...SURE OF THAT, BECAUSE THOSE DISKS WERE REAL...
...WHEN I TOOK THEM HOME.
...
HE...
...GAVE ME TWO OPPOR-TUNITIES...
...BUT...
...I WASTED THEM.
IF I HADN'T TAKEN THOSE DISKS HOME AGAIN...
...WHEN I FIRST STARTED TO SUSPECT HIM...
IF I'D GONE AFTER HIM RIGHT AFTER HE APOLOGIZED...

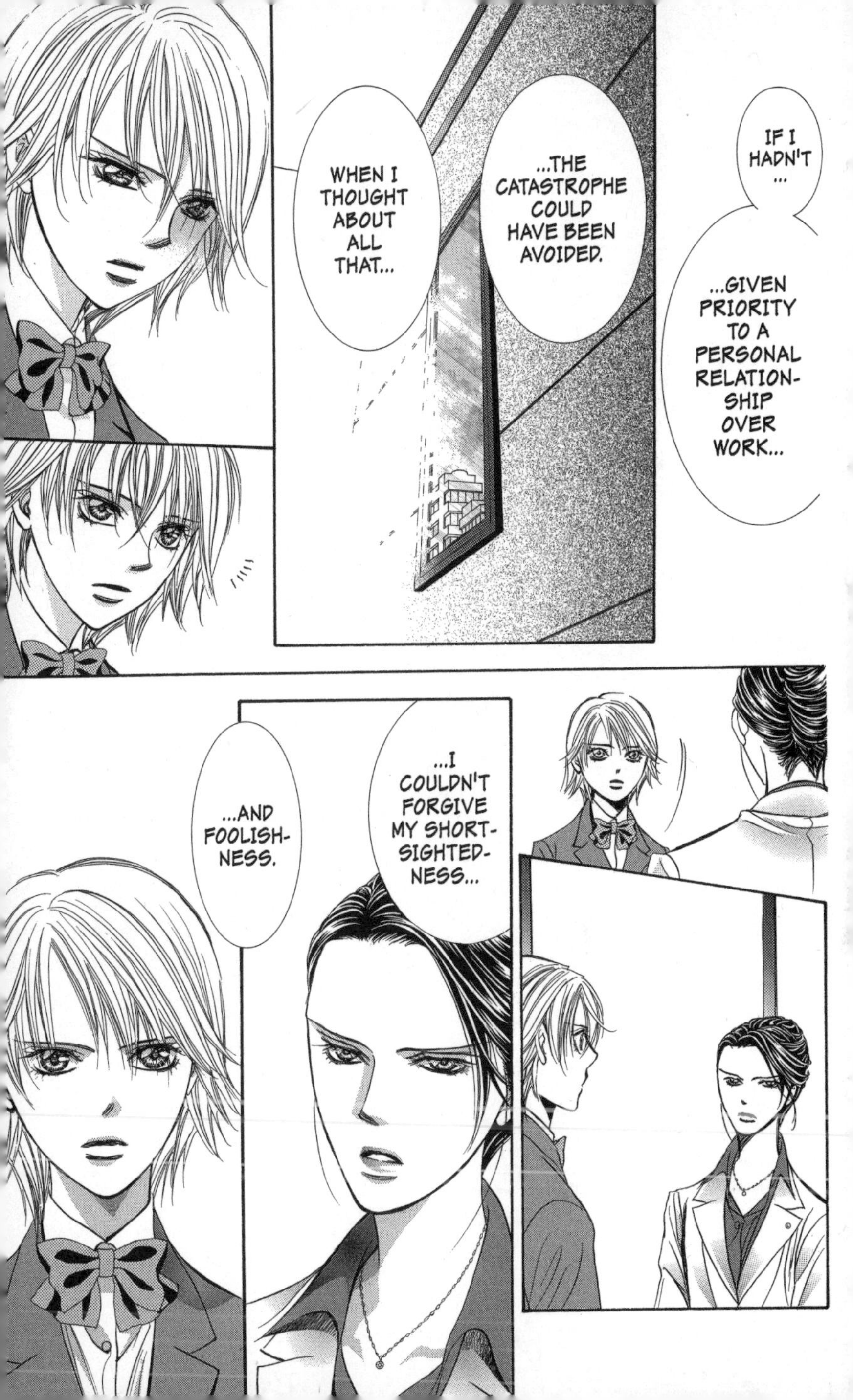
IF I HADN'T ...
...GIVEN PRIORITY TO A PERSONAL RELATION-SHIP OVER WORK...
...THE CATASTROPHE COULD HAVE BEEN AVOIDED.
WHEN I THOUGHT ABOUT ALL THAT...
...I COULDN'T FORGIVE MY SHORT-SIGHTED-NESS...
...AND FOOLISH-NESS.

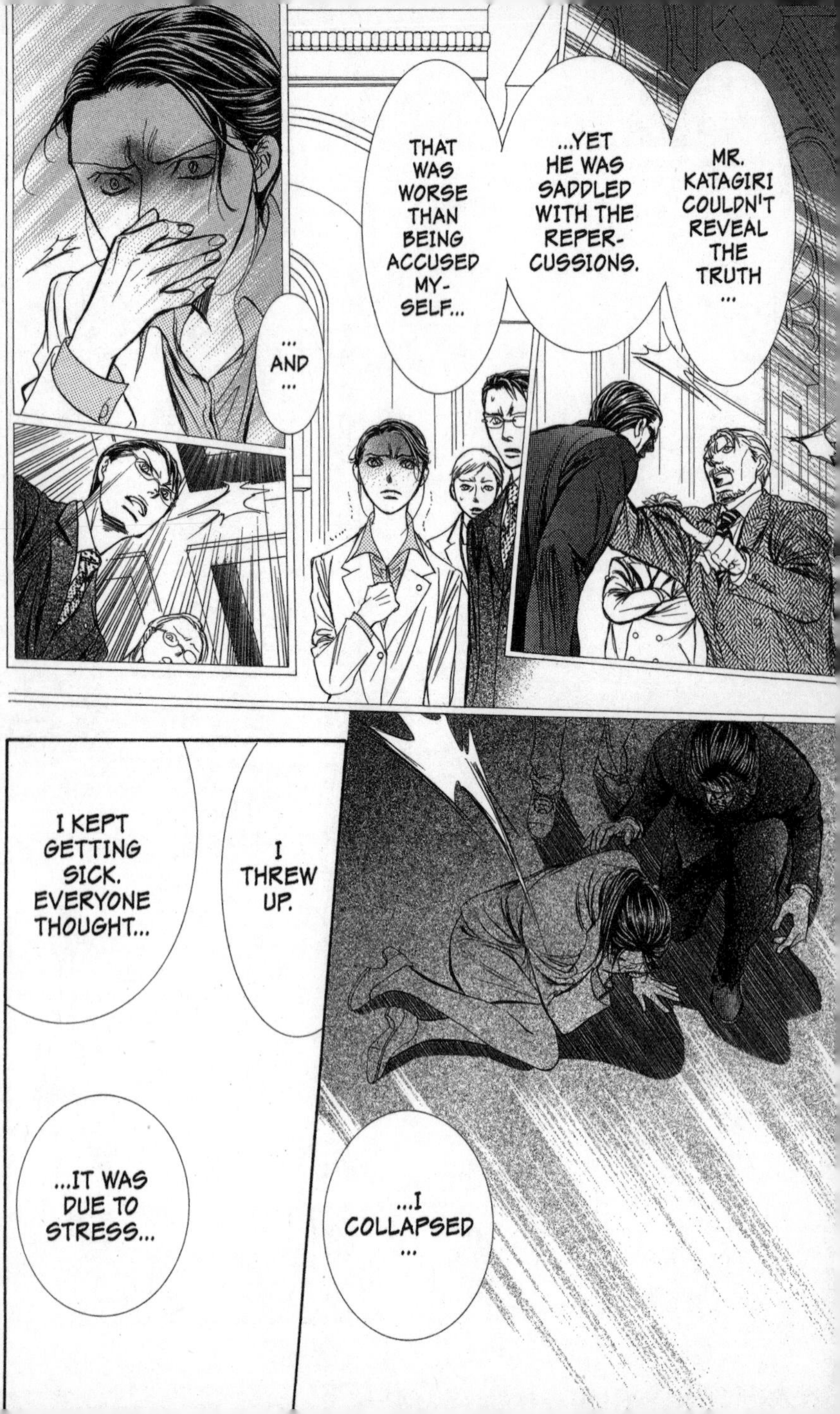
MR. KATAGIRI COULDN'T REVEAL THE TRUTH...
...YET HE WAS SADDLED WITH THE REPERCUSSIONS.
THAT WAS WORSE THAN BEING ACCUSED MYSELF...
...AND...
...I COLLAPSED...
I THREW UP.
I KEPT GETTING SICK. EVERYONE THOUGHT...
...IT WAS DUE TO STRESS...

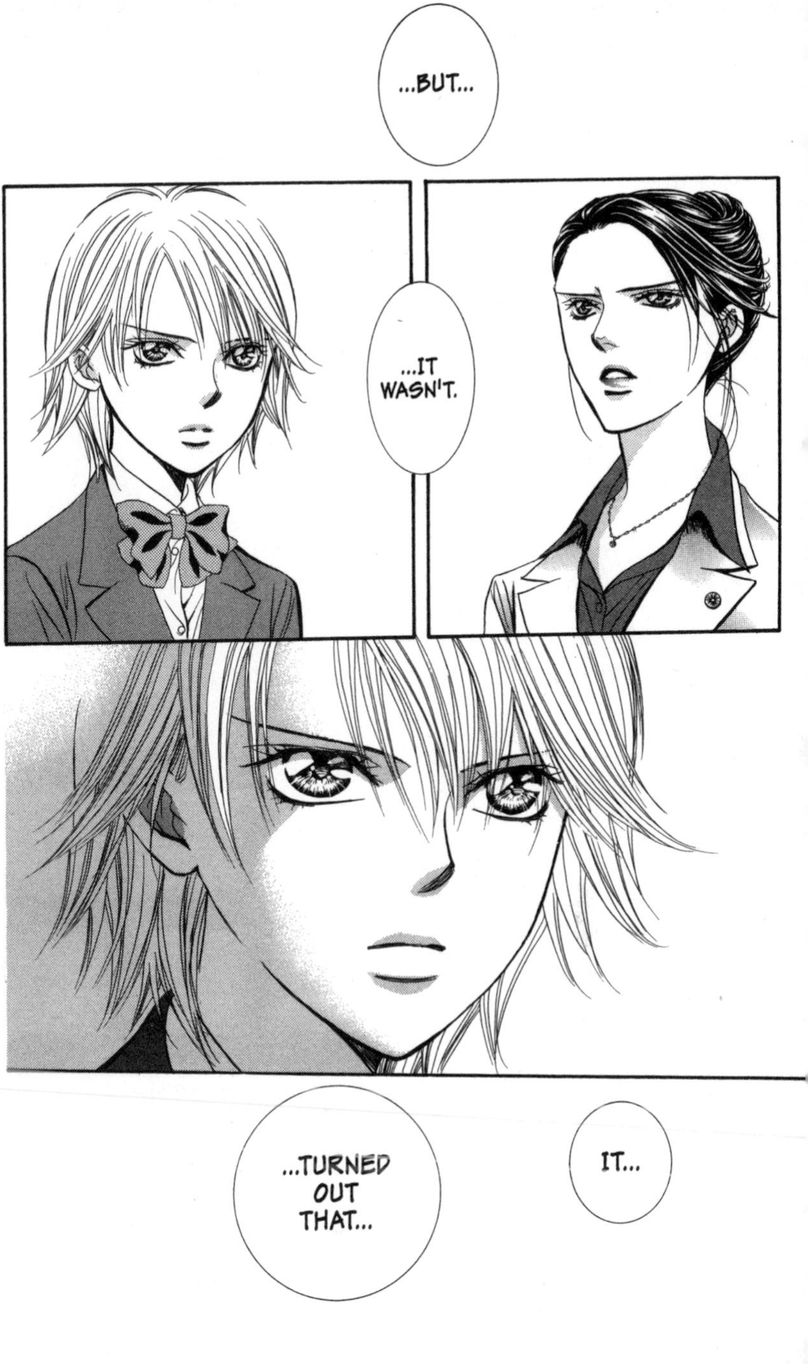
...BUT...
...IT WASN'T.
IT...
...TURNED OUT THAT...

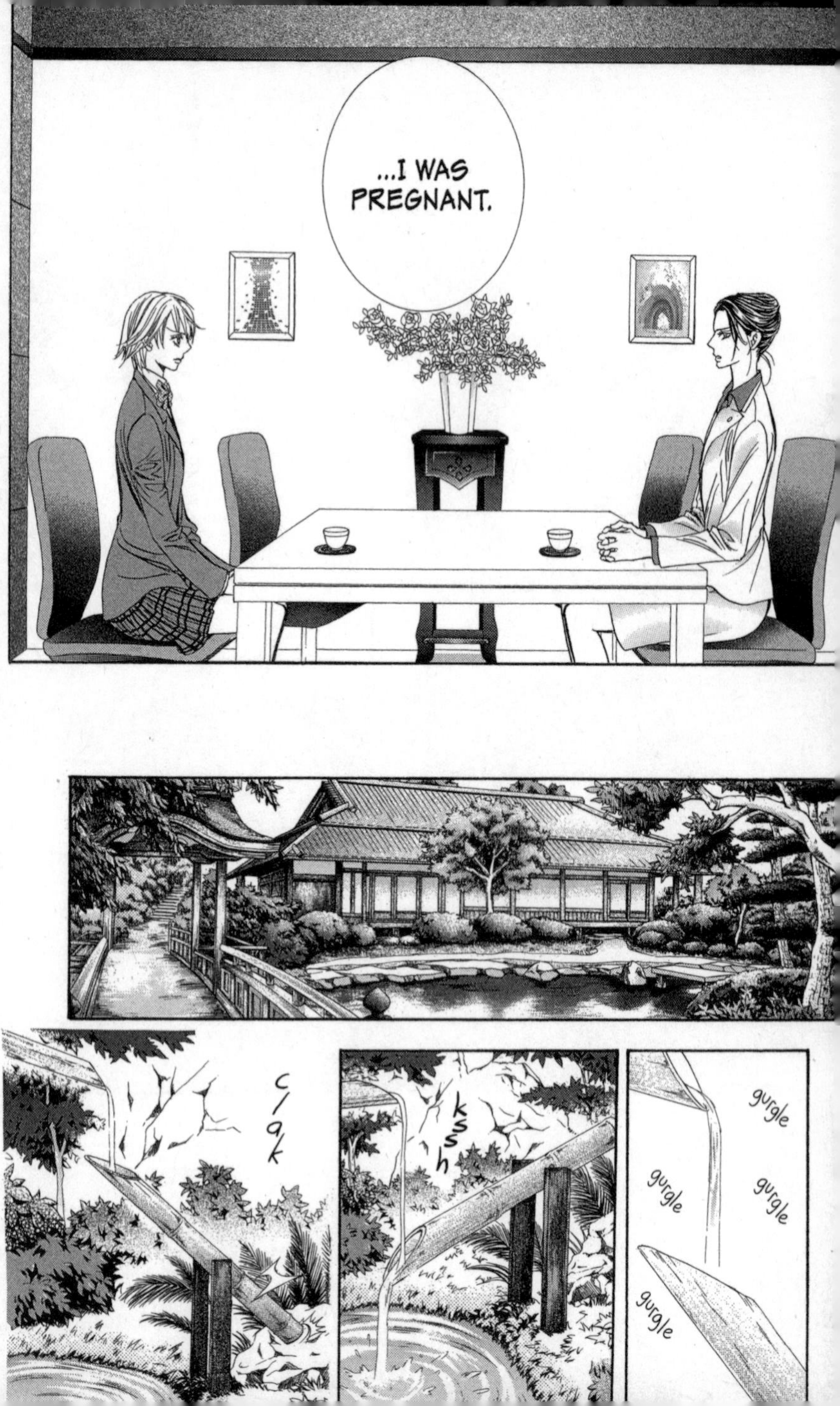
...I WAS PREGNANT.
gurgle
gurgle
gurgle
gurgle
kssh
clak

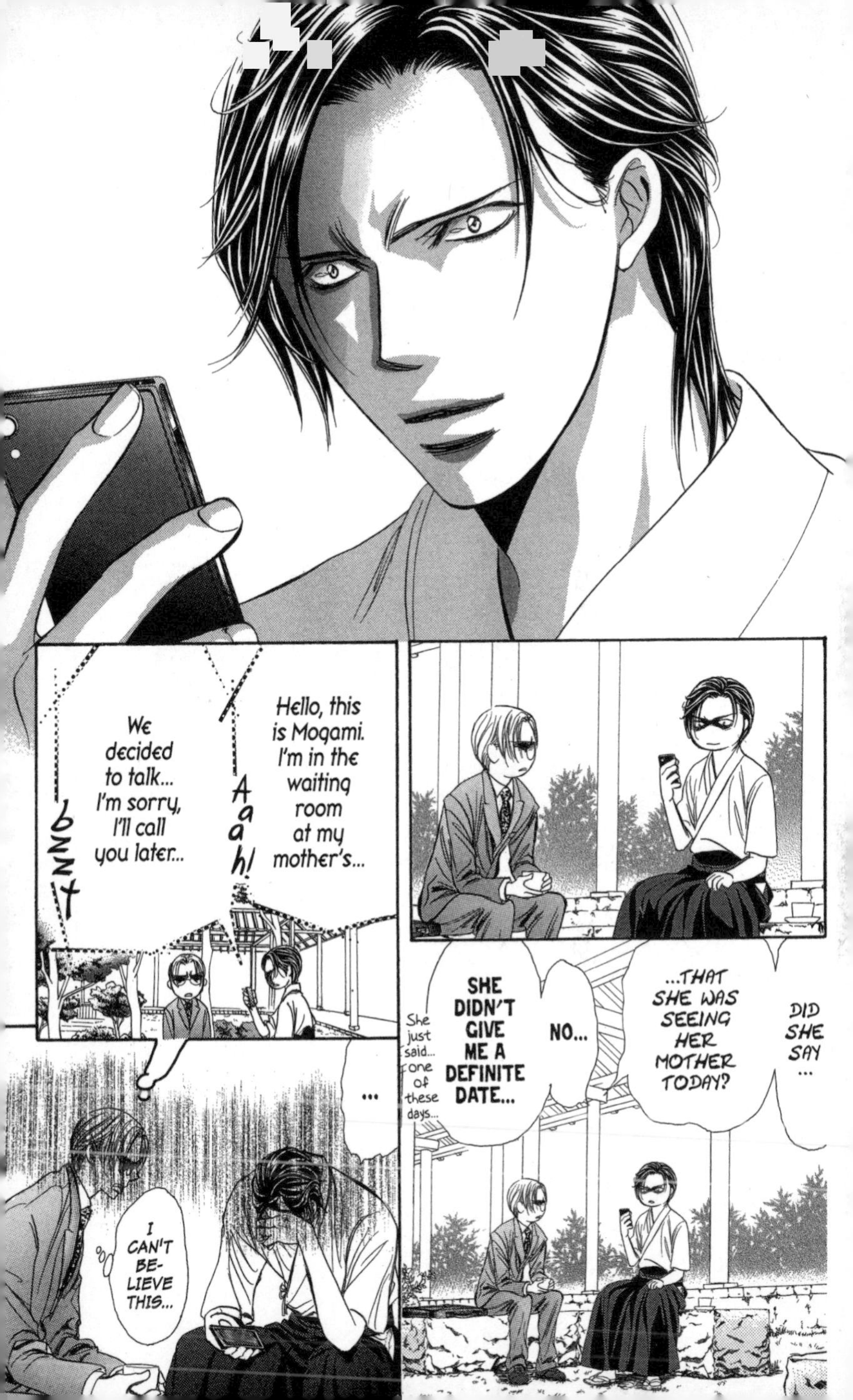
Hello, this is Mogami. I'm in the waiting room at my mother's...
Aaah!
We decided to talk... I'm sorry, I'll call you later...
bzzt
DID SHE SAY...
...THAT SHE WAS SEEING HER MOTHER TODAY?
NO...
SHE DIDN'T GIVE ME A DEFINITE DATE...
She just said... one of these days...
...
I CAN'T BELIEVE THIS...

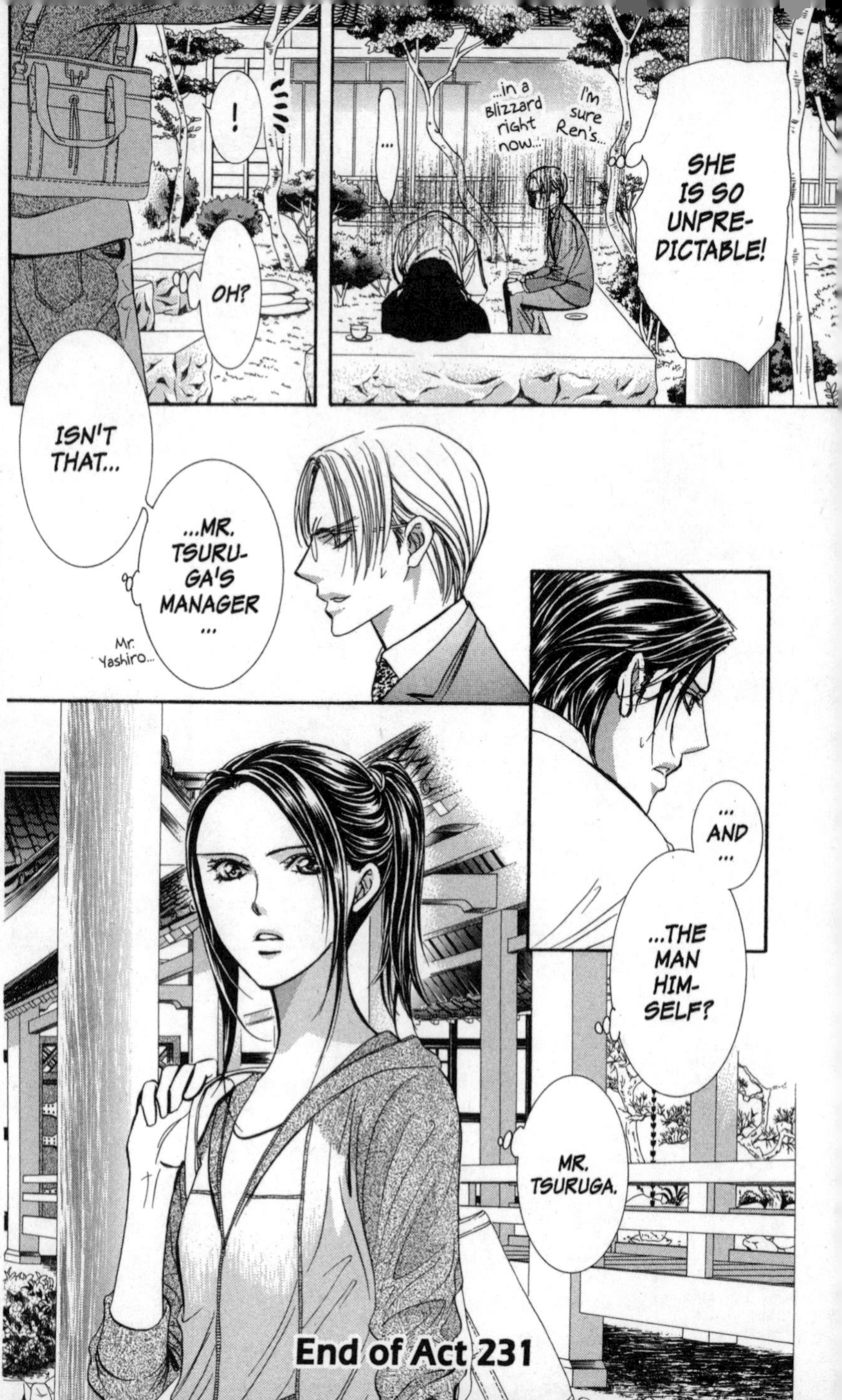
SHE IS SO UNPREDICTABLE!
I'm sure Ren's...
...in a Blizzard right now...
...
!
OH?
ISN'T THAT...
...MR. TSURUGA'S MANAGER...
Mr. Yashiro...
...AND...
...THE MAN HIMSELF?
MR. TSURUGA.
End of Act 231

Level 100
Tsuruga Weirdness

*"Making progress
with eating."*

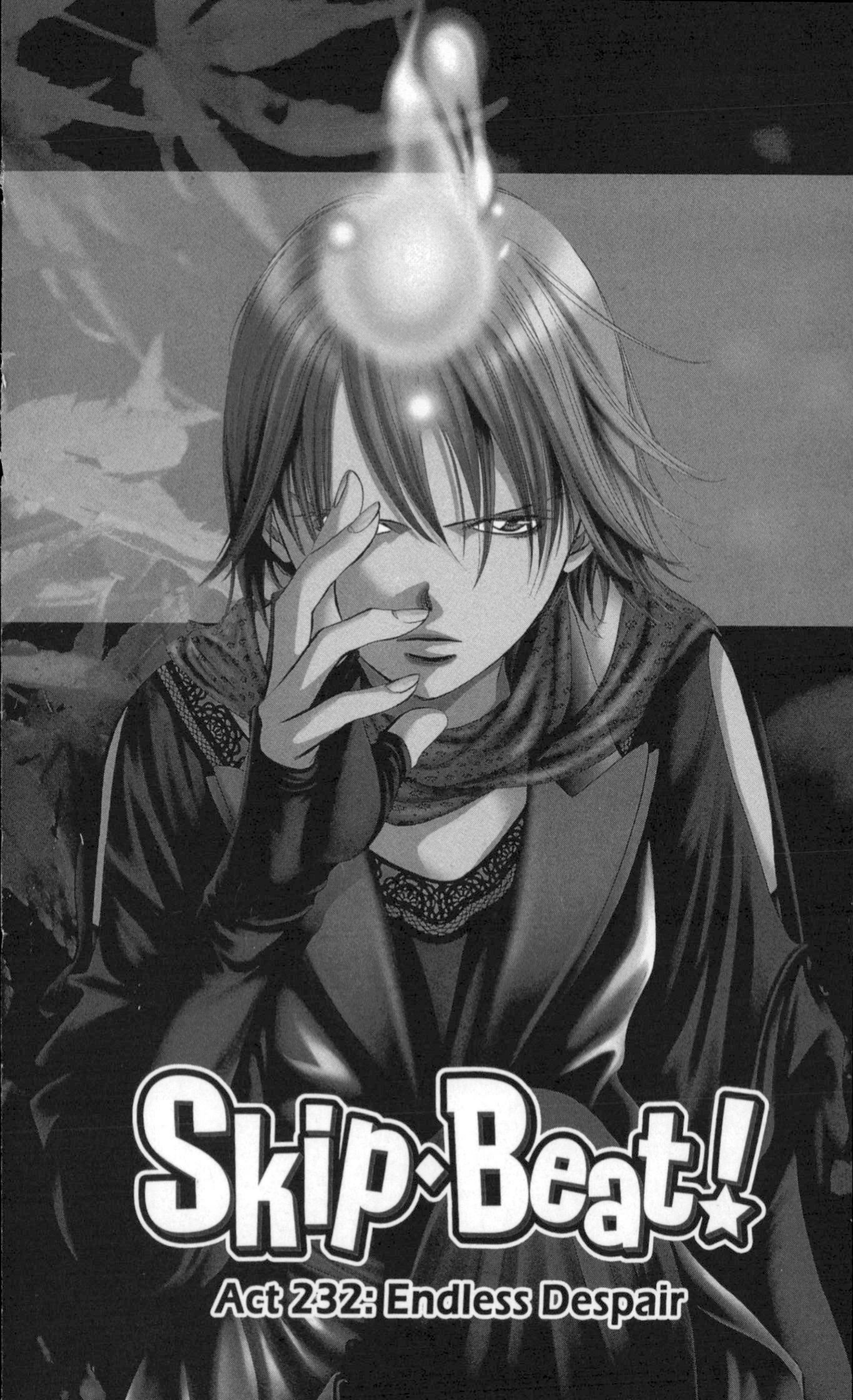
Skip·Beat!
Act 232: Endless Despair

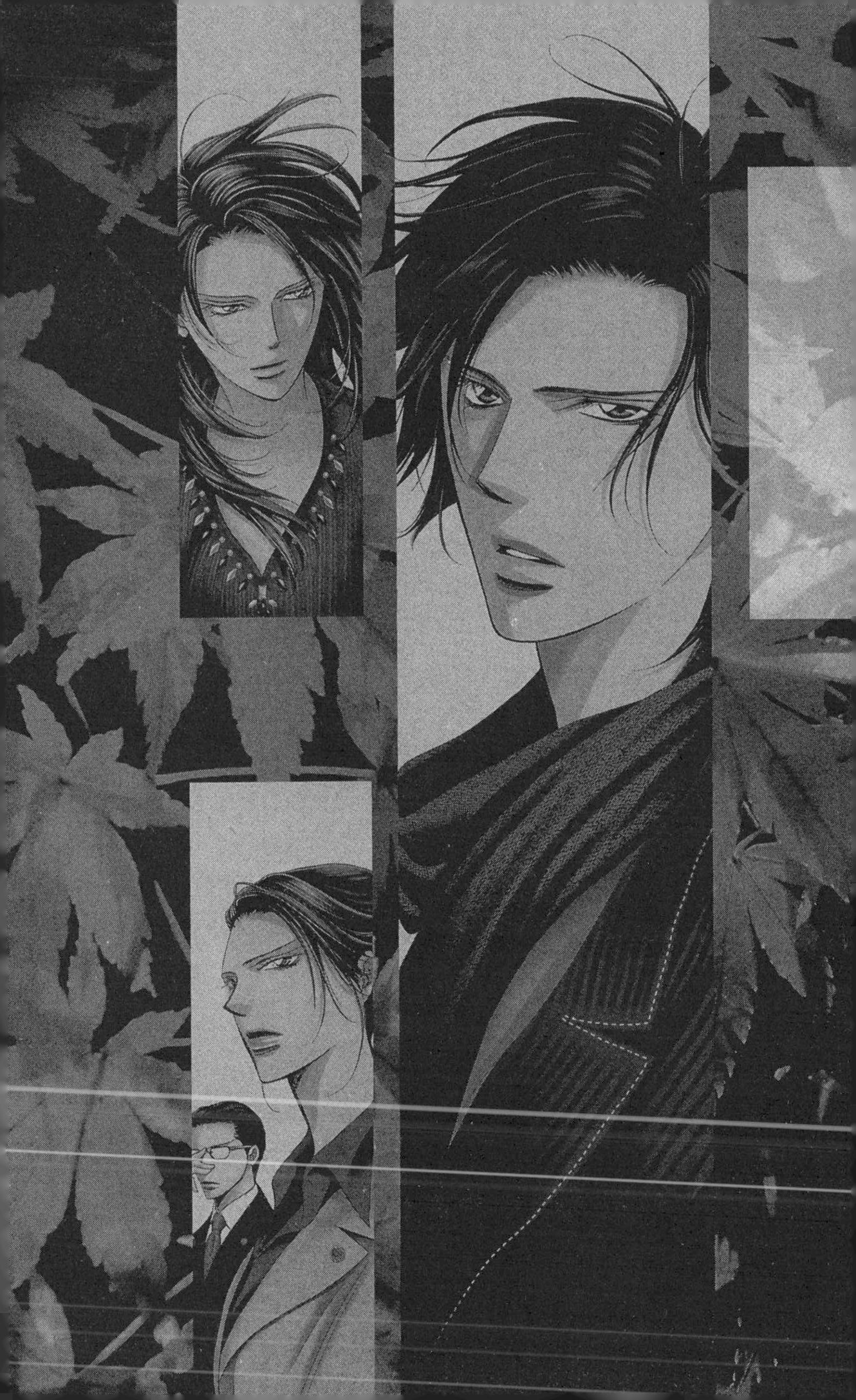

Level 100 Tsuruga Weirdness

"I don't hate this chore."

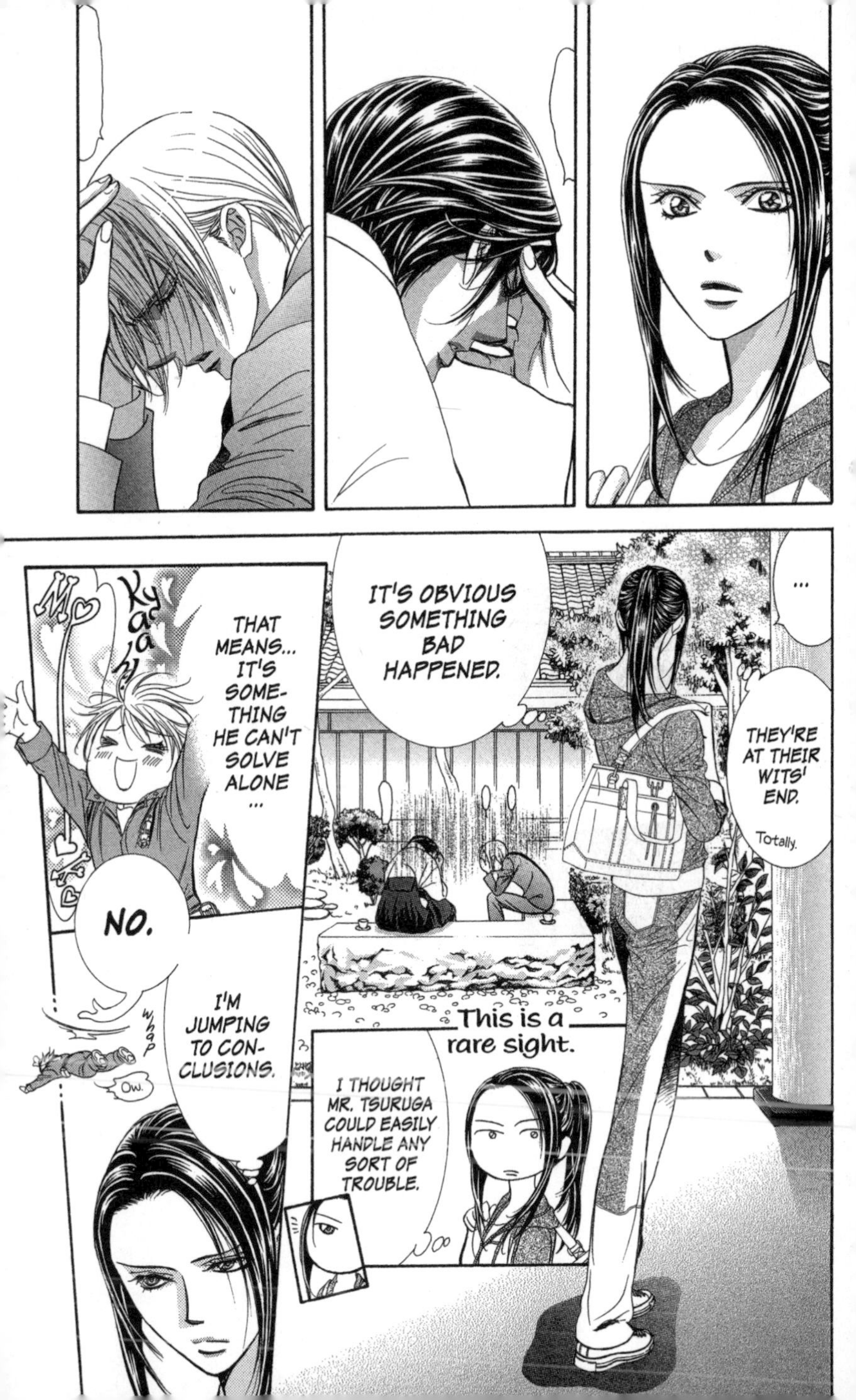
...
THEY'RE AT THEIR WITS' END.
Totally.
IT'S OBVIOUS SOMETHING BAD HAPPENED.
THAT MEANS... IT'S SOME-THING HE CAN'T SOLVE ALONE ...
Kyaah!
NO.
whap
Ow.
I'M JUMPING TO CON-CLUSIONS.
This is a rare sight.
I THOUGHT MR. TSURUGA COULD EASILY HANDLE ANY SORT OF TROUBLE.

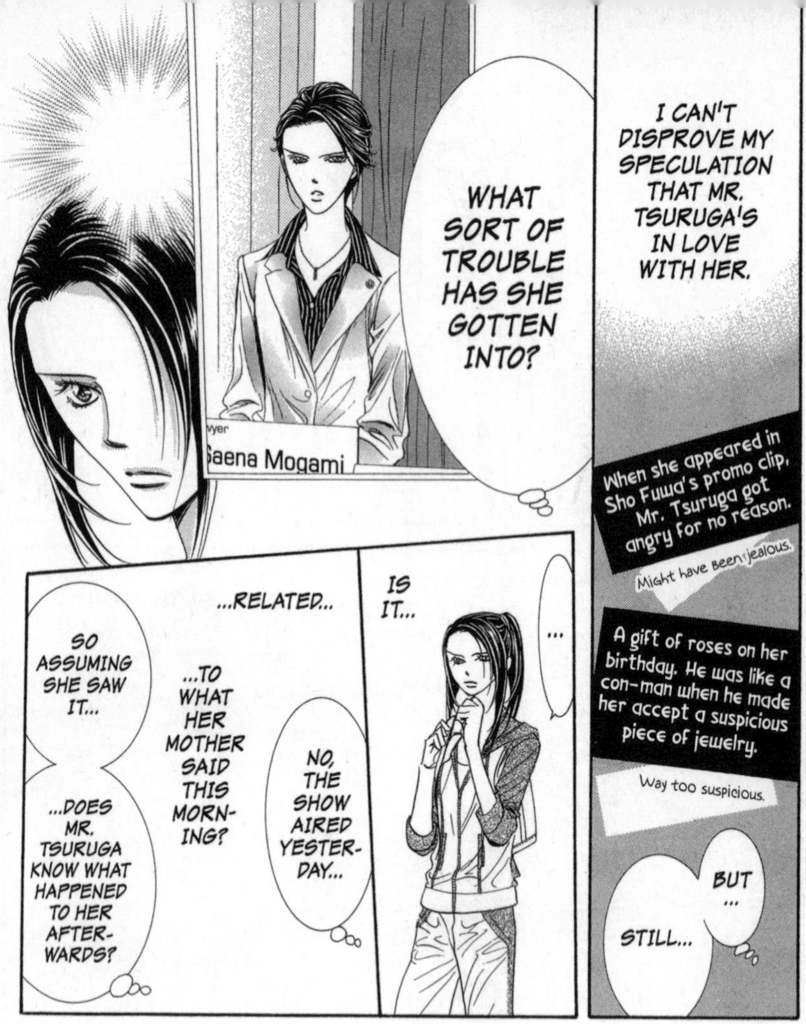
I CAN'T DISPROVE MY SPECULATION THAT MR. TSURUGA'S IN LOVE WITH HER.
When she appeared in Sho Fuwa's promo clip, Mr. Tsuruga got angry for no reason.
Might have been jealous.
A gift of roses on her birthday. He was like a con-man when he made her accept a suspicious piece of jewelry.
Way too suspicious.
BUT ...
STILL...
WHAT SORT OF TROUBLE HAS SHE GOTTEN INTO?
Saena Mogami
...
IS IT...
...RELATED...
...TO WHAT HER MOTHER SAID THIS MORNING?
NO, THE SHOW AIRED YESTERDAY...
SO ASSUMING SHE SAW IT...
...DOES MR. TSURUGA KNOW WHAT HAPPENED TO HER AFTERWARDS?

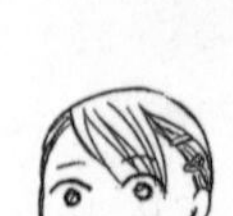

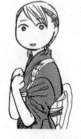

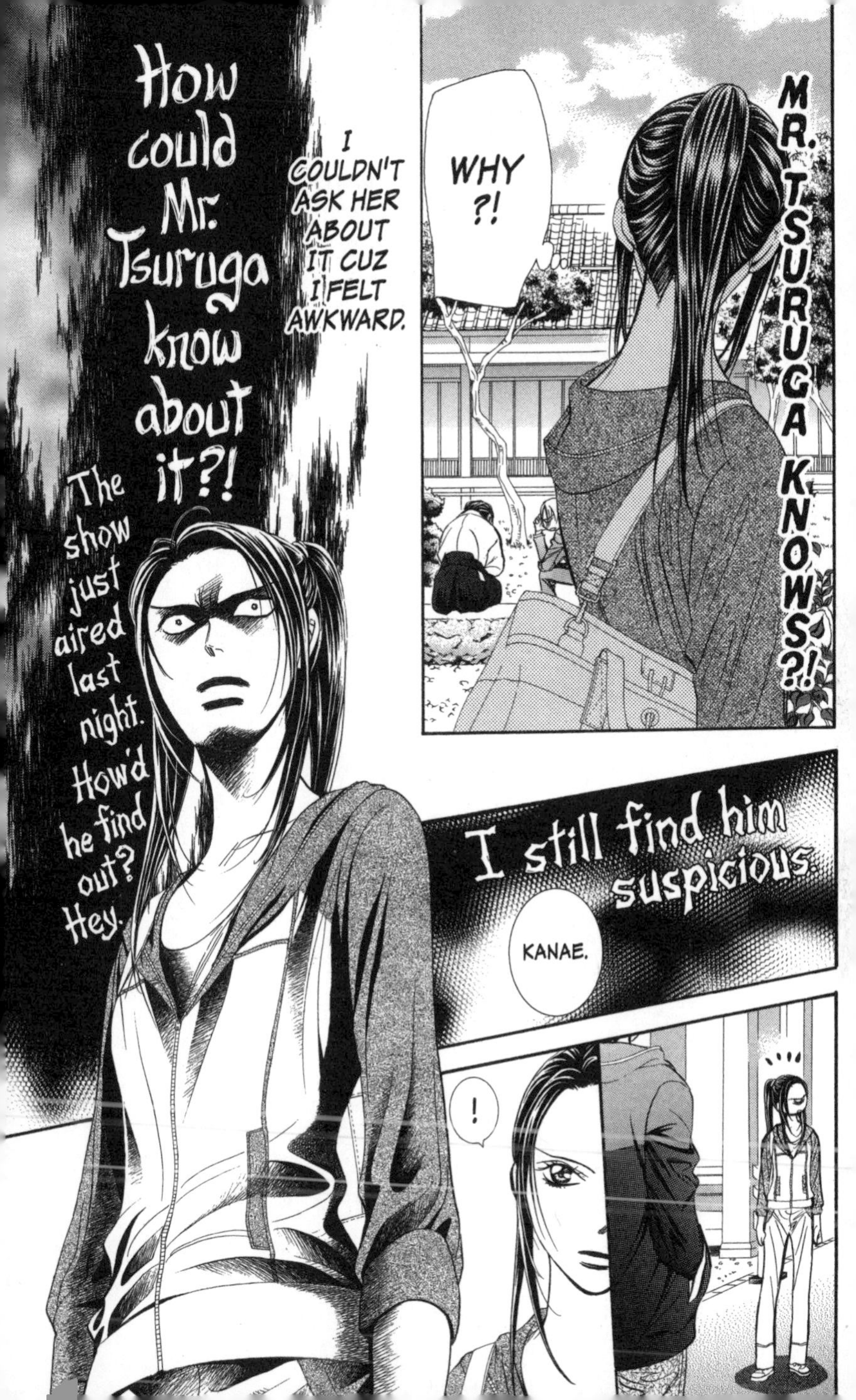
MR. TSURUGA KNOWS?!
WHY?!
I still find him suspicious.
KANAE.
!
How could Mr. Tsuruga know about it?!
I COULDN'T ASK HER ABOUT IT CUZ I FELT AWKWARD.
The show just aired last night. How'd he find out? Hey.

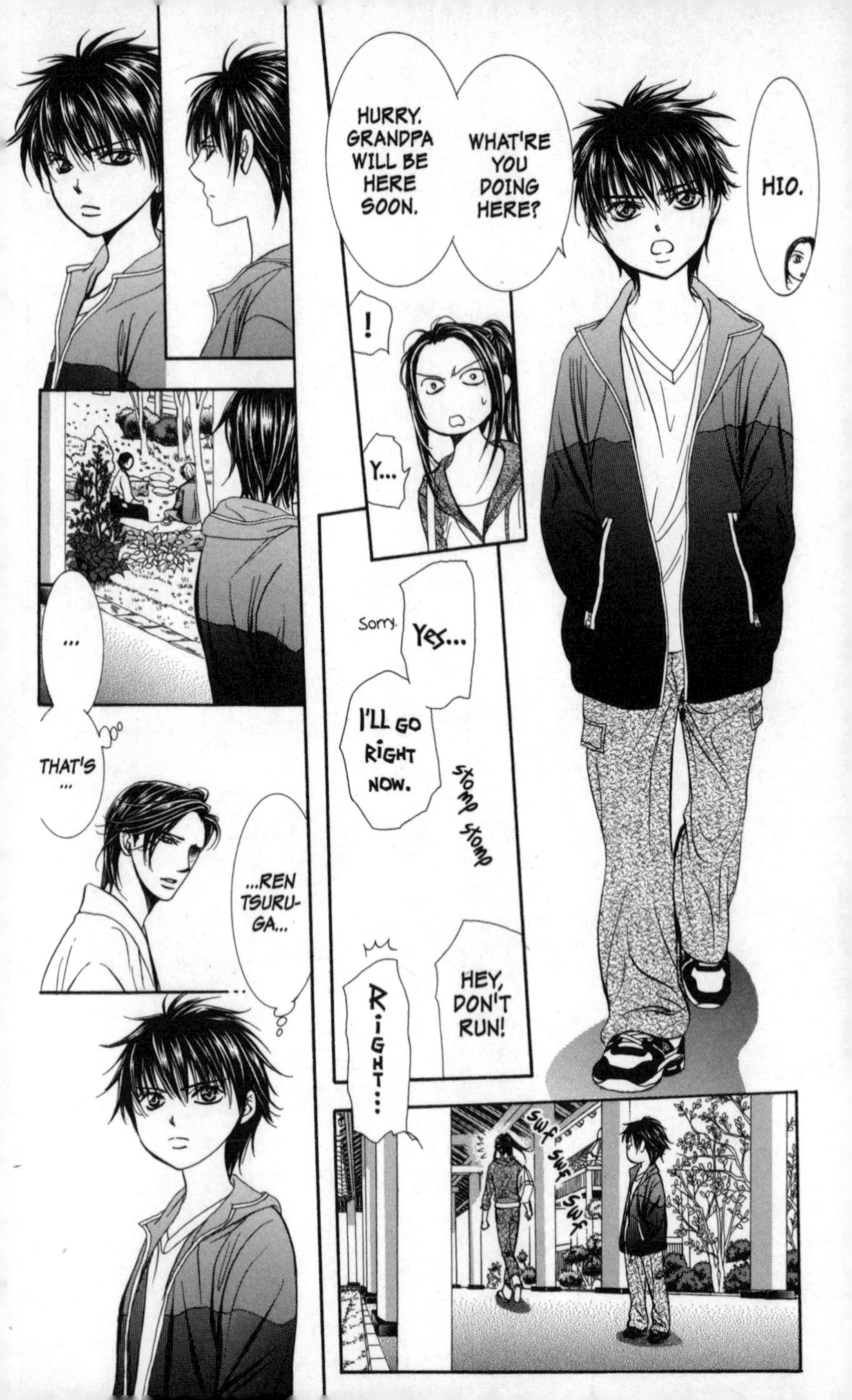
HIO.
WHAT'RE YOU DOING HERE?
HURRY. GRANDPA WILL BE HERE SOON.
!
Y...
Yes...
Sorry.
I'LL GO RIGHT NOW.
stomp stomp
HEY, DON'T RUN!
RIGHT...
SWF SWF SWF SWF
...
THAT'S ...
...REN TSURUGA...

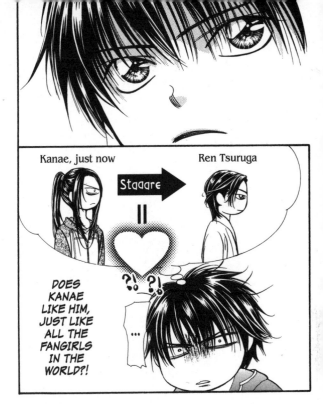

Ren Tsuruga
Staaare
Kanae, just now
?! ?!
...
DOES KANAE LIKE HIM, JUST LIKE ALL THE FANGIRLS IN THE WORLD?!
Mature. Handsome. Super tall...?
(How ordinary girls would rate him.)
...
I CAN WORK ON "HANDSOME"...
That's about it...
I MEAN...
shuffle
shuffle
WHAT THE HELL IS "SUPER TALL"? HOW TALL IS HE? LIKE TEN FEET?
IS REN TSURUGA A MONSTER?

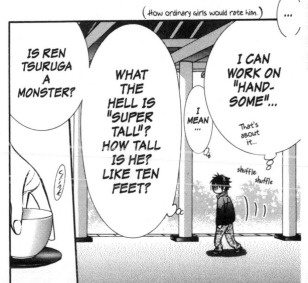

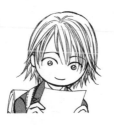

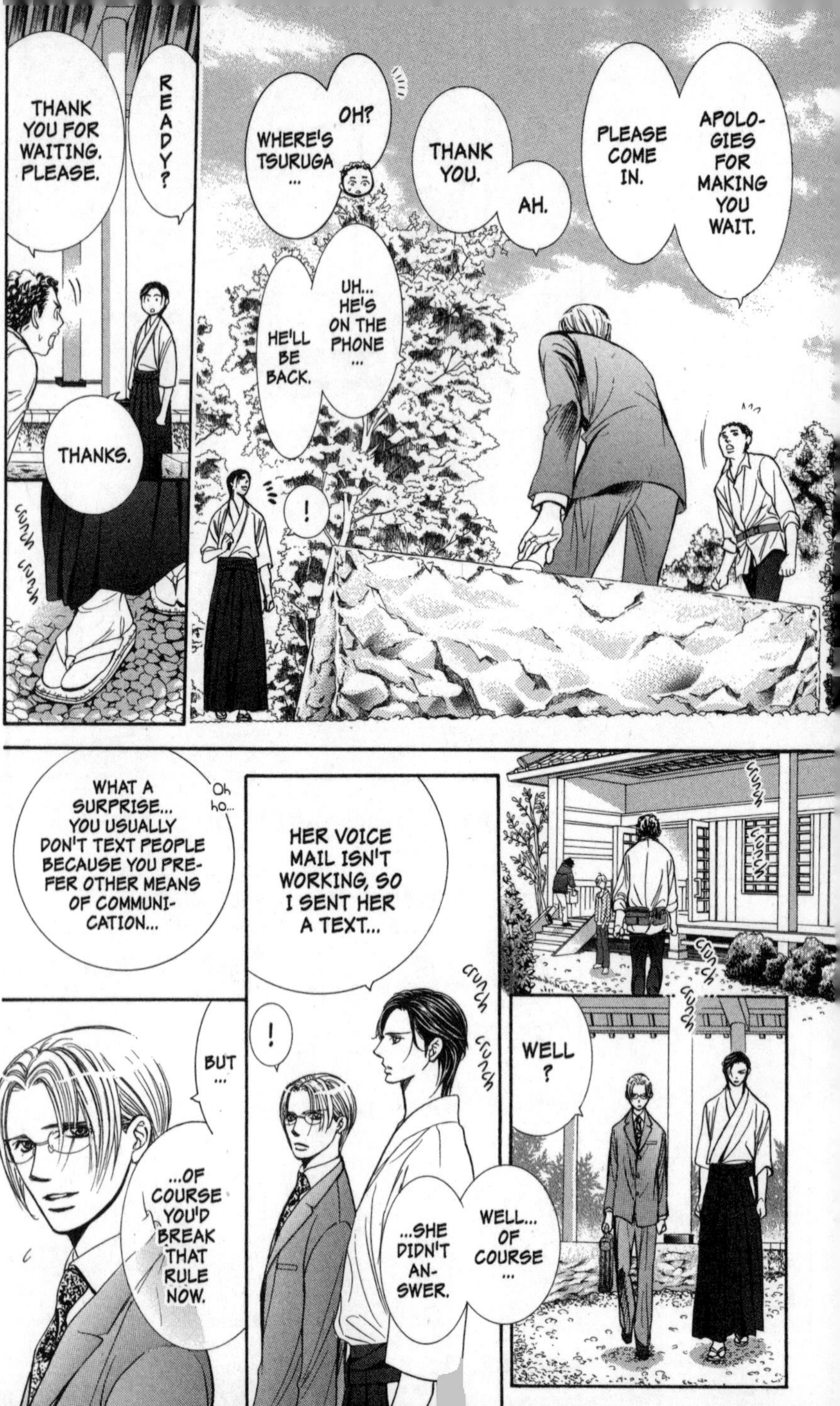
APOLOGIES FOR MAKING YOU WAIT.
PLEASE COME IN.
AH.
THANK YOU.
OH?
WHERE'S TSURUGA...
UH... HE'S ON THE PHONE...
HE'LL BE BACK.
!
READY?
THANK YOU FOR WAITING. PLEASE.
THANKS.
crunch crunch
crunch crunch crunch
WELL?
WELL... OF COURSE...
...SHE DIDN'T AN-SWER.
HER VOICE MAIL ISN'T WORKING, SO I SENT HER A TEXT...
!
crunch crunch
Oh ho...
WHAT A SURPRISE... YOU USUALLY DON'T TEXT PEOPLE BECAUSE YOU PRE-FER OTHER MEANS OF COMMUNI-CATION...
BUT...
...OF COURSE YOU'D BREAK THAT RULE NOW.

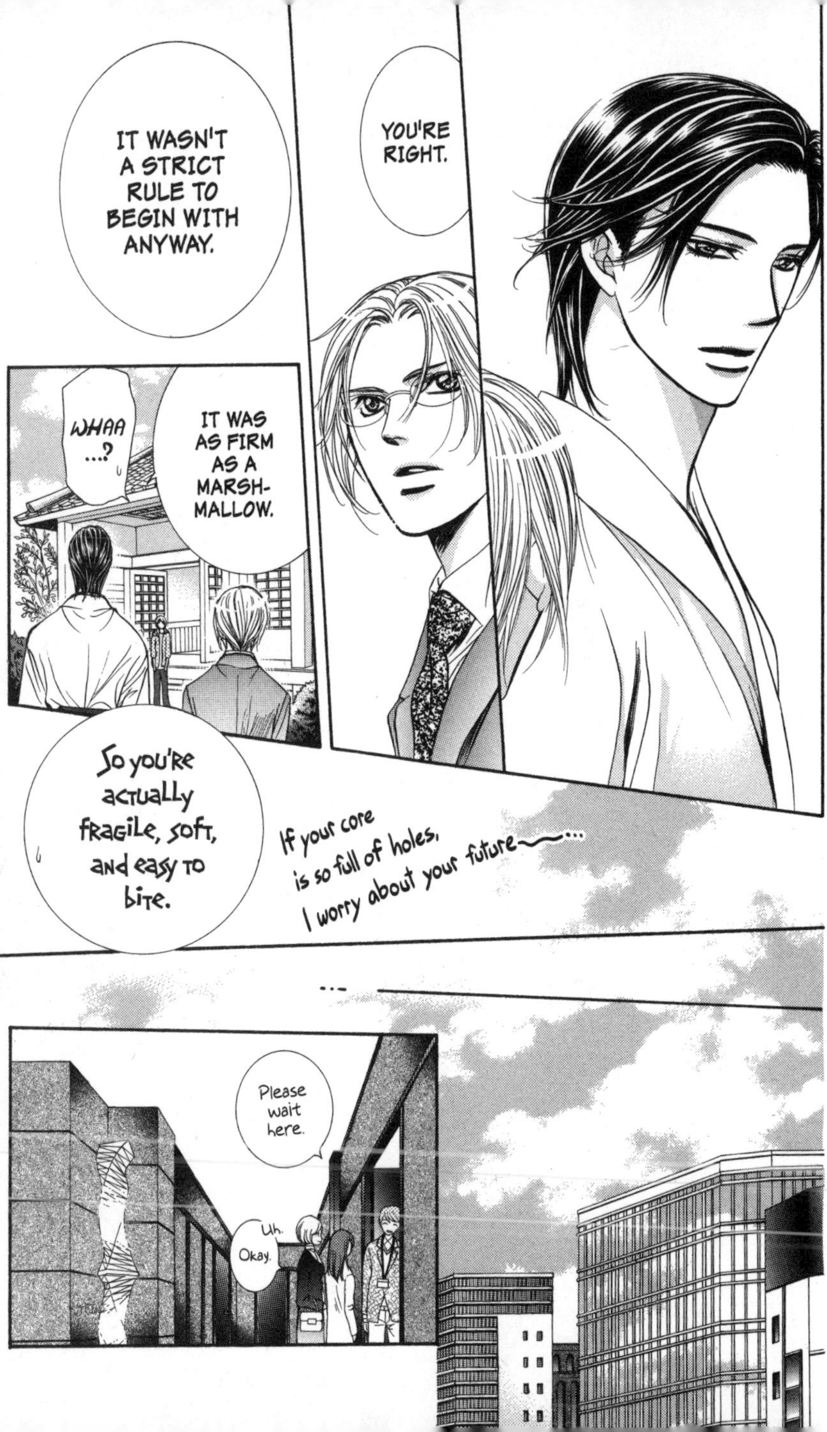
YOU'RE RIGHT.
IT WASN'T A STRICT RULE TO BEGIN WITH ANYWAY.
IT WAS AS FIRM AS A MARSHMALLOW.
WHAA ...?
So you're actually fragile, soft, and easy to bite.
If your core is so full of holes, I worry about your future~~...
Please wait here.
Uh. Okay.

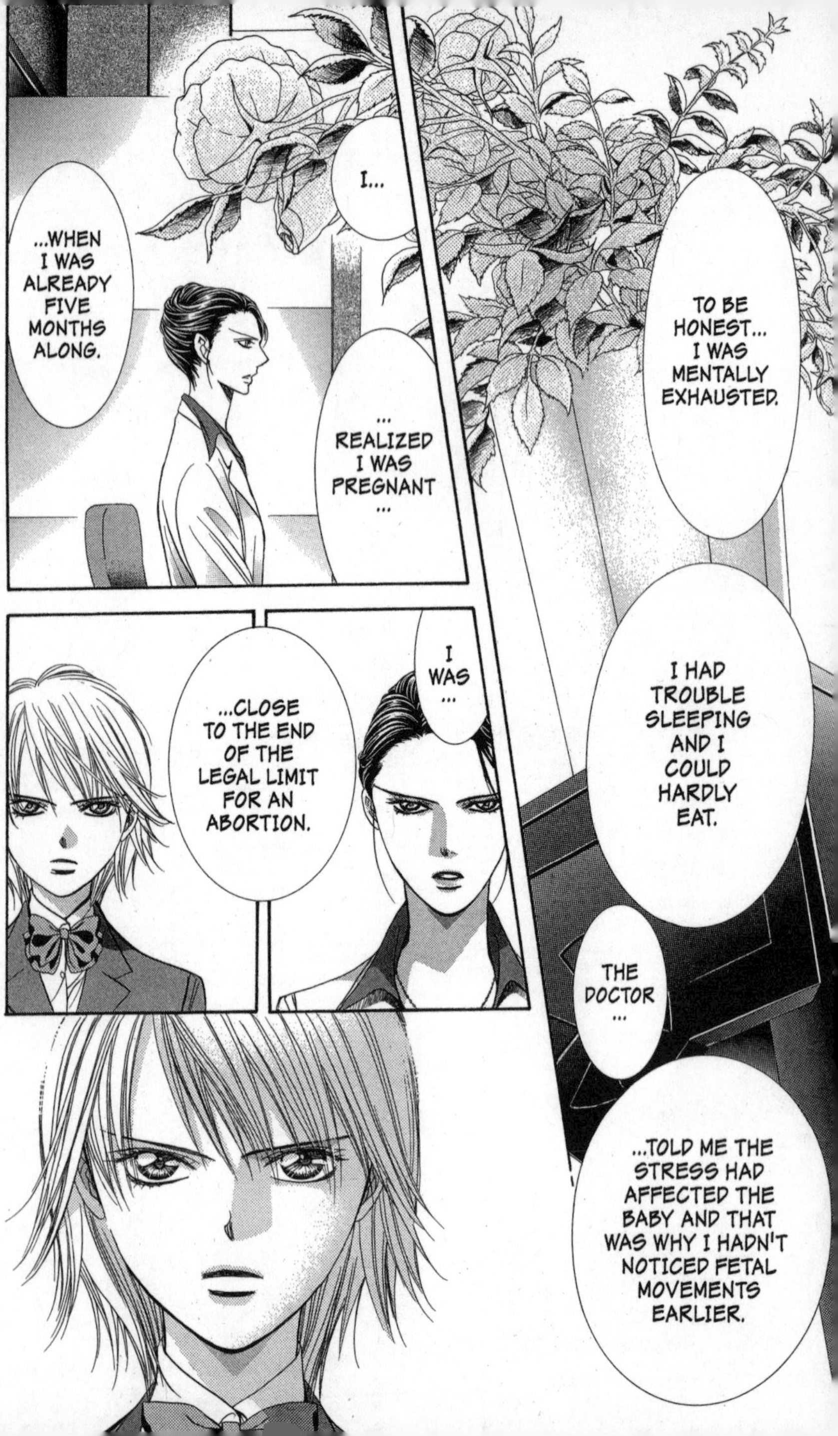
TO BE HONEST... I WAS MENTALLY EXHAUSTED.
I HAD TROUBLE SLEEPING AND I COULD HARDLY EAT.
THE DOCTOR...
...TOLD ME THE STRESS HAD AFFECTED THE BABY AND THAT WAS WHY I HADN'T NOTICED FETAL MOVEMENTS EARLIER.
I...
...REALIZED I WAS PREGNANT...
...WHEN I WAS ALREADY FIVE MONTHS ALONG.
I WAS...
...CLOSE TO THE END OF THE LEGAL LIMIT FOR AN ABORTION.

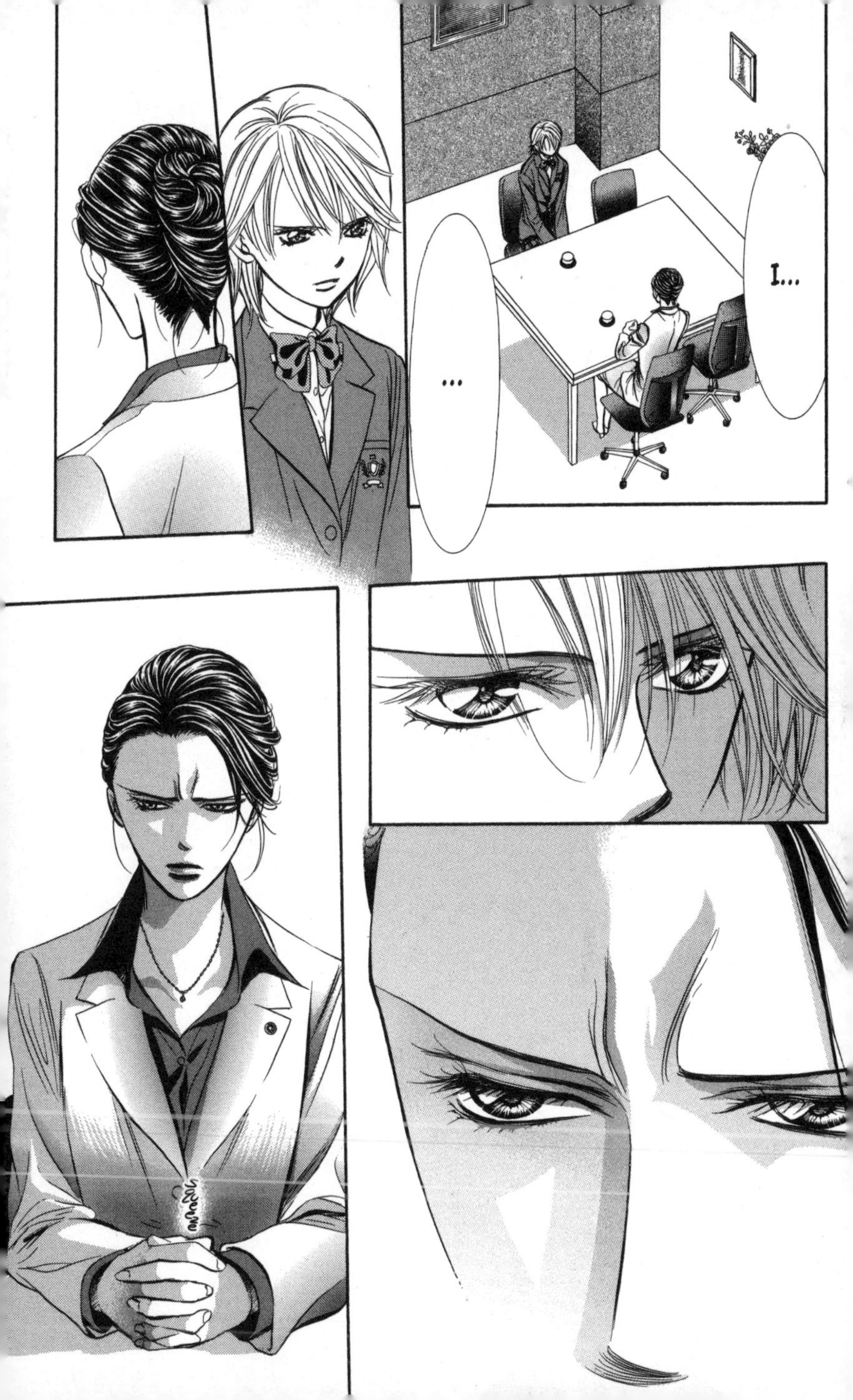
I...
...

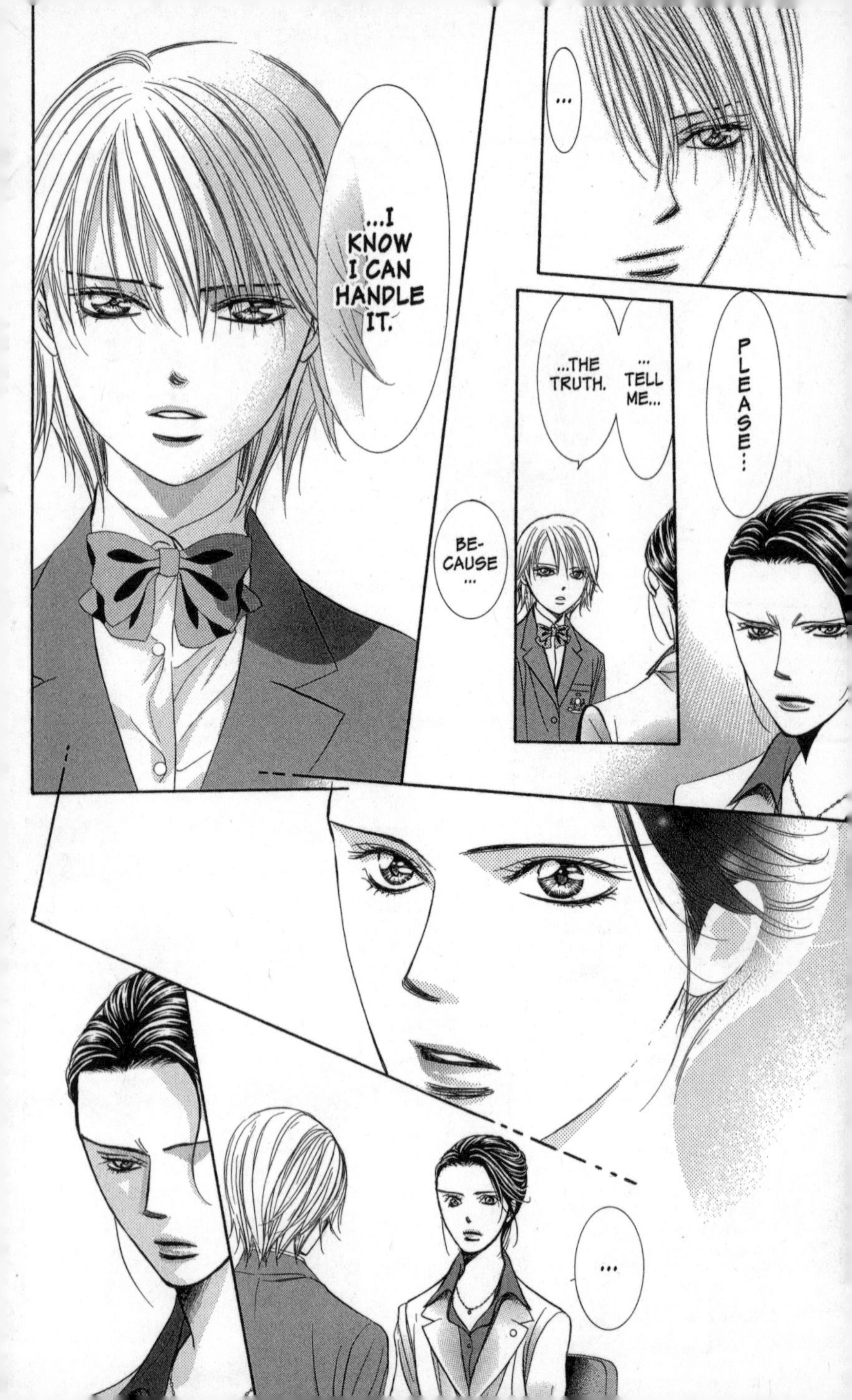
...
PLEASE...
...TELL ME...
...THE TRUTH.
BE-CAUSE...
...I KNOW I CAN HANDLE IT.
...

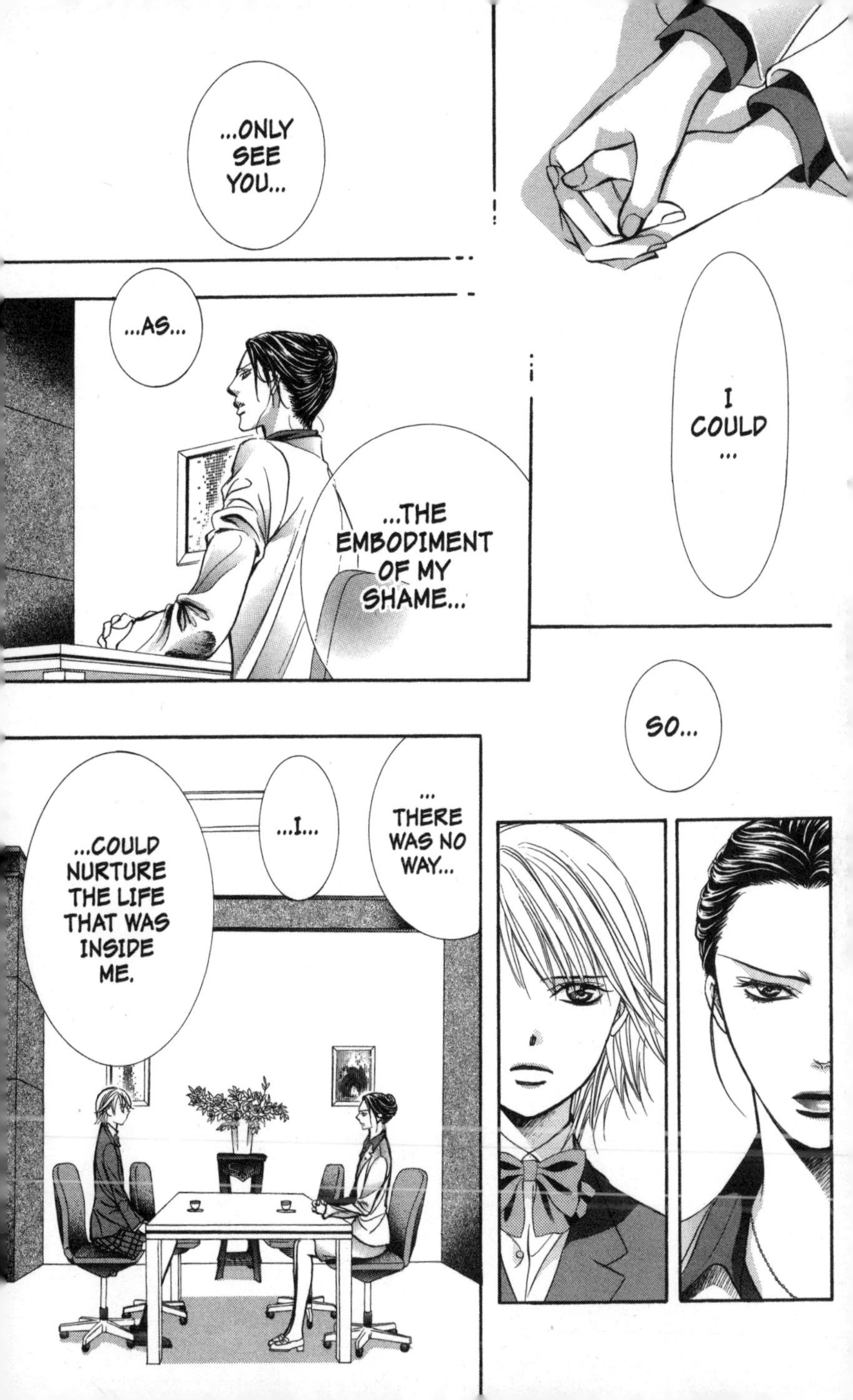
I COULD ...
...ONLY SEE YOU...
...AS...
...THE EMBODIMENT OF MY SHAME...
SO...
... THERE WAS NO WAY...
...I...
...COULD NURTURE THE LIFE THAT WAS INSIDE ME.

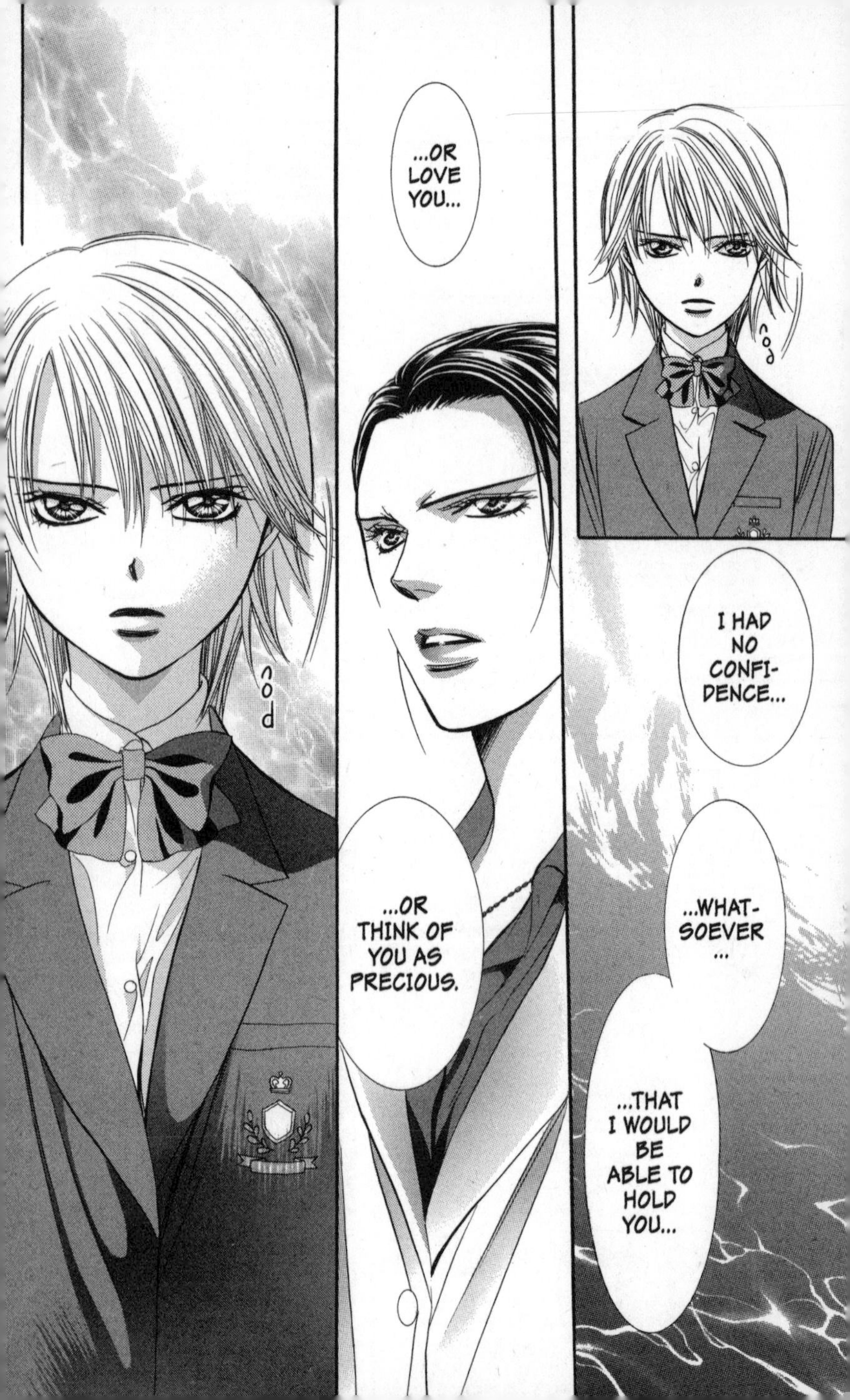
I HAD NO CONFI-DENCE...
...WHAT-SOEVER...
...THAT I WOULD BE ABLE TO HOLD YOU...
...OR LOVE YOU...
...OR THINK OF YOU AS PRECIOUS.

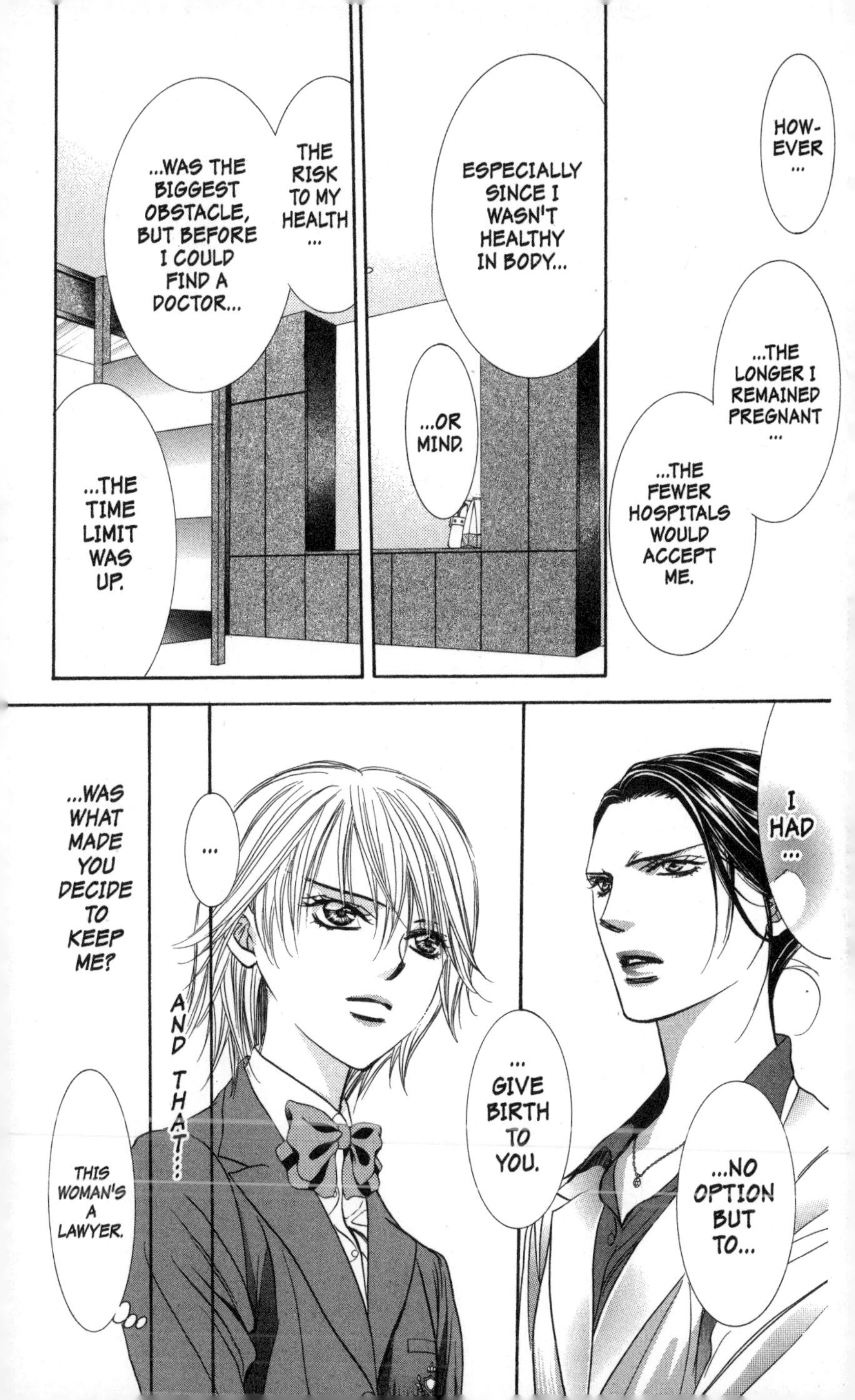
HOW-EVER...
...THE LONGER I REMAINED PREGNANT...
...THE FEWER HOSPITALS WOULD ACCEPT ME.
ESPECIALLY SINCE I WASN'T HEALTHY IN BODY...
...OR MIND.
THE RISK TO MY HEALTH...
...WAS THE BIGGEST OBSTACLE, BUT BEFORE I COULD FIND A DOCTOR...
...THE TIME LIMIT WAS UP.
I HAD...
...NO OPTION BUT TO...
...GIVE BIRTH TO YOU.
...
AND THAT...
THIS WOMAN'S A LAWYER.
...WAS WHAT MADE YOU DECIDE TO KEEP ME?

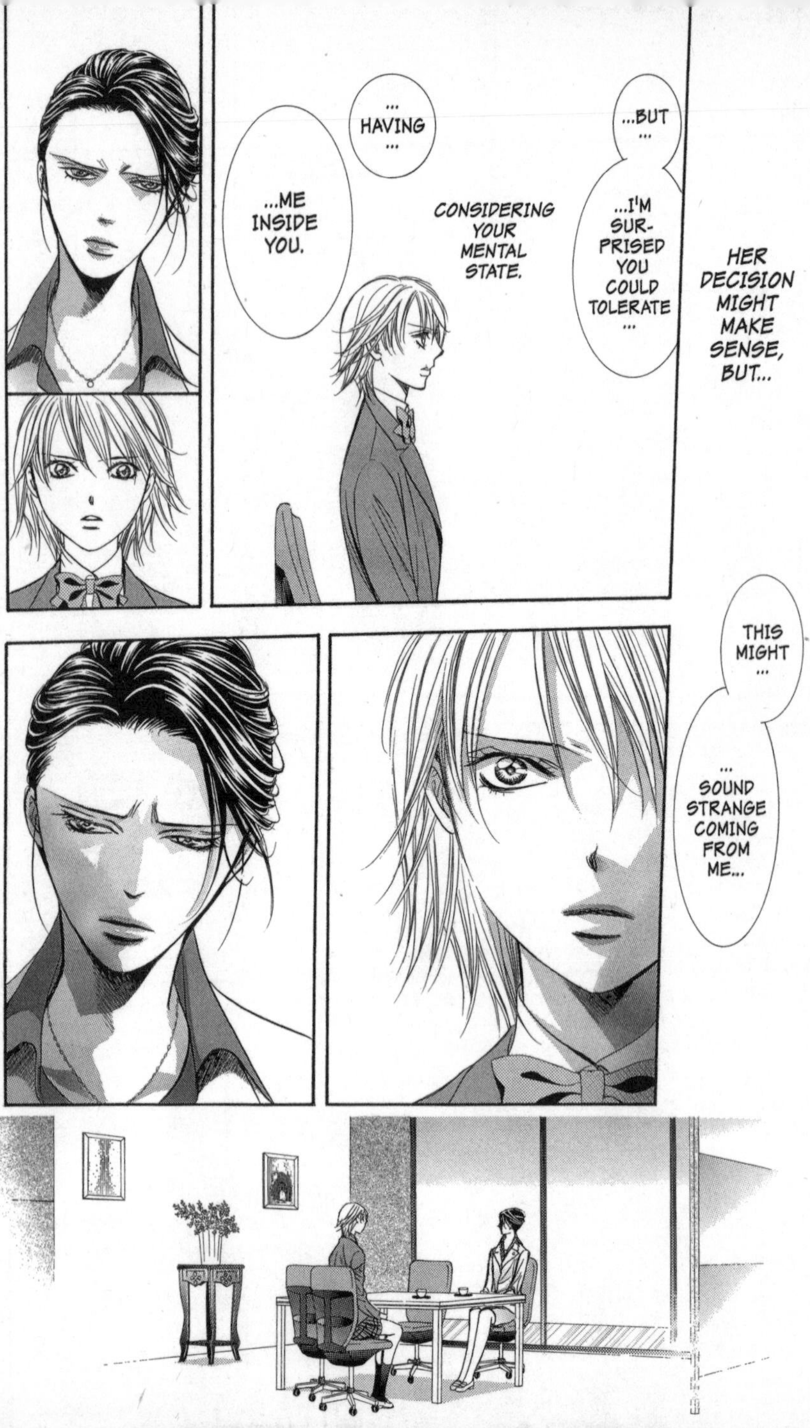
HER DECISION MIGHT MAKE SENSE, BUT...
...BUT...
...I'M SUR-PRISED YOU COULD TOLERATE...
CONSIDERING YOUR MENTAL STATE.
...HAVING...
...ME INSIDE YOU.
THIS MIGHT...
...SOUND STRANGE COMING FROM ME...

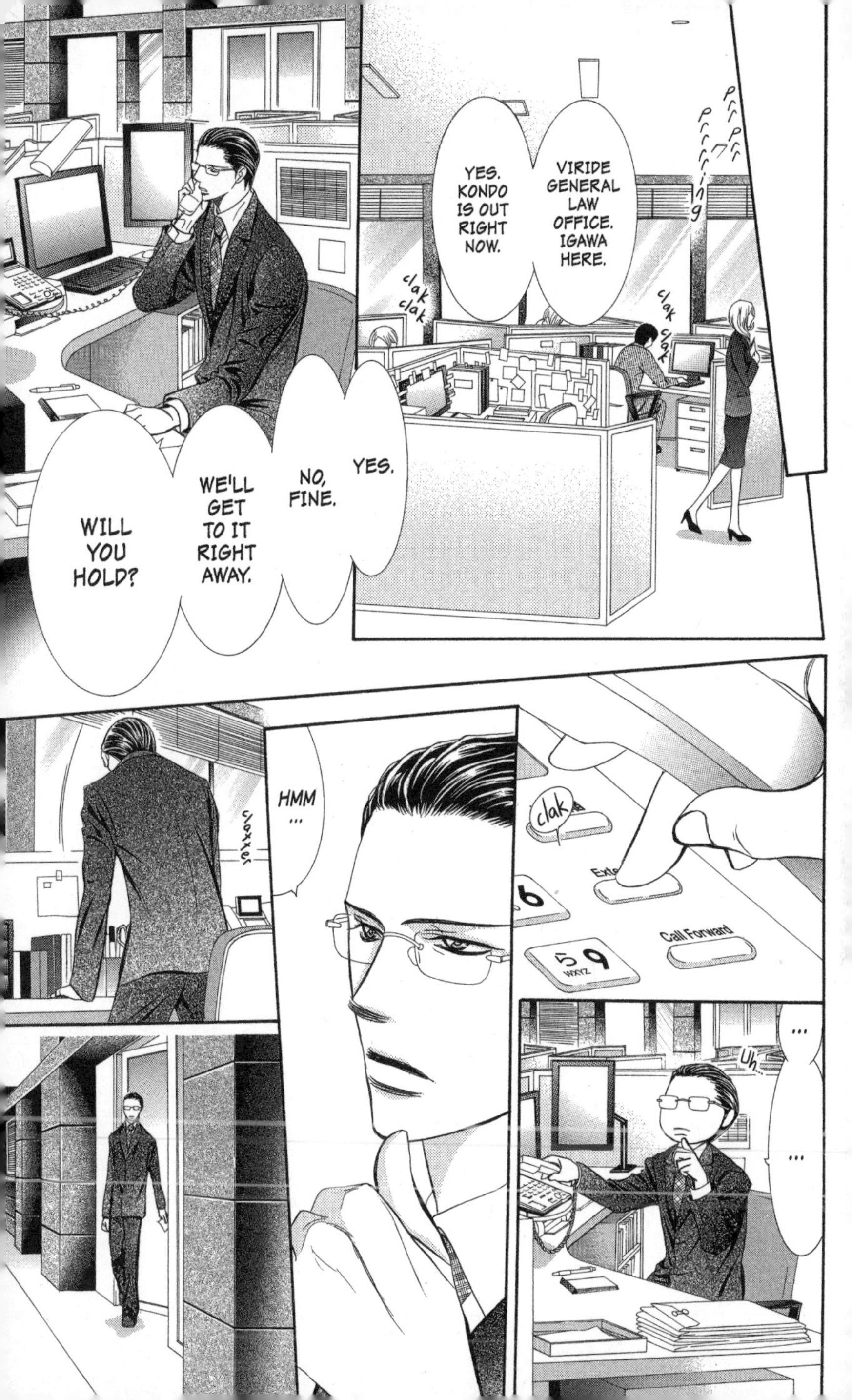
Prrrring
VIRIDE GENERAL LAW OFFICE. IGAWA HERE.
YES. KONDO IS OUT RIGHT NOW.
clak clak
clak clak
YES.
NO, FINE.
WE'LL GET TO IT RIGHT AWAY.
WILL YOU HOLD?
clak
Call Forward
Uh...
...
...
HMM...
cloxxer

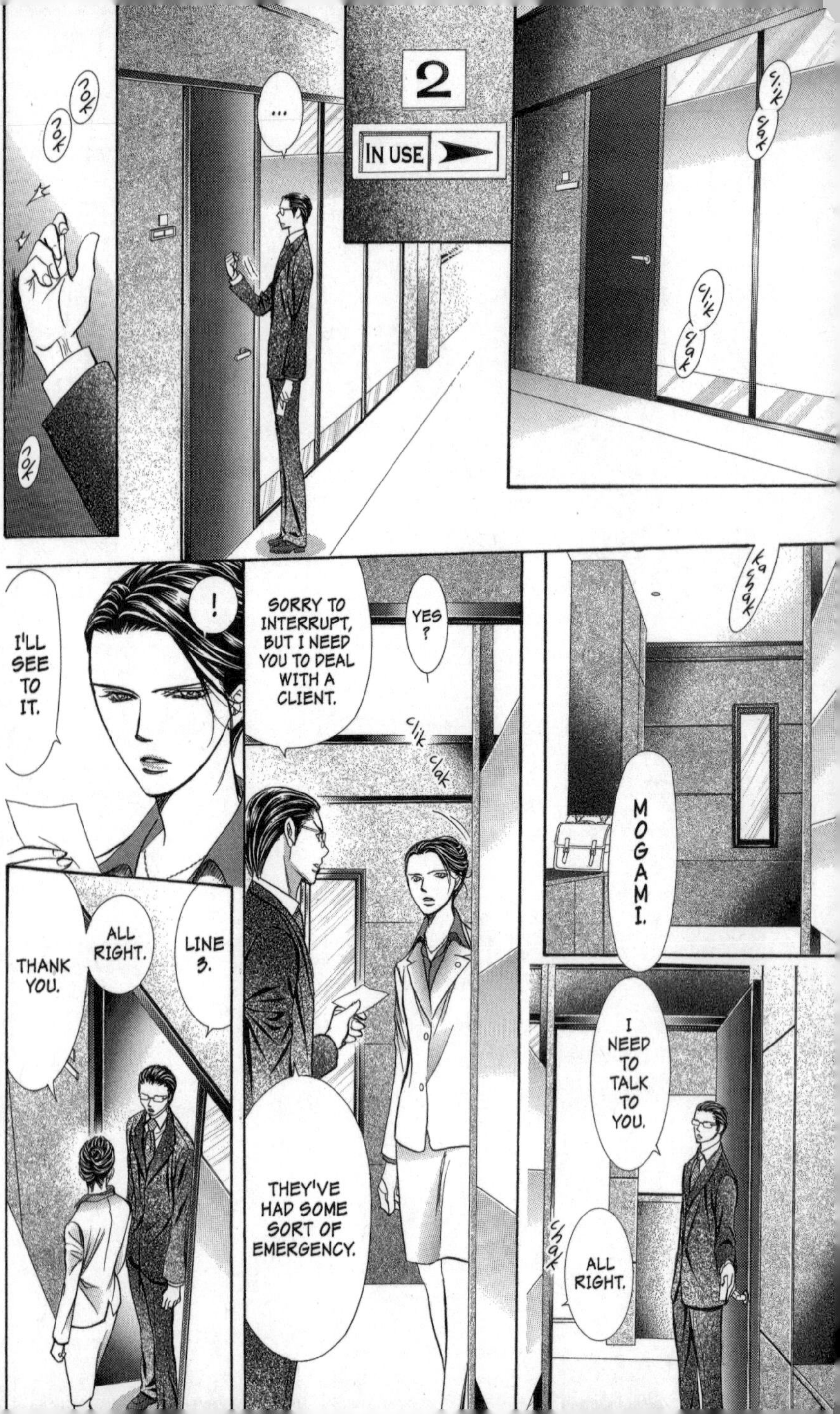
clik clak
clik clak
2
IN USE
...
nok nok
nok
ka chak
MOGAMI.
I NEED TO TALK TO YOU.
chak
ALL RIGHT.
YES?
SORRY TO INTERRUPT, BUT I NEED YOU TO DEAL WITH A CLIENT.
clik clak
THEY'VE HAD SOME SORT OF EMERGENCY.
!
I'LL SEE TO IT.
LINE 3.
ALL RIGHT.
THANK YOU.

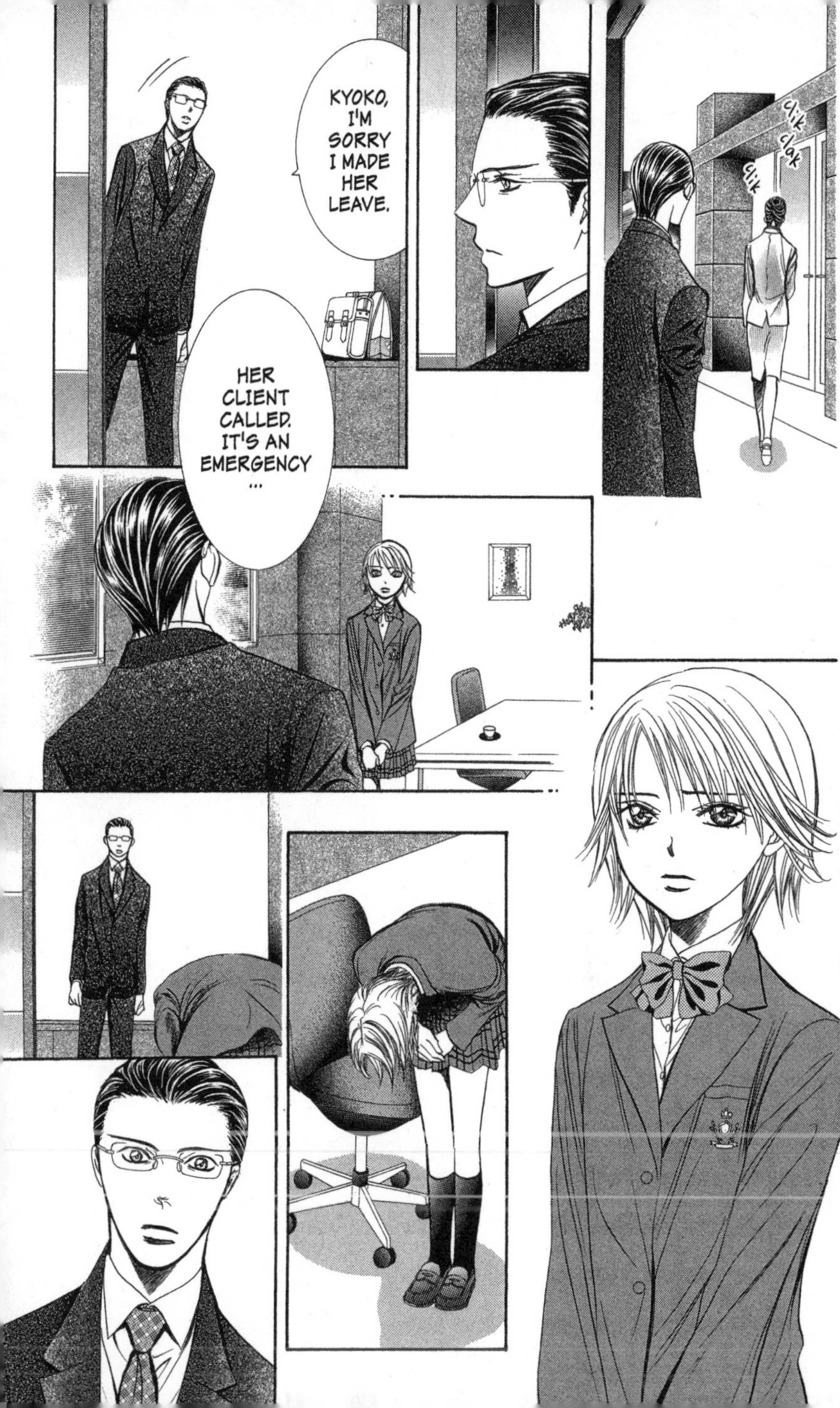
clik clak clik
KYOKO, I'M SORRY I MADE HER LEAVE.
HER CLIENT CALLED. IT'S AN EMERGENCY...

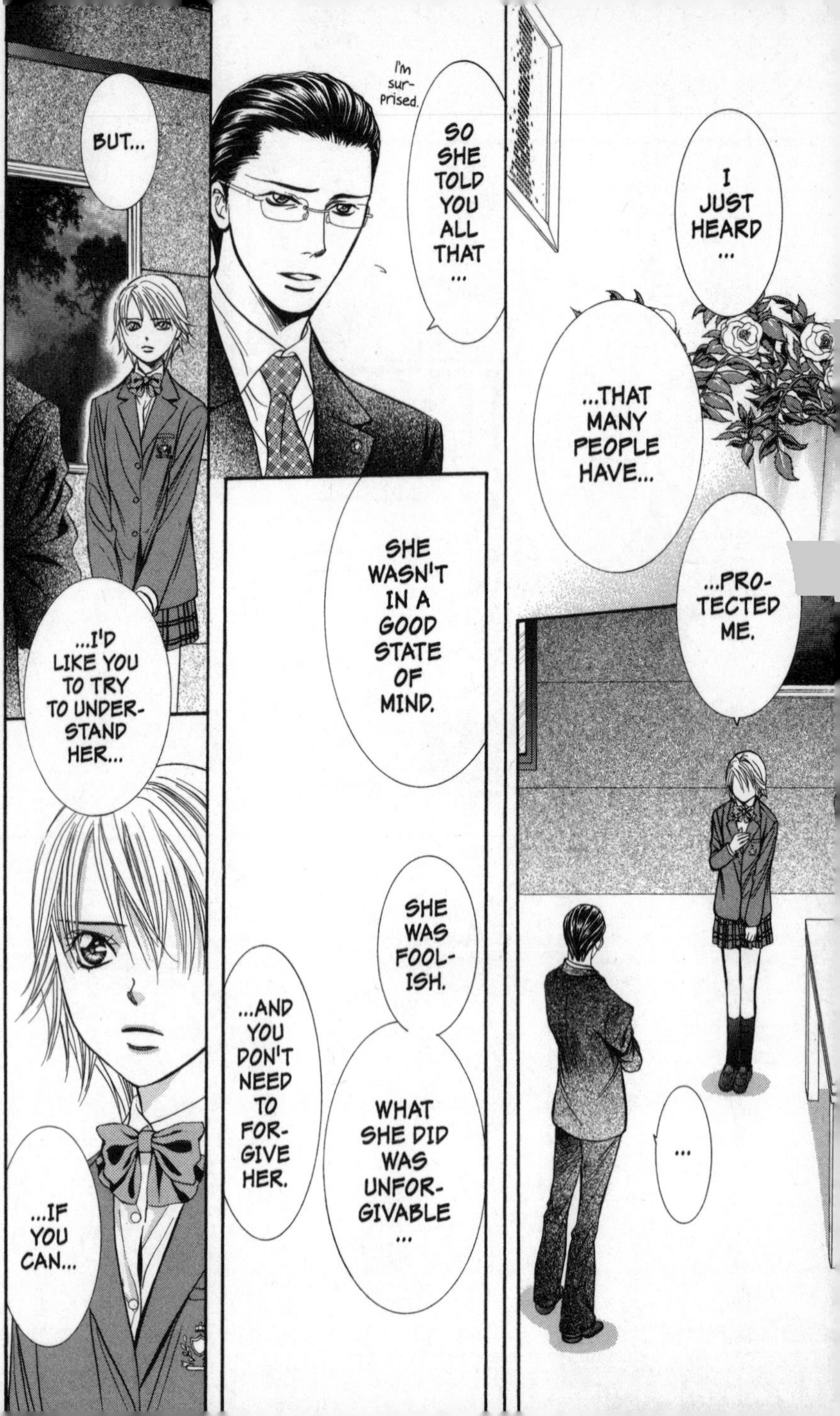
I JUST HEARD...
...THAT MANY PEOPLE HAVE...
...PROTECTED ME.
...
SO SHE TOLD YOU ALL THAT...
I'm surprised.
SHE WASN'T IN A GOOD STATE OF MIND.
SHE WAS FOOLISH.
WHAT SHE DID WAS UNFORGIVABLE...
...AND YOU DON'T NEED TO FORGIVE HER.
BUT...
...I'D LIKE YOU TO TRY TO UNDERSTAND HER...
...IF YOU CAN...

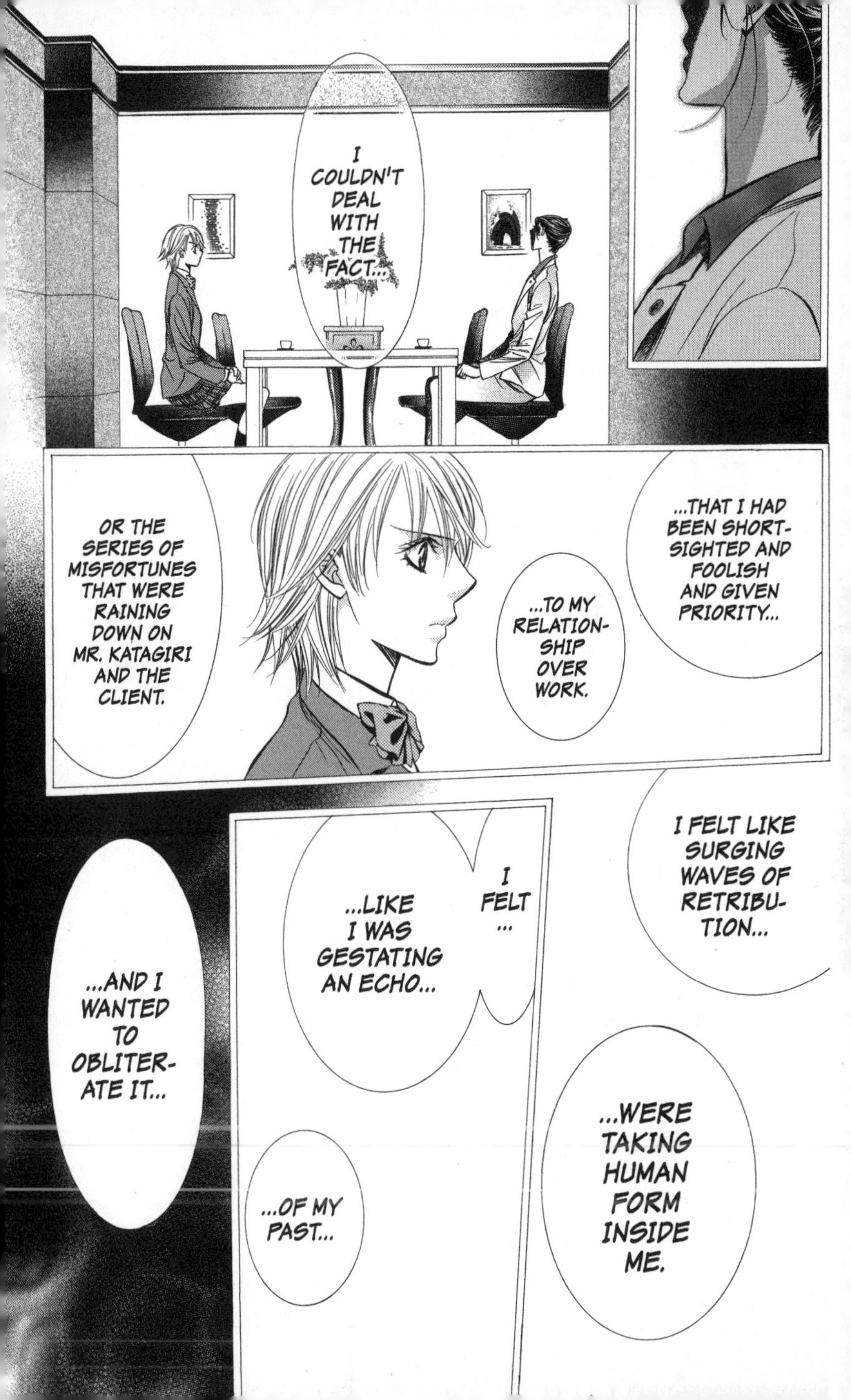
I COULDN'T DEAL WITH THE FACT...
...THAT I HAD BEEN SHORT-SIGHTED AND FOOLISH AND GIVEN PRIORITY...
...TO MY RELATIONSHIP OVER WORK.
OR THE SERIES OF MISFORTUNES THAT WERE RAINING DOWN ON MR. KATAGIRI AND THE CLIENT.
I FELT LIKE SURGING WAVES OF RETRIBU-TION...
...WERE TAKING HUMAN FORM INSIDE ME.
I FELT ...
...LIKE I WAS GESTATING AN ECHO...
...OF MY PAST...
...AND I WANTED TO OBLITER-ATE IT...

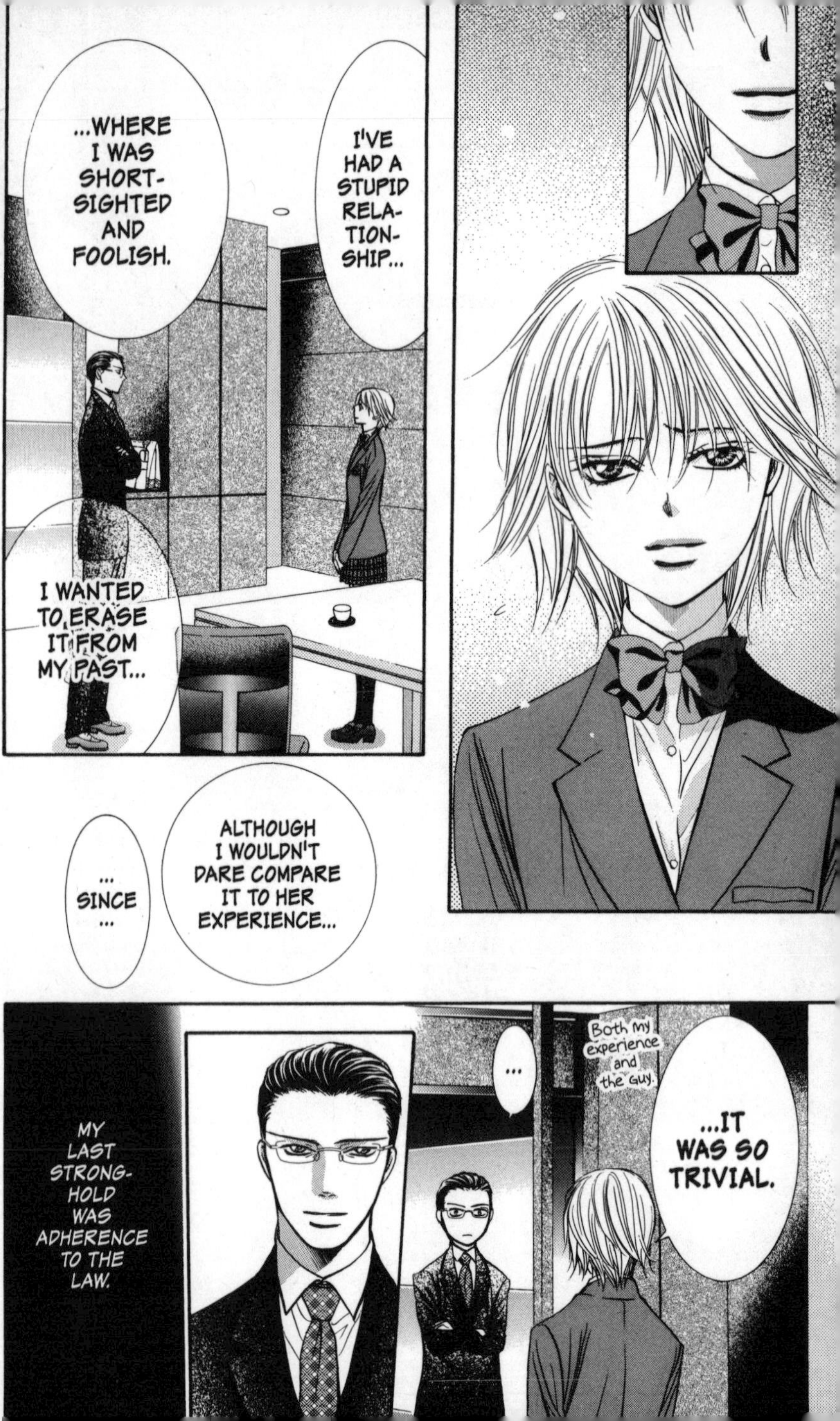
I'VE HAD A STUPID RELATIONSHIP...
...WHERE I WAS SHORT-SIGHTED AND FOOLISH.
I WANTED TO ERASE IT FROM MY PAST...
ALTHOUGH I WOULDN'T DARE COMPARE IT TO HER EXPERIENCE...
...SINCE...
...IT WAS SO TRIVIAL.
Both my experience and the guy.
...
MY LAST STRONGHOLD WAS ADHERENCE TO THE LAW.

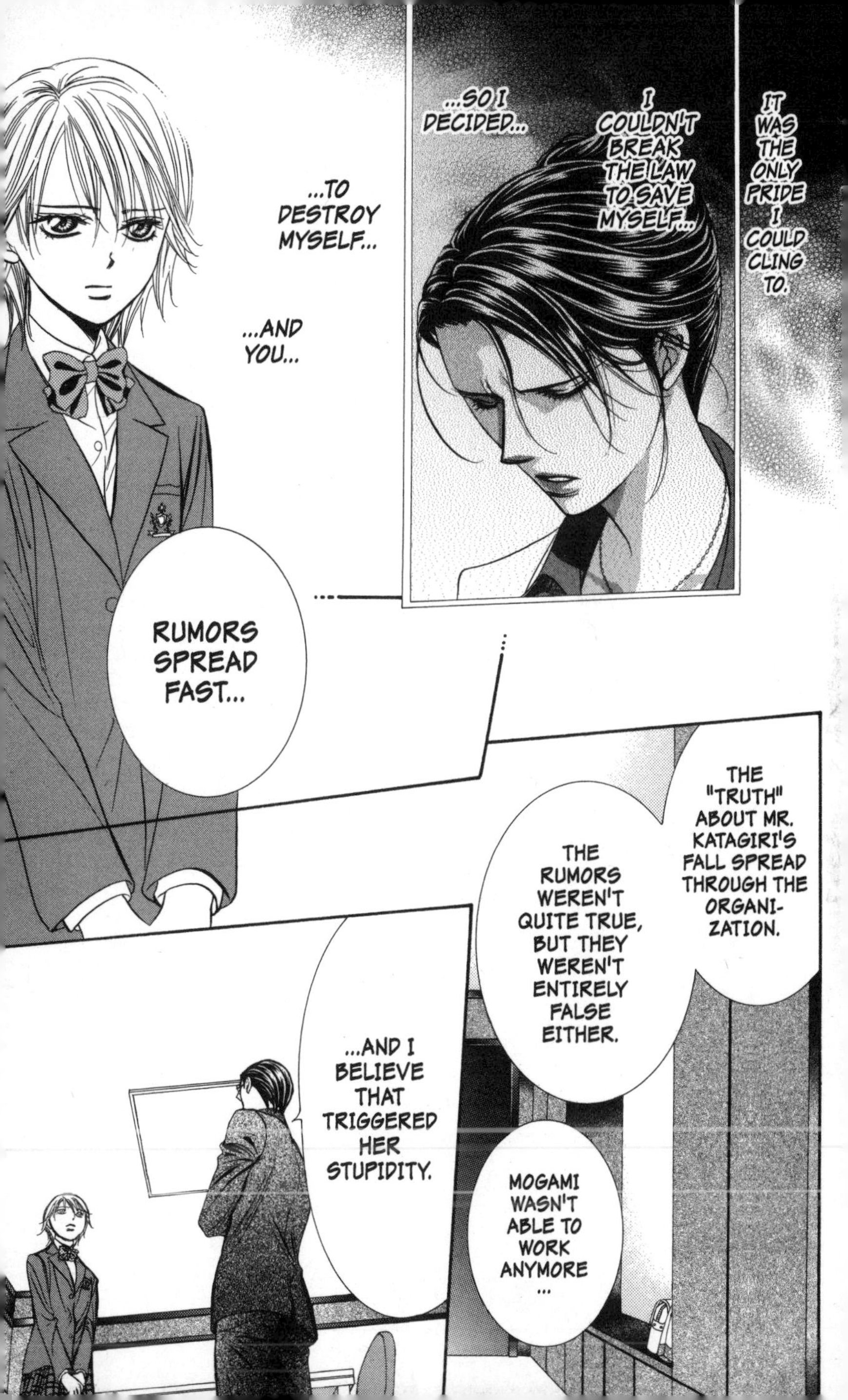
IT WAS THE ONLY PRIDE I COULD CLING TO.
I COULDN'T BREAK THE LAW TO SAVE MYSELF...
...SO I DECIDED...
...TO DESTROY MYSELF...
...AND YOU...
......
RUMORS SPREAD FAST...
THE "TRUTH" ABOUT MR. KATAGIRI'S FALL SPREAD THROUGH THE ORGANI-ZATION.
THE RUMORS WEREN'T QUITE TRUE, BUT THEY WEREN'T ENTIRELY FALSE EITHER.
MOGAMI WASN'T ABLE TO WORK ANYMORE...
...AND I BELIEVE THAT TRIGGERED HER STUPIDITY.

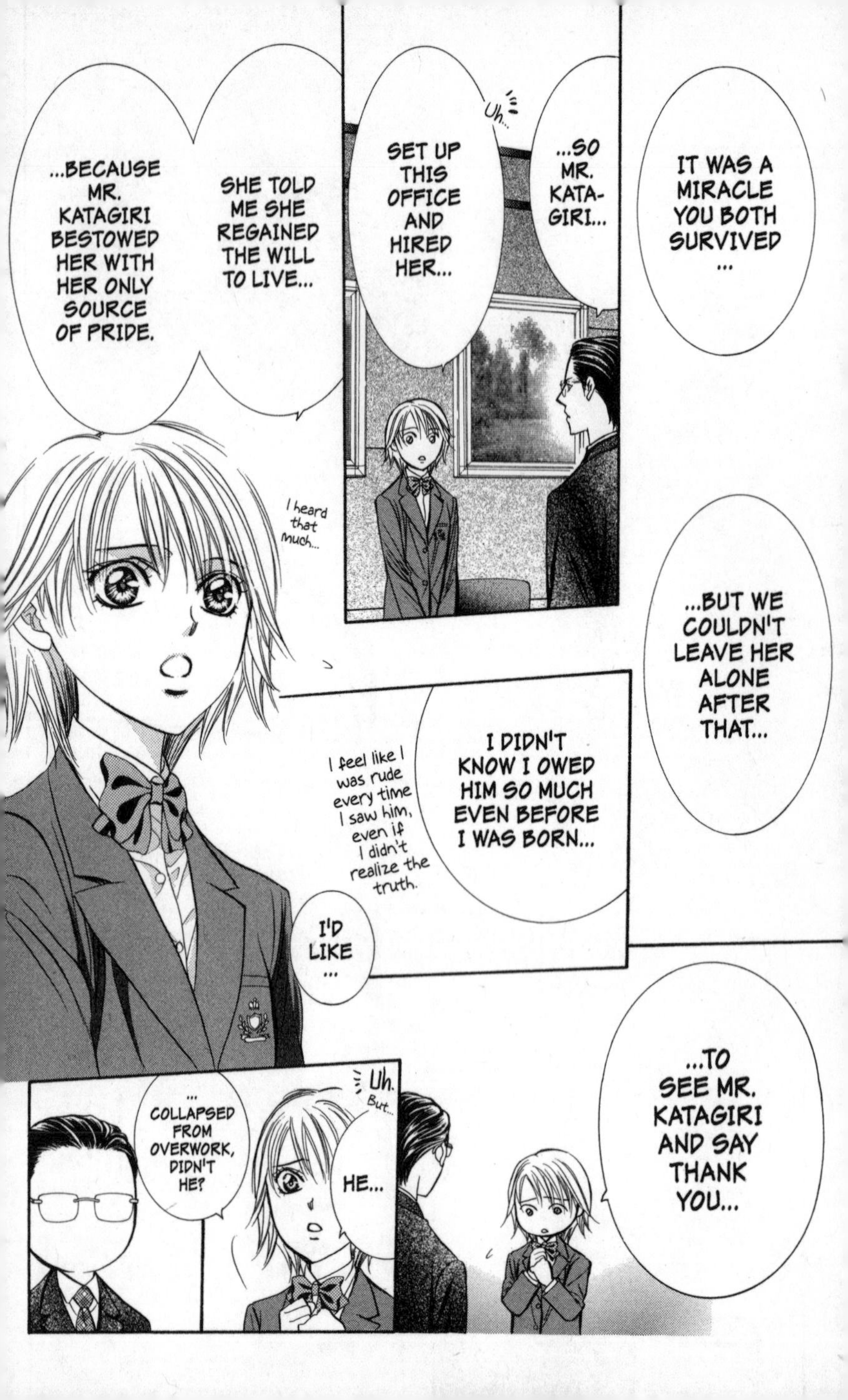
IT WAS A MIRACLE YOU BOTH SURVIVED...
...SO MR. KATAGIRI...
Uh...
SET UP THIS OFFICE AND HIRED HER...
SHE TOLD ME SHE REGAINED THE WILL TO LIVE...
...BECAUSE MR. KATAGIRI BESTOWED HER WITH HER ONLY SOURCE OF PRIDE.
...BUT WE COULDN'T LEAVE HER ALONE AFTER THAT...
I heard that much...
I DIDN'T KNOW I OWED HIM SO MUCH EVEN BEFORE I WAS BORN...
I feel like I was rude every time I saw him, even if I didn't realize the truth.
I'D LIKE...
...TO SEE MR. KATAGIRI AND SAY THANK YOU...
Uh. But...
HE...
...COLLAPSED FROM OVERWORK, DIDN'T HE?

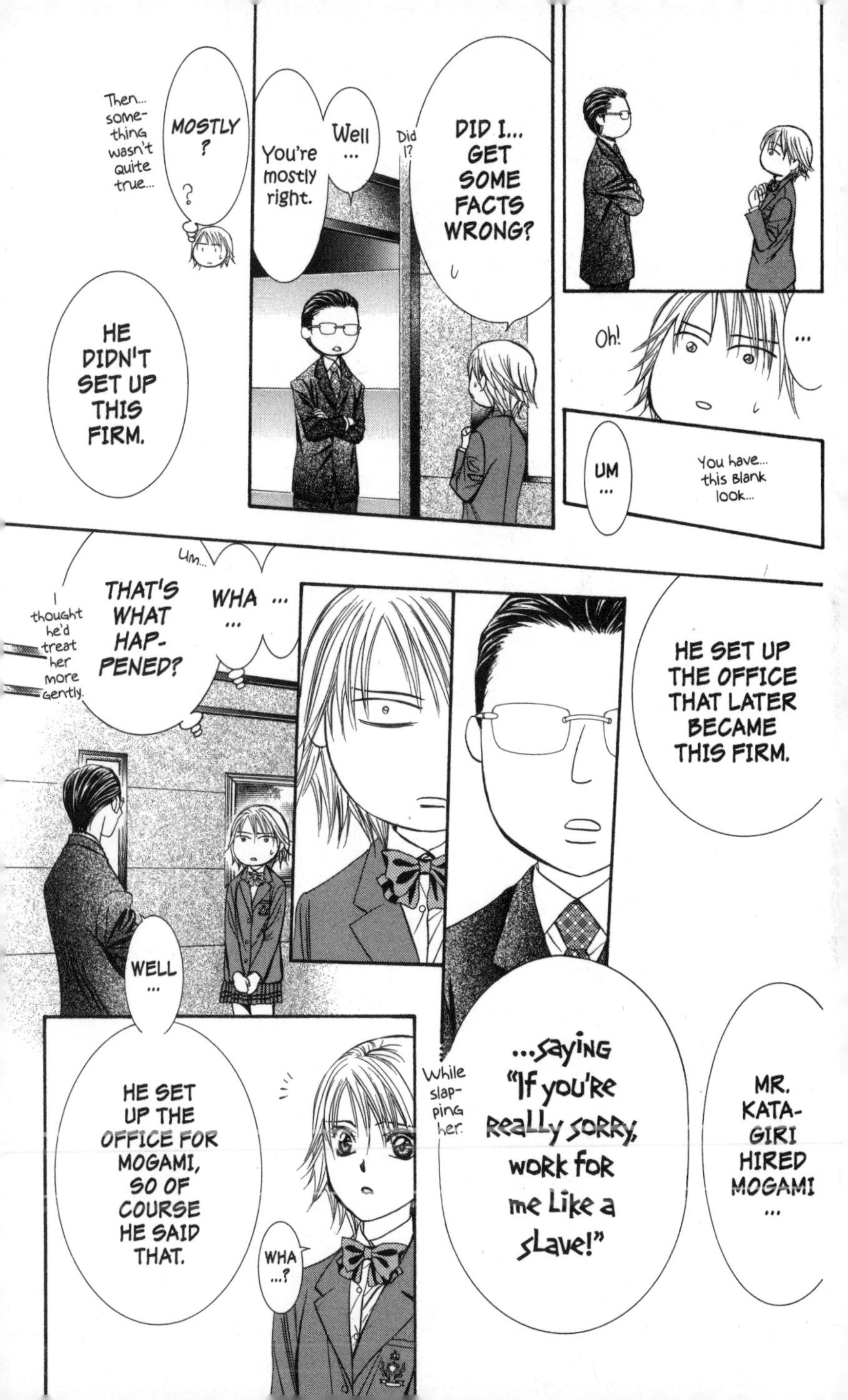
...
Oh!
You have... this blank look...
UM...
DID I... GET SOME FACTS WRONG?
Did I?
Well...
You're mostly right.
MOSTLY?
?
Then... something wasn't quite true...
HE DIDN'T SET UP THIS FIRM.
HE SET UP THE OFFICE THAT LATER BECAME THIS FIRM.
WHA... ...
Um...
THAT'S WHAT HAPPENED?
I thought he'd treat her more gently.
WELL...
MR. KATAGIRI HIRED MOGAMI...
...saying "If you're really sorry, work for me like a slave!"
While slapping her.
HE SET UP THE OFFICE FOR MOGAMI, SO OF COURSE HE SAID THAT.
WHA...?

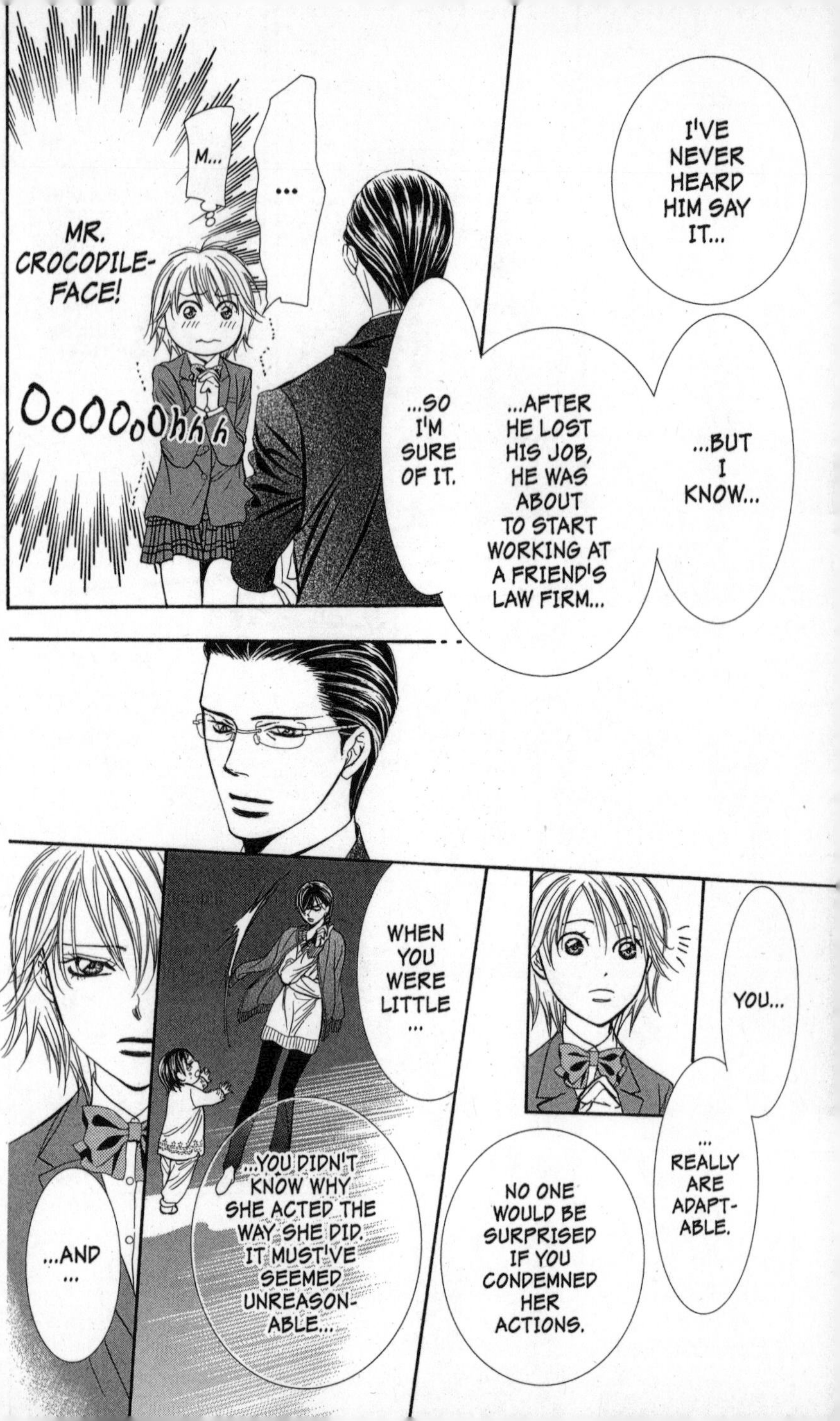
I'VE NEVER HEARD HIM SAY IT...
...BUT I KNOW...
...AFTER HE LOST HIS JOB, HE WAS ABOUT TO START WORKING AT A FRIEND'S LAW FIRM...
...SO I'M SURE OF IT.
...
M...
MR. CROCODILE-FACE!
OoOOoOhhh
YOU...
...REALLY ARE ADAPT-ABLE.
NO ONE WOULD BE SURPRISED IF YOU CONDEMNED HER ACTIONS.
WHEN YOU WERE LITTLE...
...YOU DIDN'T KNOW WHY SHE ACTED THE WAY SHE DID. IT MUST'VE SEEMED UNREASON-ABLE...
...AND...

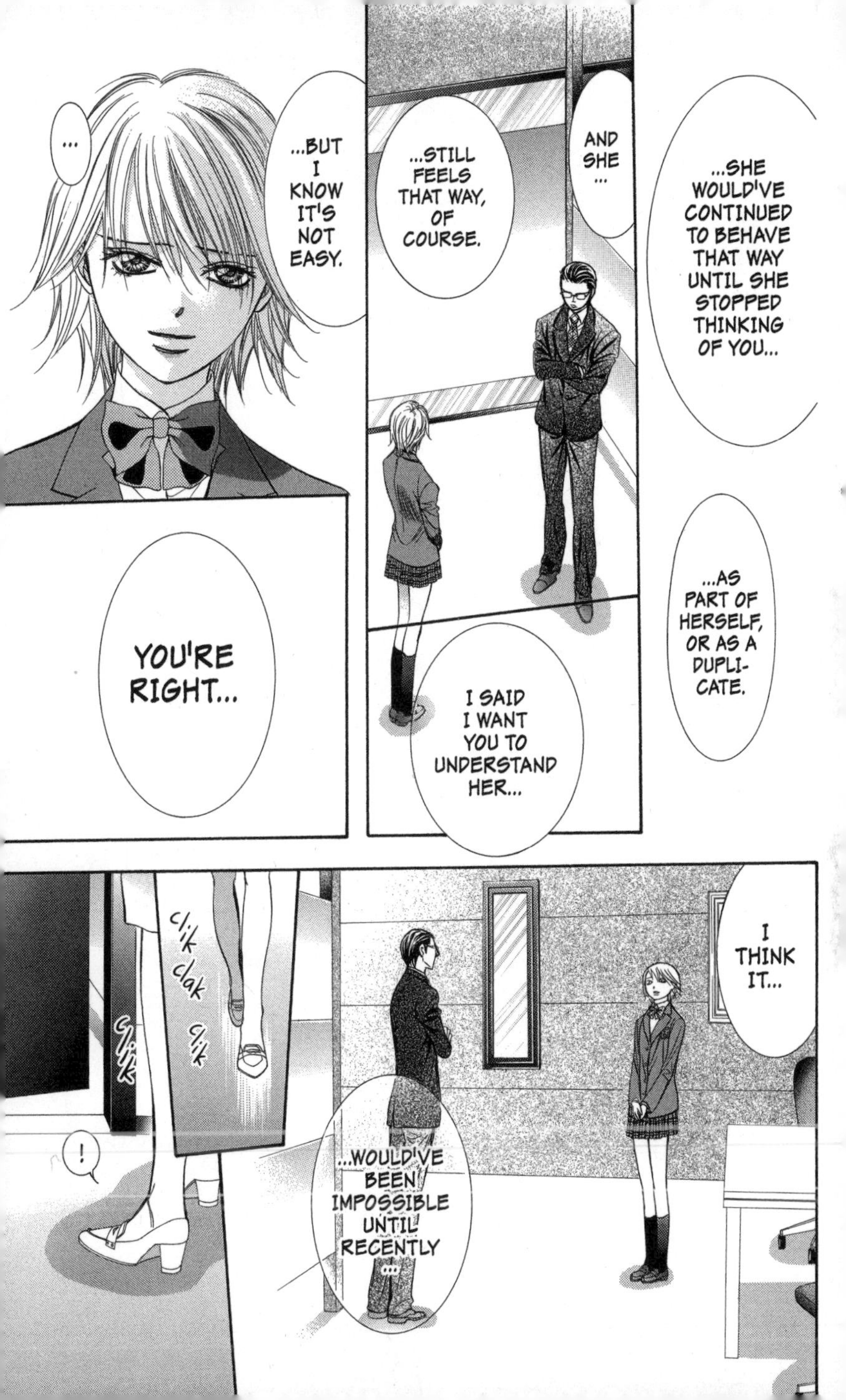
...SHE WOULD'VE CONTINUED TO BEHAVE THAT WAY UNTIL SHE STOPPED THINKING OF YOU...
...AS PART OF HERSELF, OR AS A DUPLICATE.
AND SHE...
...STILL FEELS THAT WAY, OF COURSE.
I SAID I WANT YOU TO UNDERSTAND HER...
...BUT I KNOW IT'S NOT EASY.
...
YOU'RE RIGHT...
I THINK IT...
...WOULD'VE BEEN IMPOSSIBLE UNTIL RECENTLY...
clik
clak
clik
clik
!

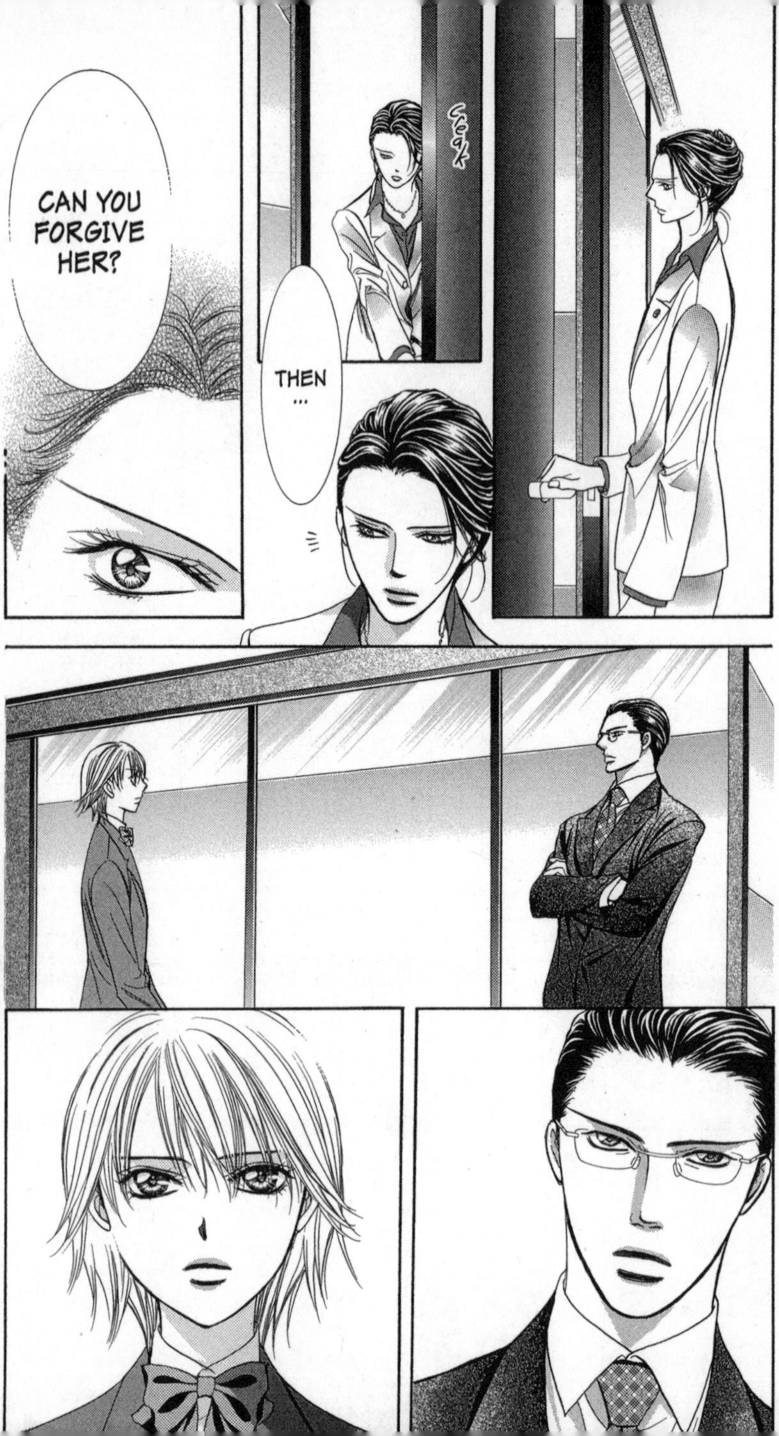
creak
THEN ...
CAN YOU FORGIVE HER?

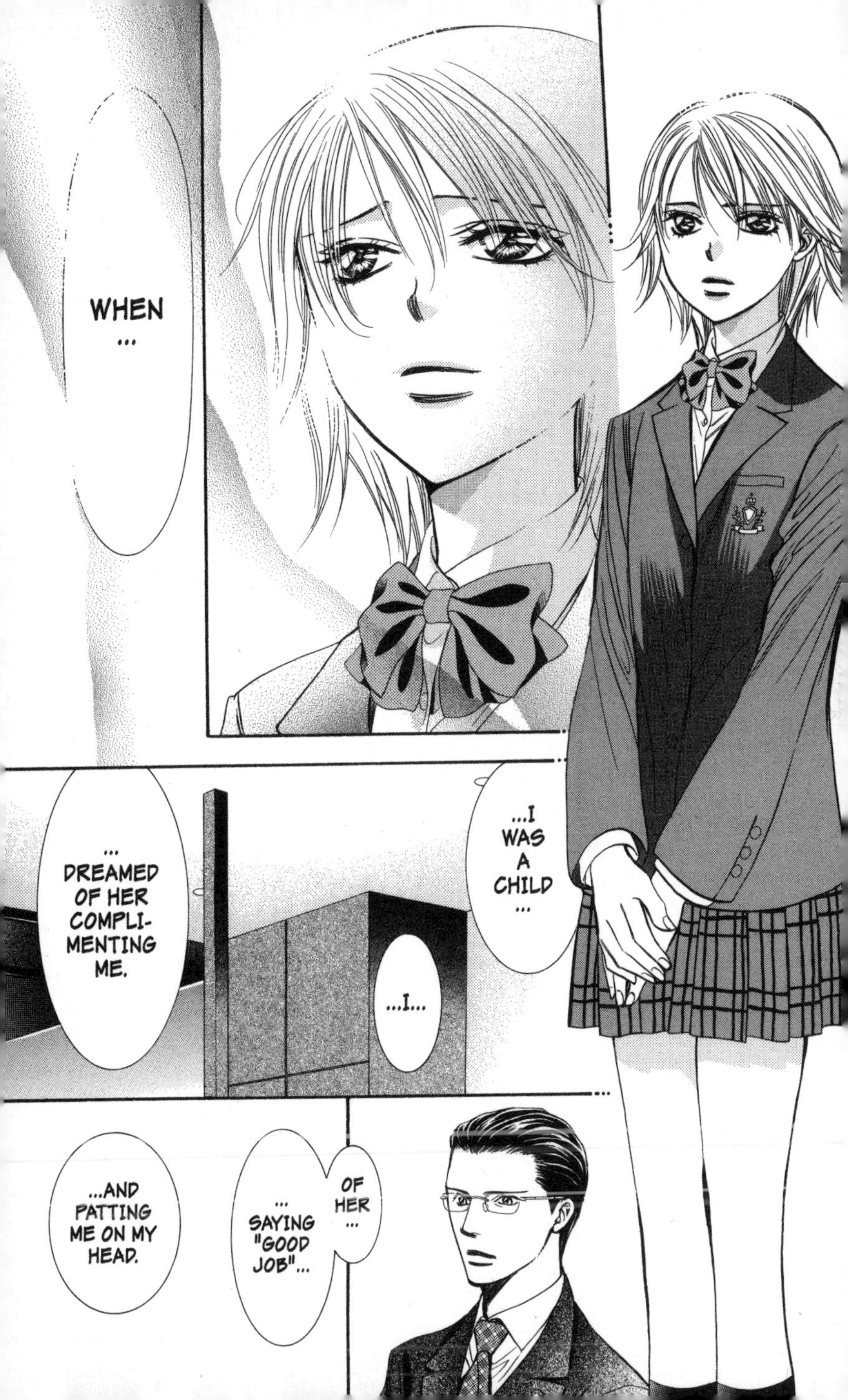
WHEN ...
...I WAS A CHILD ...
...I...
... DREAMED OF HER COMPLI-MENTING ME.
OF HER ...
... SAYING "GOOD JOB"...
...AND PATTING ME ON MY HEAD.

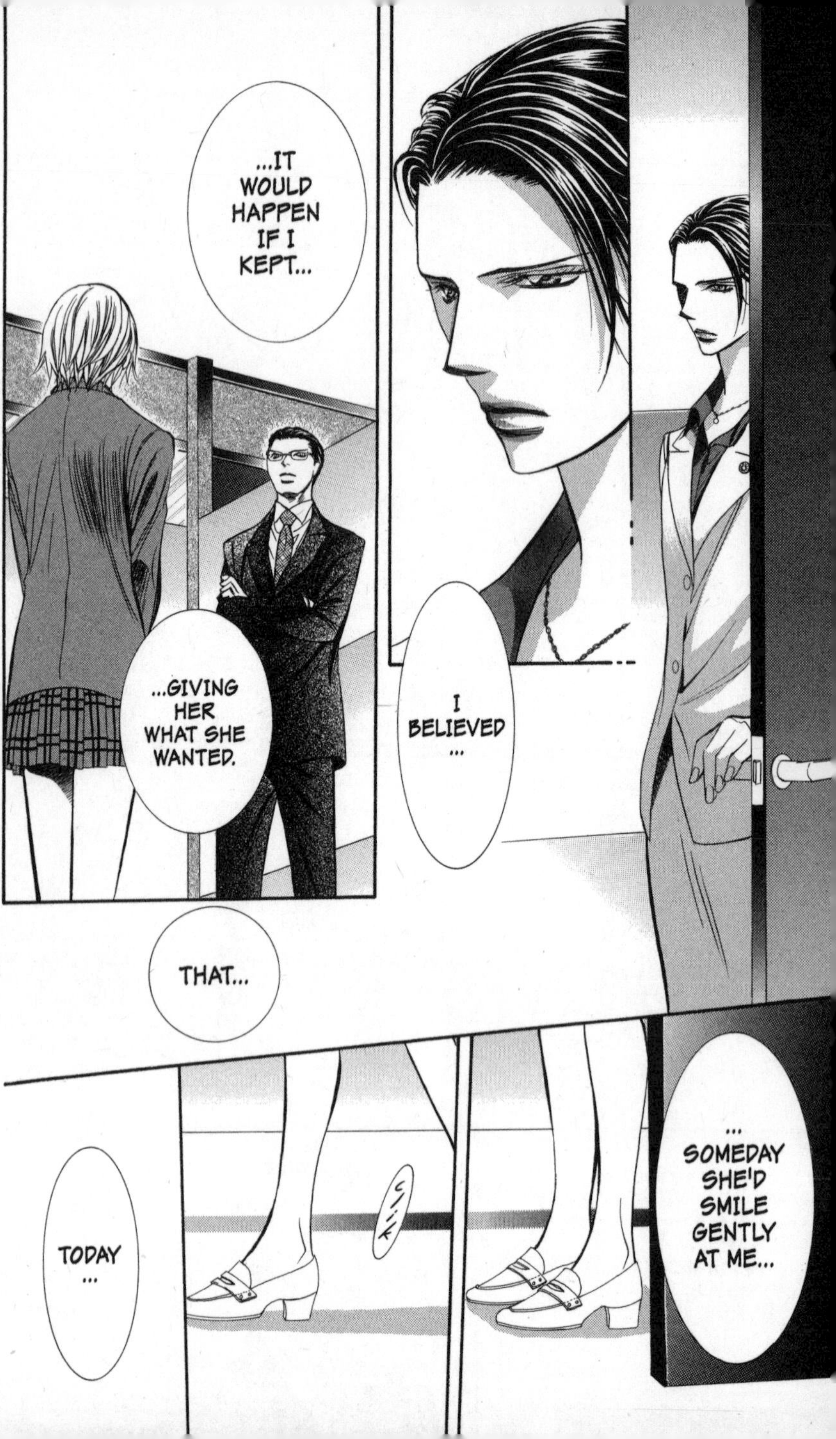
I BELIEVED...
...IT WOULD HAPPEN IF I KEPT...
...GIVING HER WHAT SHE WANTED.
THAT...
...SOMEDAY SHE'D SMILE GENTLY AT ME...
clik
TODAY...

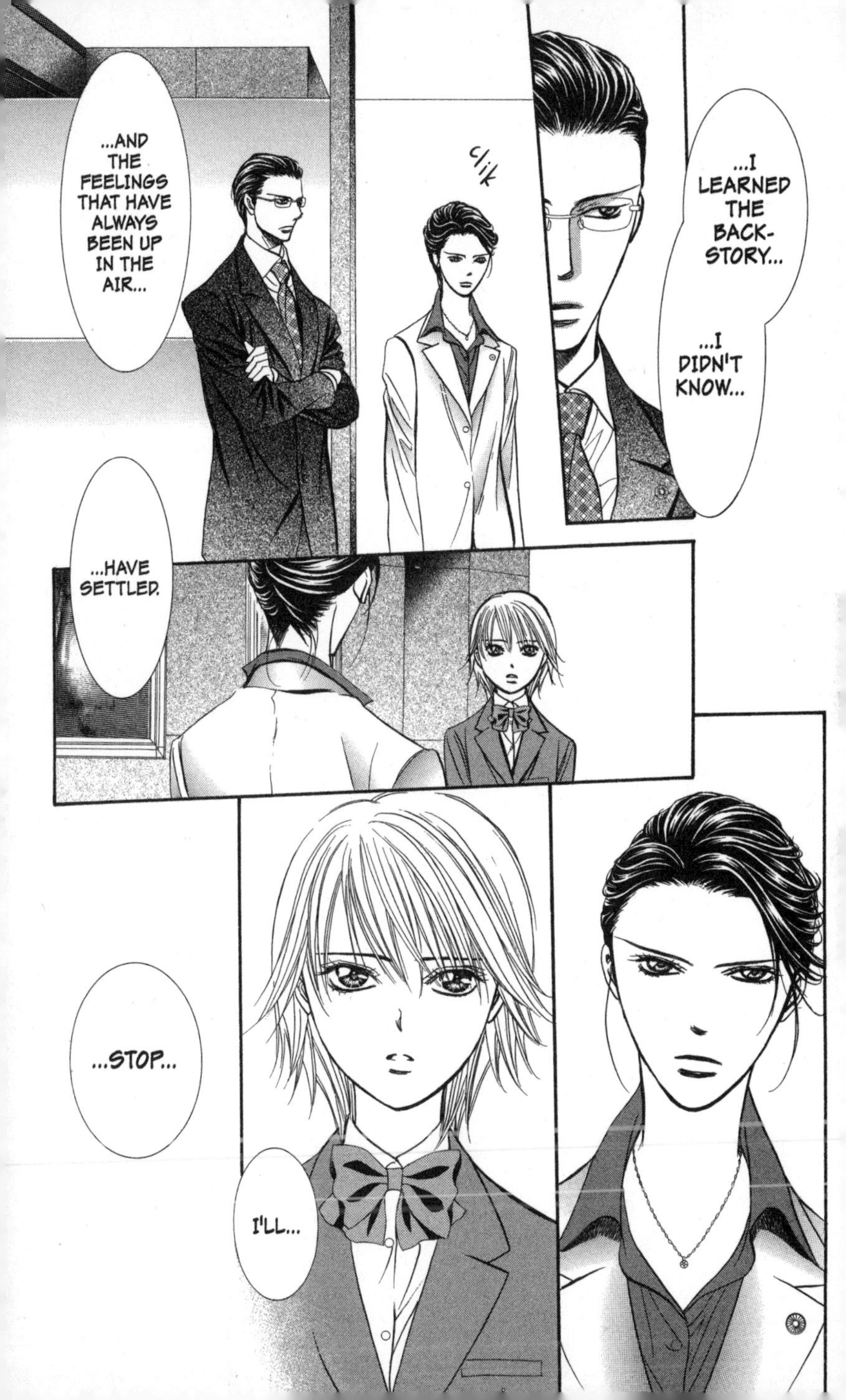
...I LEARNED THE BACK-STORY...
...I DIDN'T KNOW...
clik
...AND THE FEELINGS THAT HAVE ALWAYS BEEN UP IN THE AIR...
...HAVE SETTLED.
I'LL...
...STOP...

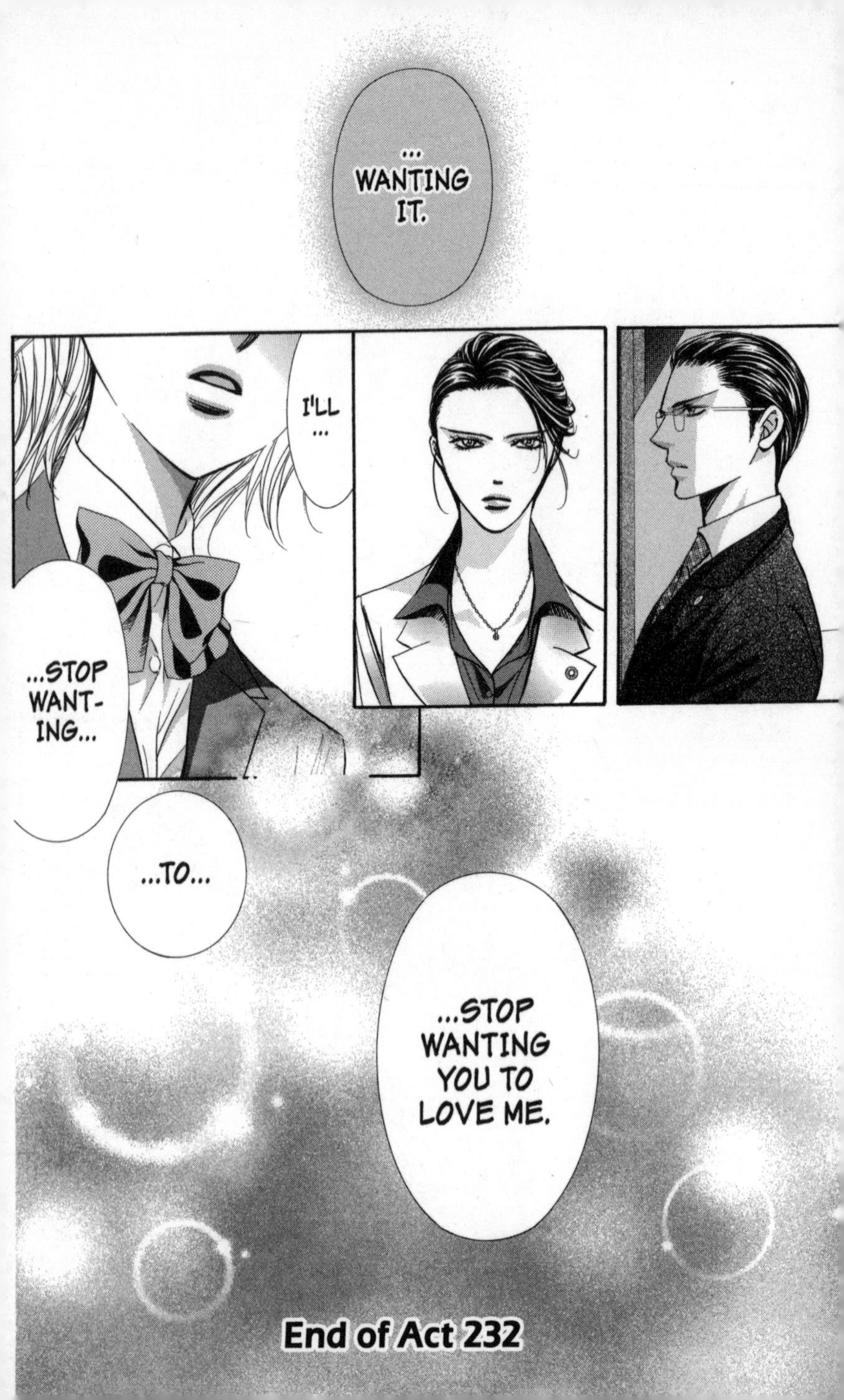
... WANTING IT.
I'LL ...
...STOP WANT-ING...
...TO...
...STOP WANTING YOU TO LOVE ME.
End of Act 232

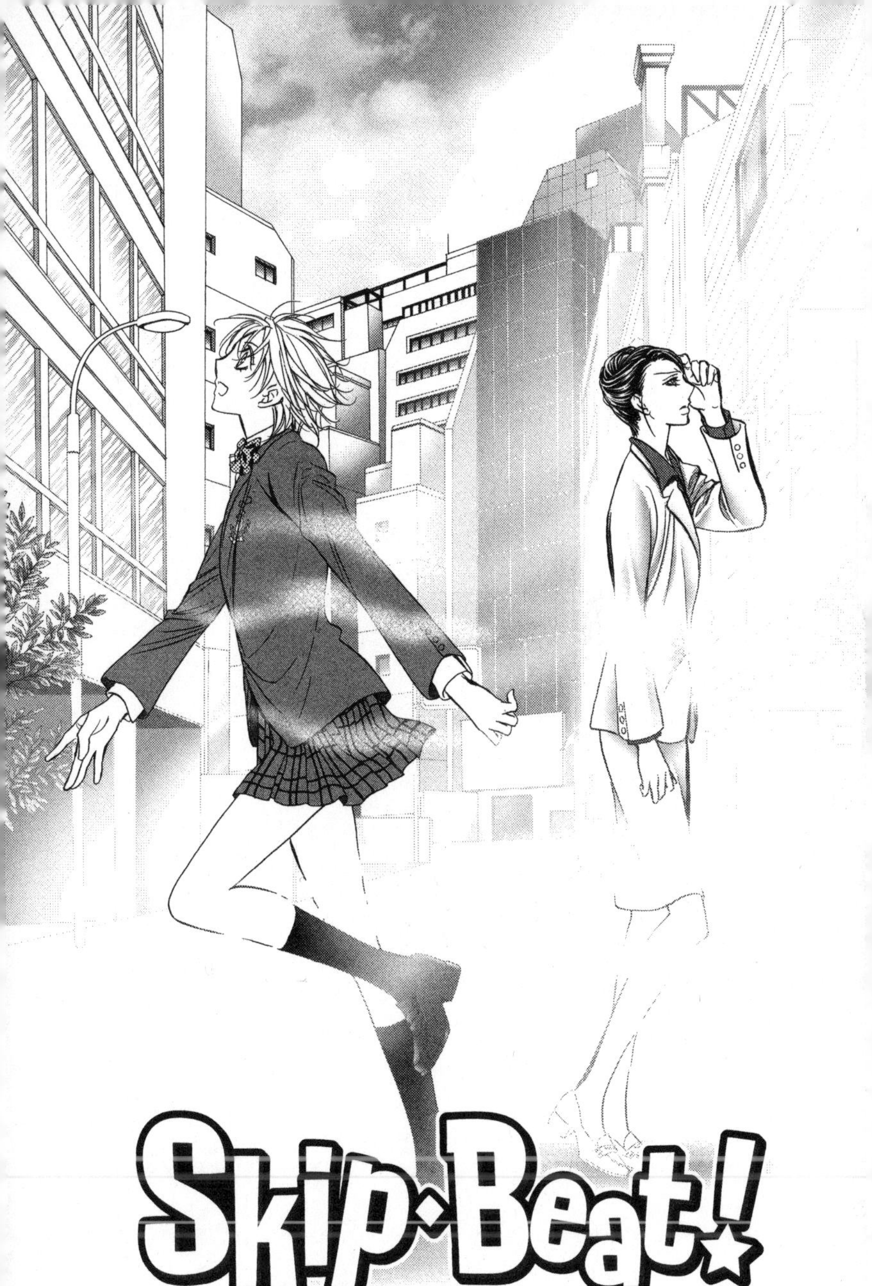
Skip·Beat!

Act 233: Clear Mist

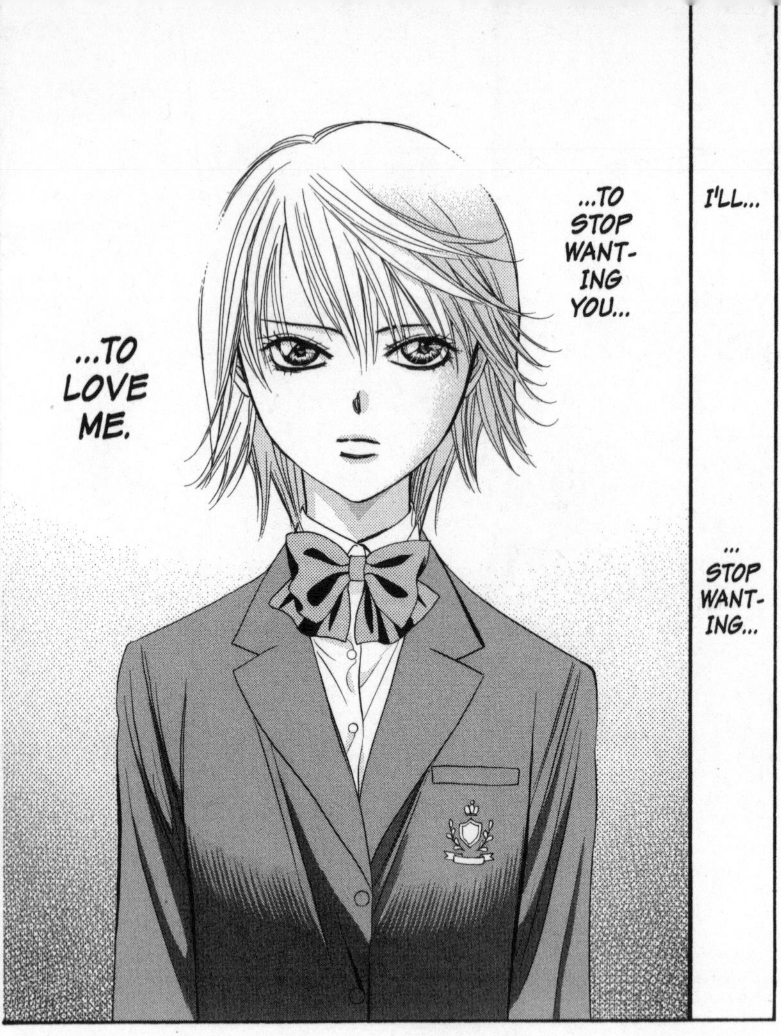
I'LL...
...STOP WANTING...
...TO STOP WANTING YOU...
...TO LOVE ME.

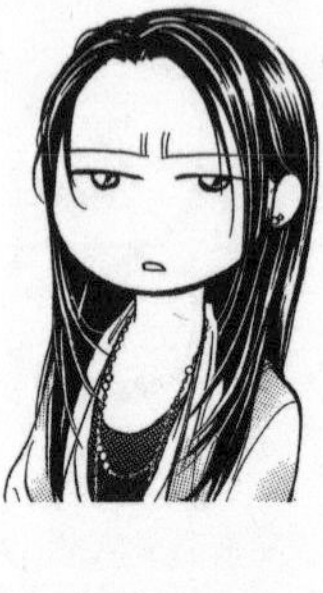

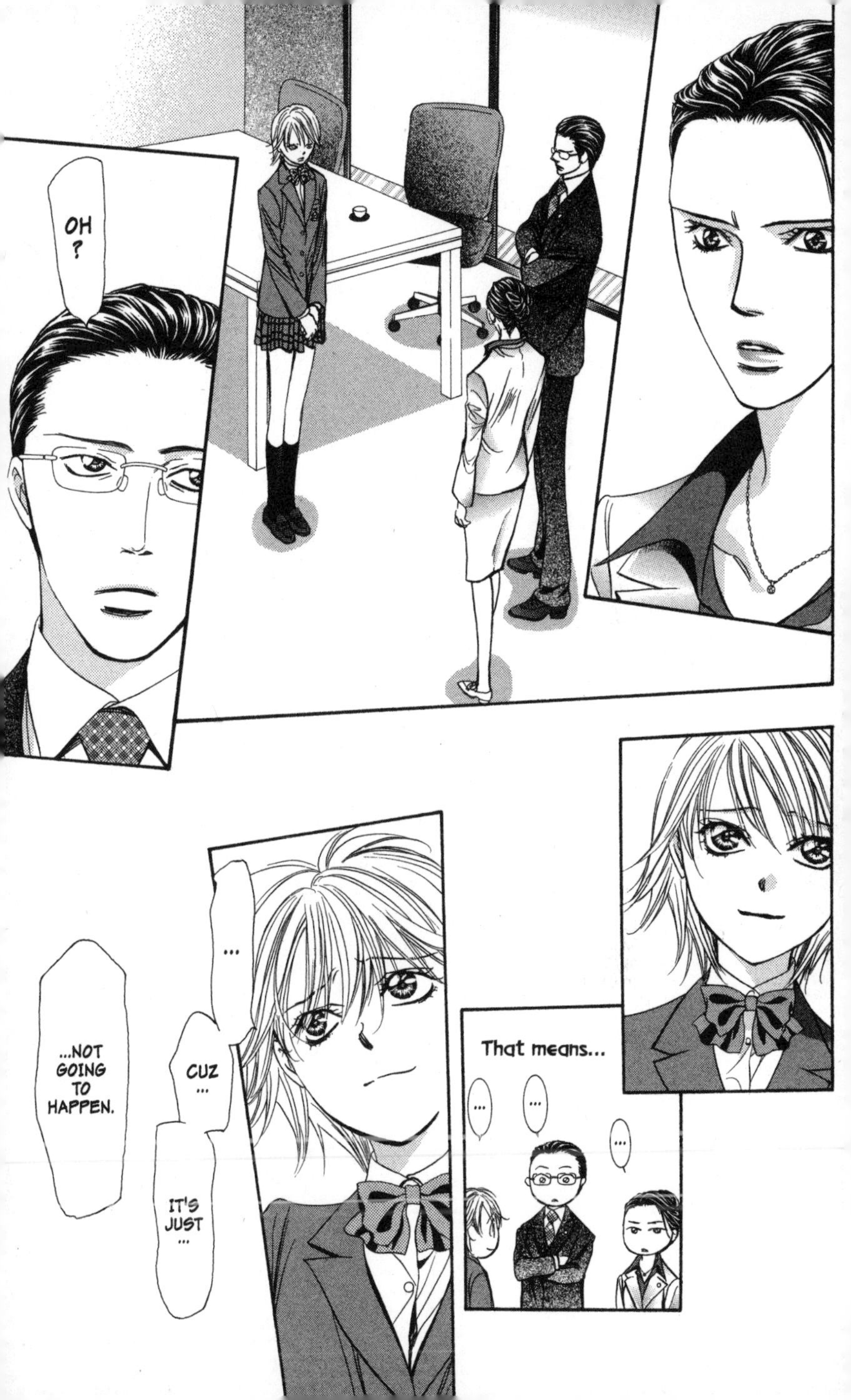
OH?
That means...
...
...
...
...
CUZ...
IT'S JUST...
...NOT GOING TO HAPPEN.

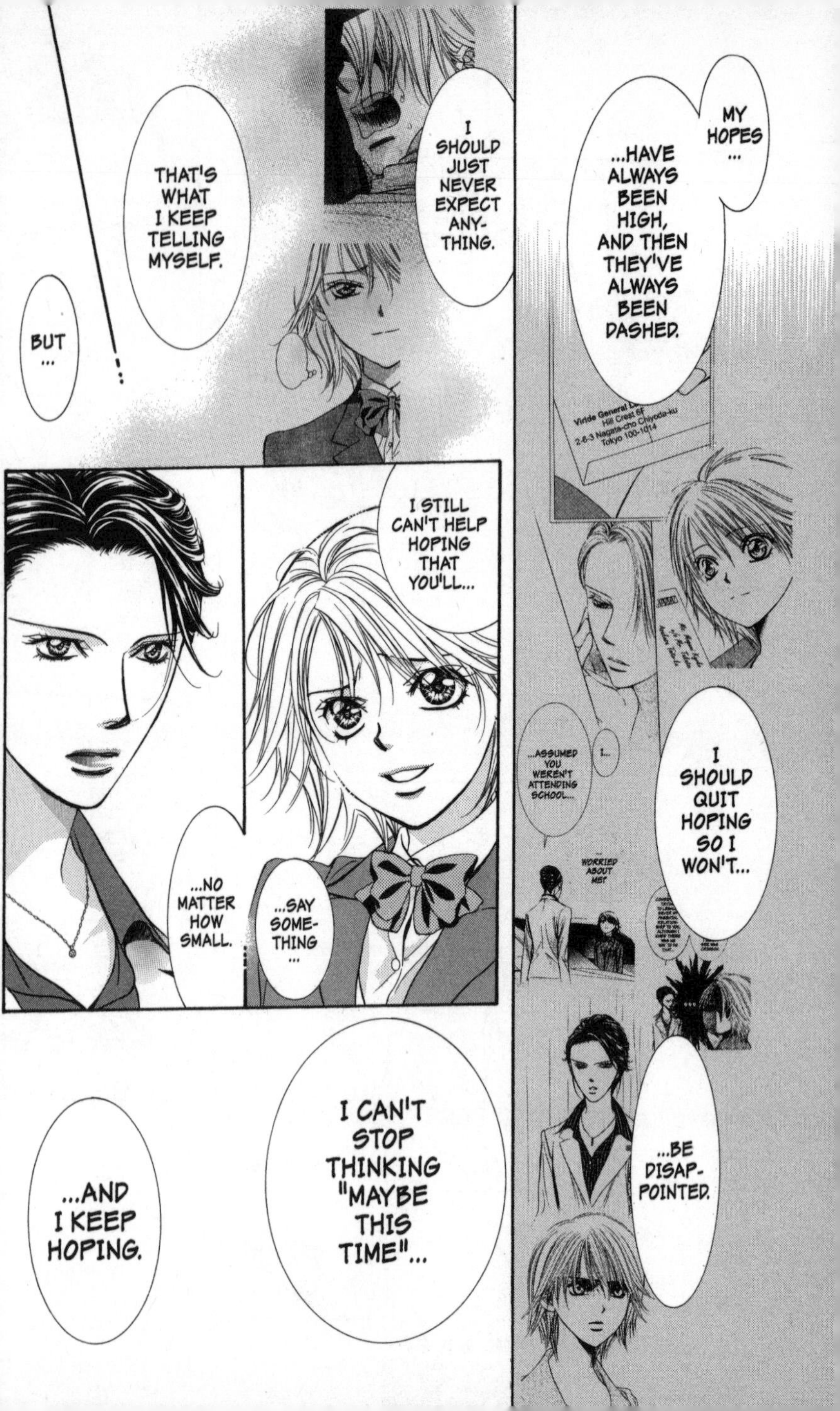
MY HOPES...
...HAVE ALWAYS BEEN HIGH, AND THEN THEY'VE ALWAYS BEEN DASHED.
I...
...ASSUMED YOU WEREN'T ATTENDING SCHOOL...
I SHOULD QUIT HOPING SO I WON'T...
WORRIED ABOUT ME?
...BE DISAPPOINTED.
I SHOULD JUST NEVER EXPECT ANYTHING.
THAT'S WHAT I KEEP TELLING MYSELF.
BUT...
I STILL CAN'T HELP HOPING THAT YOU'LL...
...SAY SOMETHING...
...NO MATTER HOW SMALL.
I CAN'T STOP THINKING "MAYBE THIS TIME"...
...AND I KEEP HOPING.

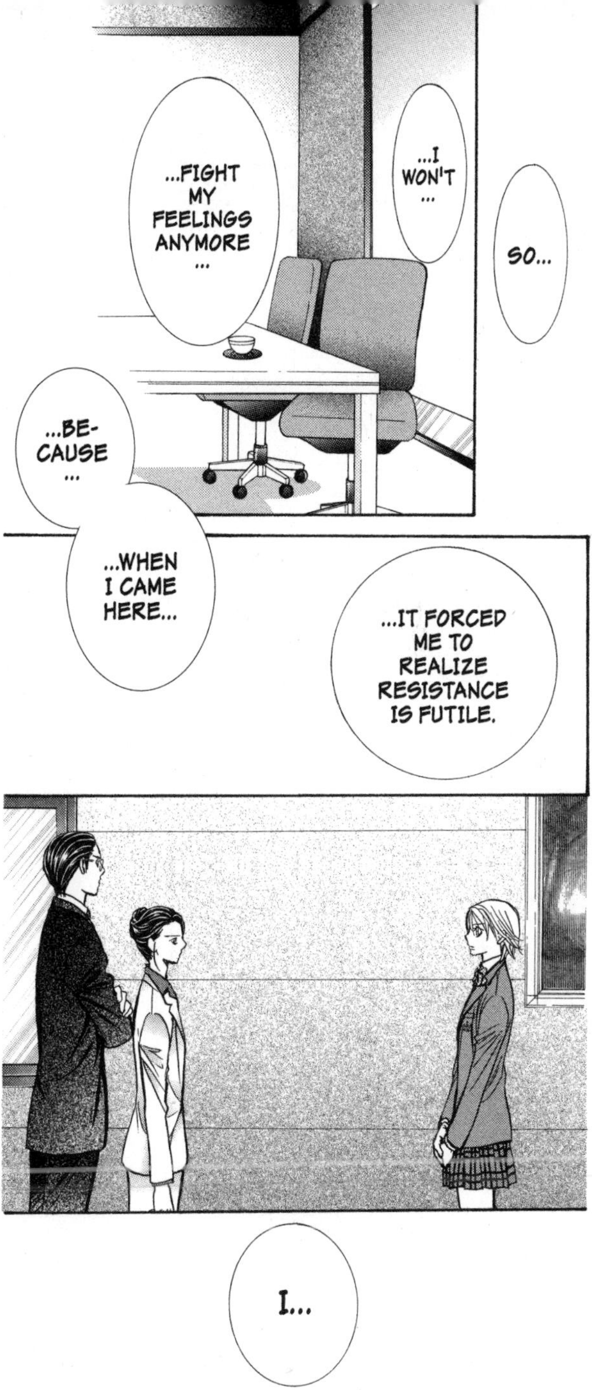
SO...
...I WON'T ...
...FIGHT MY FEELINGS ANYMORE ...
...BE-CAUSE ...
...WHEN I CAME HERE...
...IT FORCED ME TO REALIZE RESISTANCE IS FUTILE.
I...

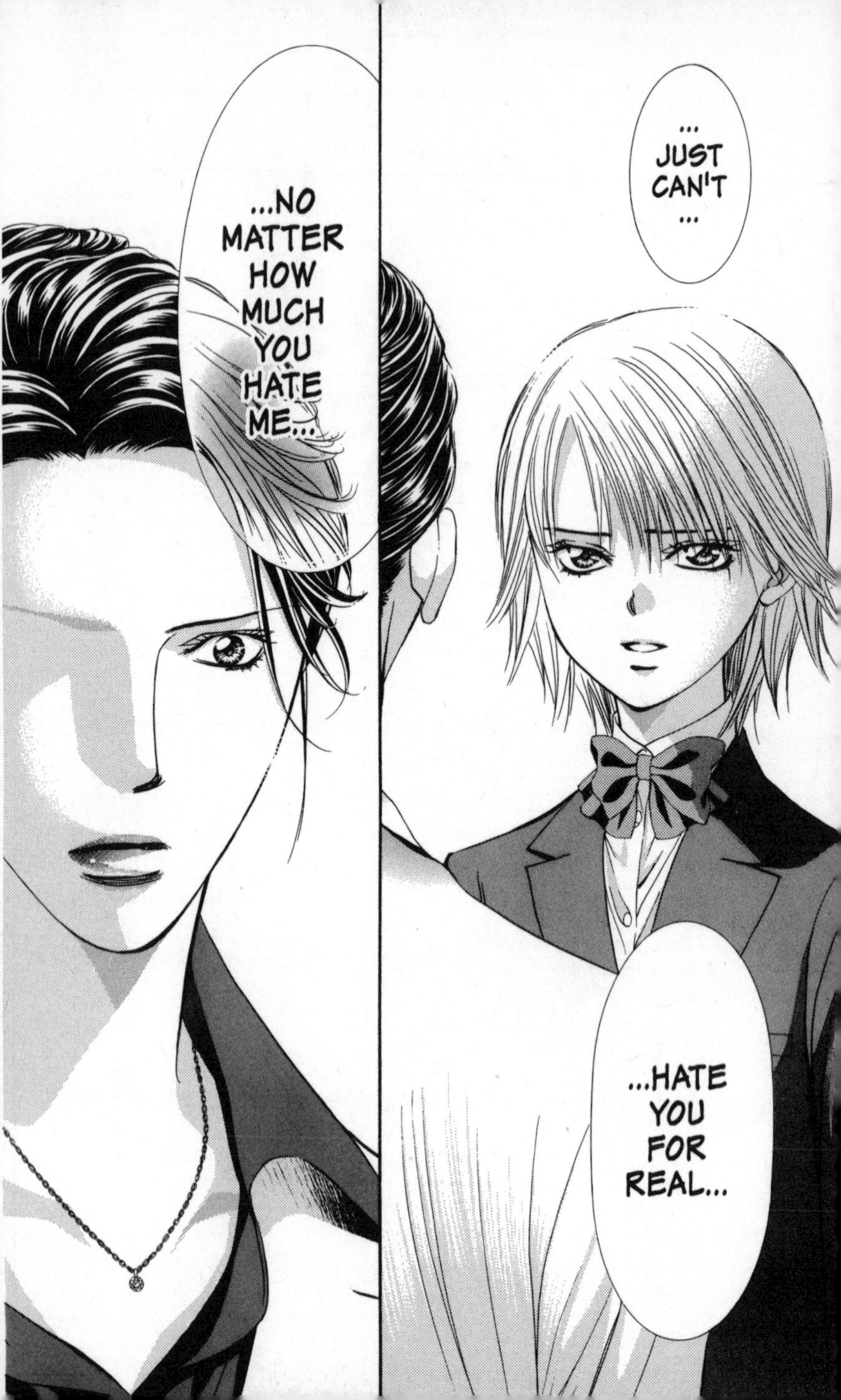
... JUST CAN'T ...
...HATE YOU FOR REAL...
...NO MATTER HOW MUCH YOU HATE ME...

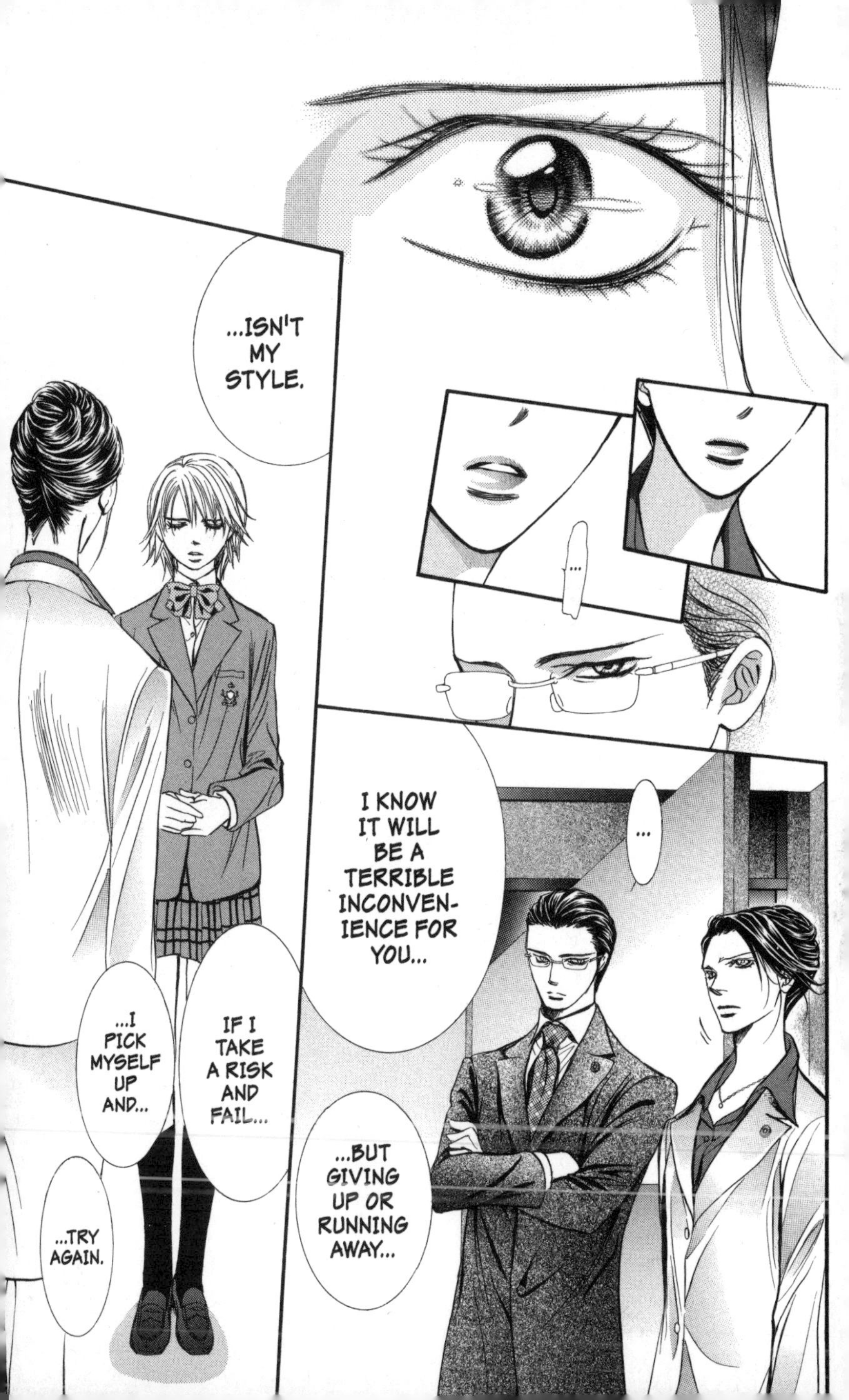
...
I KNOW IT WILL BE A TERRIBLE INCONVEN-IENCE FOR YOU...
...
...BUT GIVING UP OR RUNNING AWAY...
...ISN'T MY STYLE.
IF I TAKE A RISK AND FAIL...
...I PICK MYSELF UP AND...
...TRY AGAIN.

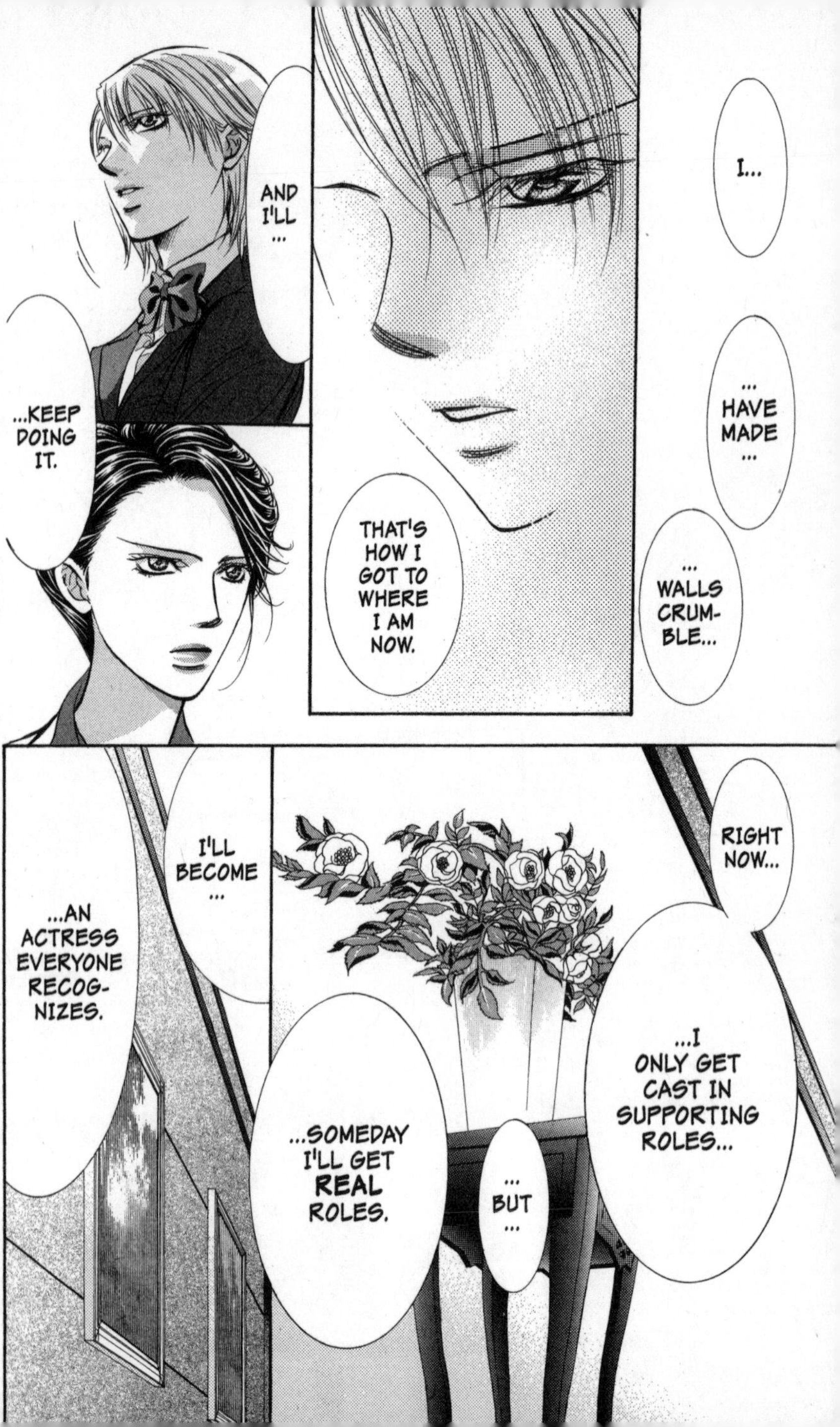
I...
...HAVE MADE...
...WALLS CRUMBLE...
THAT'S HOW I GOT TO WHERE I AM NOW.
AND I'LL...
...KEEP DOING IT.
RIGHT NOW...
...I ONLY GET CAST IN SUPPORTING ROLES...
...BUT...
...SOMEDAY I'LL GET REAL ROLES.
I'LL BECOME...
...AN ACTRESS EVERYONE RECOGNIZES.

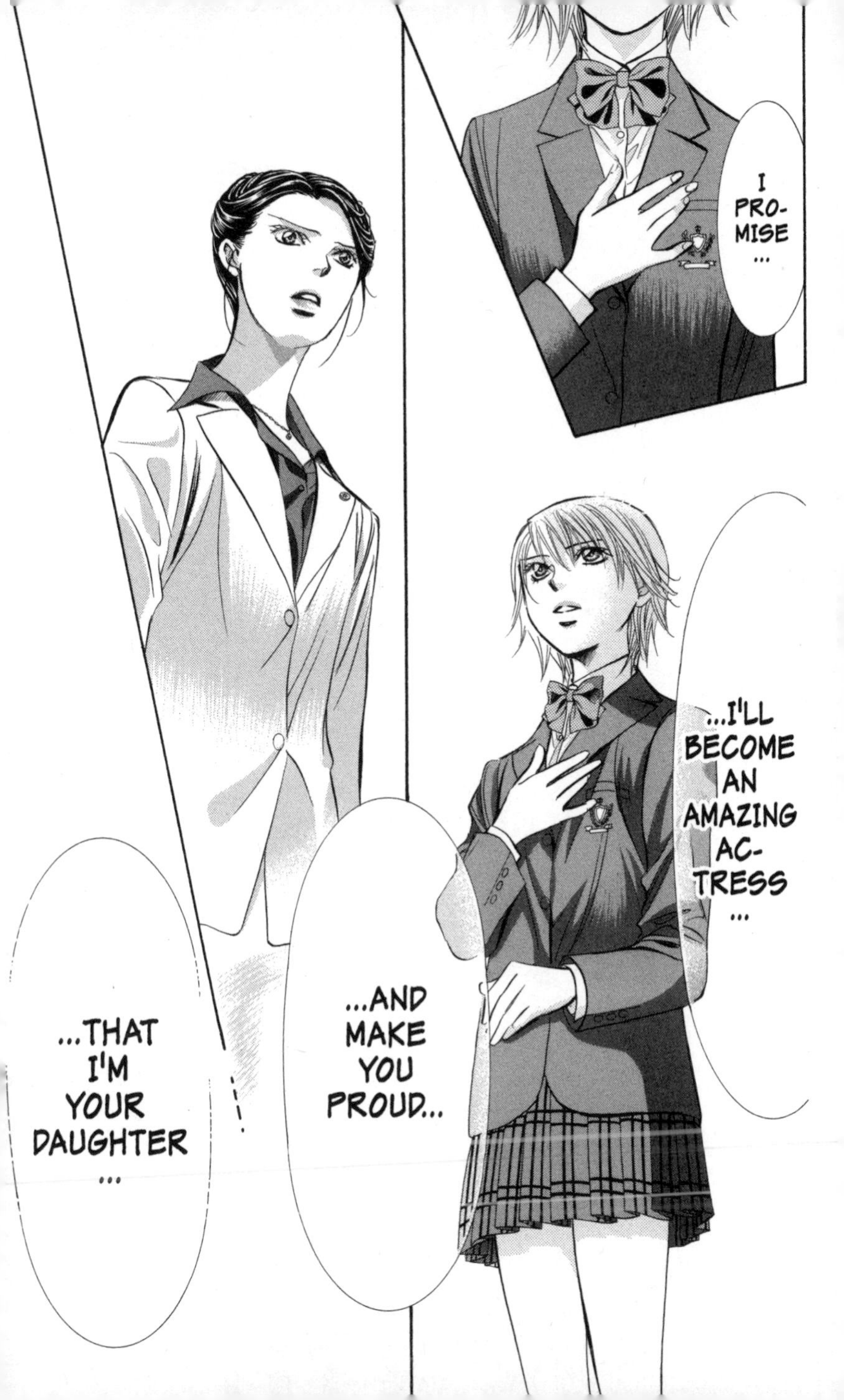
I PRO-MISE...
...I'LL BECOME AN AMAZING AC-TRESS...
...AND MAKE YOU PROUD...
...THAT I'M YOUR DAUGHTER...

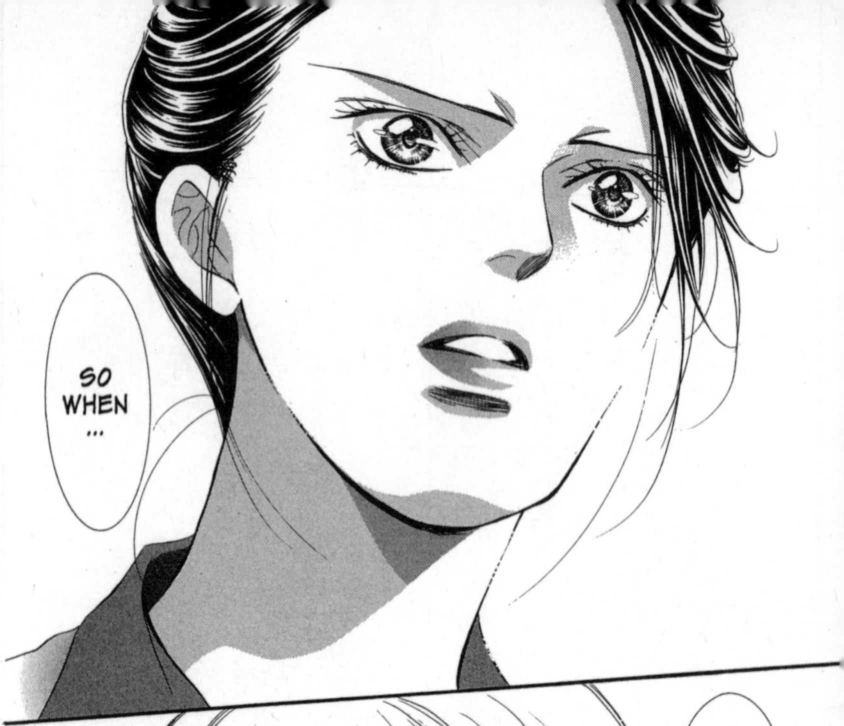
SO WHEN ...

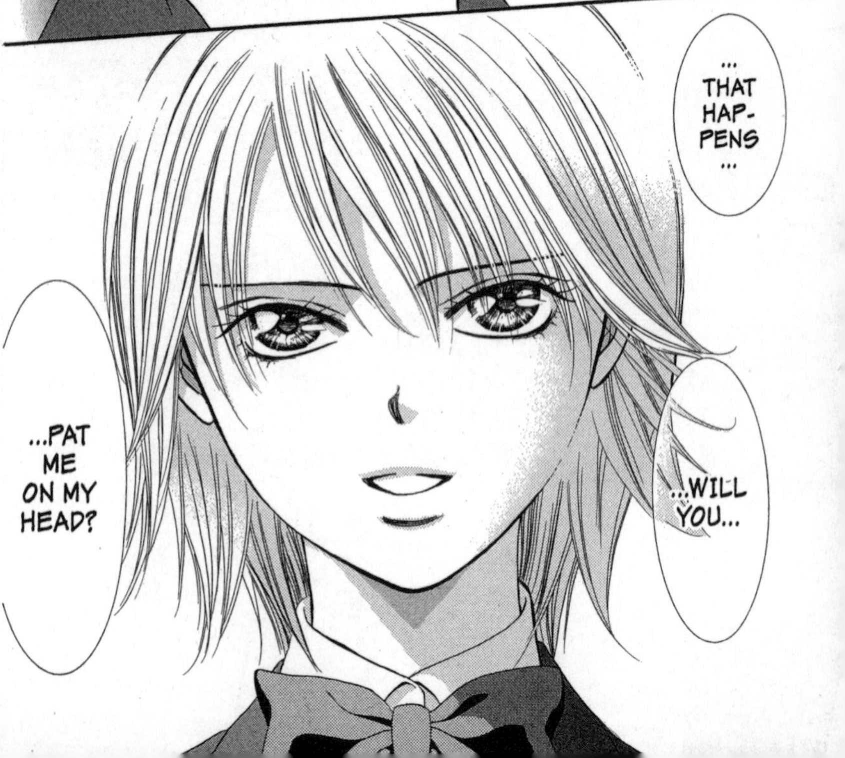
... THAT HAP-PENS ...
...WILL YOU...
...PAT ME ON MY HEAD?

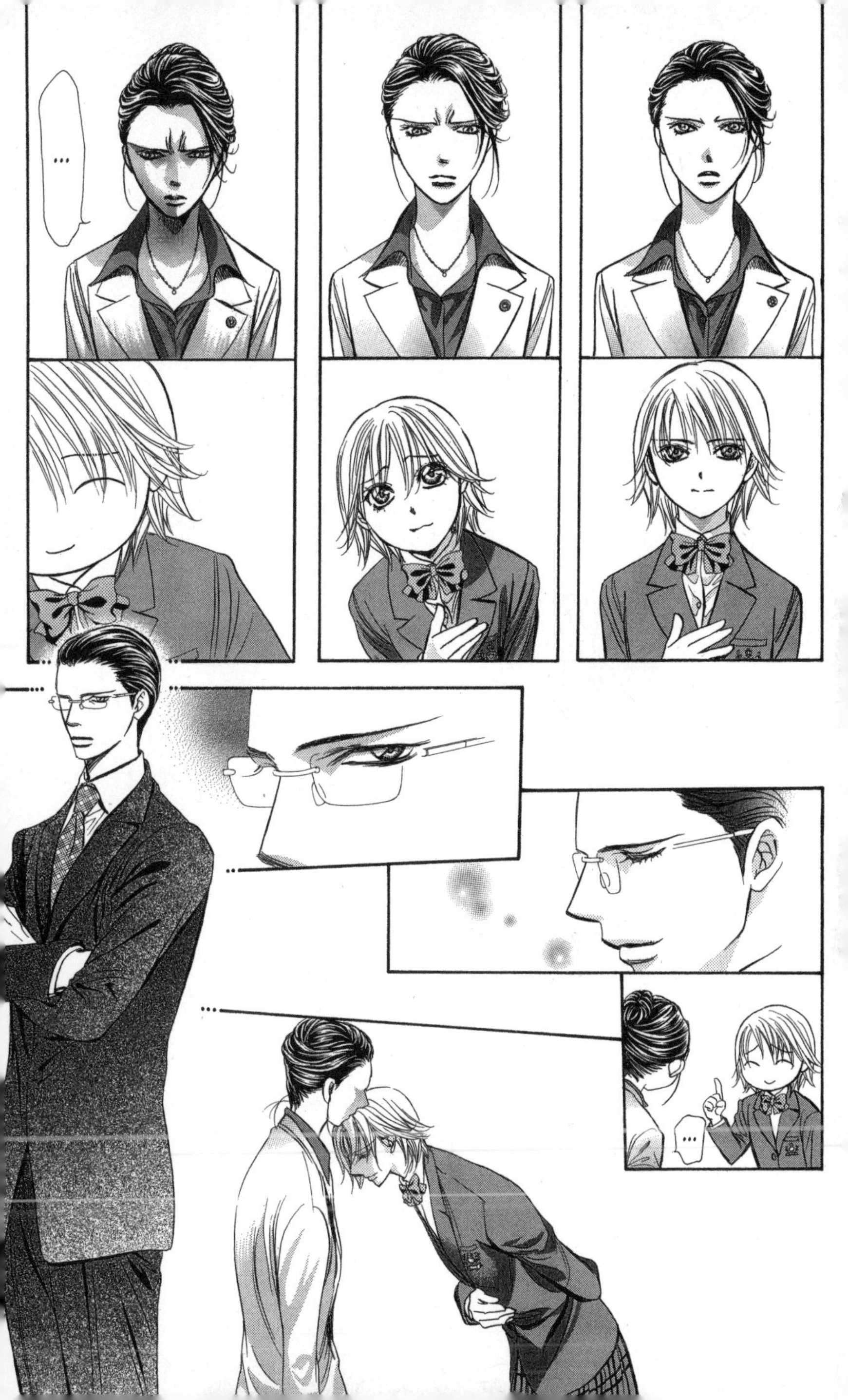
...
...

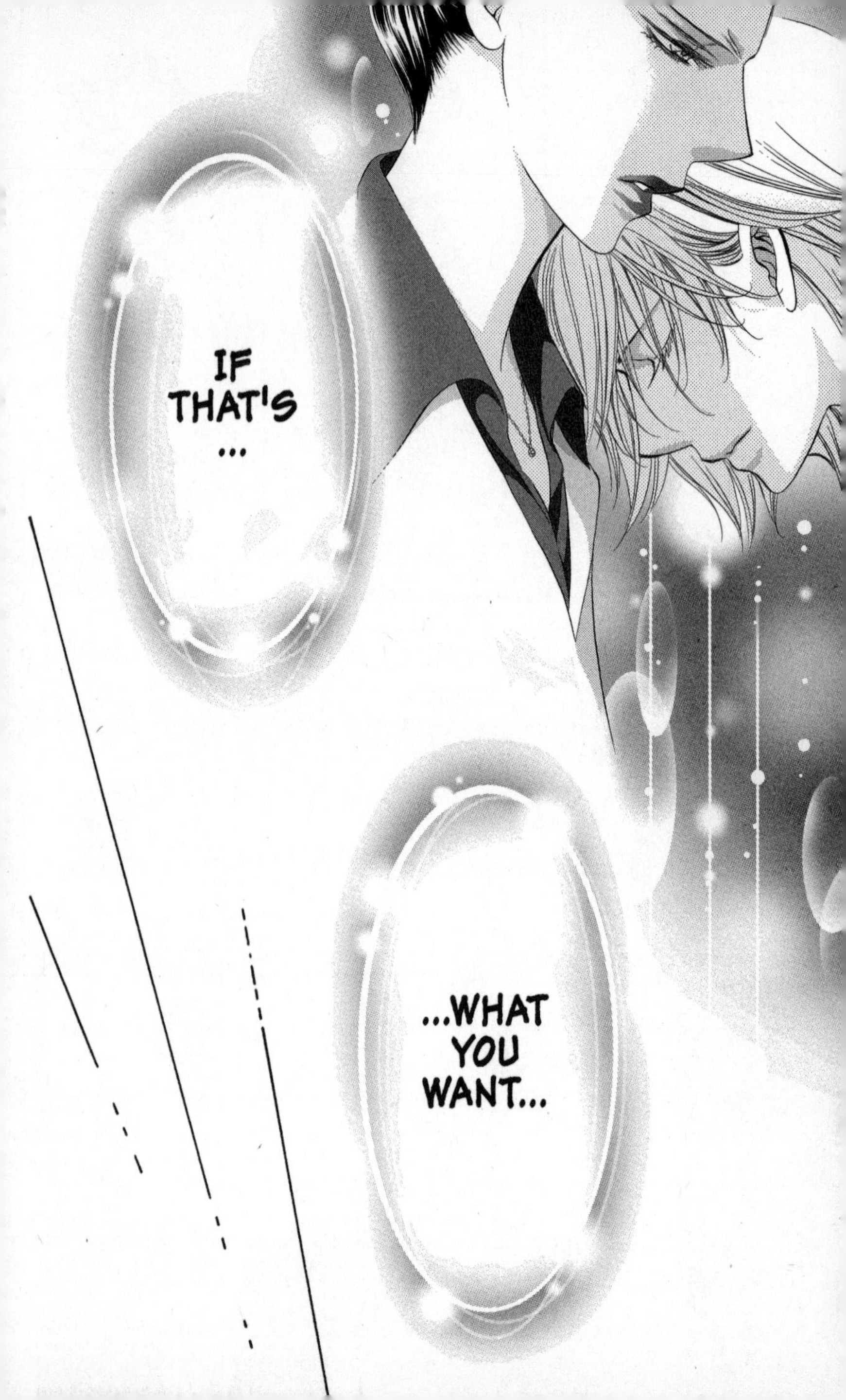
IF THAT'S ...
...WHAT YOU WANT...

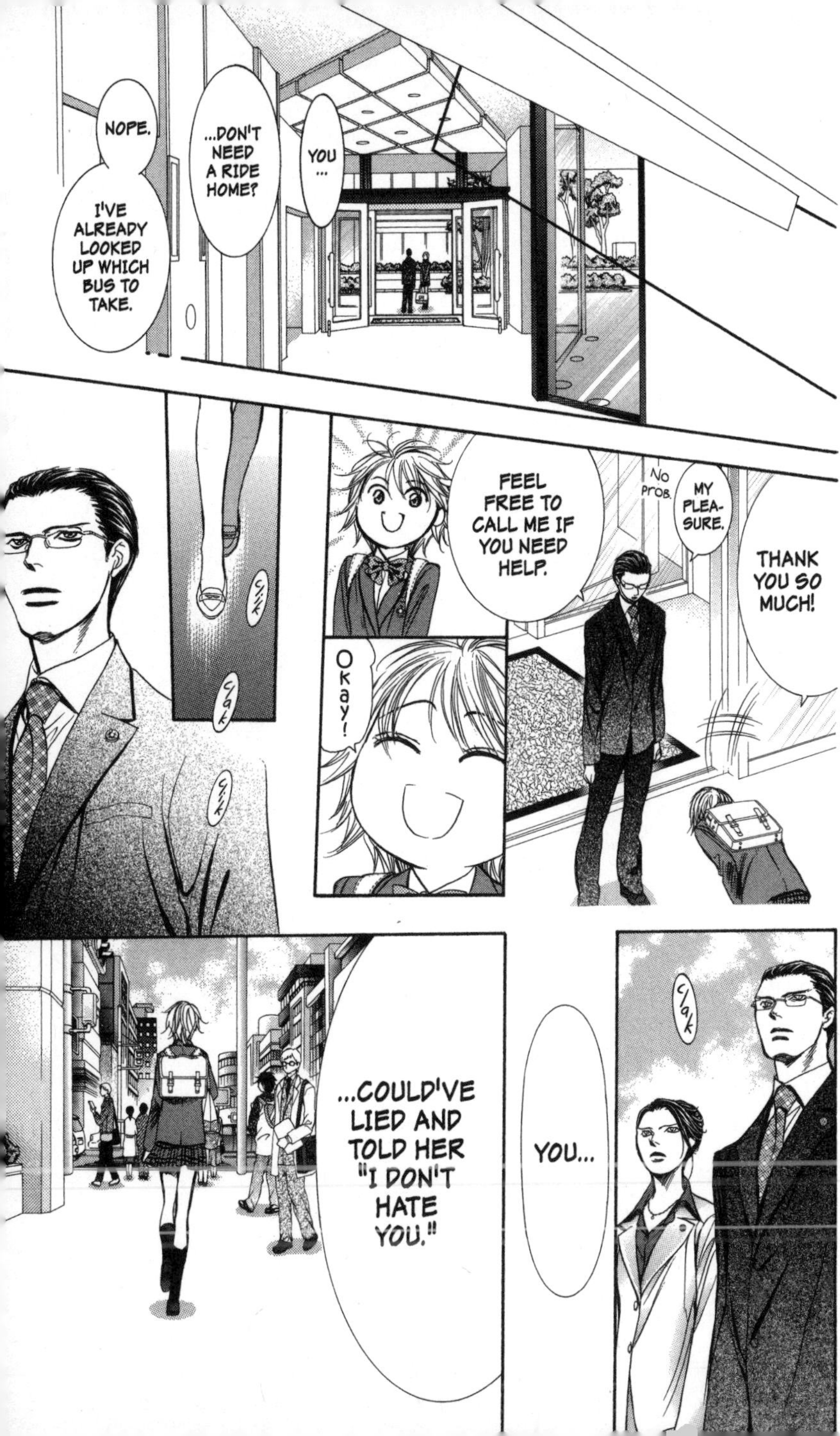
YOU ...
...DON'T NEED A RIDE HOME?
NOPE.
I'VE ALREADY LOOKED UP WHICH BUS TO TAKE.
THANK YOU SO MUCH!
MY PLEA-SURE.
No prob.
FEEL FREE TO CALL ME IF YOU NEED HELP.
Okay!
Clik
Clak
Clik
Clak
YOU...
...COULD'VE LIED AND TOLD HER "I DON'T HATE YOU."

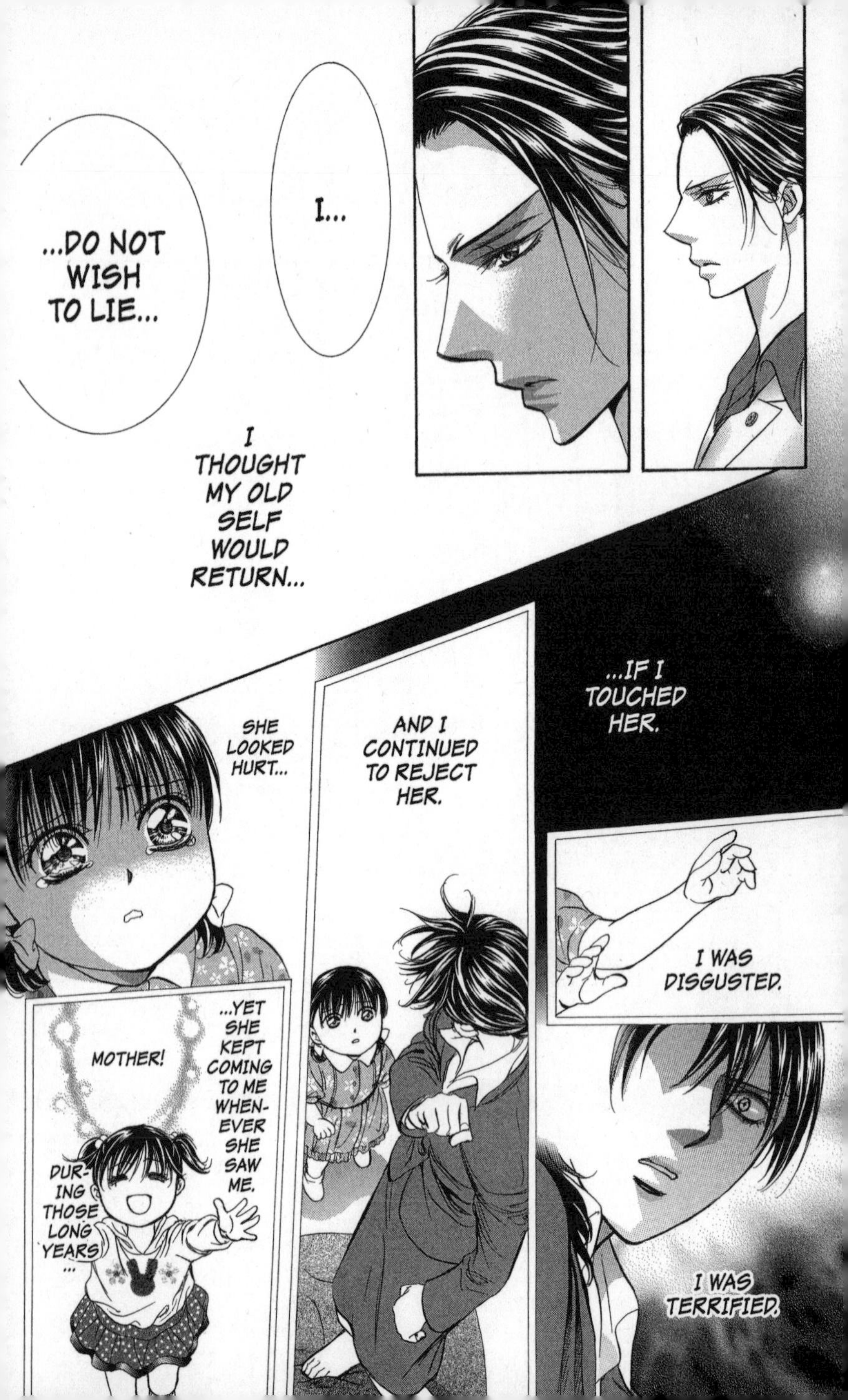
I...
...DO NOT WISH TO LIE...
I THOUGHT MY OLD SELF WOULD RETURN...
...IF I TOUCHED HER.
I WAS DISGUSTED.
I WAS TERRIFIED.
AND I CONTINUED TO REJECT HER.
SHE LOOKED HURT...
...YET SHE KEPT COMING TO ME WHENEVER SHE SAW ME.
MOTHER!
DURING THOSE LONG YEARS...

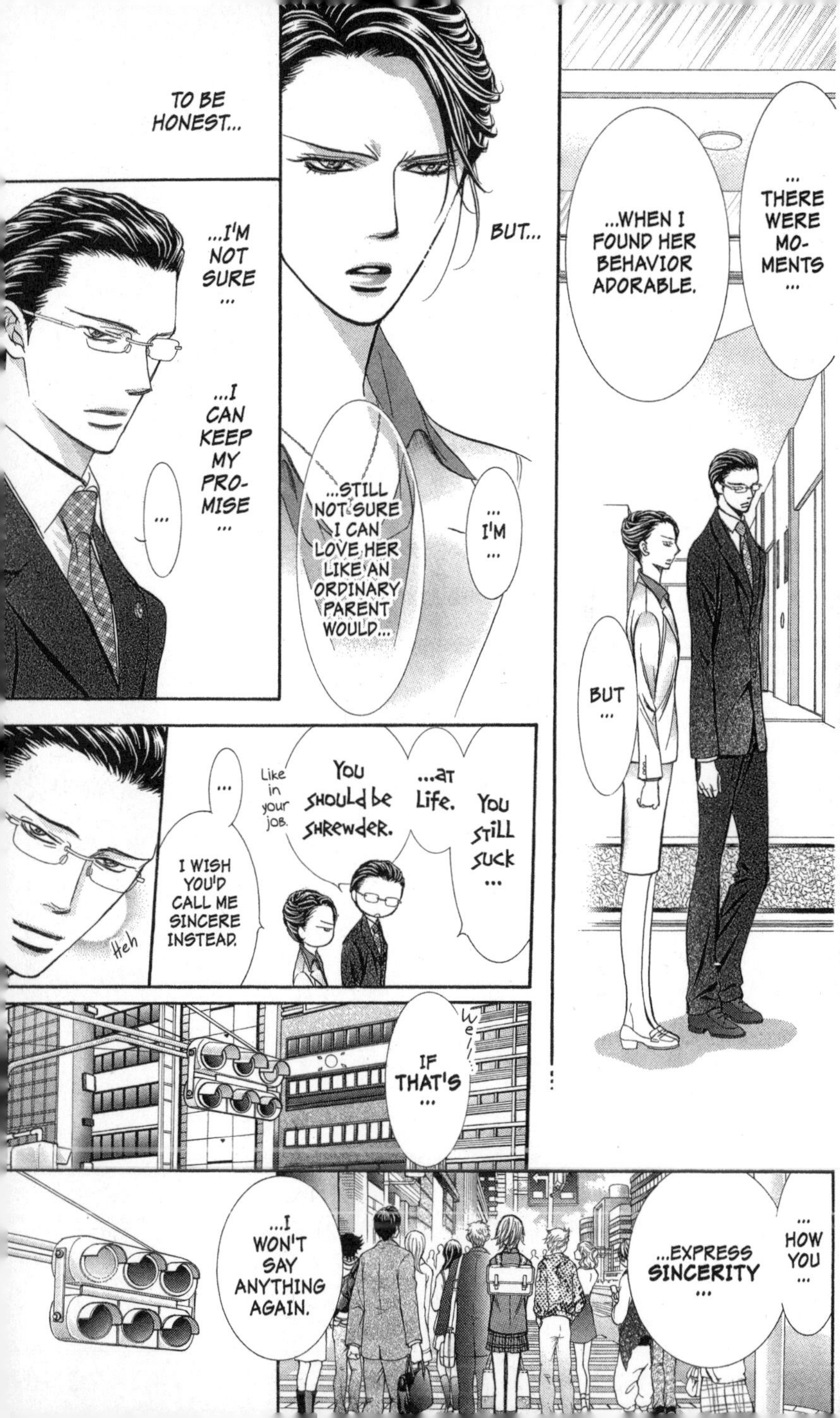

...THERE WERE MOMENTS...
...WHEN I FOUND HER BEHAVIOR ADORABLE.
BUT...
BUT...
...I'M...
...STILL NOT SURE I CAN LOVE HER LIKE AN ORDINARY PARENT WOULD...
TO BE HONEST...
...I'M NOT SURE...
...I CAN KEEP MY PROMISE...
...
You still suck...
...at life.
You should be shrewder.
Like in your job.
...
I WISH YOU'D CALL ME SINCERE INSTEAD.
Heh
Well...
IF THAT'S...
...HOW YOU...
...EXPRESS SINCERITY...
...I WON'T SAY ANYTHING AGAIN.

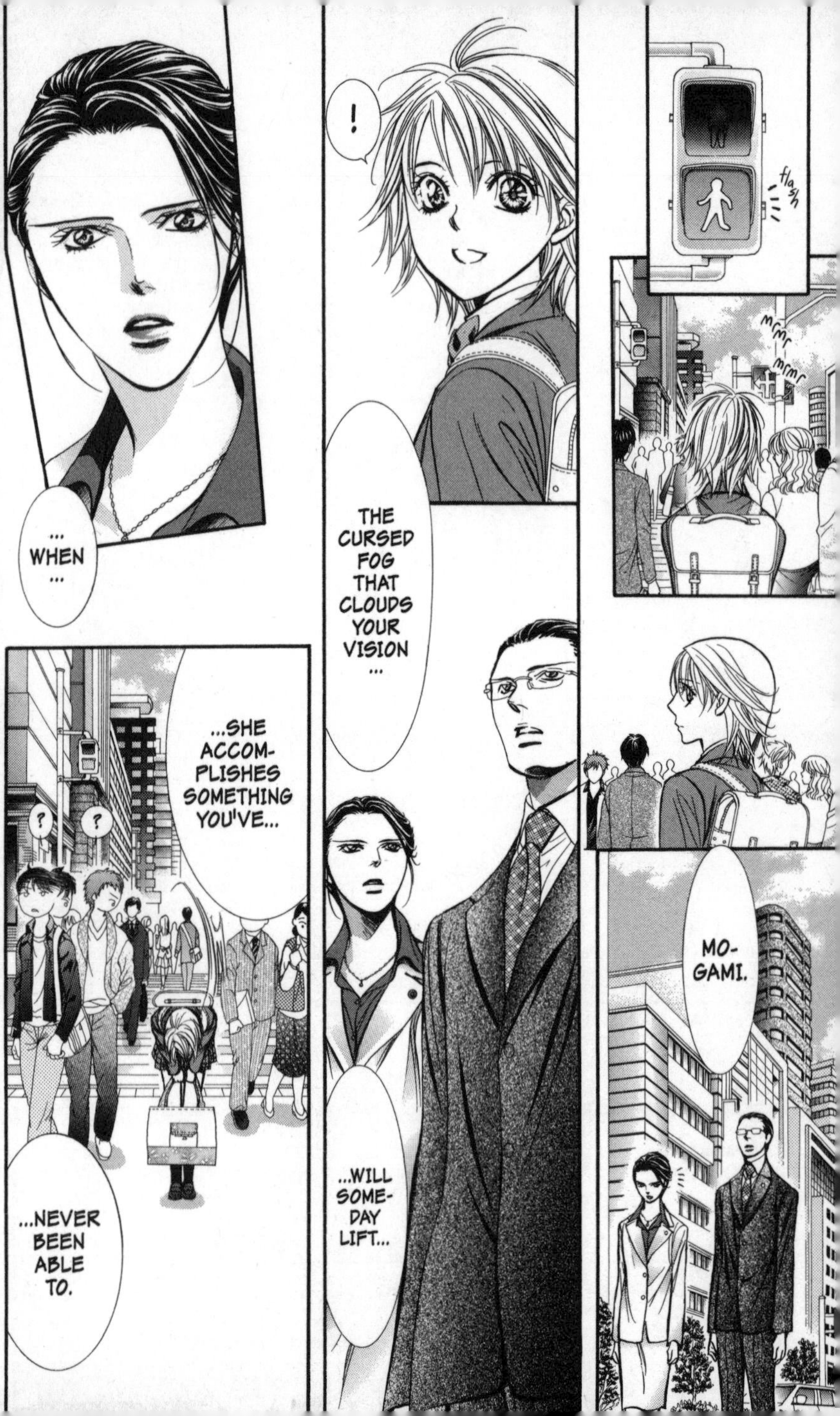
flash
mrmr mrmr
!
...WHEN...
MO-GAMI.
THE CURSED FOG THAT CLOUDS YOUR VISION...
...WILL SOMEDAY LIFT...
...SHE ACCOMPLISHES SOMETHING YOU'VE...
?
?
...NEVER BEEN ABLE TO.

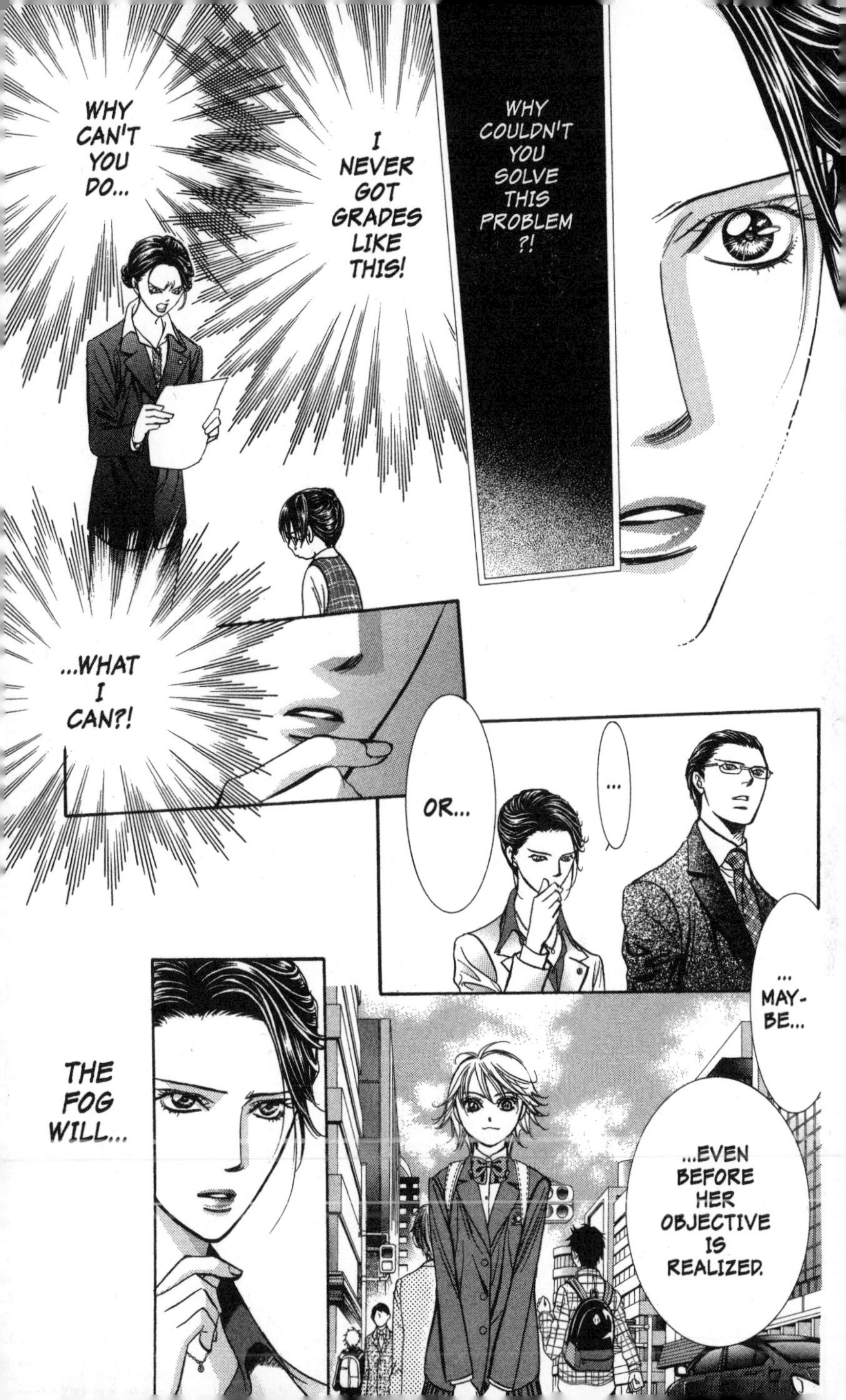
WHY COULDN'T YOU SOLVE THIS PROBLEM ?!
I NEVER GOT GRADES LIKE THIS!
WHY CAN'T YOU DO...
...WHAT I CAN?!
...
OR...
... MAY-BE...
...EVEN BEFORE HER OBJECTIVE IS REALIZED.
THE FOG WILL...

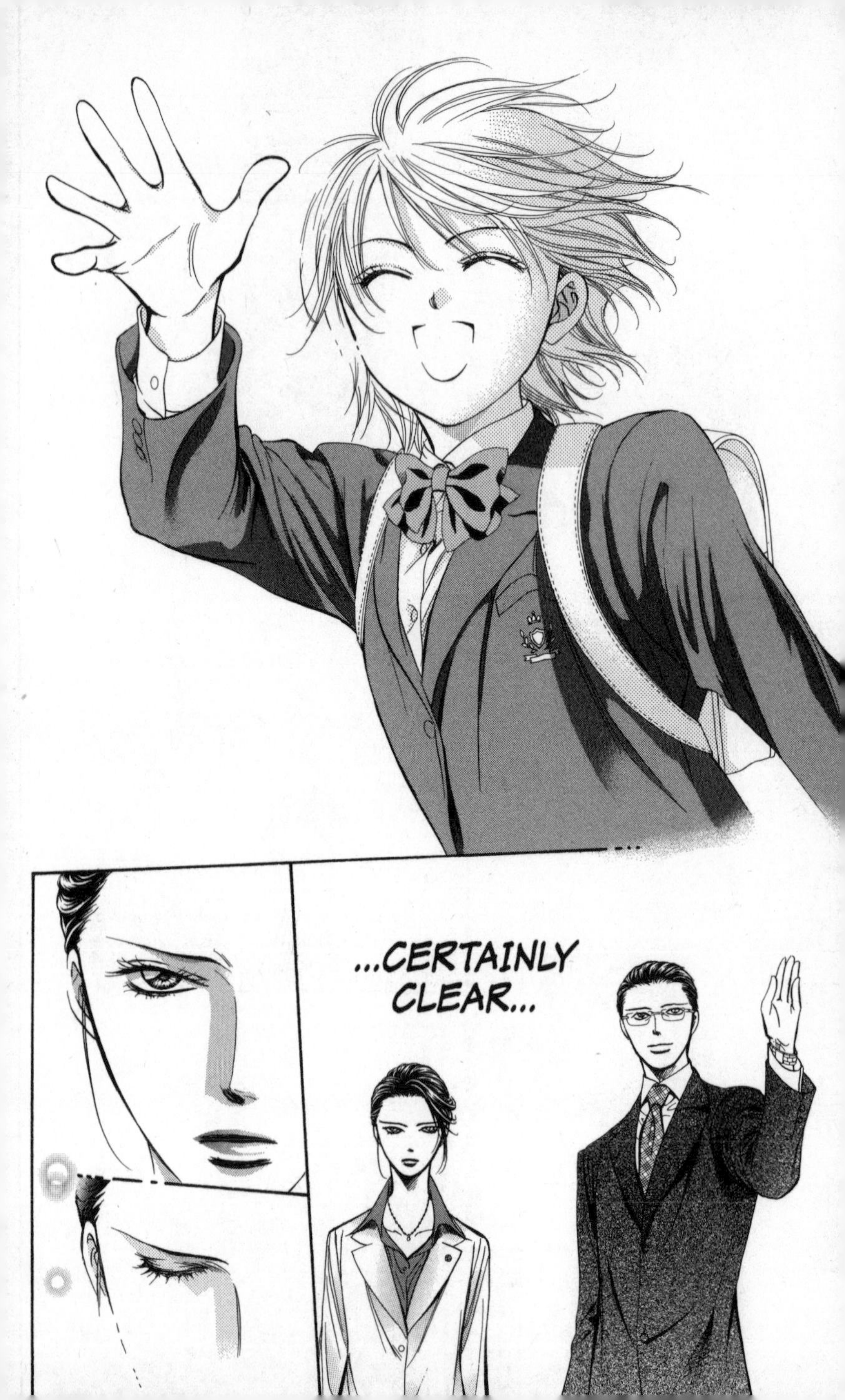
...CERTAINLY
CLEAR...

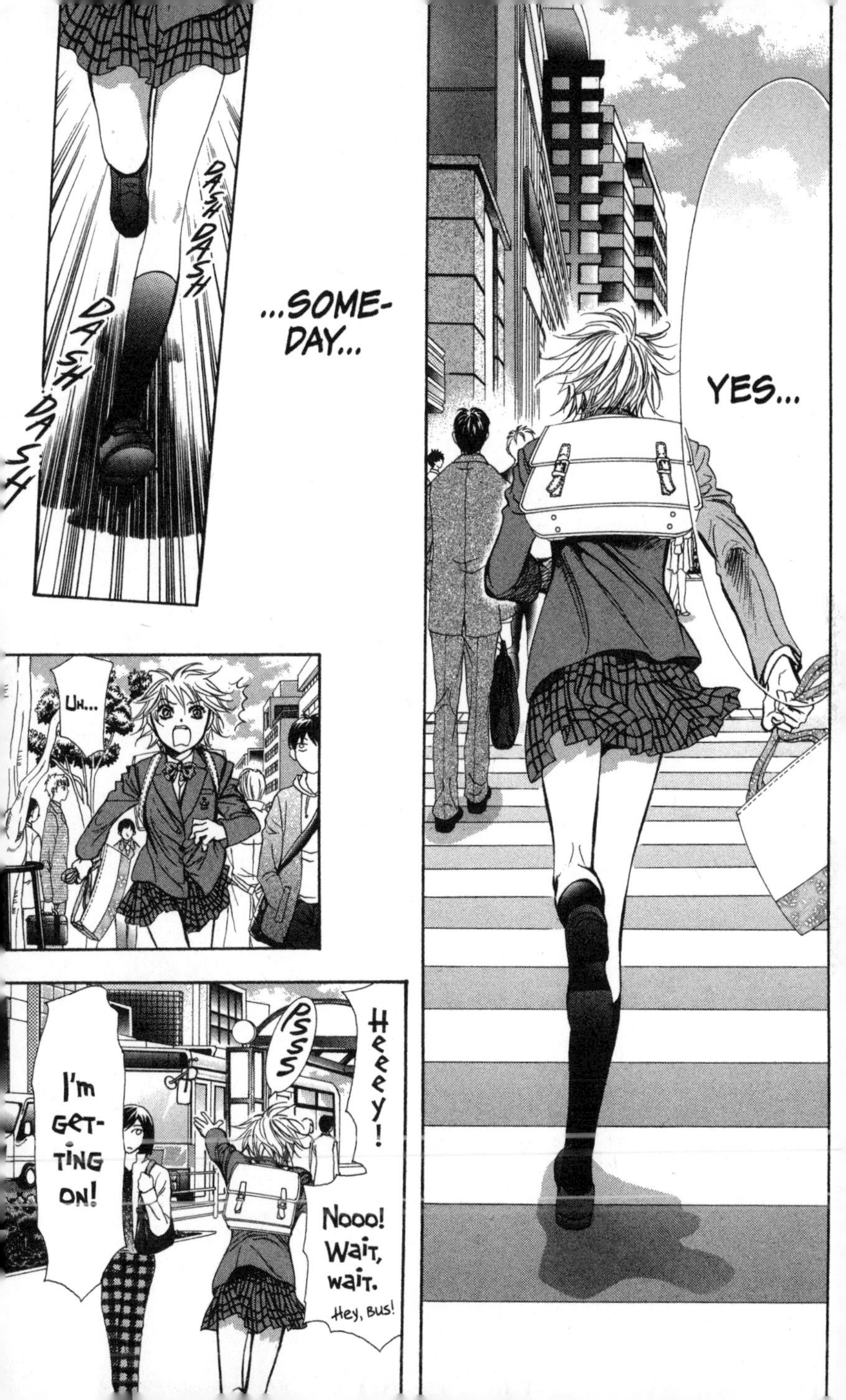
YES...
...SOME-DAY...
DASH DASH
DASH DASH
DASH
UH...
Heeey!
PSSS
Nooo! Wait, wait.
Hey, bus!
I'm GET-TING ON!

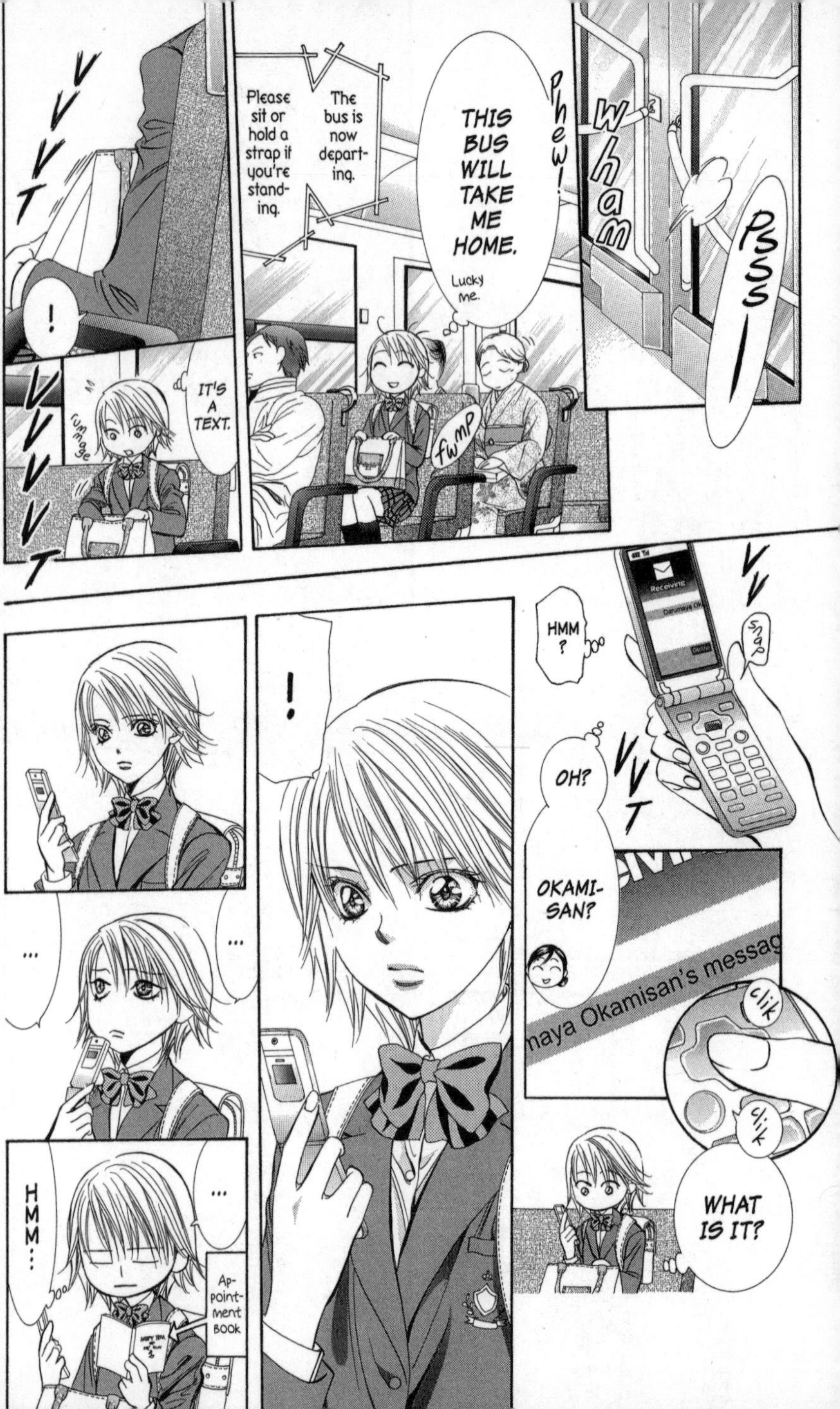
PSSS
Wham
Phew!
THIS BUS WILL TAKE ME HOME.
Lucky me.
The bus is now departing.
Please sit or hold a strap if you're standing.
fwmP
VVVT
!
IT'S A TEXT.
rummage
VVVVVT
Receiving
VV
snap
HMM?
OH?
VVT
OKAMI-SAN?
maya Okamisan's messag
clik
clik
WHAT IS IT?
!
...
...
...
HMM...
Appointment Book

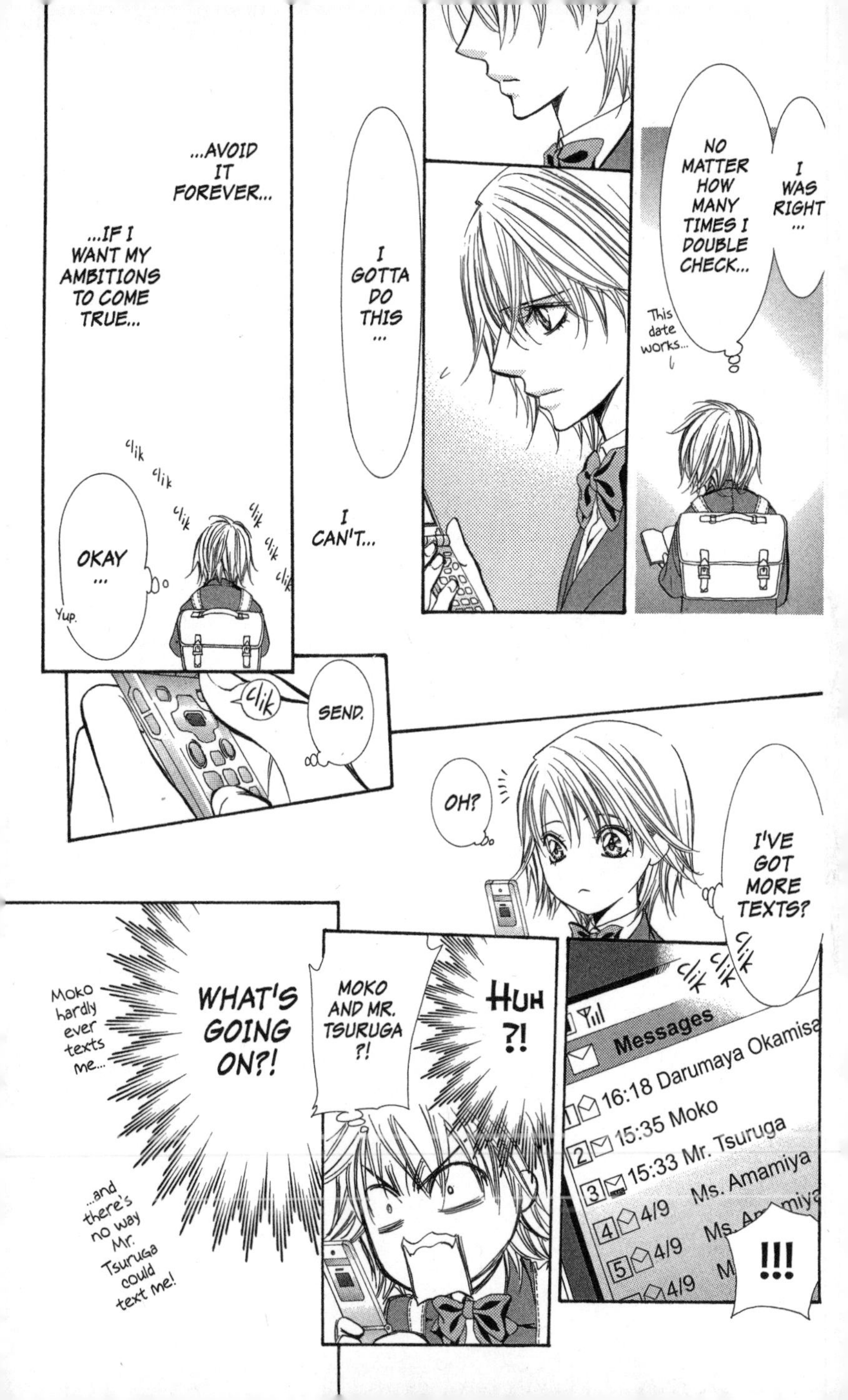

I WAS RIGHT...
NO MATTER HOW MANY TIMES I DOUBLE CHECK...
This date works...
I GOTTA DO THIS...
I CAN'T...
...AVOID IT FOREVER...
...IF I WANT MY AMBITIONS TO COME TRUE...
clik clik clik clik clik clik
OKAY...
Yup.
SEND.
clik
I'VE GOT MORE TEXTS?
OH?
clik clik
Messages
16:18 Darumaya Okamisa
1 15:35 Moko
2 15:33 Mr. Tsuruga
3 4/9 Ms. Amamiya
4 4/9 Ms. Amamiya
5 4/9
!!!
HUH?!
MOKO AND MR. TSURUGA?!
WHAT'S GOING ON?!
Moko hardly ever texts me...
...and there's no way Mr. Tsuruga could text me!

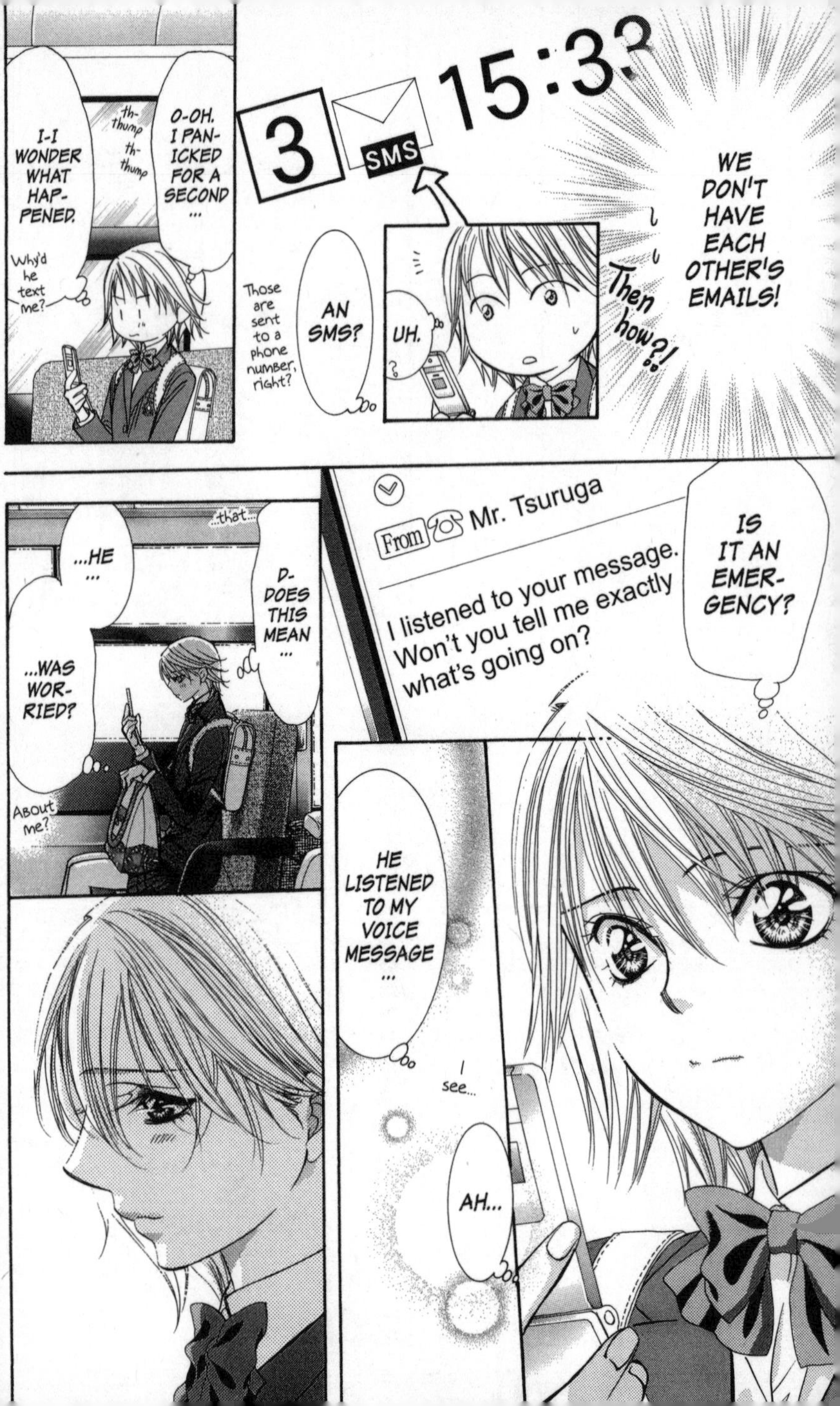
3
SMS
15:33
WE DON'T HAVE EACH OTHER'S EMAILS!
Then how?!
UH.
AN SMS?
Those are sent to a phone number, right?
O-OH. I PANICKED FOR A SECOND...
th-thump th-thump
I-I WONDER WHAT HAPPENED.
Why'd he text me?
From Mr. Tsuruga
I listened to your message. Won't you tell me exactly what's going on?
IS IT AN EMERGENCY?
D-DOES THIS MEAN...
...that...
...HE...
...WAS WORRIED?
About me?
HE LISTENED TO MY VOICE MESSAGE...
I see...
AH...

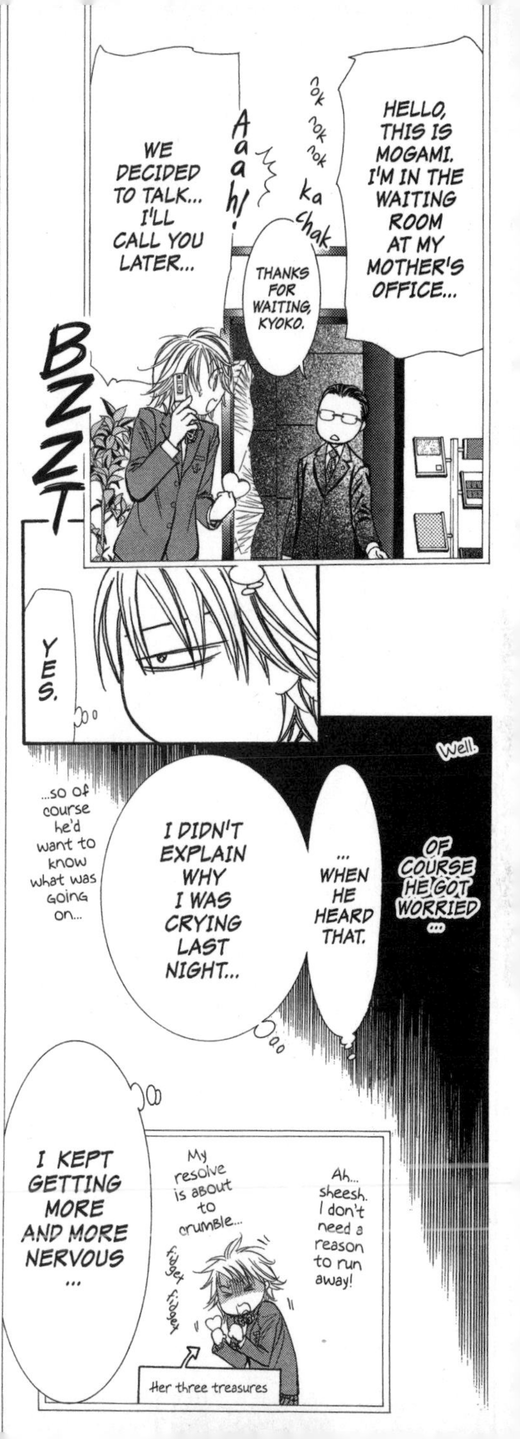
HELLO, THIS IS MOGAMI. I'M IN THE WAITING ROOM AT MY MOTHER'S OFFICE...
nok nok nok
Aaah!
ka chak
WE DECIDED TO TALK... I'LL CALL YOU LATER...
THANKS FOR WAITING, KYOKO.
BZZZT
YES.
Well.
OF COURSE HE GOT WORRIED...
...WHEN HE HEARD THAT.
I DIDN'T EXPLAIN WHY I WAS CRYING LAST NIGHT...
...so of course he'd want to know what was going on...
I KEPT GETTING MORE AND MORE NERVOUS...
Ah... sheesh. I don't need a reason to run away!
My resolve is about to crumble...
fidget fidget
Her three treasures
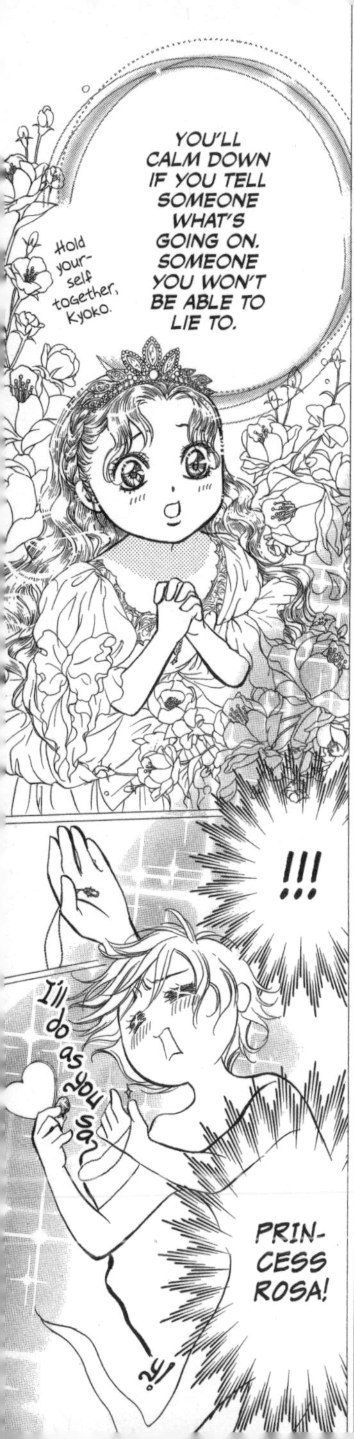
YOU'LL CALM DOWN IF YOU TELL SOMEONE WHAT'S GOING ON. SOMEONE YOU WON'T BE ABLE TO LIE TO.
Hold yourself together, Kyoko.
!!!
PRINCESS ROSA!
I'll do as you say
?!

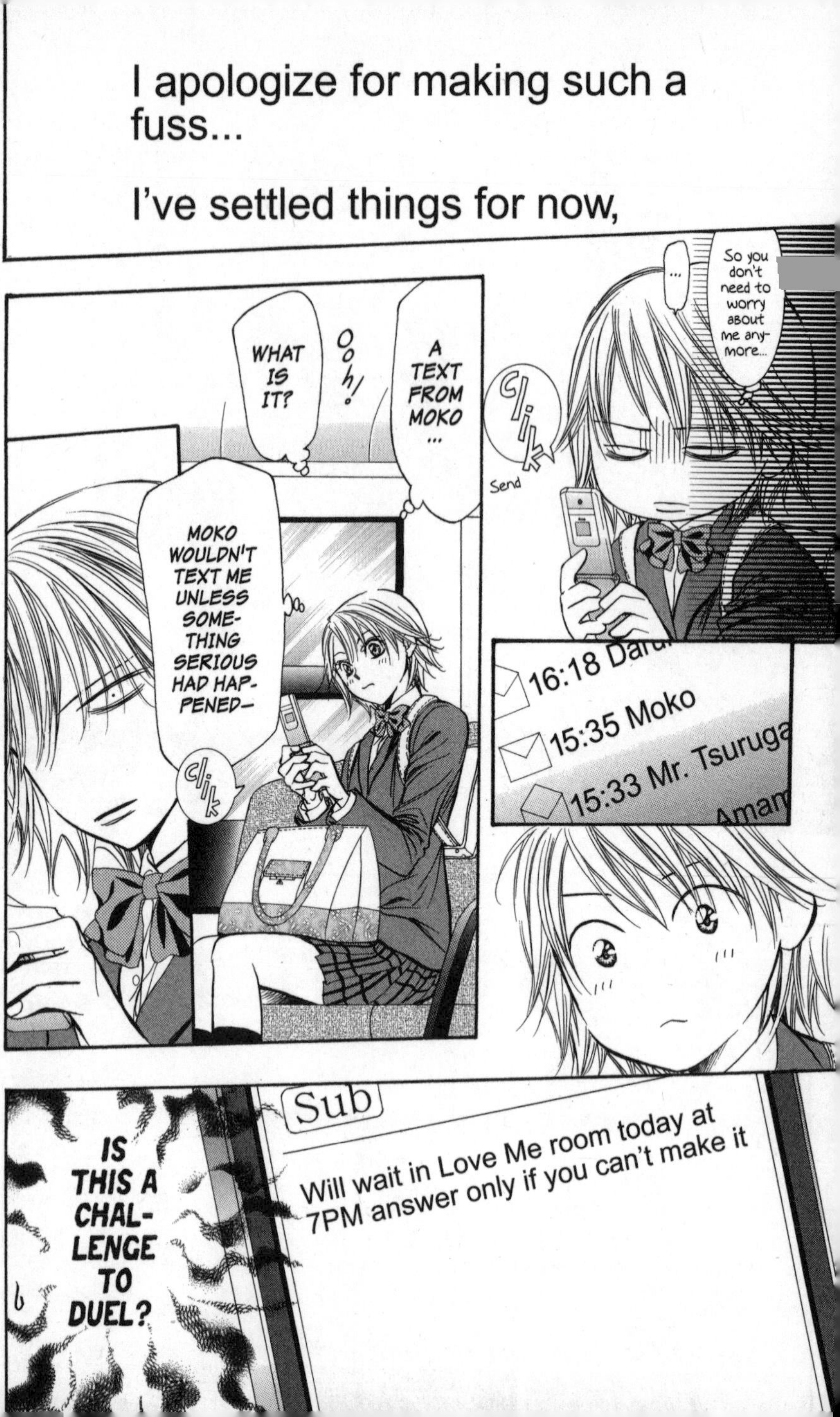
I apologize for making such a fuss...
I've settled things for now,
...
So you don't need to worry about me any-more...
Clik
Send
16:18 Daru
15:35 Moko
15:33 Mr. Tsuruga
Amam
A TEXT FROM MOKO...
Ooh!
WHAT IS IT?
MOKO WOULDN'T TEXT ME UNLESS SOME-THING SERIOUS HAD HAP-PENED—
Clik
Sub
Will wait in Love Me room today at 7PM answer only if you can't make it
IS THIS A CHAL-LENGE TO DUEL?

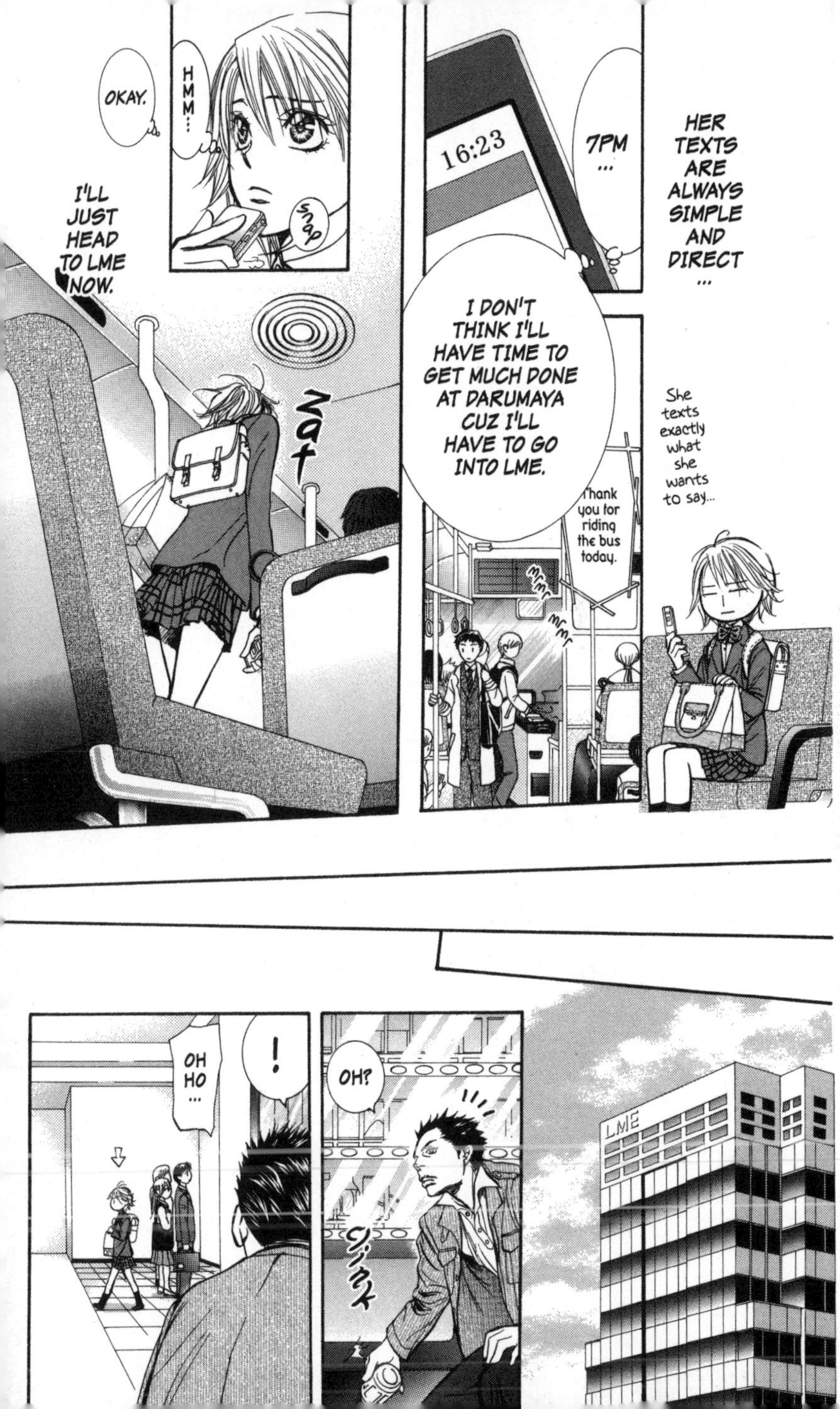
HER TEXTS ARE ALWAYS SIMPLE AND DIRECT...
7PM...
16:23
I DON'T THINK I'LL HAVE TIME TO GET MUCH DONE AT DARUMAYA CUZ I'LL HAVE TO GO INTO LME.
She texts exactly what she wants to say...
Thank you for riding the bus today.
mrmr
mrmr
HMM...
OKAY.
snap
I'LL JUST HEAD TO LME NOW.
zat
LME
OH?
!
jink
OH HO...

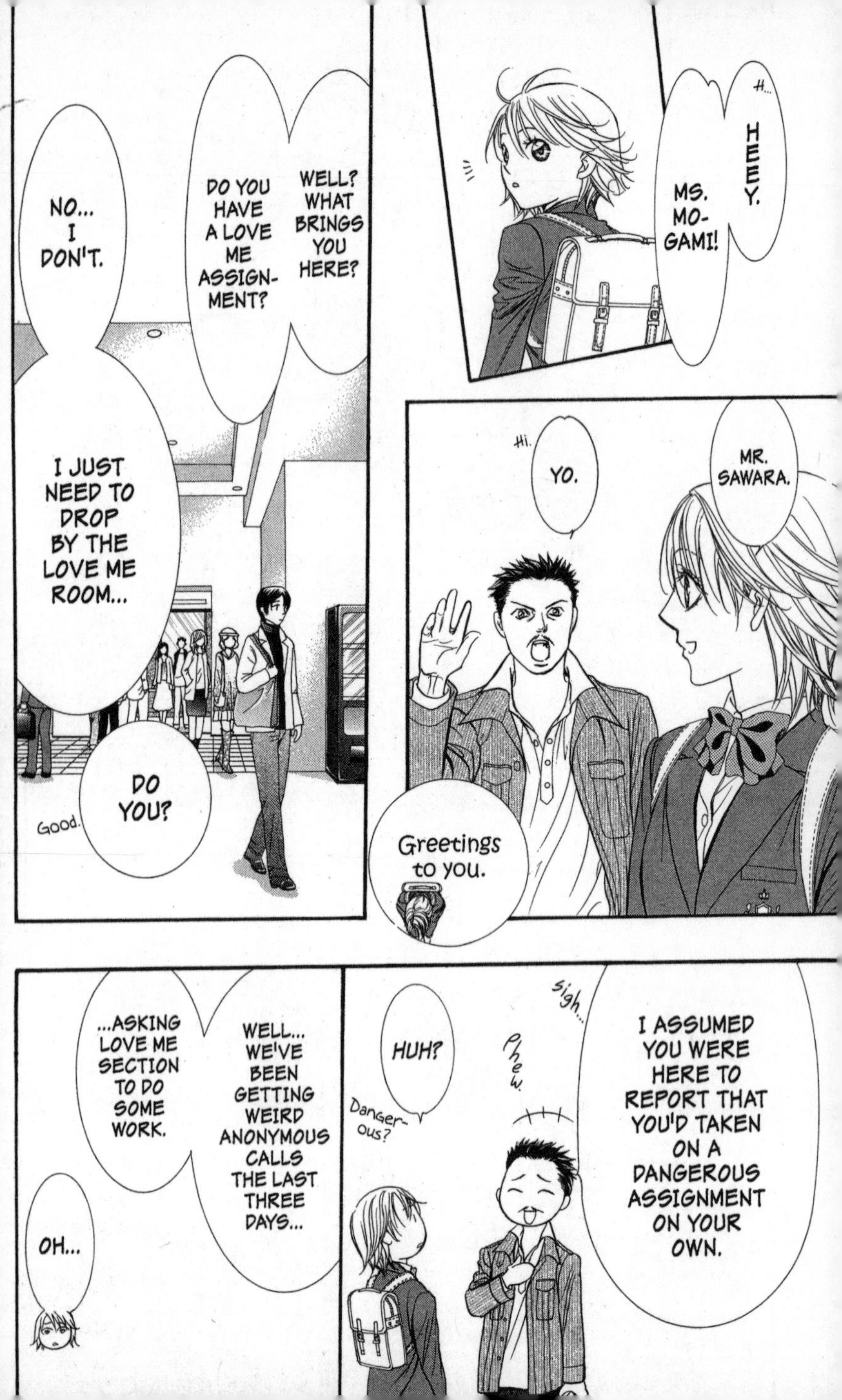
H... HEEY.
MS. MO-GAMI!
MR. SAWARA.
Hi.
YO.
Greetings to you.
WELL? WHAT BRINGS YOU HERE?
DO YOU HAVE A LOVE ME ASSIGN-MENT?
NO... I DON'T.
I JUST NEED TO DROP BY THE LOVE ME ROOM...
DO YOU?
Good.
I ASSUMED YOU WERE HERE TO REPORT THAT YOU'D TAKEN ON A DANGEROUS ASSIGNMENT ON YOUR OWN.
sigh...
Phew.
HUH?
Danger-ous?
WELL... WE'VE BEEN GETTING WEIRD ANONYMOUS CALLS THE LAST THREE DAYS...
...ASKING LOVE ME SECTION TO DO SOME WORK.
OH...

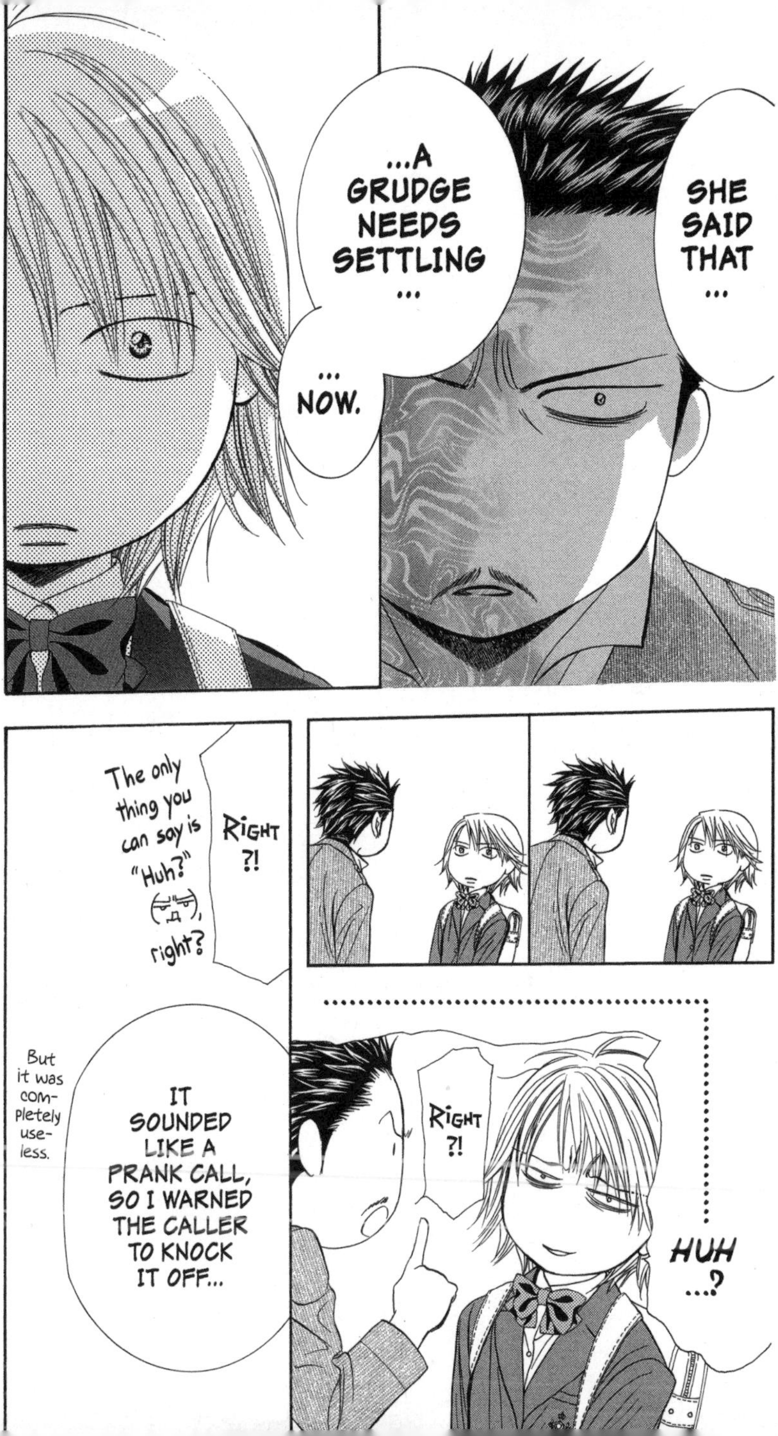
SHE SAID THAT ...
...A GRUDGE NEEDS SETTLING ...
... NOW.
RIGHT ?!
The only thing you can say is "Huh?" , right?
HUH ...?
RIGHT ?!
IT SOUNDED LIKE A PRANK CALL, SO I WARNED THE CALLER TO KNOCK IT OFF...
But it was completely useless.

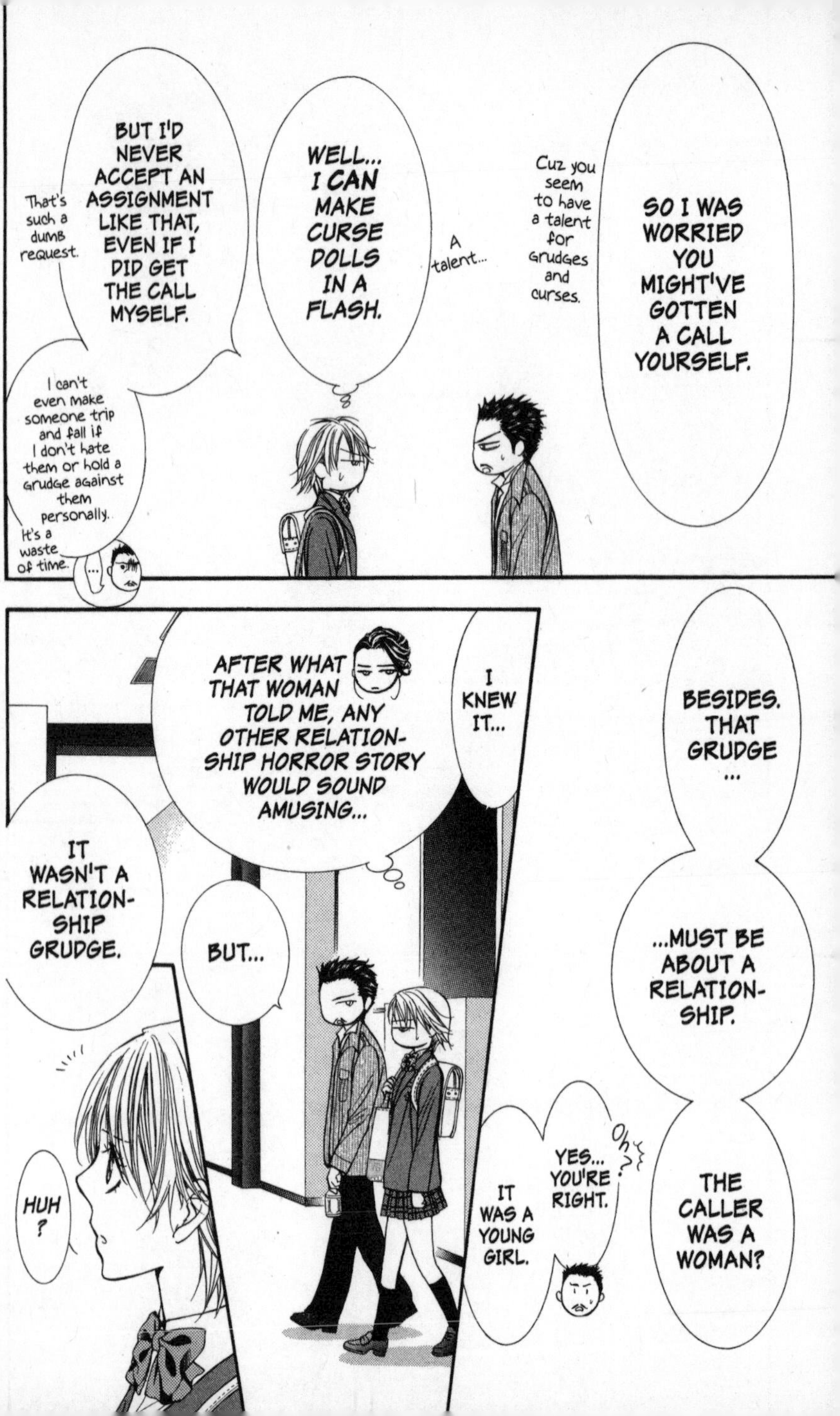
SO I WAS WORRIED YOU MIGHT'VE GOTTEN A CALL YOURSELF.
Cuz you seem to have a talent for grudges and curses.
A talent...
WELL... I CAN MAKE CURSE DOLLS IN A FLASH.
BUT I'D NEVER ACCEPT AN ASSIGNMENT LIKE THAT, EVEN IF I DID GET THE CALL MYSELF.
That's such a dumb request.
I can't even make someone trip and fall if I don't hate them or hold a grudge against them personally.
It's a waste of time.
...
BESIDES. THAT GRUDGE ...
...MUST BE ABOUT A RELATION-SHIP.
THE CALLER WAS A WOMAN?
I KNEW IT...
AFTER WHAT THAT WOMAN TOLD ME, ANY OTHER RELATION-SHIP HORROR STORY WOULD SOUND AMUSING...
YES... YOU'RE RIGHT.
Oh?
IT WAS A YOUNG GIRL.
BUT...
IT WASN'T A RELATION-SHIP GRUDGE.
HUH?

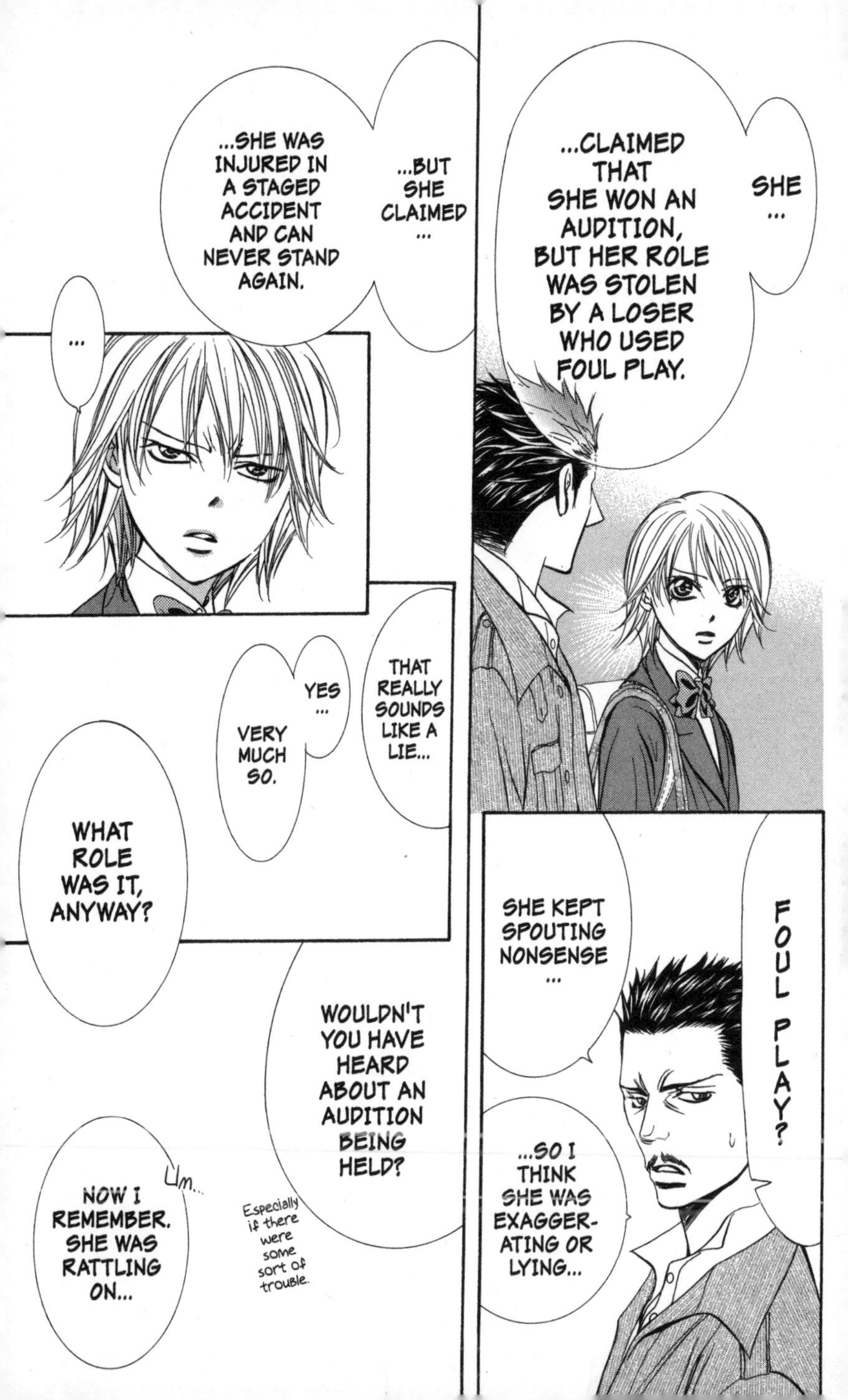
SHE ...
...CLAIMED THAT SHE WON AN AUDITION, BUT HER ROLE WAS STOLEN BY A LOSER WHO USED FOUL PLAY.
FOUL PLAY?
SHE KEPT SPOUTING NONSENSE ...
...SO I THINK SHE WAS EXAGGER-ATING OR LYING...
...BUT SHE CLAIMED ...
...SHE WAS INJURED IN A STAGED ACCIDENT AND CAN NEVER STAND AGAIN.
...
THAT REALLY SOUNDS LIKE A LIE...
YES ...
VERY MUCH SO.
WHAT ROLE WAS IT, ANYWAY?
WOULDN'T YOU HAVE HEARD ABOUT AN AUDITION BEING HELD?
Especially if there were some sort of trouble.
Um...
NOW I REMEMBER. SHE WAS RATTLING ON...

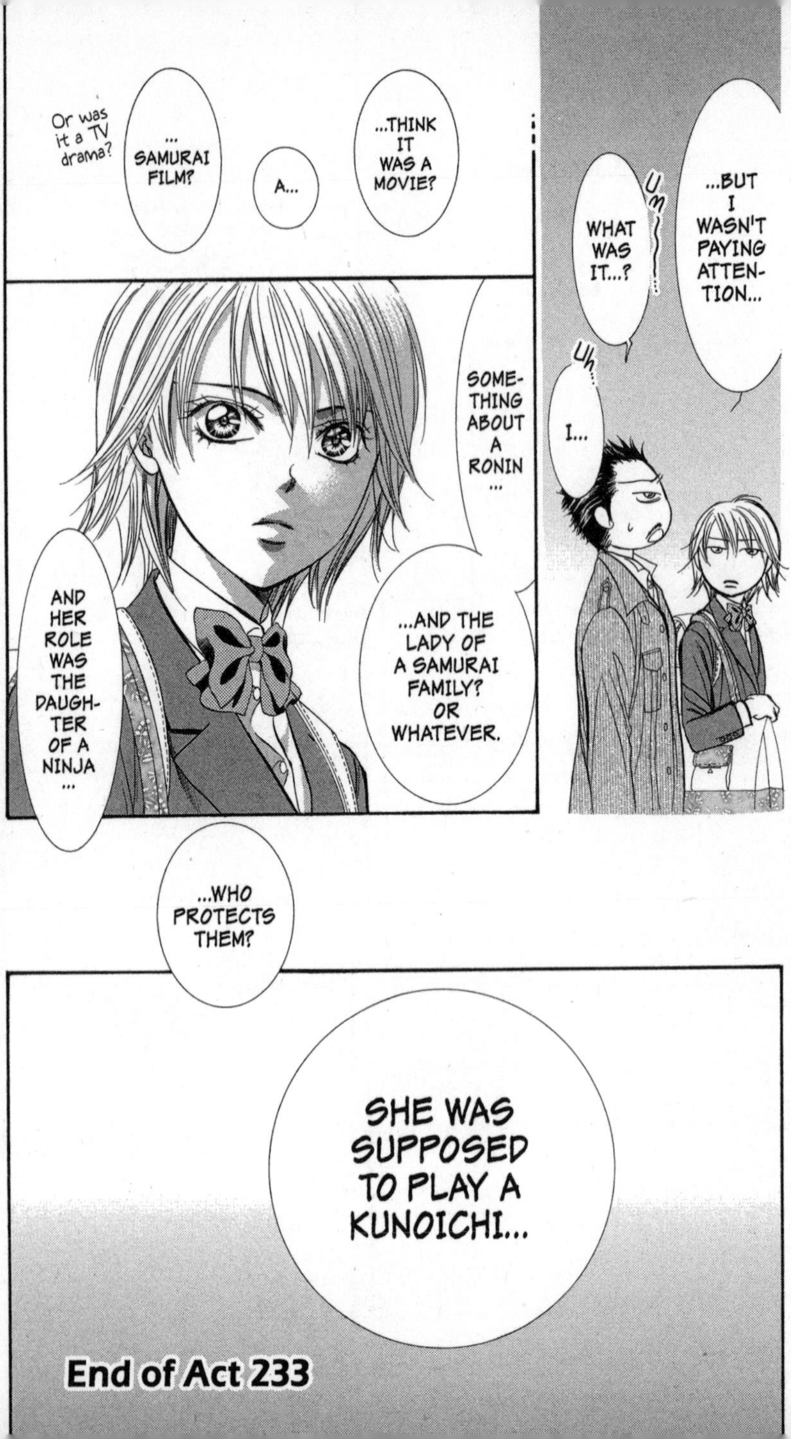
...BUT I WASN'T PAYING ATTEN-TION...
Um~~...
WHAT WAS IT...?
Uh...
I...
...THINK IT WAS A MOVIE?
A...
... SAMURAI FILM?
Or was it a TV drama?
SOME-THING ABOUT A RONIN ...
...AND THE LADY OF A SAMURAI FAMILY? OR WHATEVER.
AND HER ROLE WAS THE DAUGH-TER OF A NINJA ...
...WHO PROTECTS THEM?
SHE WAS SUPPOSED TO PLAY A KUNOICHI...
End of Act 233

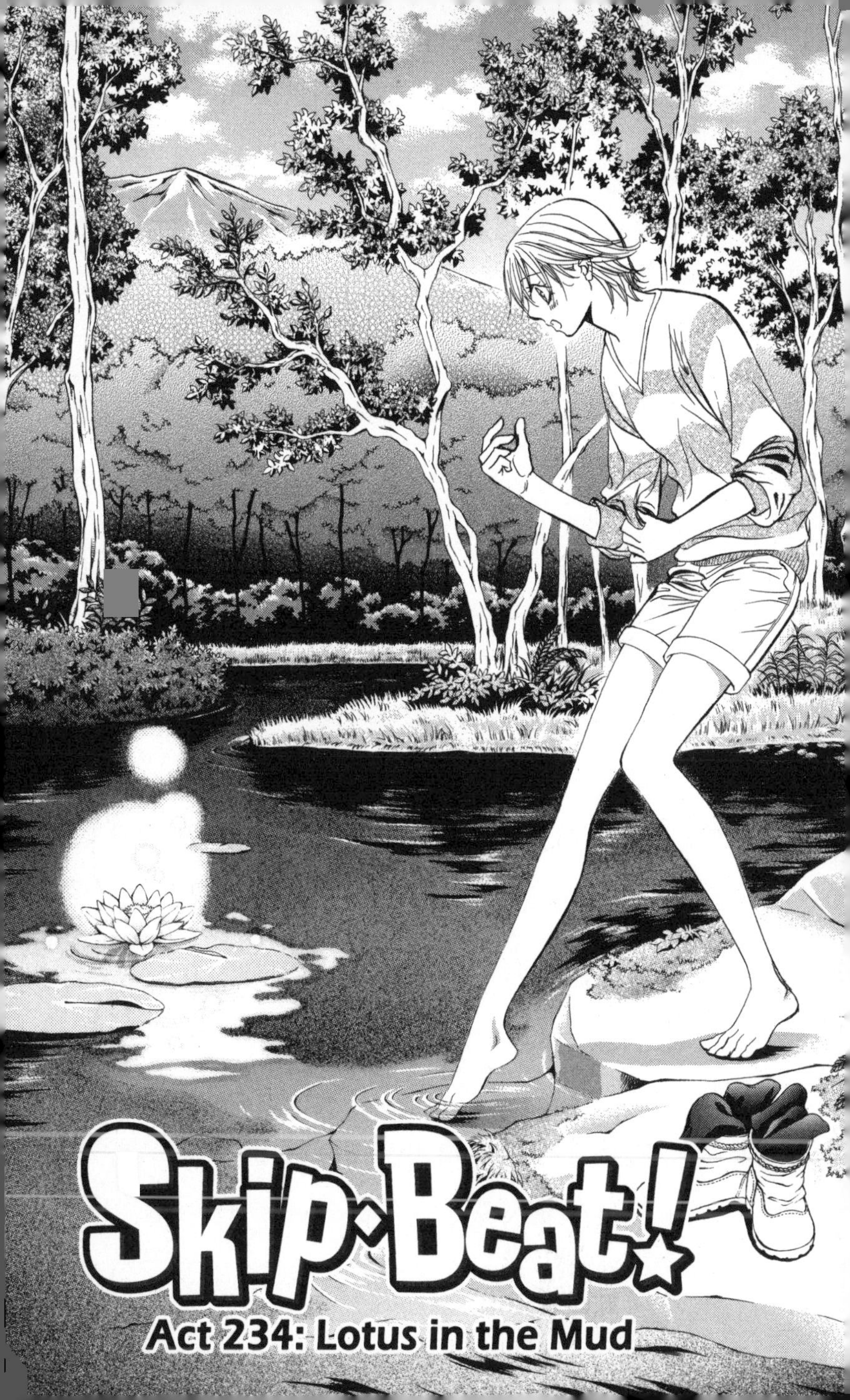
Skip·Beat!
Act 234: Lotus in the Mud

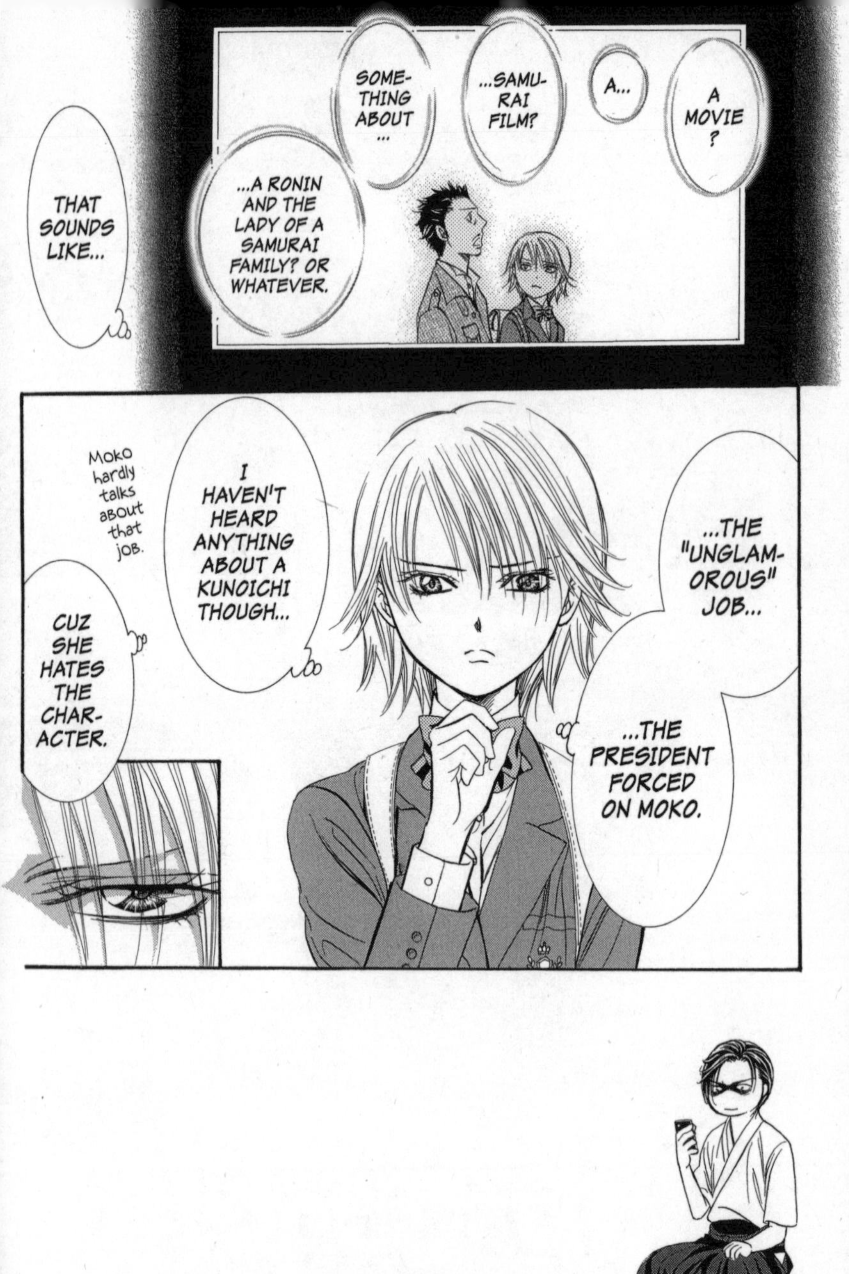
A MOVIE?
A...
...SAMURAI FILM?
SOMETHING ABOUT...
...A RONIN AND THE LADY OF A SAMURAI FAMILY? OR WHATEVER.
THAT SOUNDS LIKE...
...THE "UNGLAMOROUS" JOB...
...THE PRESIDENT FORCED ON MOKO.
I HAVEN'T HEARD ANYTHING ABOUT A KUNOICHI THOUGH...
Moko hardly talks about that job.
CUZ SHE HATES THE CHARACTER.

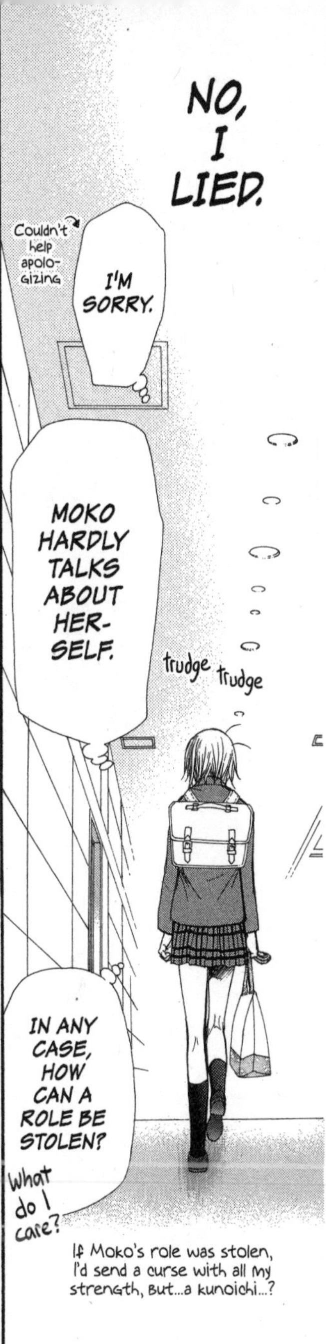
NO, I LIED.
Couldn't help apologizing
I'M SORRY.
MOKO HARDLY TALKS ABOUT HERSELF.
trudge trudge
IN ANY CASE, HOW CAN A ROLE BE STOLEN?
What do I care?
If Moko's role was stolen, I'd send a curse with all my strength, but...a kunoichi...?
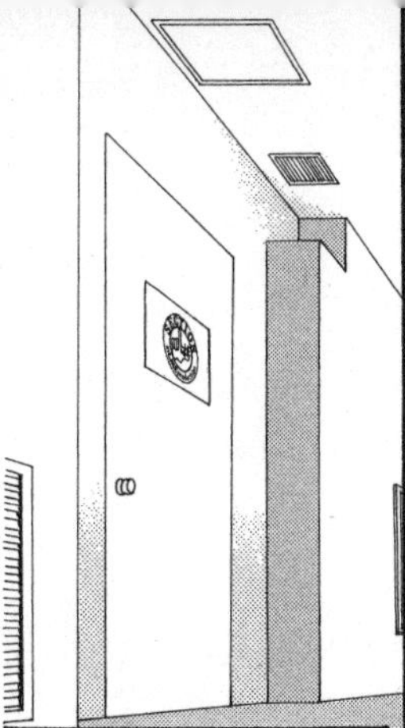
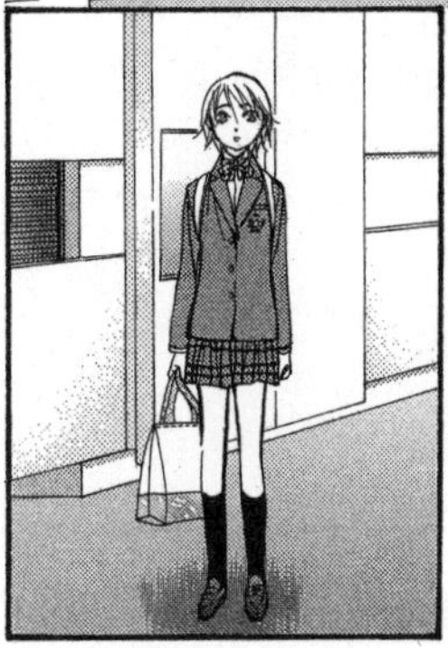
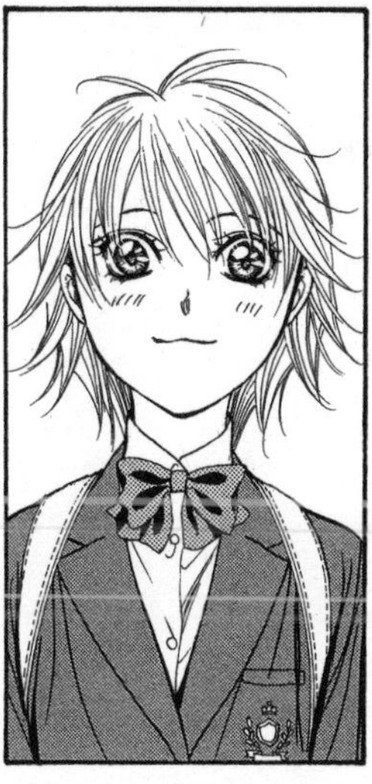
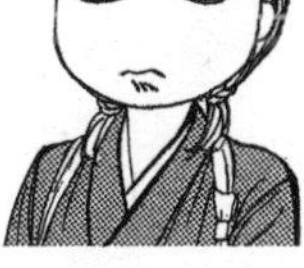

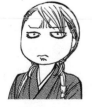

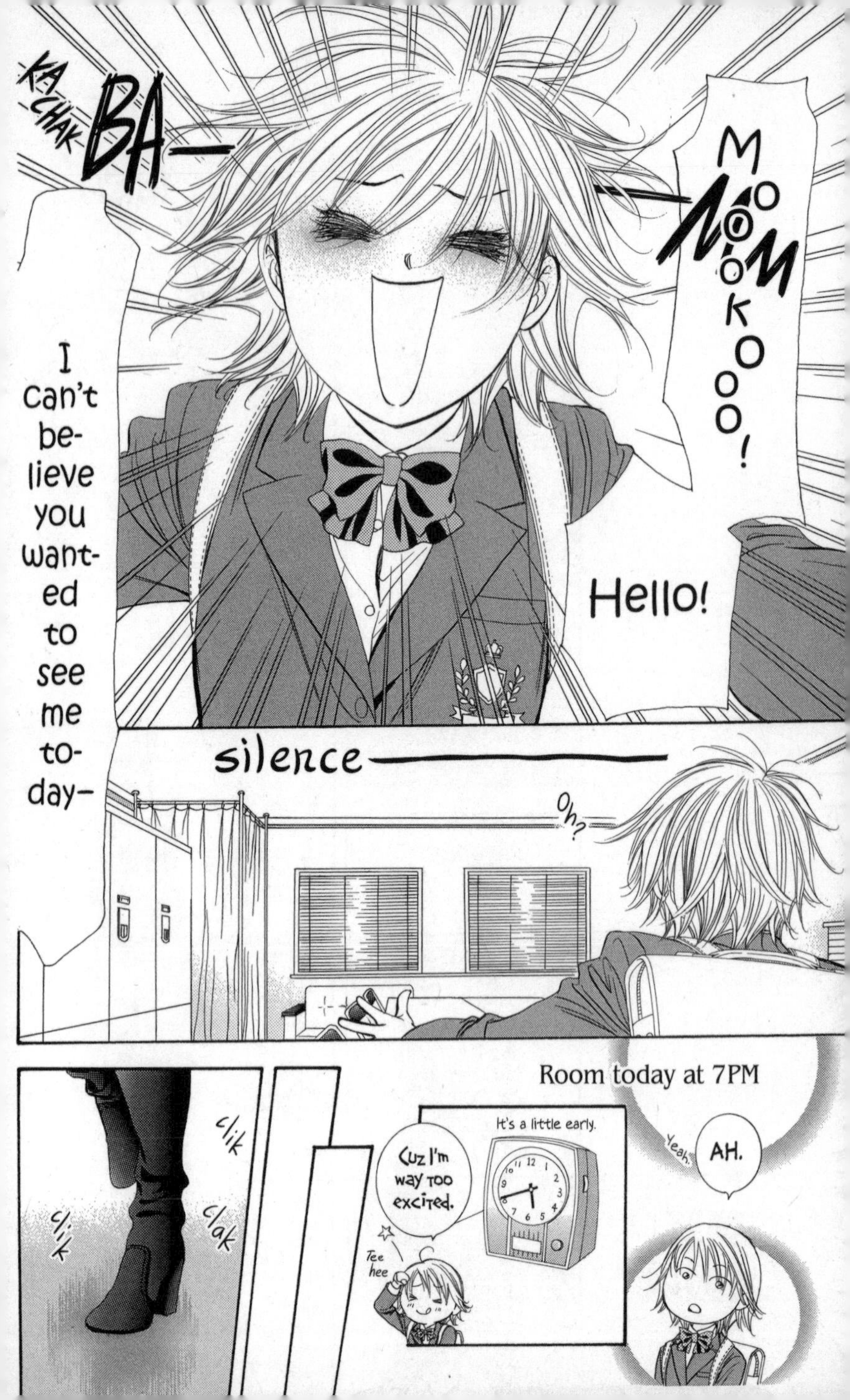
MOMOKOOOO!
Hello!
KA-CHAK
BA—
I can't be-lieve you want-ed to see me to-day—
silence——
Oh?
Room today at 7PM
Yeah.
AH.
It's a little early.
Cuz I'm way too excited.
Tee hee
clik
clak
clik

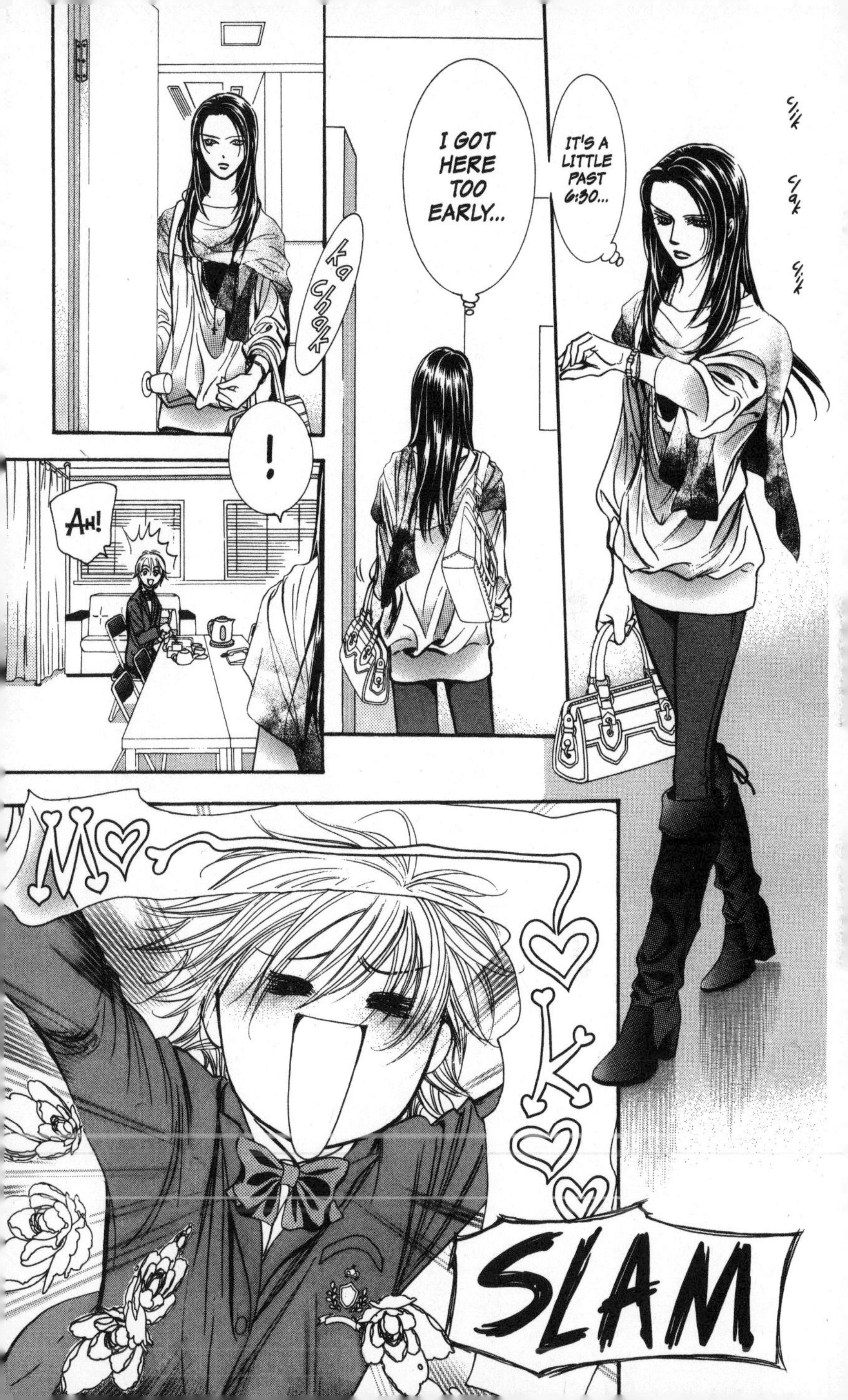

clik
clak
clik
IT'S A LITTLE PAST 6:30...
I GOT HERE TOO EARLY...
ka chak
!
AH!
M♥ K♥
SLAM

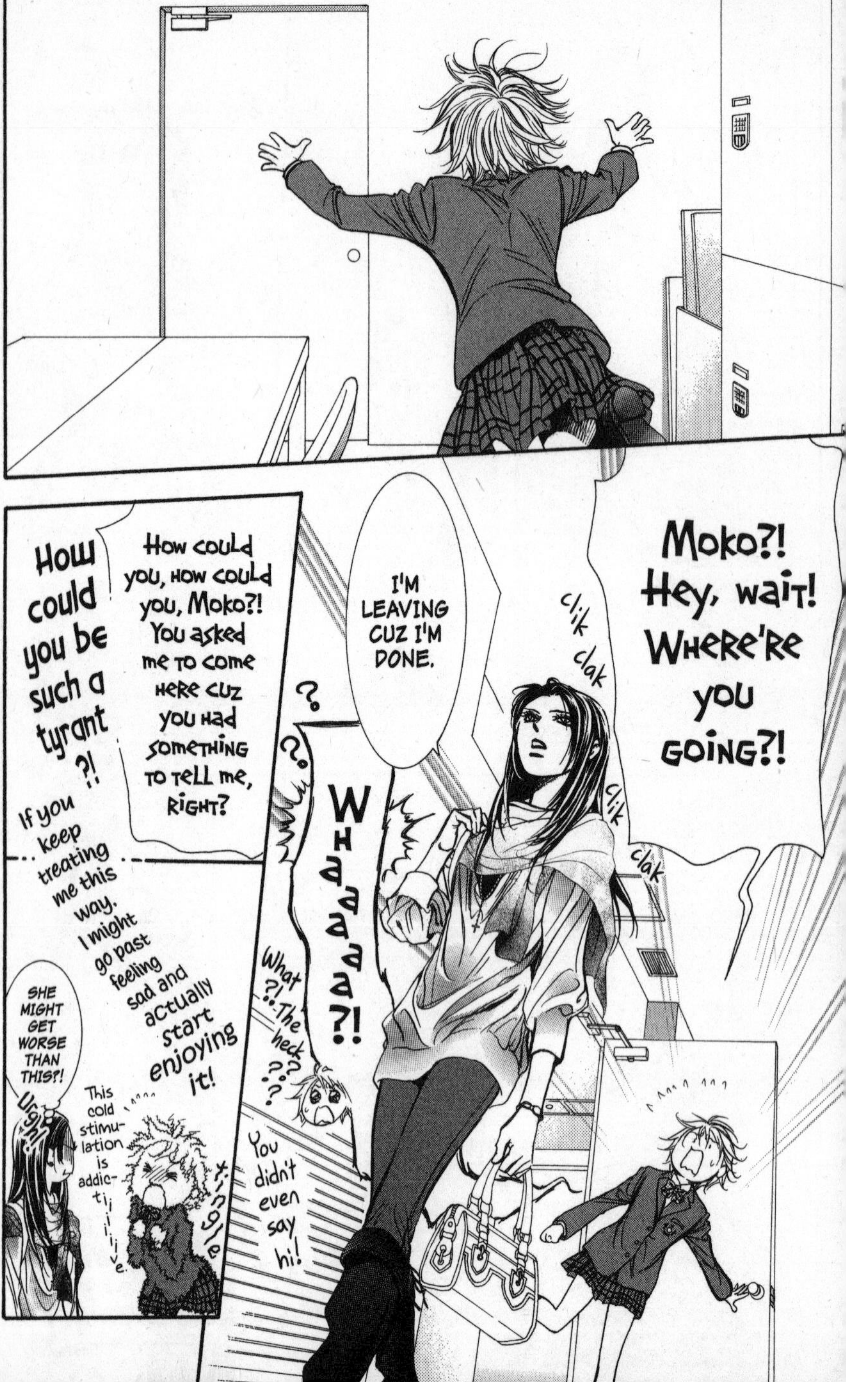
Moko?! Hey, wait! Where're you going?!
clik clak
clik clak
I'M LEAVING CUZ I'M DONE.
?
?
Whaaaaaa?!
What?! The heck???
You didn't even say hi!
How could you, how could you, Moko?! You asked me to come here cuz you had something to tell me, right?
How could you be such a tyrant?!
If you keep treating me this way, I might go past feeling sad and actually start enjoying it!
SHE MIGHT GET WORSE THAN THIS?!
Urgh!
This cold stimulation is addic-tiiiive.
tingle

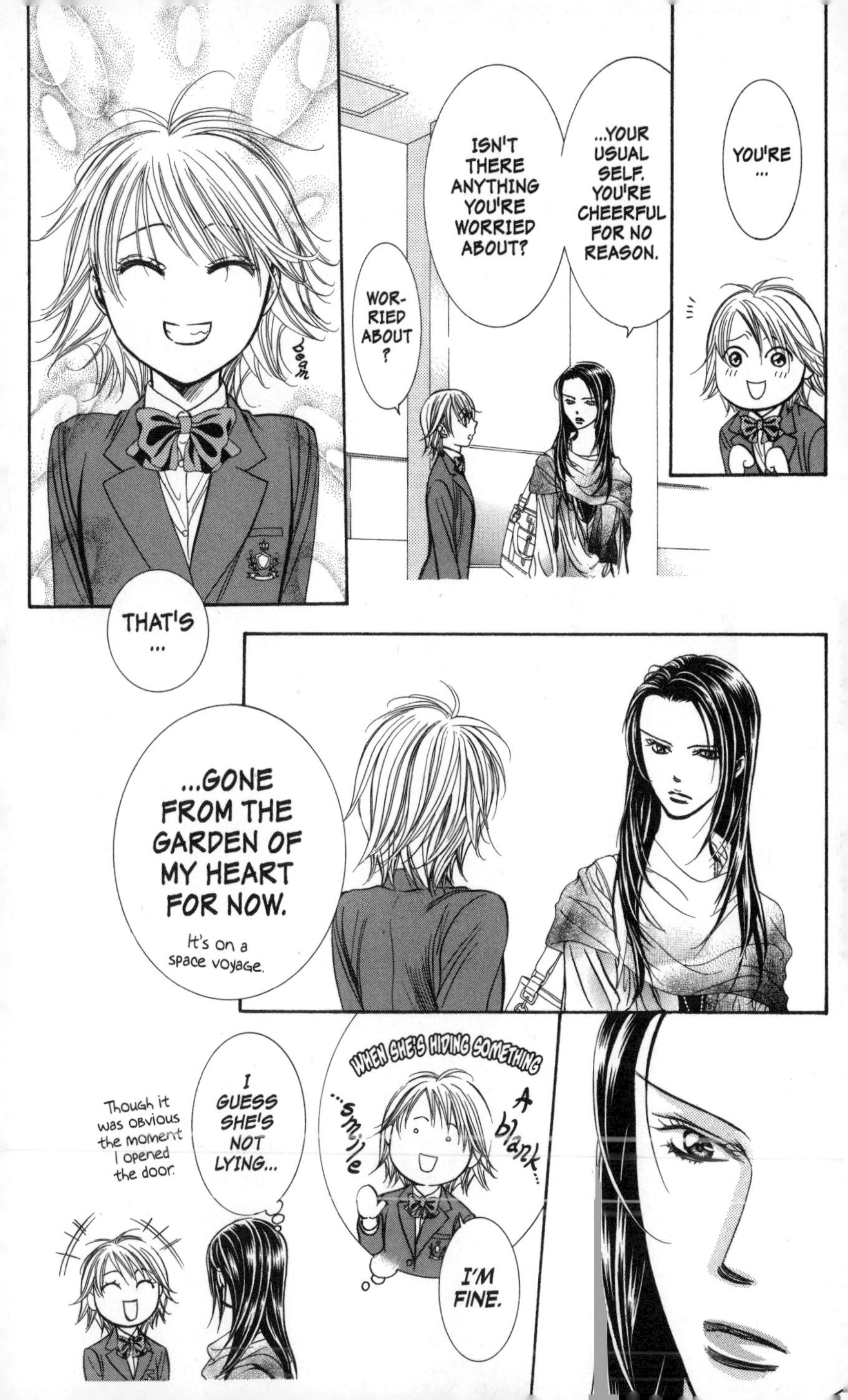
YOU'RE ...
...YOUR USUAL SELF. YOU'RE CHEERFUL FOR NO REASON.
ISN'T THERE ANYTHING YOU'RE WORRIED ABOUT?
WOR-RIED ABOUT?
beam
THAT'S ...
...GONE FROM THE GARDEN OF MY HEART FOR NOW.
It's on a space voyage.
WHEN SHE'S HIDING SOMETHING
A blank...
...smile
I'M FINE.
I GUESS SHE'S NOT LYING...
Though it was obvious the moment I opened the door.

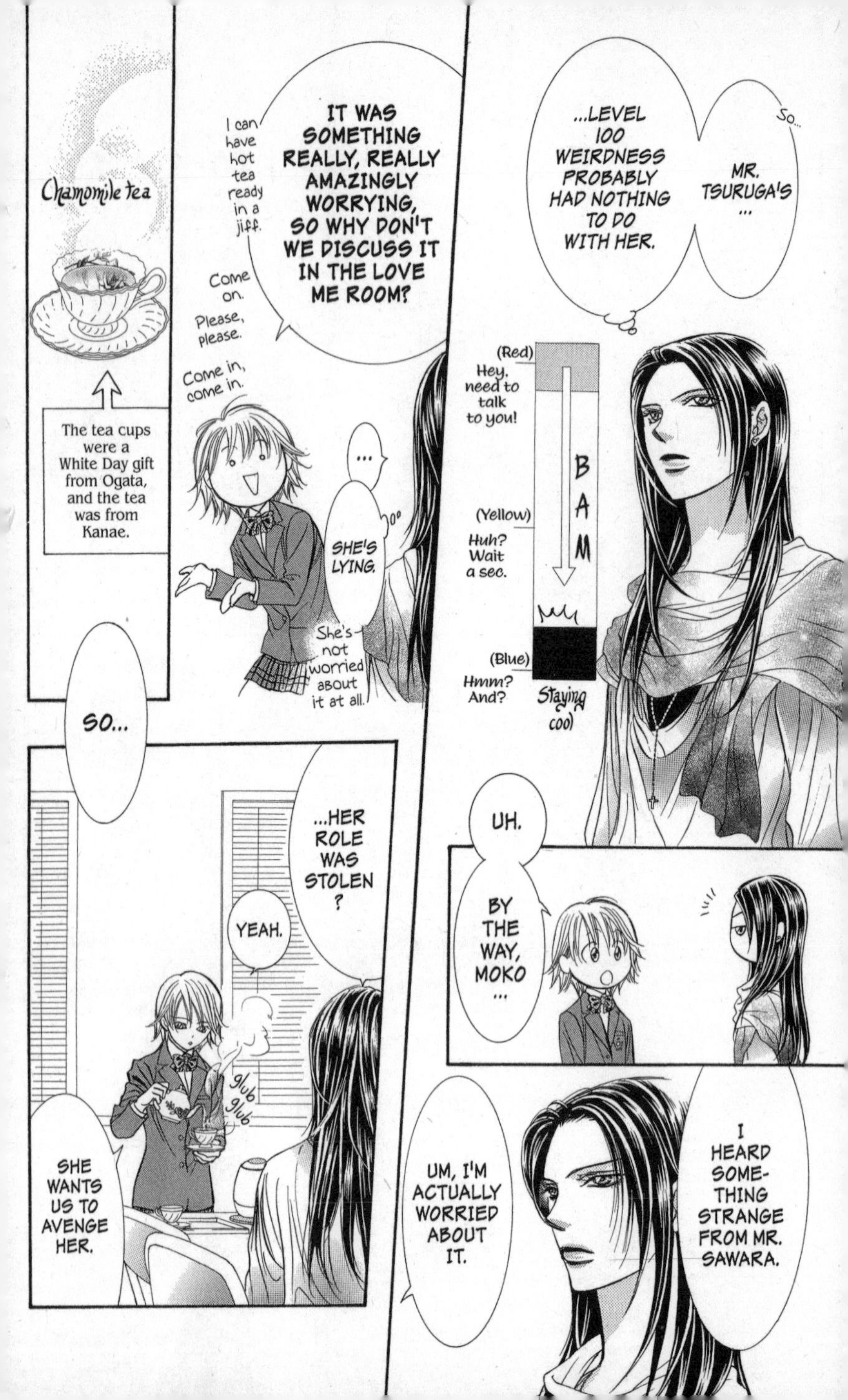
So...
MR. TSURUGA'S ...
...LEVEL 100 WEIRDNESS PROBABLY HAD NOTHING TO DO WITH HER.
(Red) Hey, need to talk to you!
BAM
(Yellow) Huh? Wait a sec.
(Blue) Hmm? And?
Staying cool
UH.
BY THE WAY, MOKO ...
I HEARD SOMETHING STRANGE FROM MR. SAWARA.
UM, I'M ACTUALLY WORRIED ABOUT IT.
IT WAS SOMETHING REALLY, REALLY AMAZINGLY WORRYING, SO WHY DON'T WE DISCUSS IT IN THE LOVE ME ROOM?
I can have hot tea ready in a jiff.
Come on.
Please, please.
Come in, come in.
...
SHE'S LYING.
She's not worried about it at all.
Chamomile tea
The tea cups were a White Day gift from Ogata, and the tea was from Kanae.
SO...
...HER ROLE WAS STOLEN?
YEAH.
glub glub
SHE WANTS US TO AVENGE HER.

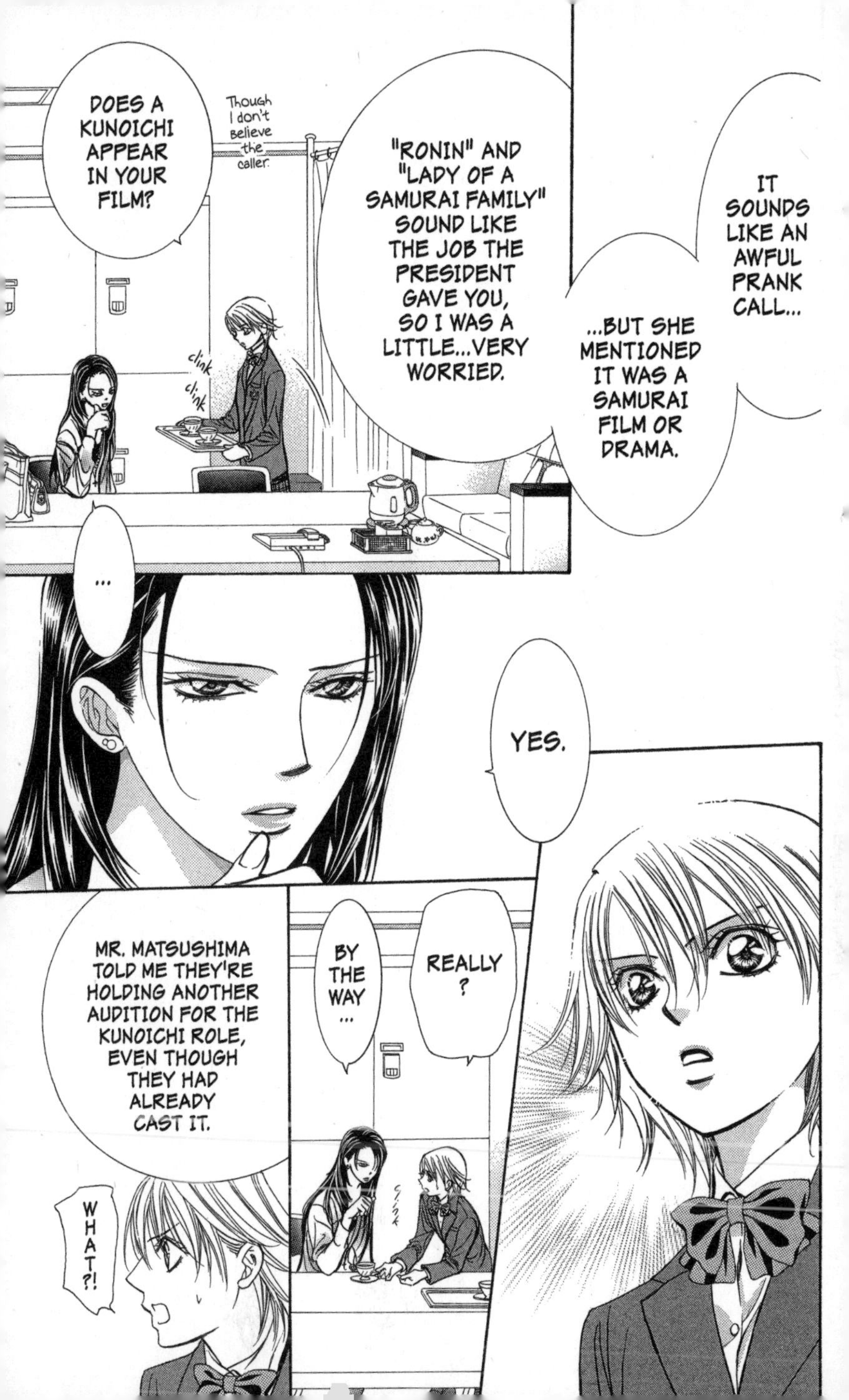
IT SOUNDS LIKE AN AWFUL PRANK CALL...
...BUT SHE MENTIONED IT WAS A SAMURAI FILM OR DRAMA.
"RONIN" AND "LADY OF A SAMURAI FAMILY" SOUND LIKE THE JOB THE PRESIDENT GAVE YOU, SO I WAS A LITTLE...VERY WORRIED.
DOES A KUNOICHI APPEAR IN YOUR FILM?
Though I don't believe the caller.
clink clink
YES.
...
REALLY?
BY THE WAY...
MR. MATSUSHIMA TOLD ME THEY'RE HOLDING ANOTHER AUDITION FOR THE KUNOICHI ROLE, EVEN THOUGH THEY HAD ALREADY CAST IT.
WHAT?!

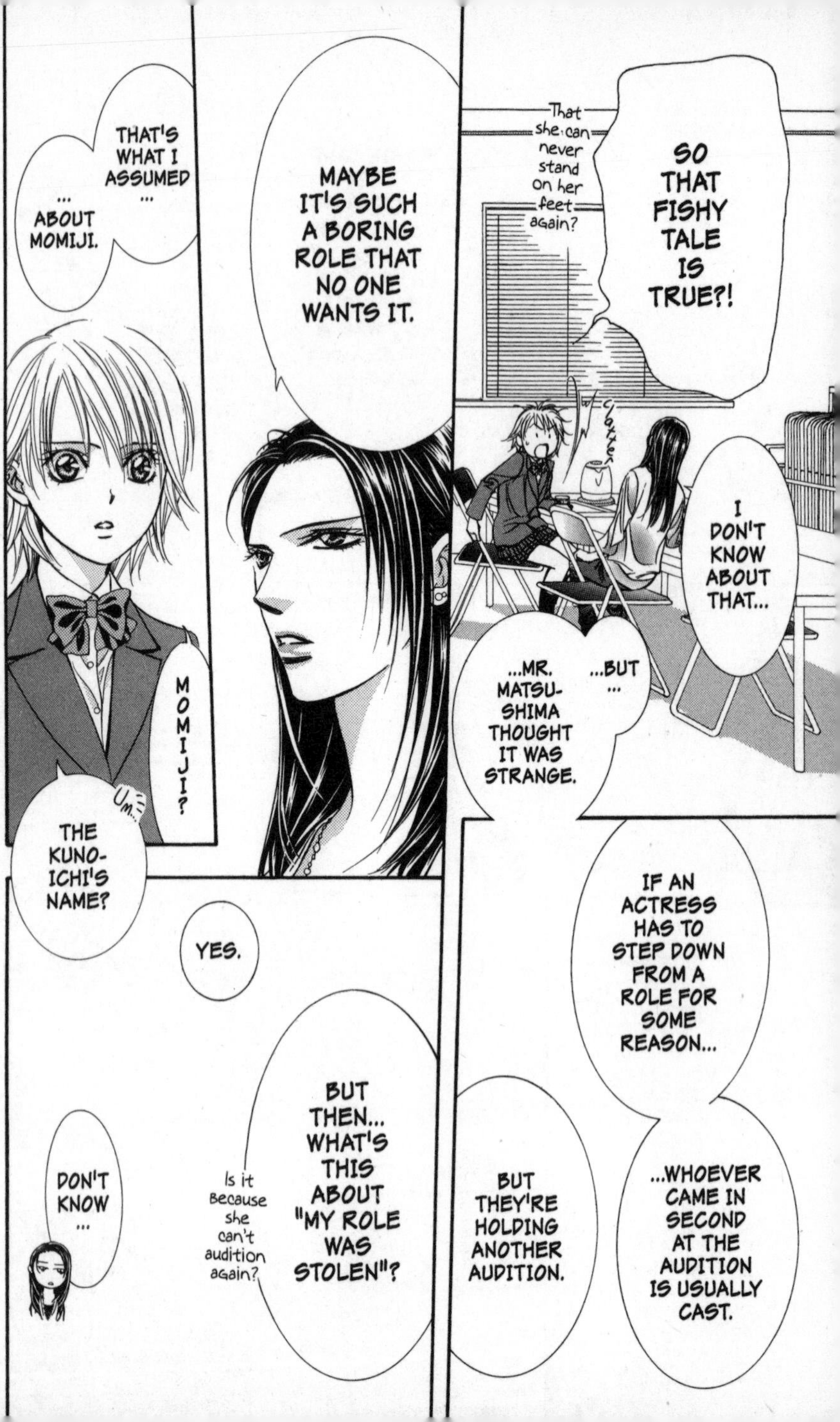

SO THAT FISHY TALE IS TRUE?!
That she can never stand on her feet again?
clatter
I DON'T KNOW ABOUT THAT...
...BUT ...
...MR. MATSU-SHIMA THOUGHT IT WAS STRANGE.
MAYBE IT'S SUCH A BORING ROLE THAT NO ONE WANTS IT.
THAT'S WHAT I ASSUMED ...
... ABOUT MOMIJI.
MOMIJI?
Um...
THE KUNO-ICHI'S NAME?
IF AN ACTRESS HAS TO STEP DOWN FROM A ROLE FOR SOME REASON...
...WHOEVER CAME IN SECOND AT THE AUDITION IS USUALLY CAST.
BUT THEY'RE HOLDING ANOTHER AUDITION.
YES.
BUT THEN... WHAT'S THIS ABOUT "MY ROLE WAS STOLEN"?
Is it because she can't audition again?
DON'T KNOW ...

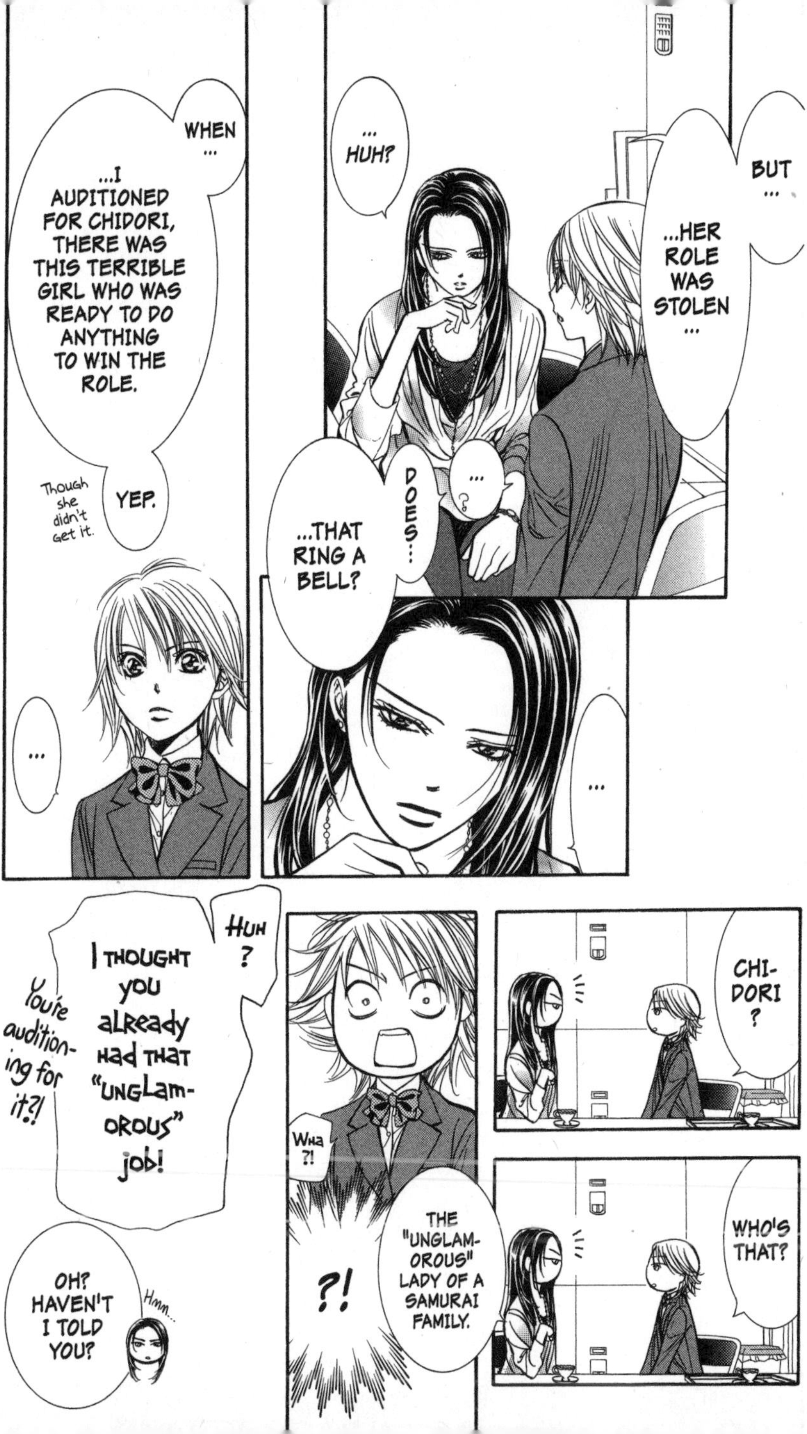

BUT...
...HER ROLE WAS STOLEN...
...HUH?
...?
DOES...
...THAT RING A BELL?
...
WHEN...
...I AUDITIONED FOR CHIDORI, THERE WAS THIS TERRIBLE GIRL WHO WAS READY TO DO ANYTHING TO WIN THE ROLE.
YEP.
Though she didn't get it.
...
CHI-DORI?
WHO'S THAT?
THE "UNGLAMOROUS" LADY OF A SAMURAI FAMILY.
?!
Wha ?!
Huh ?
I thought you already had that "unglamorous" job!
You're auditioning for it?!
OH? HAVEN'T I TOLD YOU?
Hmm...

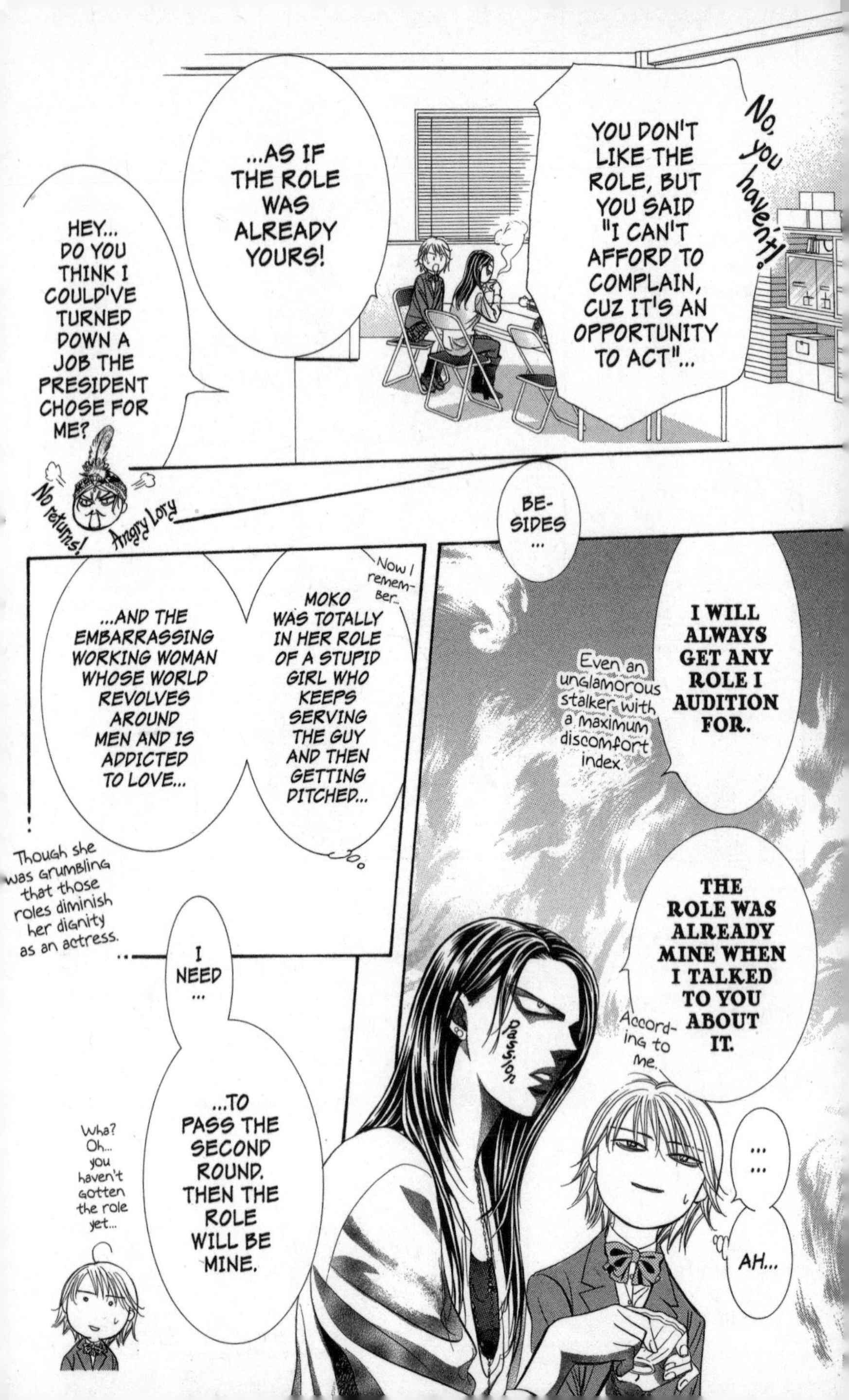
No, you haven't!
YOU DON'T LIKE THE ROLE, BUT YOU SAID "I CAN'T AFFORD TO COMPLAIN, CUZ IT'S AN OPPORTUNITY TO ACT"...
...AS IF THE ROLE WAS ALREADY YOURS!
HEY... DO YOU THINK I COULD'VE TURNED DOWN A JOB THE PRESIDENT CHOSE FOR ME?
No returns!
Angry Lory
BESIDES...
I WILL ALWAYS GET ANY ROLE I AUDITION FOR.
Even an unglamorous stalker with a maximum discomfort index.
THE ROLE WAS ALREADY MINE WHEN I TALKED TO YOU ABOUT IT.
According to me.
passion
......
AH...
Now I remember...
MOKO WAS TOTALLY IN HER ROLE OF A STUPID GIRL WHO KEEPS SERVING THE GUY AND THEN GETTING DITCHED...
...AND THE EMBARRASSING WORKING WOMAN WHOSE WORLD REVOLVES AROUND MEN AND IS ADDICTED TO LOVE...
Though she was grumbling that those roles diminish her dignity as an actress.
I NEED...
...TO PASS THE SECOND ROUND. THEN THE ROLE WILL BE MINE.
Wha? Oh... you haven't gotten the role yet...

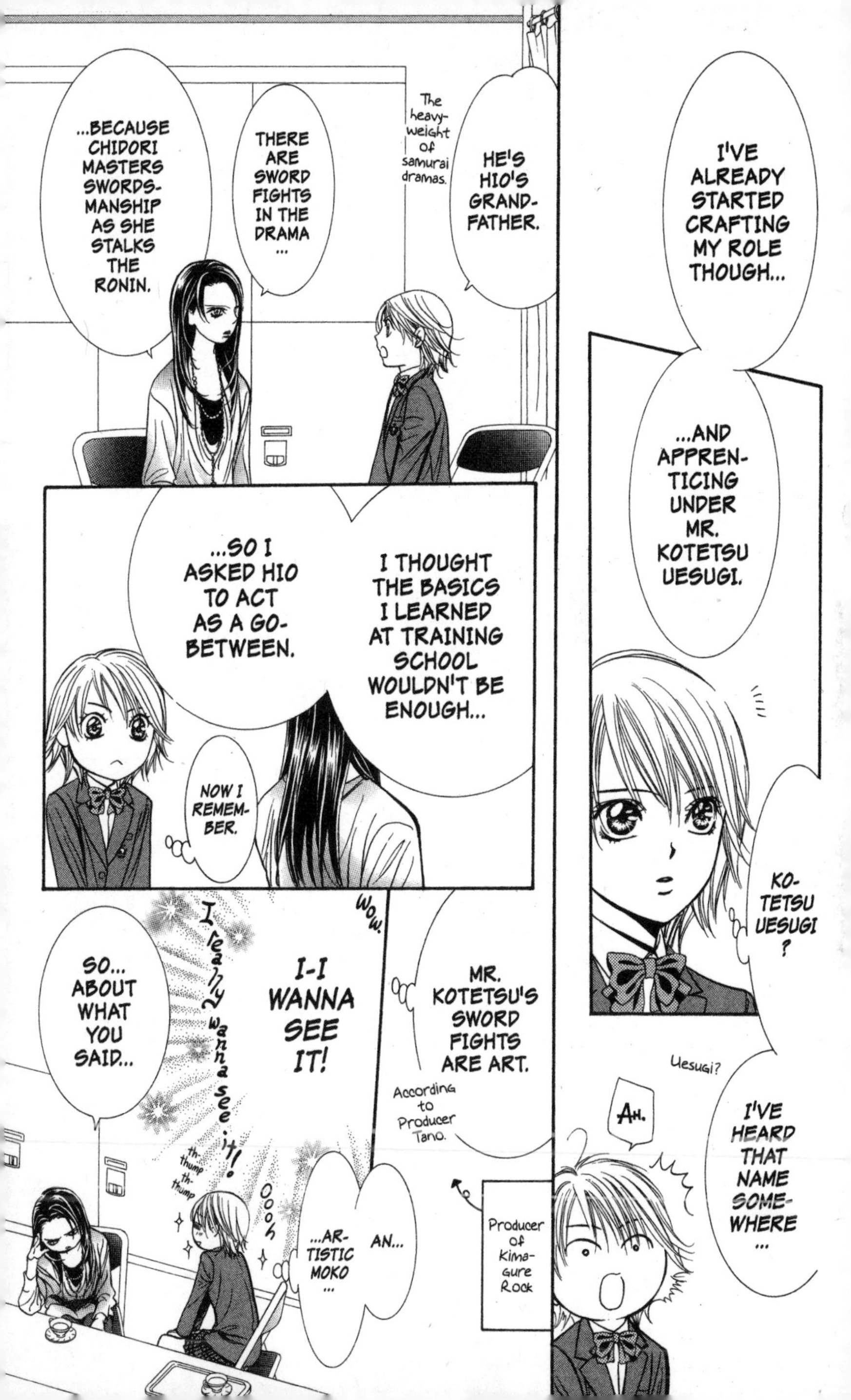
I'VE ALREADY STARTED CRAFTING MY ROLE THOUGH...
...AND APPRENTICING UNDER MR. KOTETSU UESUGI.
KOTETSU UESUGI?
Uesugi?
AH.
I'VE HEARD THAT NAME SOMEWHERE...
HE'S HIO'S GRANDFATHER.
The heavyweight of samurai dramas.
THERE ARE SWORD FIGHTS IN THE DRAMA...
...BECAUSE CHIDORI MASTERS SWORDSMANSHIP AS SHE STALKS THE RONIN.
I THOUGHT THE BASICS I LEARNED AT TRAINING SCHOOL WOULDN'T BE ENOUGH...
...SO I ASKED HIO TO ACT AS A GO-BETWEEN.
NOW I REMEMBER.
MR. KOTETSU'S SWORD FIGHTS ARE ART.
According to Producer Tano.
Producer of Kimagure Rock
AN...
...ARTISTIC MOKO...
WOW.
I-I WANNA SEE IT!
I really wanna see it!
th-thump th-thump
Oooh
SO... ABOUT WHAT YOU SAID...

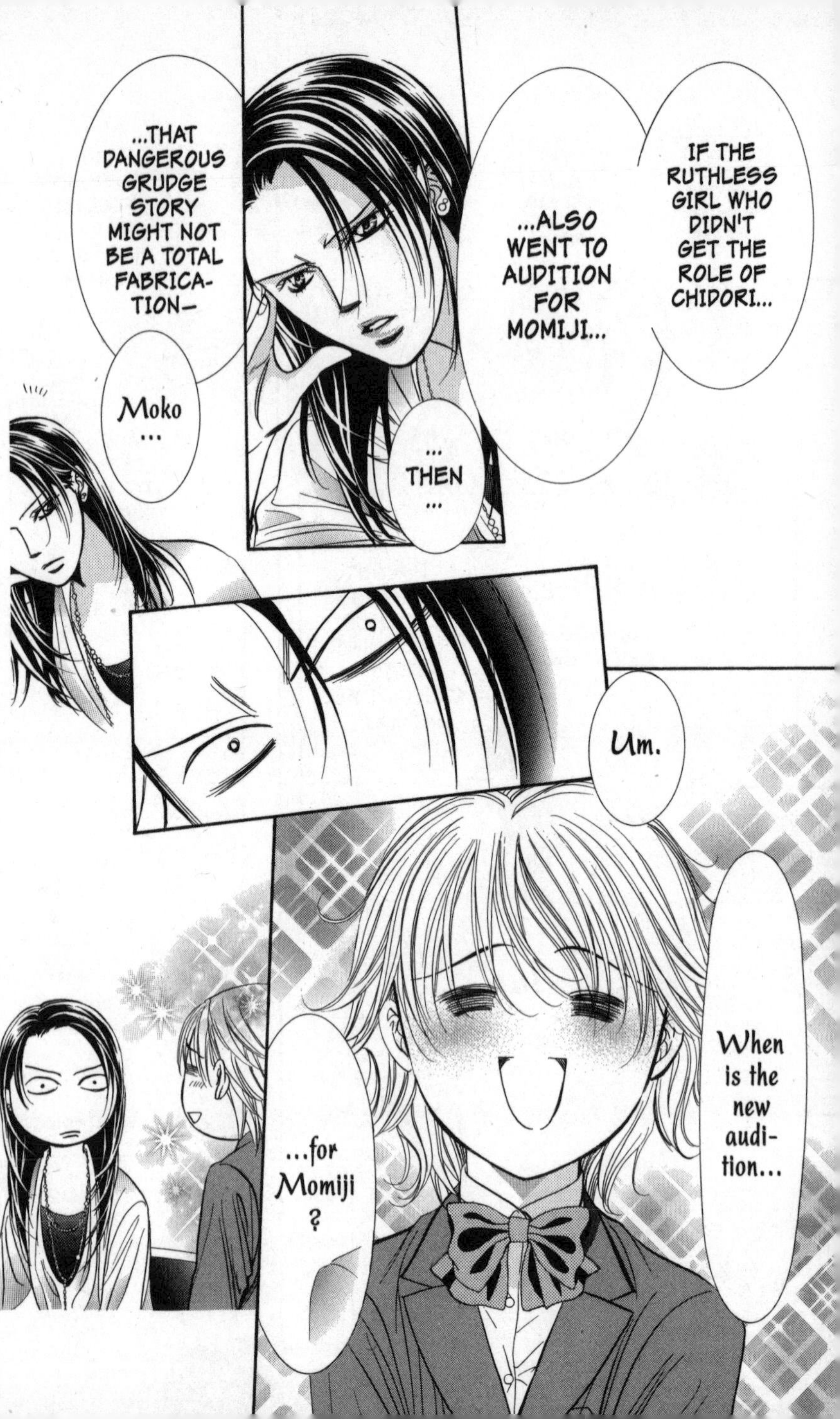
IF THE RUTHLESS GIRL WHO DIDN'T GET THE ROLE OF CHIDORI...
...ALSO WENT TO AUDITION FOR MOMIJI...
...THEN...
...THAT DANGEROUS GRUDGE STORY MIGHT NOT BE A TOTAL FABRICATION—
Moko...
Um.
When is the new audition...
...for Momiji?

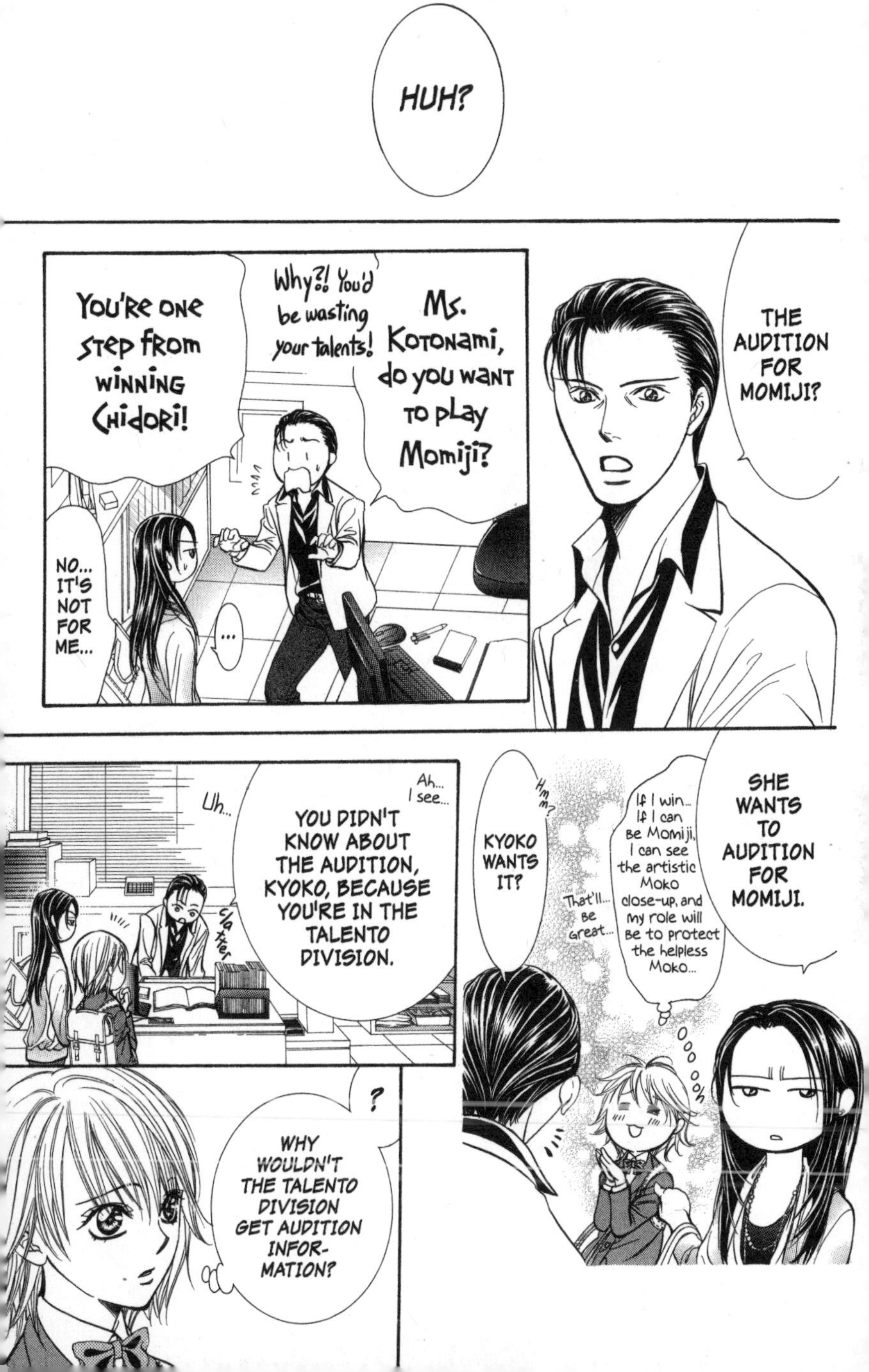
HUH?
THE AUDITION FOR MOMIJI?
Ms. Kotonami, do you want to play Momiji?
Why?!! You'd be wasting your talents!
You're one step from winning Chidori!
No... it's not for me...
...
SHE WANTS TO AUDITION FOR MOMIJI.
If I win... If I can be Momiji, I can see the artistic Moko close-up, and my role will be to protect the helpless Moko...
That'll... be great...
Hmm?
KYOKO WANTS IT?
Ooo ooh
Ah... I see...
YOU DIDN'T KNOW ABOUT THE AUDITION, KYOKO, BECAUSE YOU'RE IN THE TALENTO DIVISION.
Uh...
clatter
?
WHY WOULDN'T THE TALENTO DIVISION GET AUDITION INFORMATION?

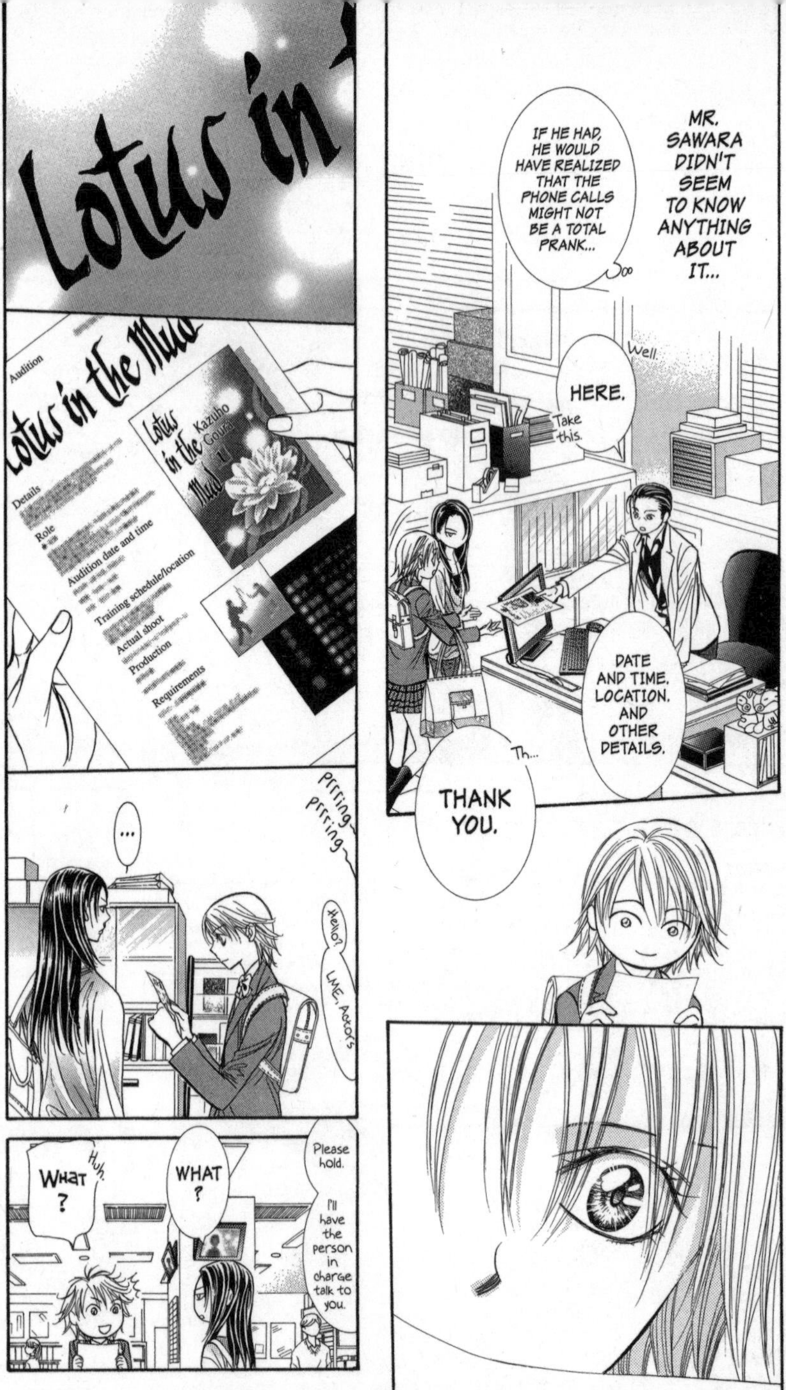
MR. SAWARA DIDN'T SEEM TO KNOW ANYTHING ABOUT IT...
IF HE HAD, HE WOULD HAVE REALIZED THAT THE PHONE CALLS MIGHT NOT BE A TOTAL PRANK...
Well.
HERE.
Take this.
DATE AND TIME, LOCATION, AND OTHER DETAILS.
Th...
THANK YOU.
Lotus in
Audition
Lotus in the Mud
Lotus in the Mud 1
Kazuho Goura
Details
Role
Audition date and time
Training schedule/location
Actual shoot
Production
Requirements
Prrring prrring
...
Hello? LME, Actors
Please hold.
I'll have the person in charge talk to you.
WHAT?
Huh.
WHAT?

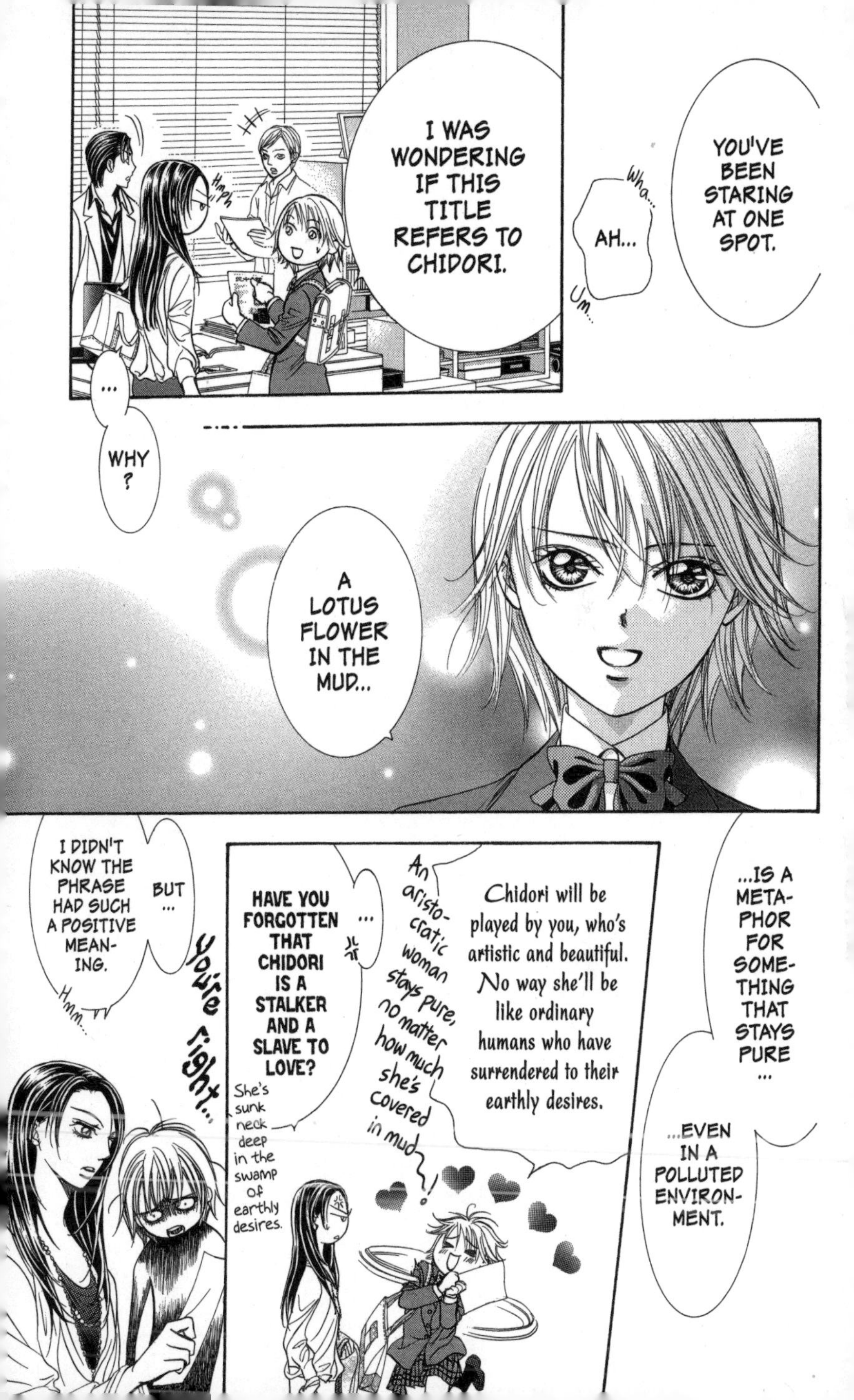
YOU'VE BEEN STARING AT ONE SPOT.
Wha...
AH...
Um...
I WAS WONDERING IF THIS TITLE REFERS TO CHIDORI.
Hmph
...
WHY?
A LOTUS FLOWER IN THE MUD...
...IS A METAPHOR FOR SOMETHING THAT STAYS PURE ...
...EVEN IN A POLLUTED ENVIRONMENT.
Chidori will be played by you, who's artistic and beautiful. No way she'll be like ordinary humans who have surrendered to their earthly desires.
An aristocratic woman stays pure, no matter how much she's covered in mud.
...
HAVE YOU FORGOTTEN THAT CHIDORI IS A STALKER AND A SLAVE TO LOVE?
She's sunk neck deep in the swamp of earthly desires.
BUT ...
I DIDN'T KNOW THE PHRASE HAD SUCH A POSITIVE MEANING.
Hmm...
You're right...

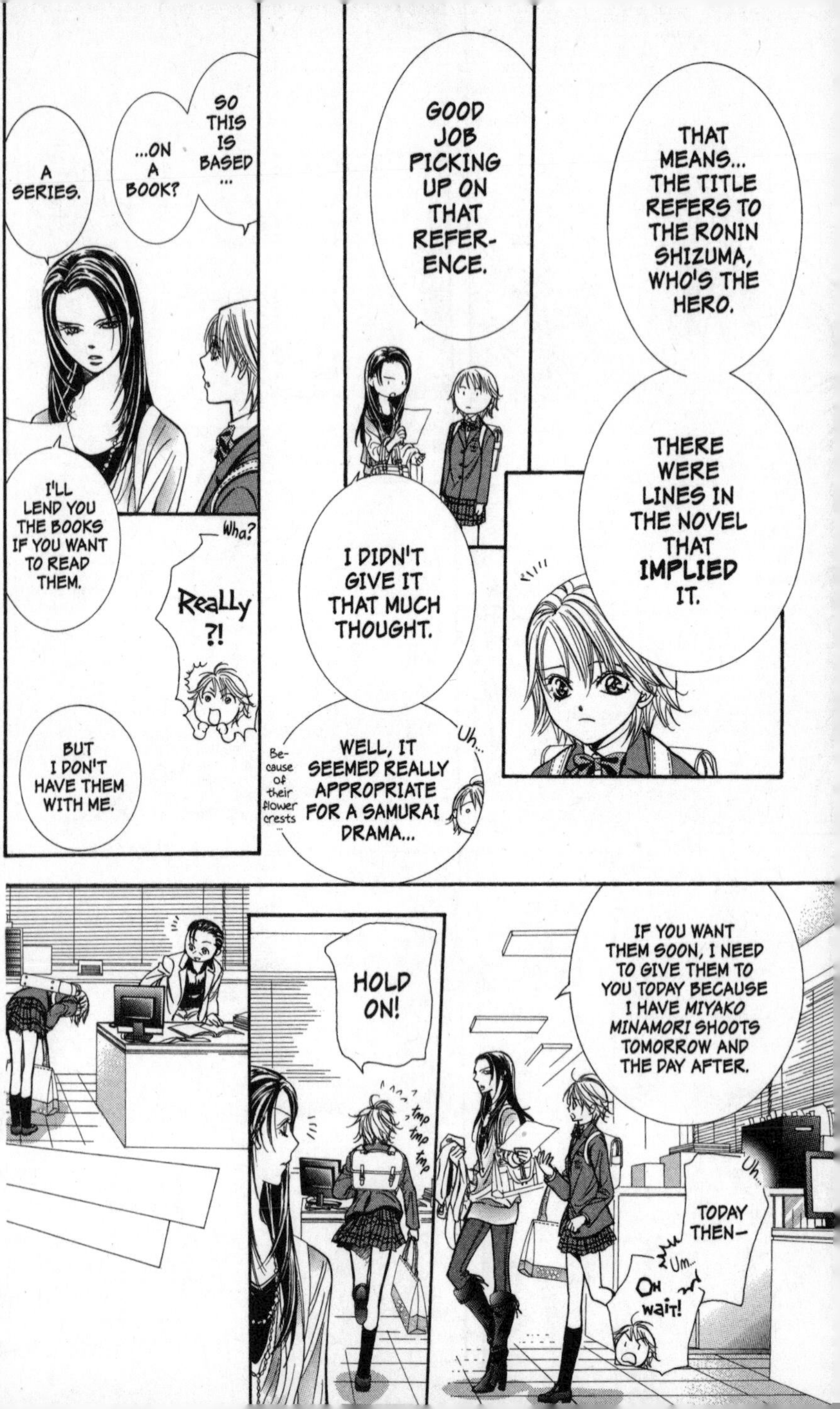
THAT MEANS... THE TITLE REFERS TO THE RONIN SHIZUMA, WHO'S THE HERO.
GOOD JOB PICKING UP ON THAT REFERENCE.
THERE WERE LINES IN THE NOVEL THAT IMPLIED IT.
I DIDN'T GIVE IT THAT MUCH THOUGHT.
Uh...
WELL, IT SEEMED REALLY APPROPRIATE FOR A SAMURAI DRAMA...
Because of their flower crests...
SO THIS IS BASED...
...ON A BOOK?
A SERIES.
I'LL LEND YOU THE BOOKS IF YOU WANT TO READ THEM.
Wha?
Really ?!
BUT I DON'T HAVE THEM WITH ME.
IF YOU WANT THEM SOON, I NEED TO GIVE THEM TO YOU TODAY BECAUSE I HAVE MIYAKO MINAMORI SHOOTS TOMORROW AND THE DAY AFTER.
Uh...
TODAY THEN—
Um...
Oh wait!
HOLD ON!
tmp tmp tmp

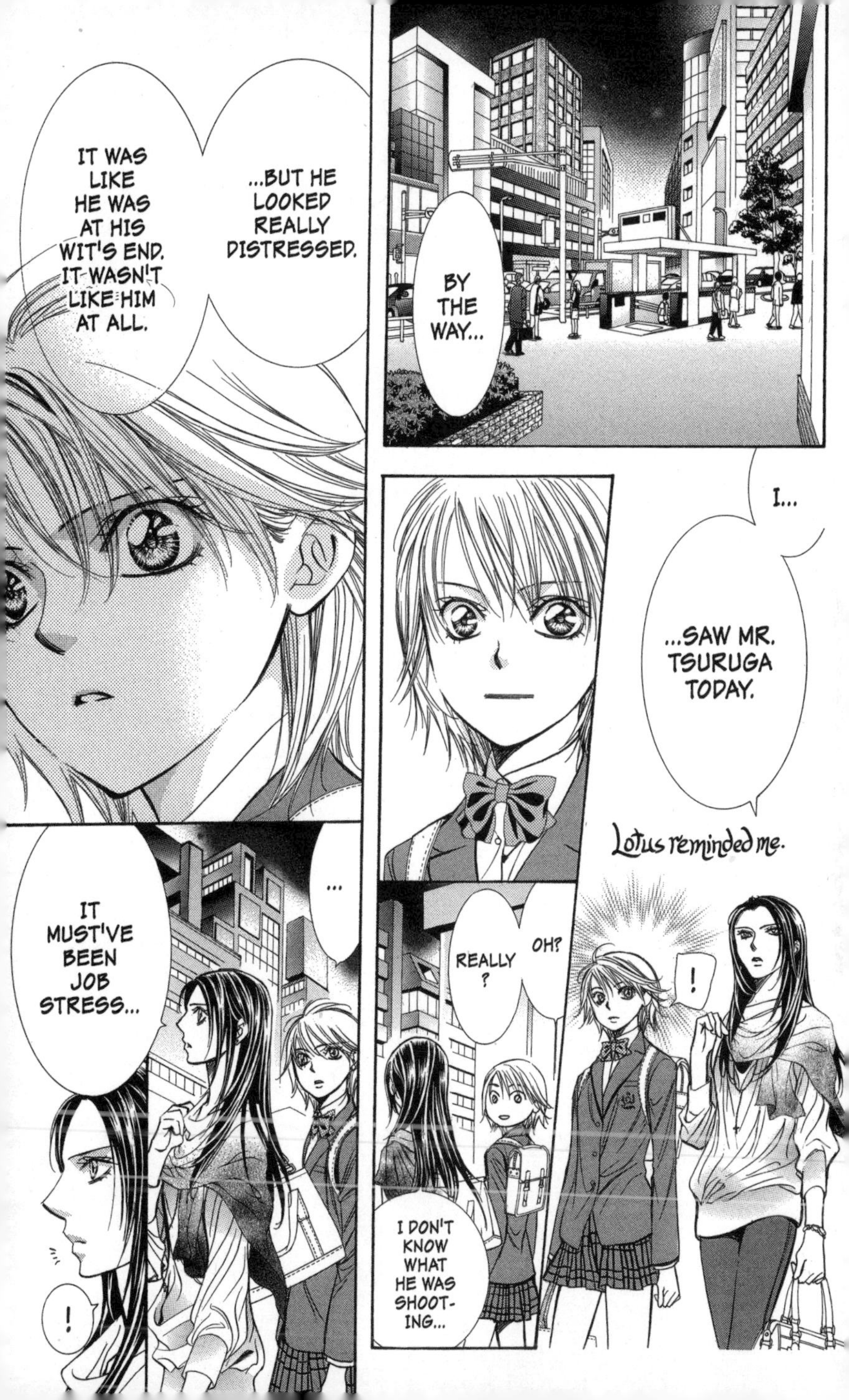
BY THE WAY...
I...
...SAW MR. TSURUGA TODAY.
Lotus reminded me.
!
OH?
REALLY?
I DON'T KNOW WHAT HE WAS SHOOTING...
...BUT HE LOOKED REALLY DISTRESSED.
IT WAS LIKE HE WAS AT HIS WIT'S END. IT WASN'T LIKE HIM AT ALL.
...
IT MUST'VE BEEN JOB STRESS...
!

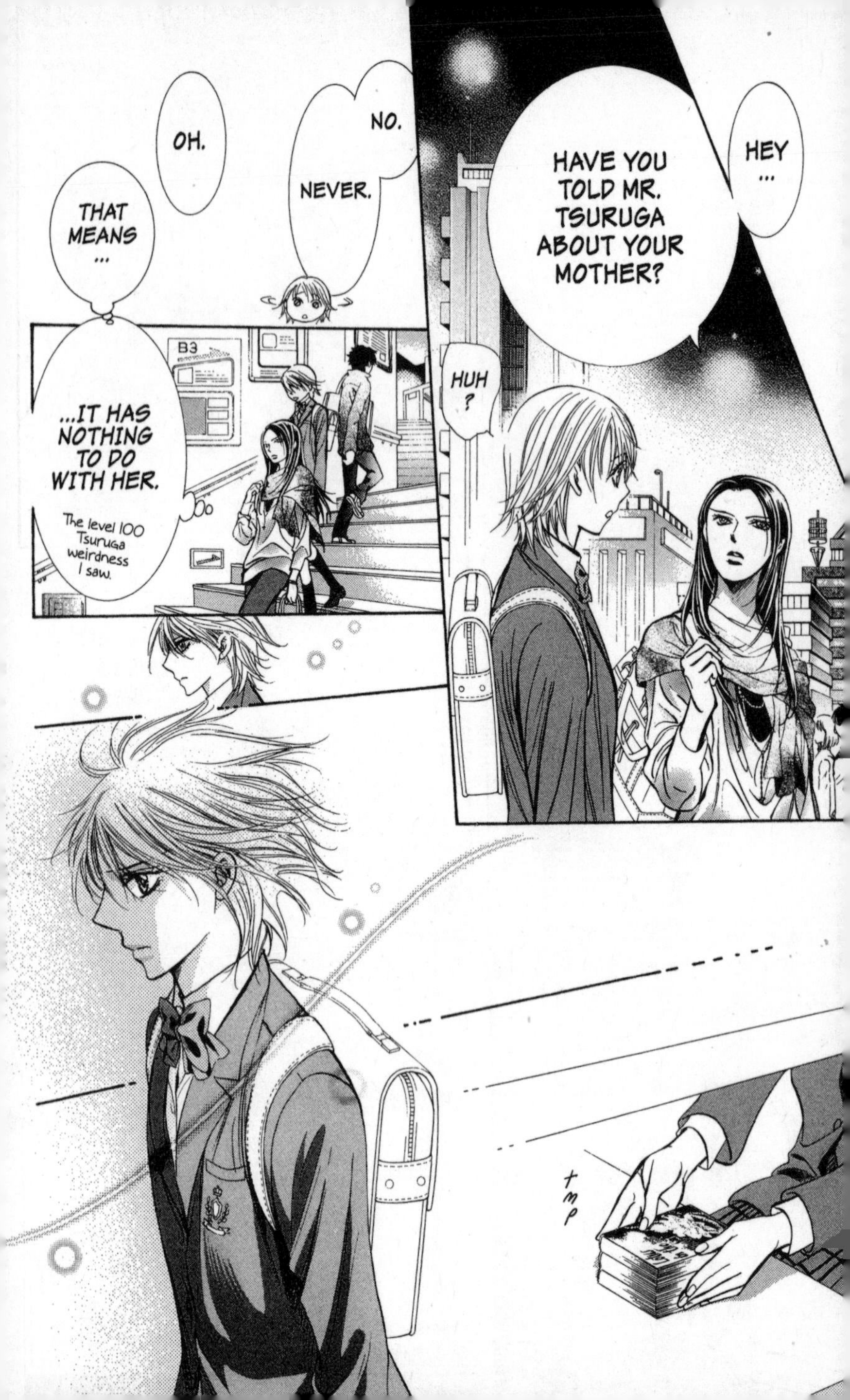
HEY ...
HAVE YOU TOLD MR. TSURUGA ABOUT YOUR MOTHER?
HUH?
NO.
NEVER.
OH.
THAT MEANS ...
...IT HAS NOTHING TO DO WITH HER.
The level 100 Tsuruga weirdness I saw.
B3
tmp

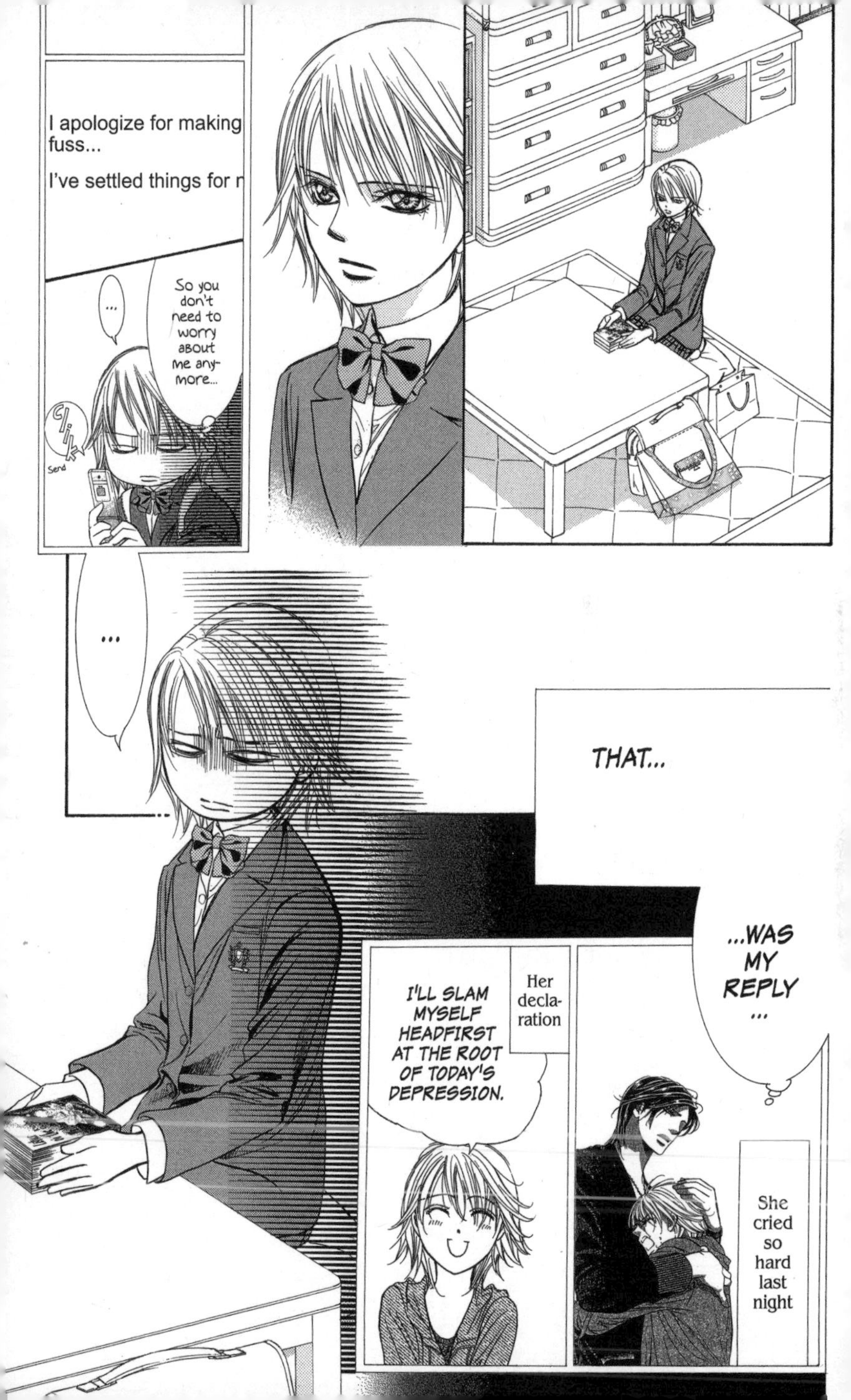
I apologize for making fuss...
I've settled things for r
...
So you don't need to worry about me any-more...
Clik
Send
THAT...
...WAS MY REPLY...
She cried so hard last night
Her declaration
I'LL SLAM MYSELF HEADFIRST AT THE ROOT OF TODAY'S DEPRESSION.
...

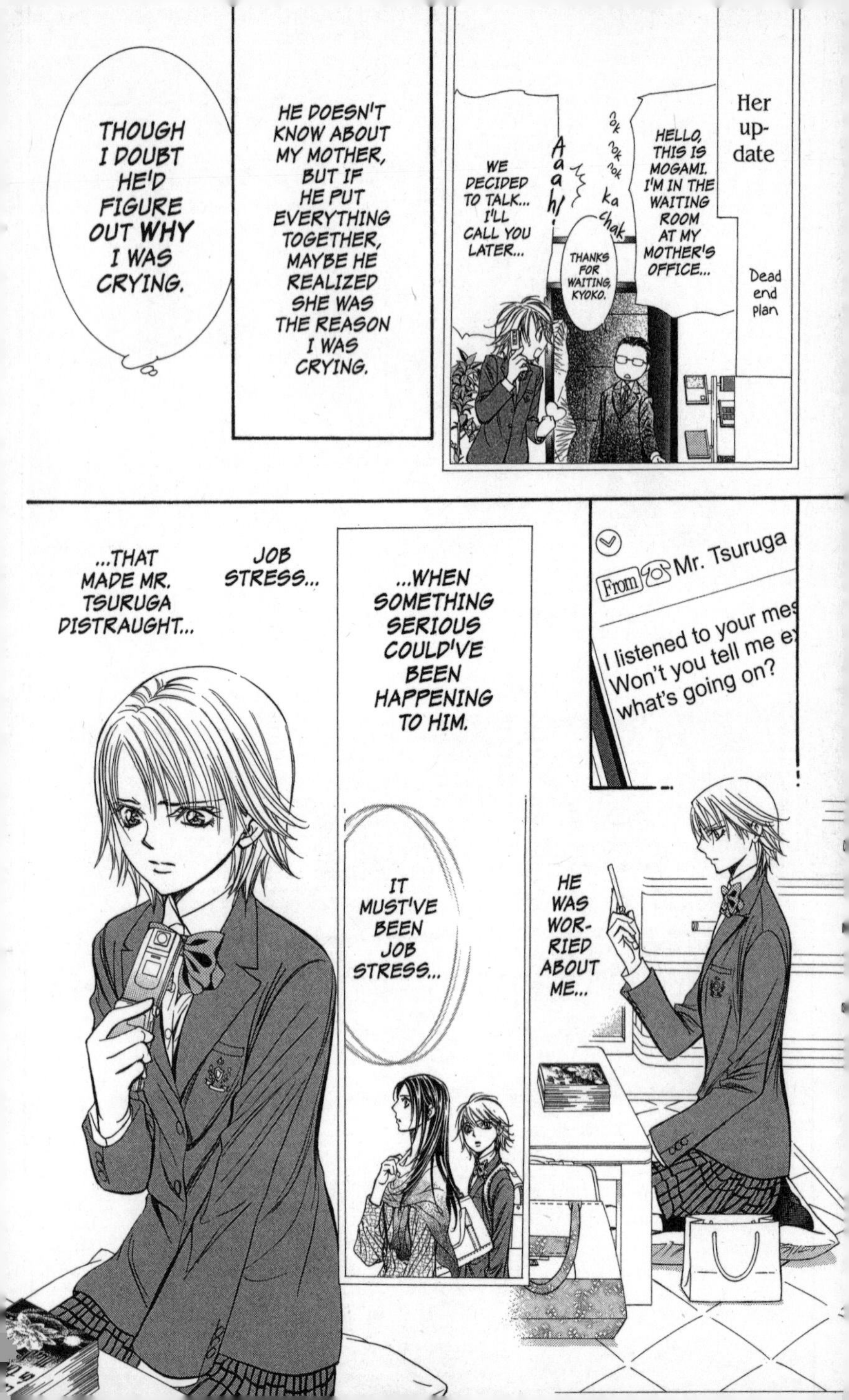
Her update
Dead end plan
HELLO, THIS IS MOGAMI. I'M IN THE WAITING ROOM AT MY MOTHER'S OFFICE...
nok nok nok
ka chak
Aaaah!
WE DECIDED TO TALK... I'LL CALL YOU LATER...
THANKS FOR WAITING, KYOKO.
HE DOESN'T KNOW ABOUT MY MOTHER, BUT IF HE PUT EVERYTHING TOGETHER, MAYBE HE REALIZED SHE WAS THE REASON I WAS CRYING.
THOUGH I DOUBT HE'D FIGURE OUT WHY I WAS CRYING.
From Mr. Tsuruga
I listened to your mes
Won't you tell me ex
what's going on?
HE WAS WOR-RIED ABOUT ME...
...WHEN SOMETHING SERIOUS COULD'VE BEEN HAPPENING TO HIM.
IT MUST'VE BEEN JOB STRESS...
JOB STRESS...
...THAT MADE MR. TSURUGA DISTRAUGHT...

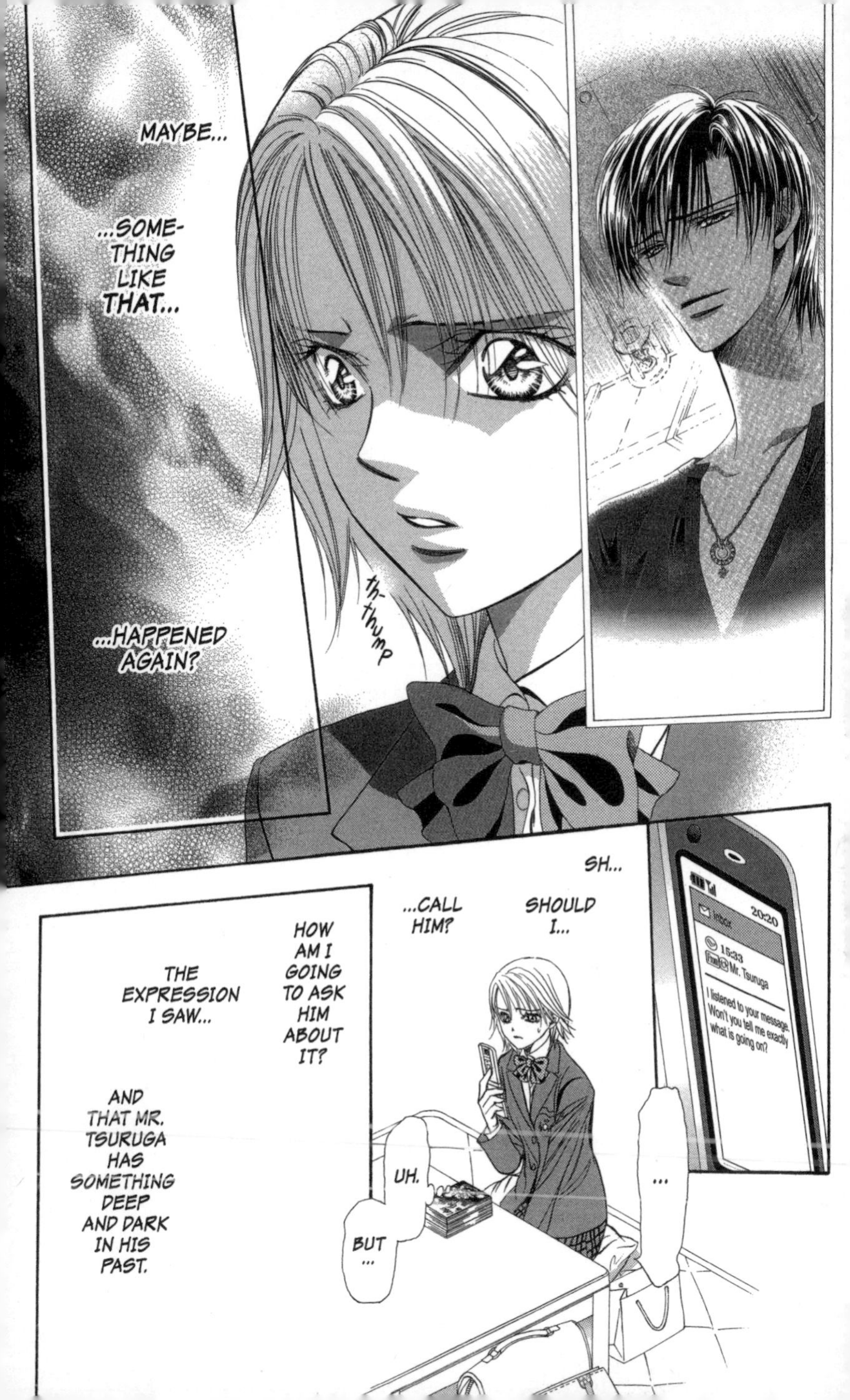
MAYBE...
...SOMETHING LIKE THAT...
...HAPPENED AGAIN?
th-thump
SH...
SHOULD I...
...CALL HIM?
Inbox
20:20
15:33
Mr. Tsuruga
I listened to your message. Won't you tell me exactly what is going on?
HOW AM I GOING TO ASK HIM ABOUT IT?
THE EXPRESSION I SAW...
AND THAT MR. TSURUGA HAS SOMETHING DEEP AND DARK IN HIS PAST.
...
UH.
BUT ...

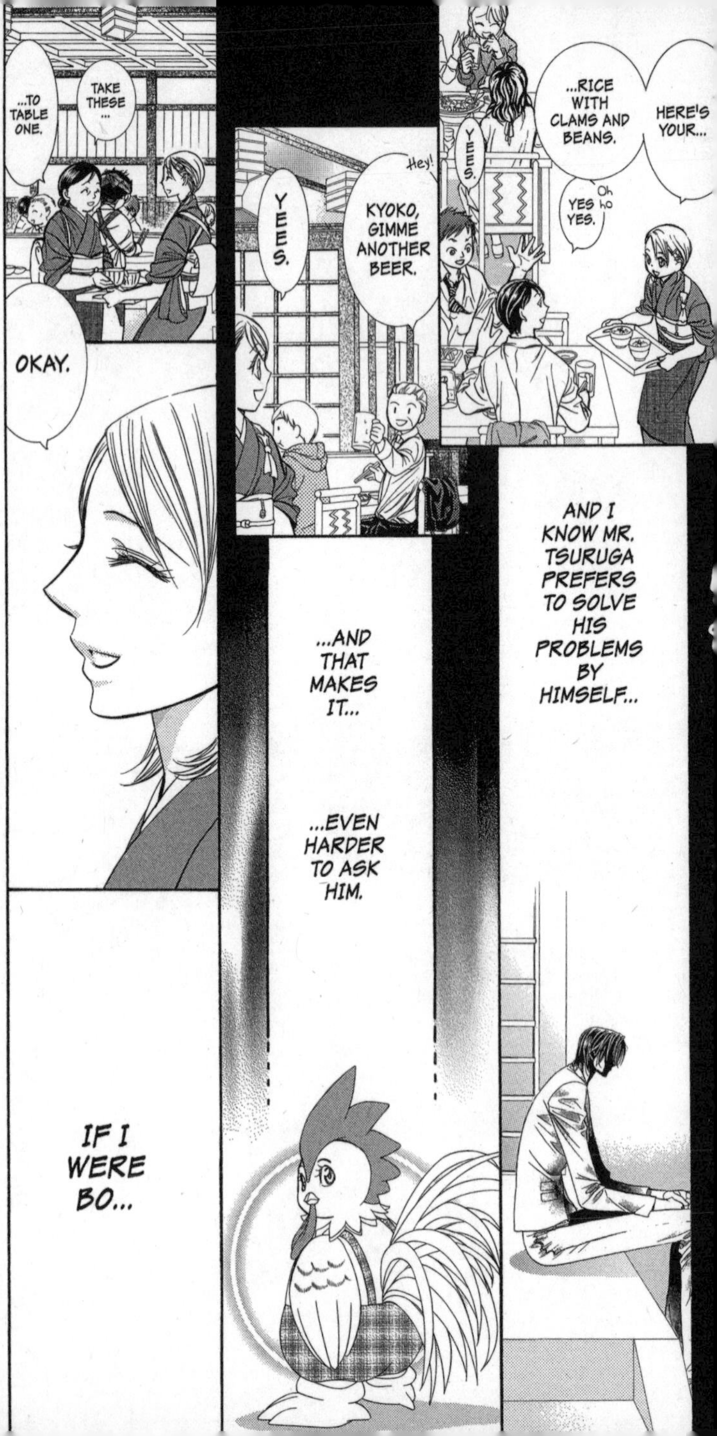
HERE'S YOUR...
...RICE WITH CLAMS AND BEANS.
YEES.
Oh ho
YES YES.
Hey!
KYOKO, GIMME ANOTHER BEER.
YEES.
TAKE THESE...
...TO TABLE ONE.
OKAY.
AND I KNOW MR. TSURUGA PREFERS TO SOLVE HIS PROBLEMS BY HIMSELF...
...AND THAT MAKES IT...
...EVEN HARDER TO ASK HIM.
IF I WERE BO...

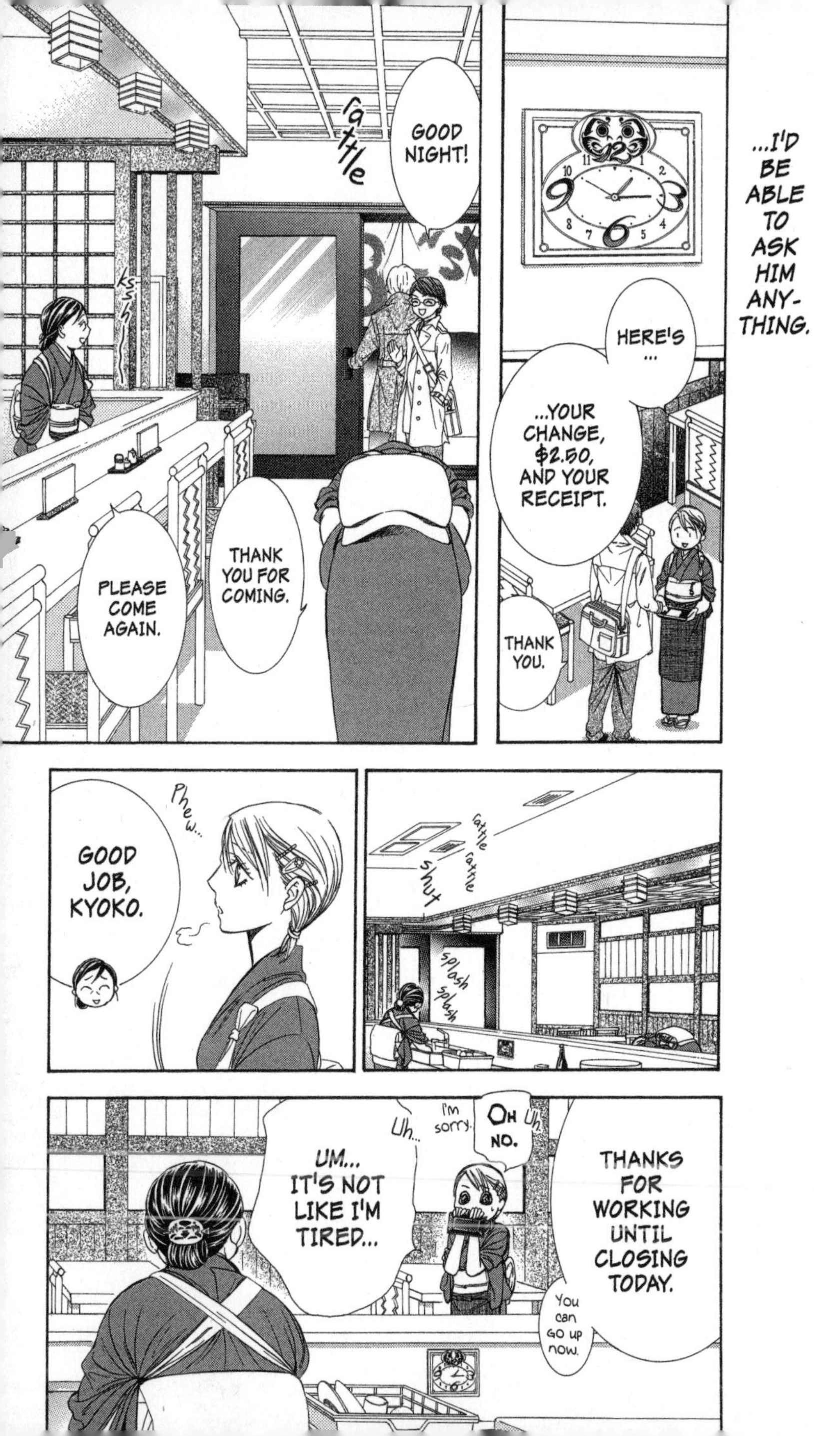
...I'D BE ABLE TO ASK HIM ANYTHING.
HERE'S...
...YOUR CHANGE, $2.50, AND YOUR RECEIPT.
THANK YOU.
rattle
GOOD NIGHT!
ksh
THANK YOU FOR COMING.
PLEASE COME AGAIN.
rattle
rattle
shut
splash
splash
Phew...
GOOD JOB, KYOKO.
THANKS FOR WORKING UNTIL CLOSING TODAY.
You can go up now.
Uh.
OH NO.
I'm sorry.
Uh...
UM... IT'S NOT LIKE I'M TIRED...

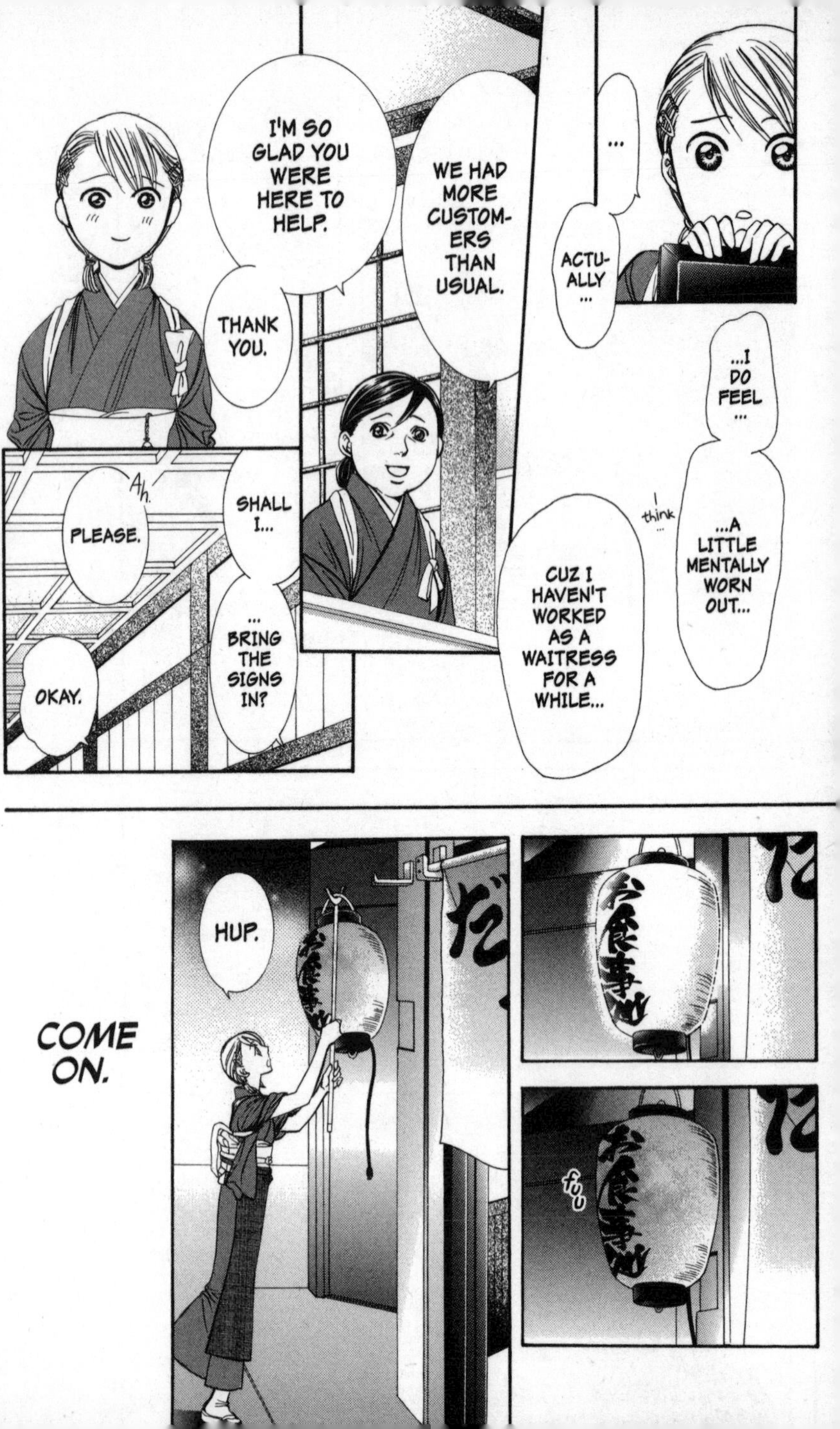
...
ACTUALLY...
...I DO FEEL...
...A LITTLE MENTALLY WORN OUT...
I think...
CUZ I HAVEN'T WORKED AS A WAITRESS FOR A WHILE...
WE HAD MORE CUSTOMERS THAN USUAL.
I'M SO GLAD YOU WERE HERE TO HELP.
THANK YOU.
SHALL I...
...BRING THE SIGNS IN?
Ah.
PLEASE.
OKAY.
fuu
HUP.
COME ON.

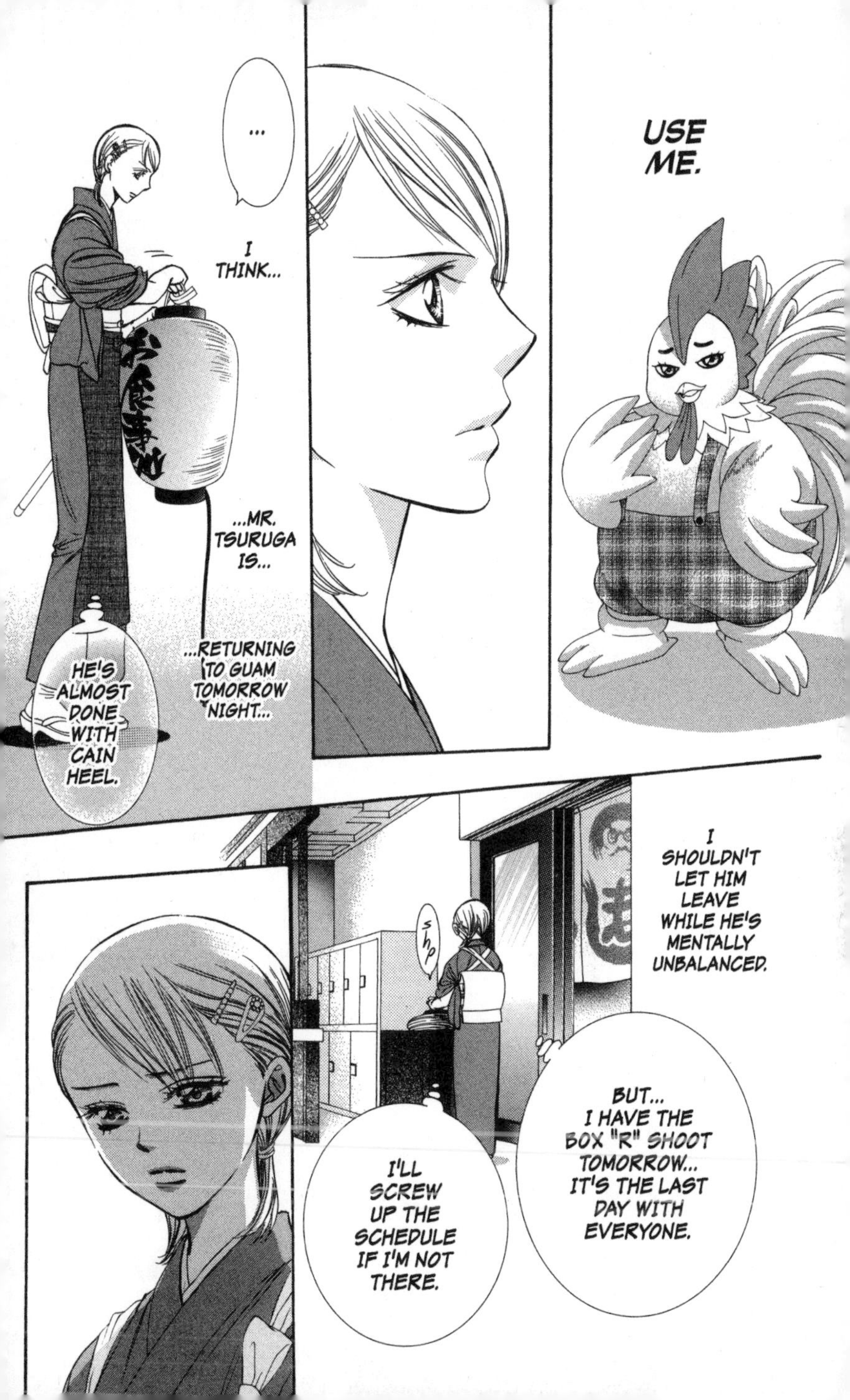
USE ME.
...
I THINK...
...MR. TSURUGA IS...
...RETURNING TO GUAM TOMORROW NIGHT...
HE'S ALMOST DONE WITH CAIN HEEL.
I SHOULDN'T LET HIM LEAVE WHILE HE'S MENTALLY UNBALANCED.
shp
BUT... I HAVE THE BOX "R" SHOOT TOMORROW... IT'S THE LAST DAY WITH EVERYONE.
I'LL SCREW UP THE SCHEDULE IF I'M NOT THERE.

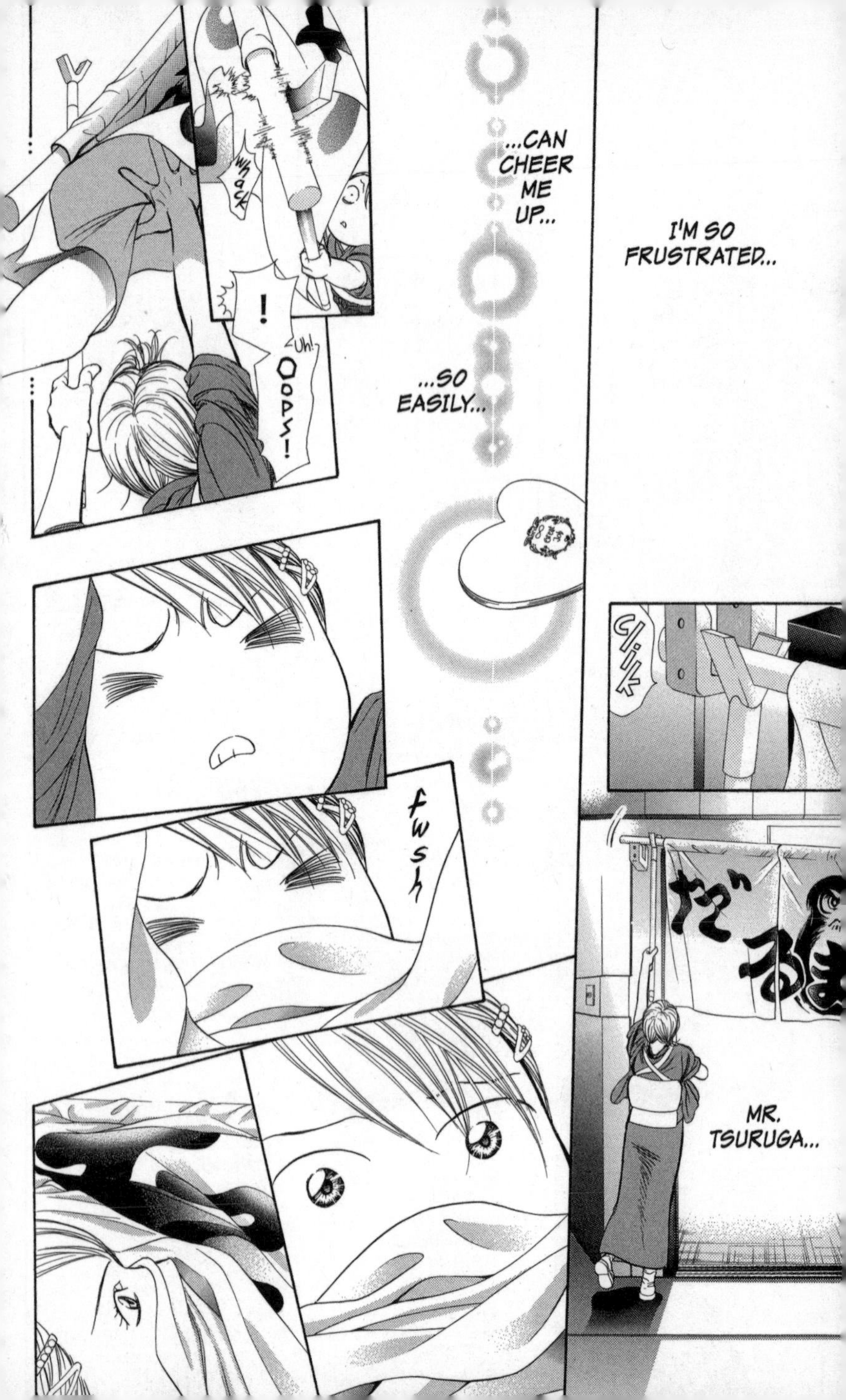

I'M SO FRUSTRATED...
Clik
MR. TSURUGA...
...CAN CHEER ME UP...
Whack
!
Uh!
OOPS!
...
...
...SO EASILY...
fwsh

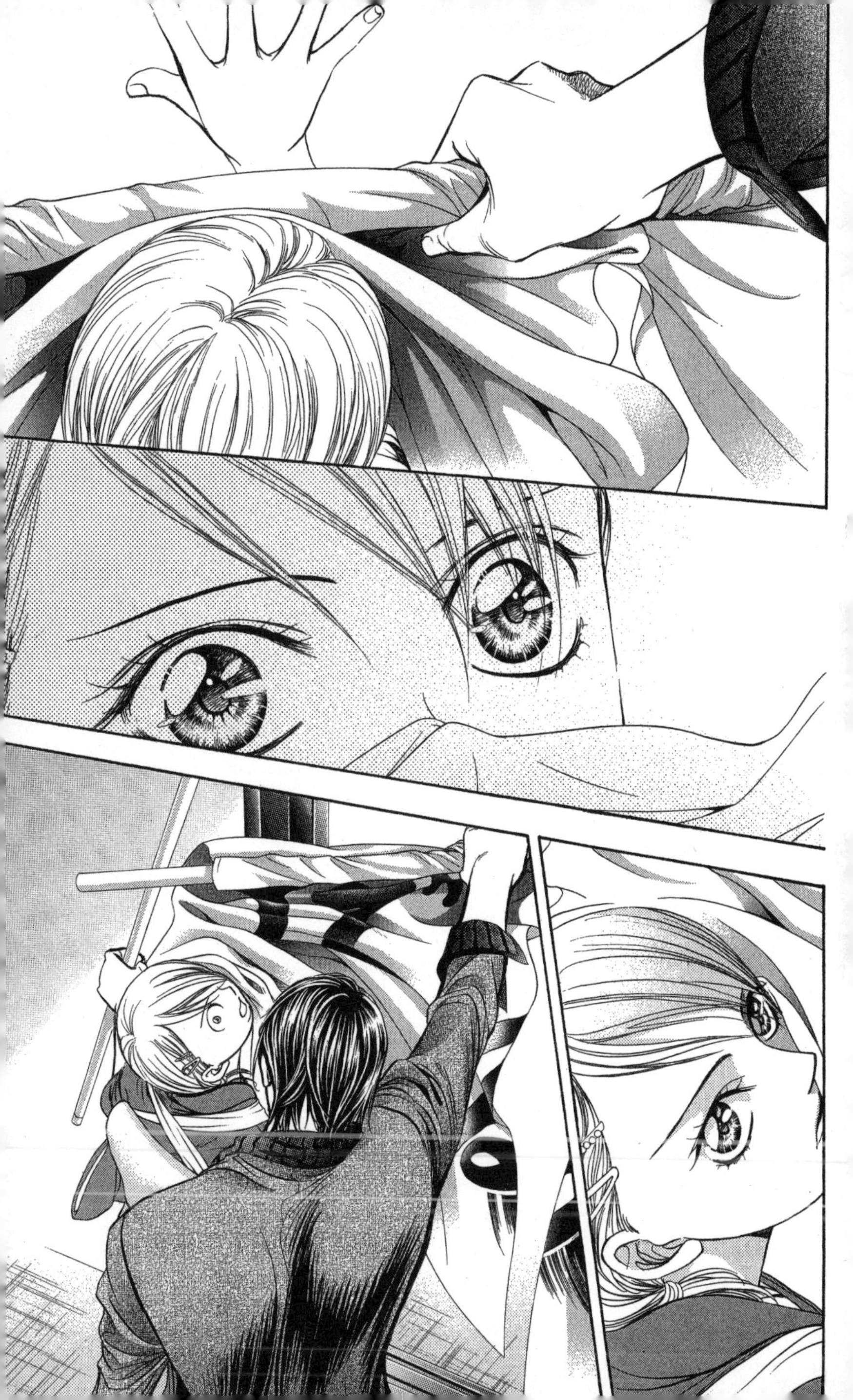

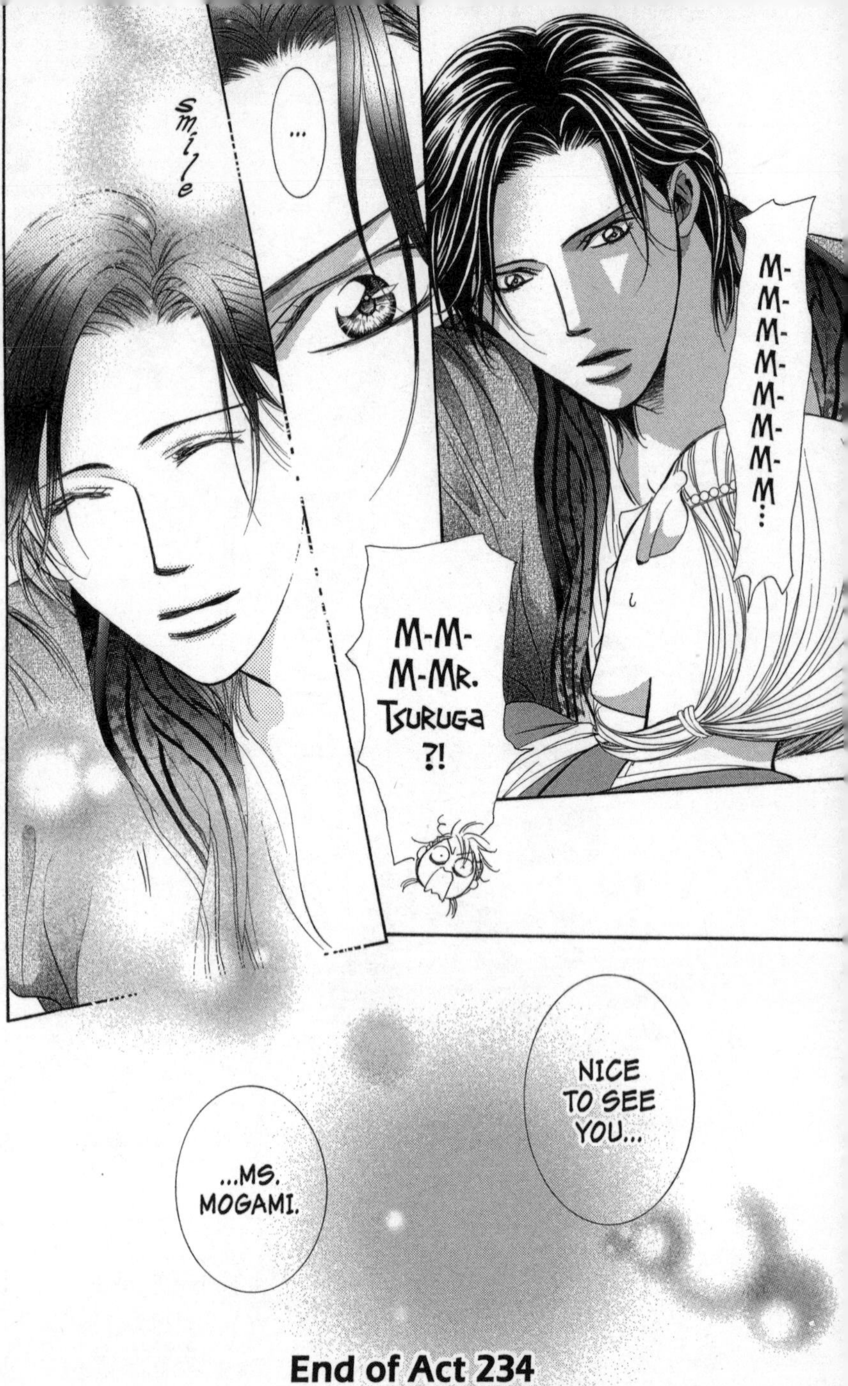
M-M-M-M-M-M-M...
M-M-M-Mr. Tsuruga ?!
...
smile
NICE TO SEE YOU...
...MS. MOGAMI.

End of Act 234

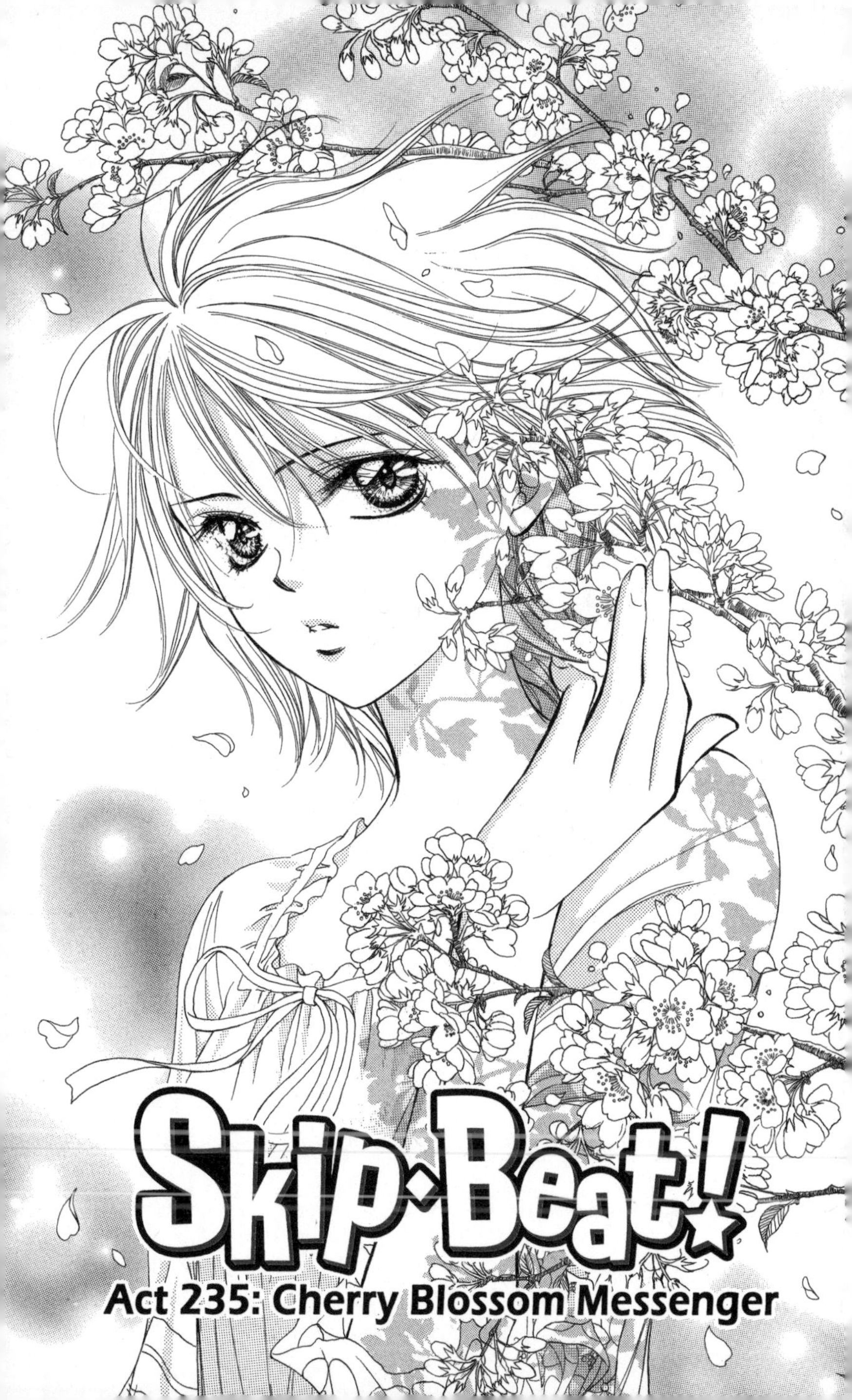
Skip·Beat!
Act 235: Cherry Blossom Messenger

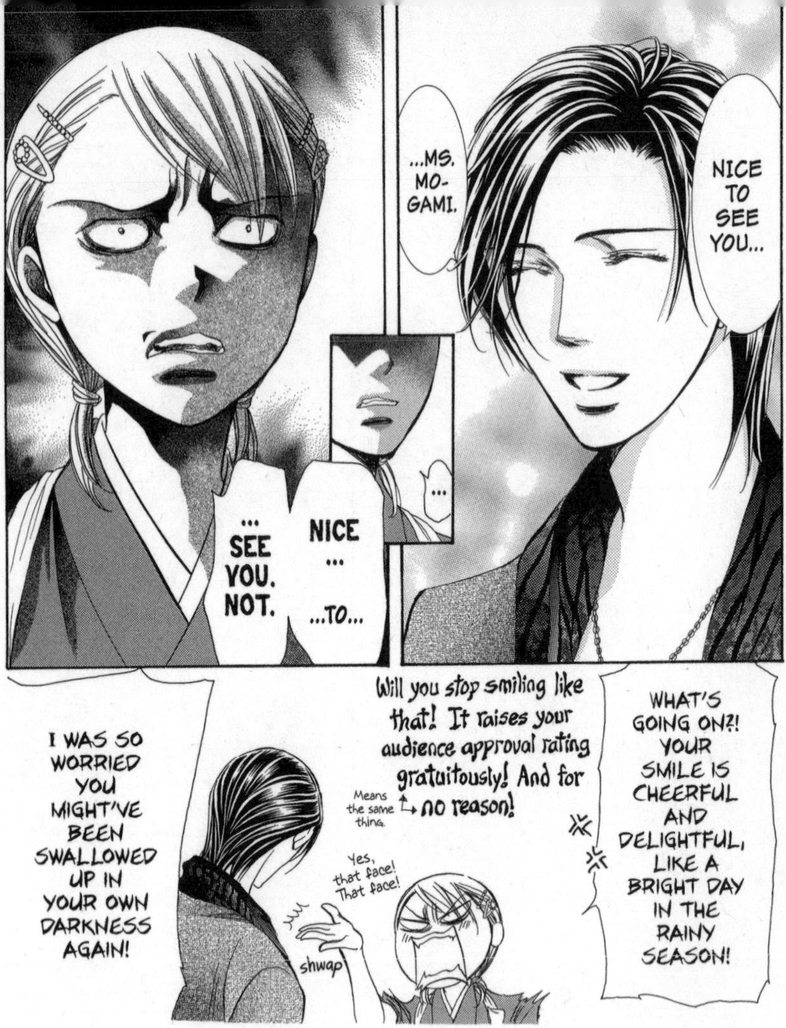
NICE TO SEE YOU...
...MS. MO-GAMI.
...
NICE ... ...TO...
... SEE YOU. NOT.
WHAT'S GOING ON?! YOUR SMILE IS CHEERFUL AND DELIGHTFUL, LIKE A BRIGHT DAY IN THE RAINY SEASON!
Will you stop smiling like that! It raises your audience approval rating gratuitously! And for no reason!
Means the same thing.
Yes, that face! That face!
shwap
I WAS SO WORRIED YOU MIGHT'VE BEEN SWALLOWED UP IN YOUR OWN DARKNESS AGAIN!

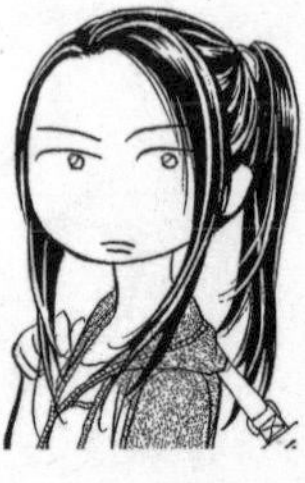

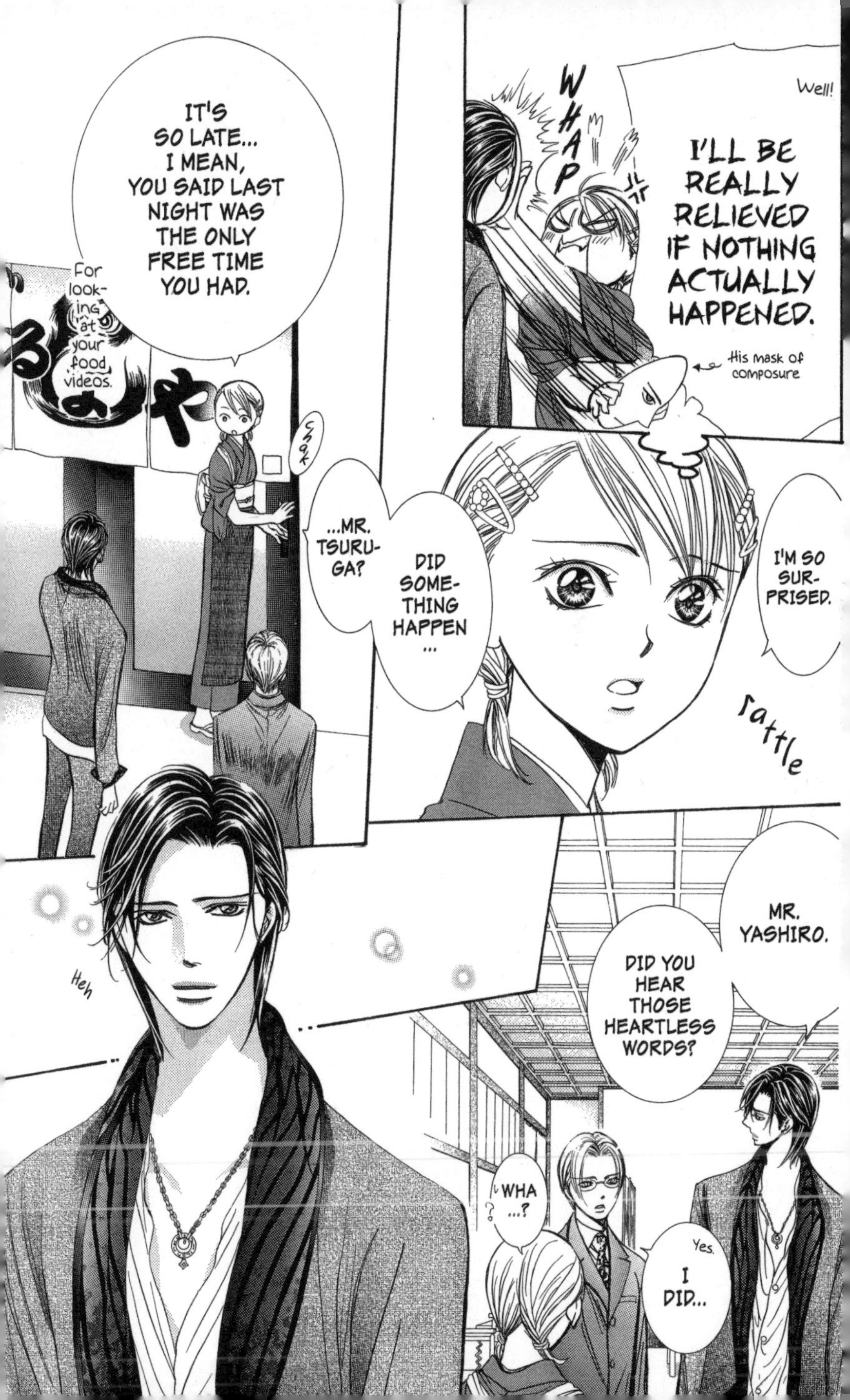
WHAP
Well!
I'LL BE REALLY RELIEVED IF NOTHING ACTUALLY HAPPENED.
His mask of composure
I'M SO SURPRISED.
rattle
...MR. TSURUGA?
DID SOMETHING HAPPEN...
IT'S SO LATE... I MEAN, YOU SAID LAST NIGHT WAS THE ONLY FREE TIME YOU HAD.
For looking at your food videos.
clack
MR. YASHIRO.
DID YOU HEAR THOSE HEARTLESS WORDS?
Yes.
I DID...
WHA...?
Heh
...
...

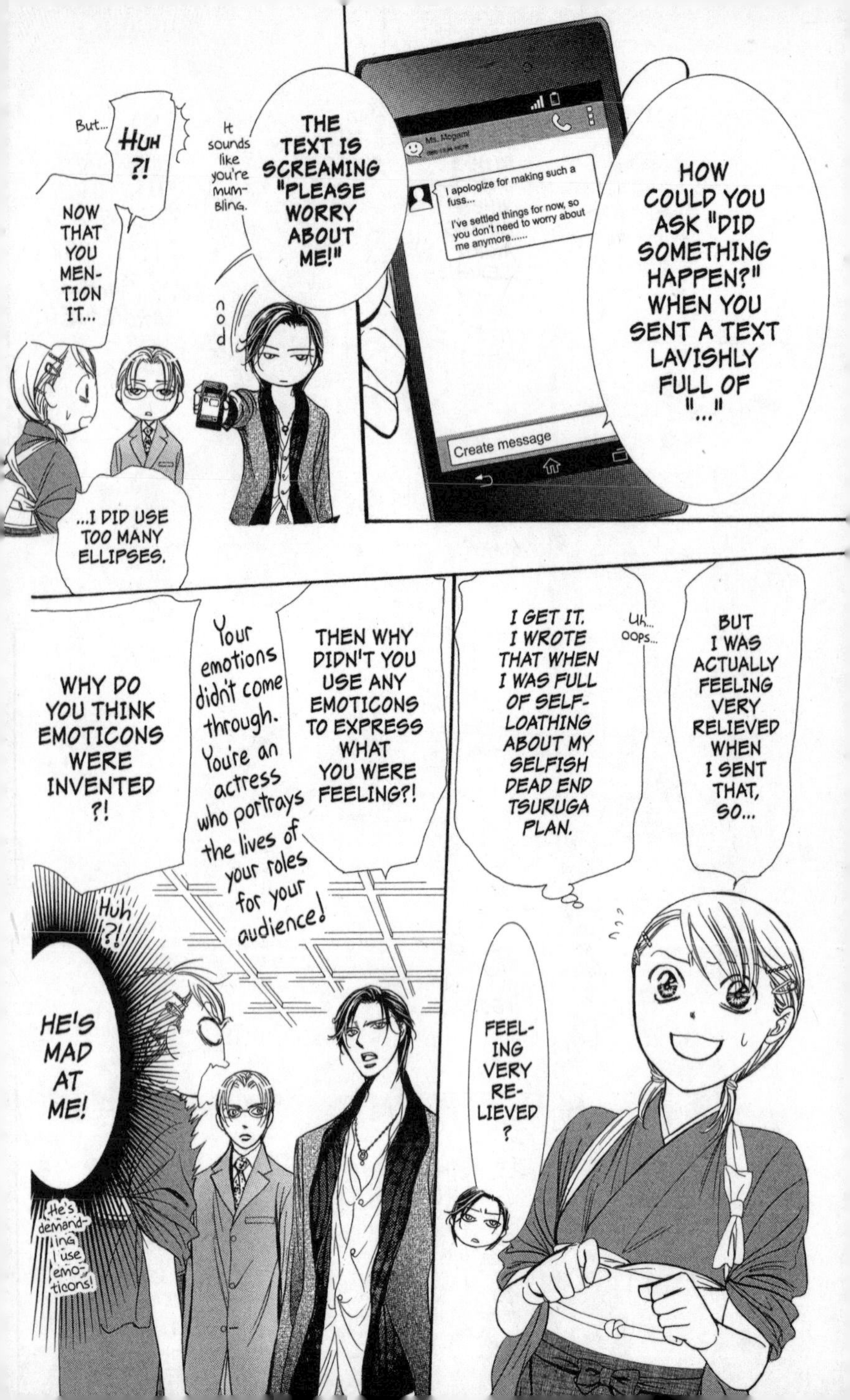
HOW COULD YOU ASK "DID SOMETHING HAPPEN?" WHEN YOU SENT A TEXT LAVISHLY FULL OF "..."
Ms. Mogami
I apologize for making such a fuss...
I've settled things for now, so you don't need to worry about me anymore......
Create message
THE TEXT IS SCREAMING "PLEASE WORRY ABOUT ME!"
It sounds like you're mumbling.
nod
HUH ?!
But...
NOW THAT YOU MENTION IT...
...I DID USE TOO MANY ELLIPSES.
BUT I WAS ACTUALLY FEELING VERY RELIEVED WHEN I SENT THAT, SO...
Uh... oops...
I GET IT. I WROTE THAT WHEN I WAS FULL OF SELF-LOATHING ABOUT MY SELFISH DEAD END TSURUGA PLAN.
FEELING VERY RELIEVED ?
THEN WHY DIDN'T YOU USE ANY EMOTICONS TO EXPRESS WHAT YOU WERE FEELING?!
Your emotions didn't come through. You're an actress who portrays the lives of your roles for your audience!
WHY DO YOU THINK EMOTICONS WERE INVENTED ?!
Huh ?!
HE'S MAD AT ME!
He's demanding I use emoticons!

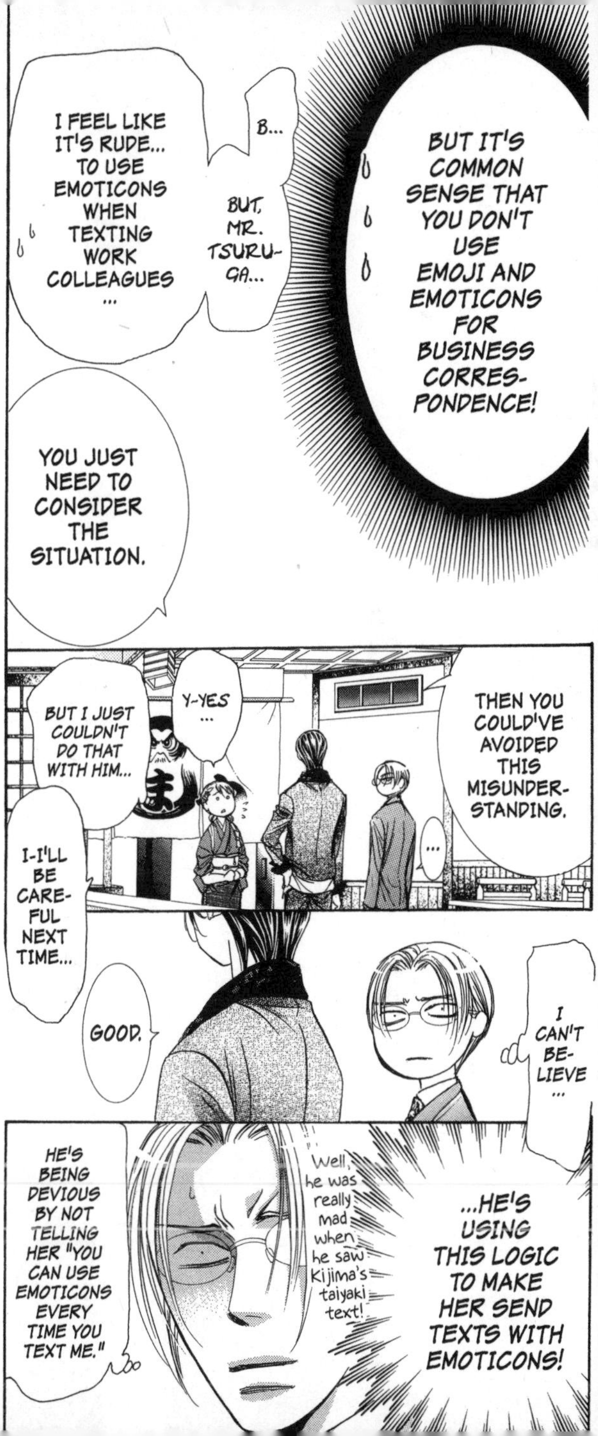
BUT IT'S COMMON SENSE THAT YOU DON'T USE EMOJI AND EMOTICONS FOR BUSINESS CORRES-PONDENCE!
B...
BUT, MR. TSURU-GA...
I FEEL LIKE IT'S RUDE... TO USE EMOTICONS WHEN TEXTING WORK COLLEAGUES ...
YOU JUST NEED TO CONSIDER THE SITUATION.
THEN YOU COULD'VE AVOIDED THIS MISUNDER-STANDING.
...
Y-YES ...
BUT I JUST COULDN'T DO THAT WITH HIM...
I-I'LL BE CARE-FUL NEXT TIME...
I CAN'T BE-LIEVE ...
GOOD.
...HE'S USING THIS LOGIC TO MAKE HER SEND TEXTS WITH EMOTICONS!
Well, he was really mad when he saw Kijima's taiyaki text!
HE'S BEING DEVIOUS BY NOT TELLING HER "YOU CAN USE EMOTICONS EVERY TIME YOU TEXT ME."
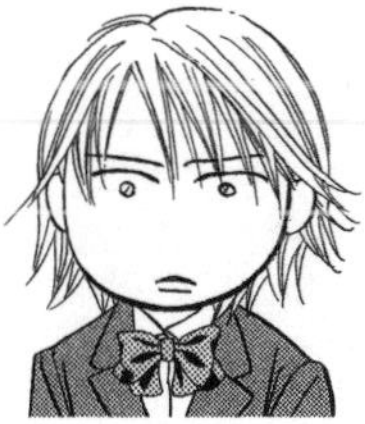

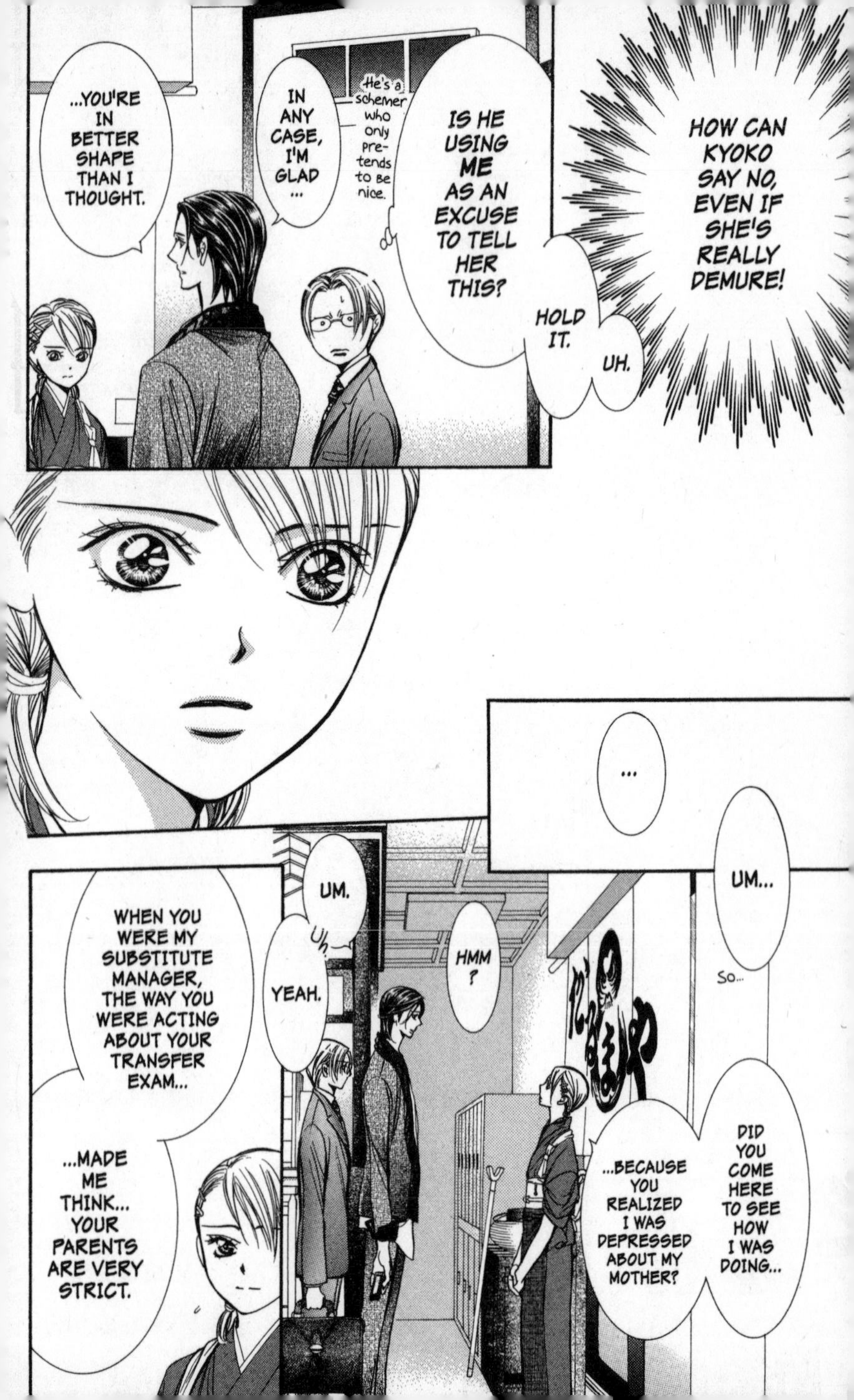
HOW CAN KYOKO SAY NO, EVEN IF SHE'S REALLY DEMURE!
UH.
HOLD IT.
IS HE USING ME AS AN EXCUSE TO TELL HER THIS?
He's a schemer who only pretends to be nice.
IN ANY CASE, I'M GLAD...
...YOU'RE IN BETTER SHAPE THAN I THOUGHT.
...
UM...
So...
DID YOU COME HERE TO SEE HOW I WAS DOING...
...BECAUSE YOU REALIZED I WAS DEPRESSED ABOUT MY MOTHER?
HMM?
UM.
Uh.
YEAH.
WHEN YOU WERE MY SUBSTITUTE MANAGER, THE WAY YOU WERE ACTING ABOUT YOUR TRANSFER EXAM...
...MADE ME THINK... YOUR PARENTS ARE VERY STRICT.

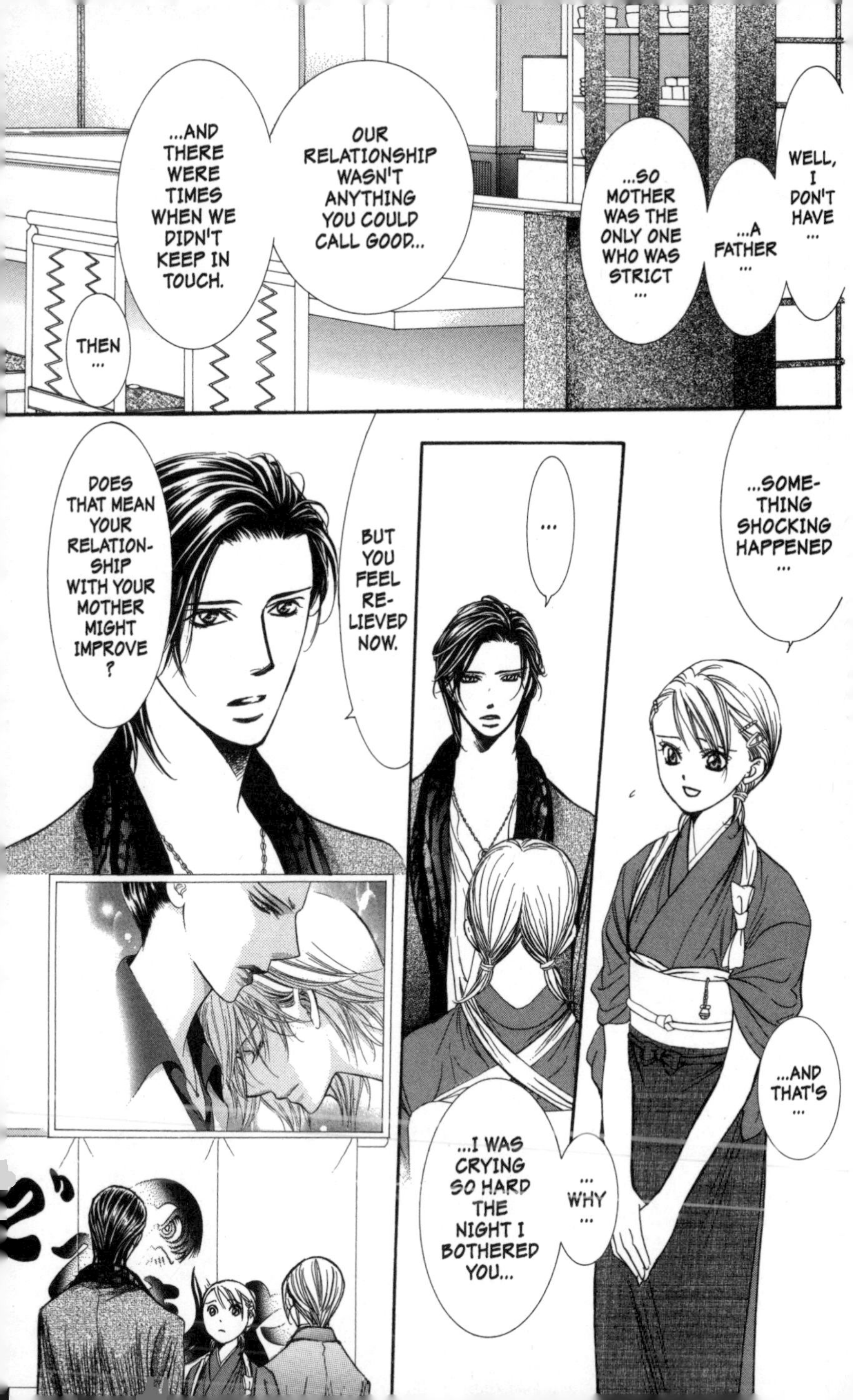
WELL, I DON'T HAVE ...
...A FATHER ...
...SO MOTHER WAS THE ONLY ONE WHO WAS STRICT ...
OUR RELATIONSHIP WASN'T ANYTHING YOU COULD CALL GOOD...
...AND THERE WERE TIMES WHEN WE DIDN'T KEEP IN TOUCH.
THEN ...
...SOME-THING SHOCKING HAPPENED ...
...AND THAT'S ...
... WHY ...
...I WAS CRYING SO HARD THE NIGHT I BOTHERED YOU...
...
BUT YOU FEEL RE-LIEVED NOW.
DOES THAT MEAN YOUR RELATION-SHIP WITH YOUR MOTHER MIGHT IMPROVE ?

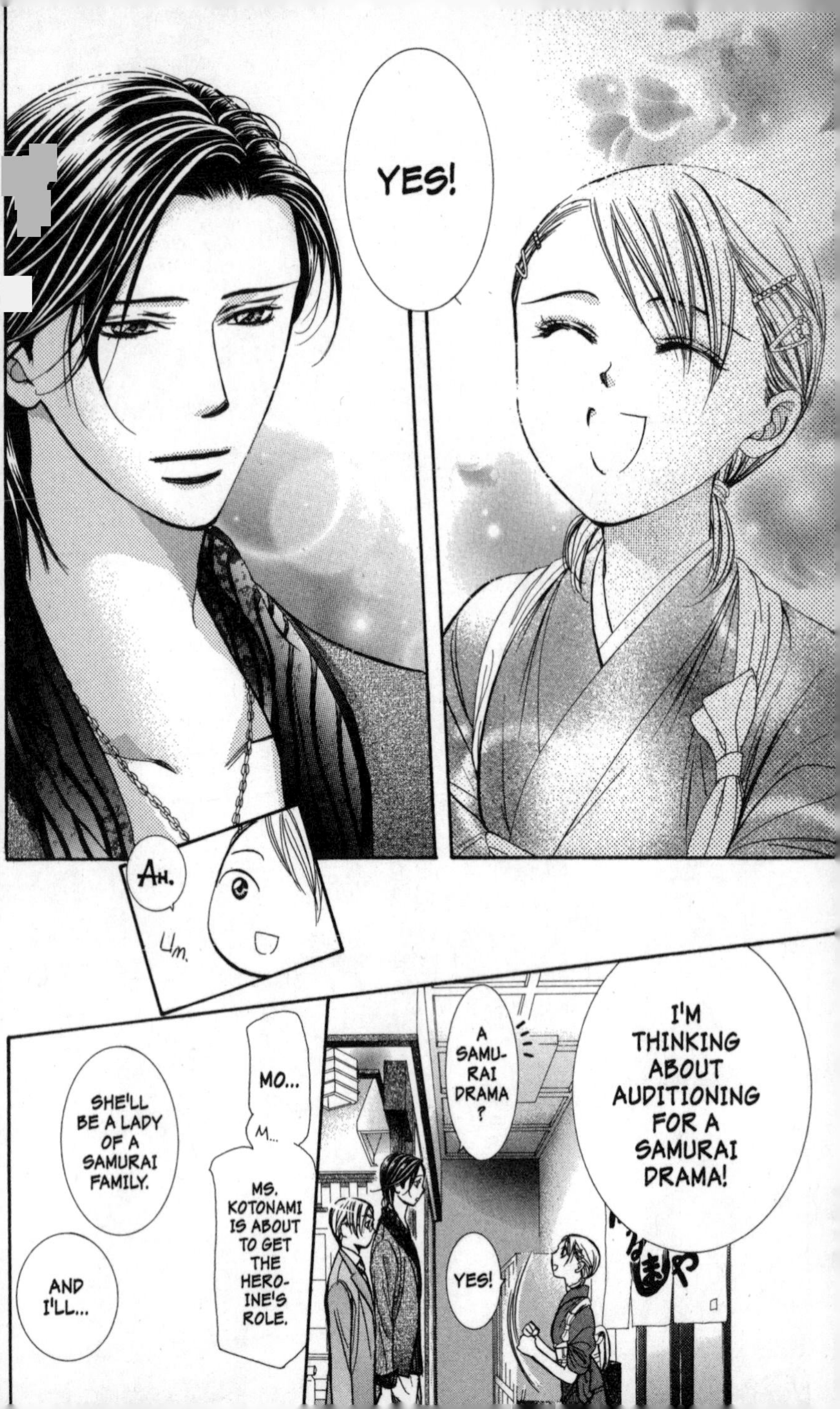
YES!
Ah.
Um.
I'M THINKING ABOUT AUDITIONING FOR A SAMURAI DRAMA!
A SAMU-RAI DRAMA?
YES!
MO...
M...
MS. KOTONAMI IS ABOUT TO GET THE HERO-INE'S ROLE.
SHE'LL BE A LADY OF A SAMURAI FAMILY.
AND I'LL...

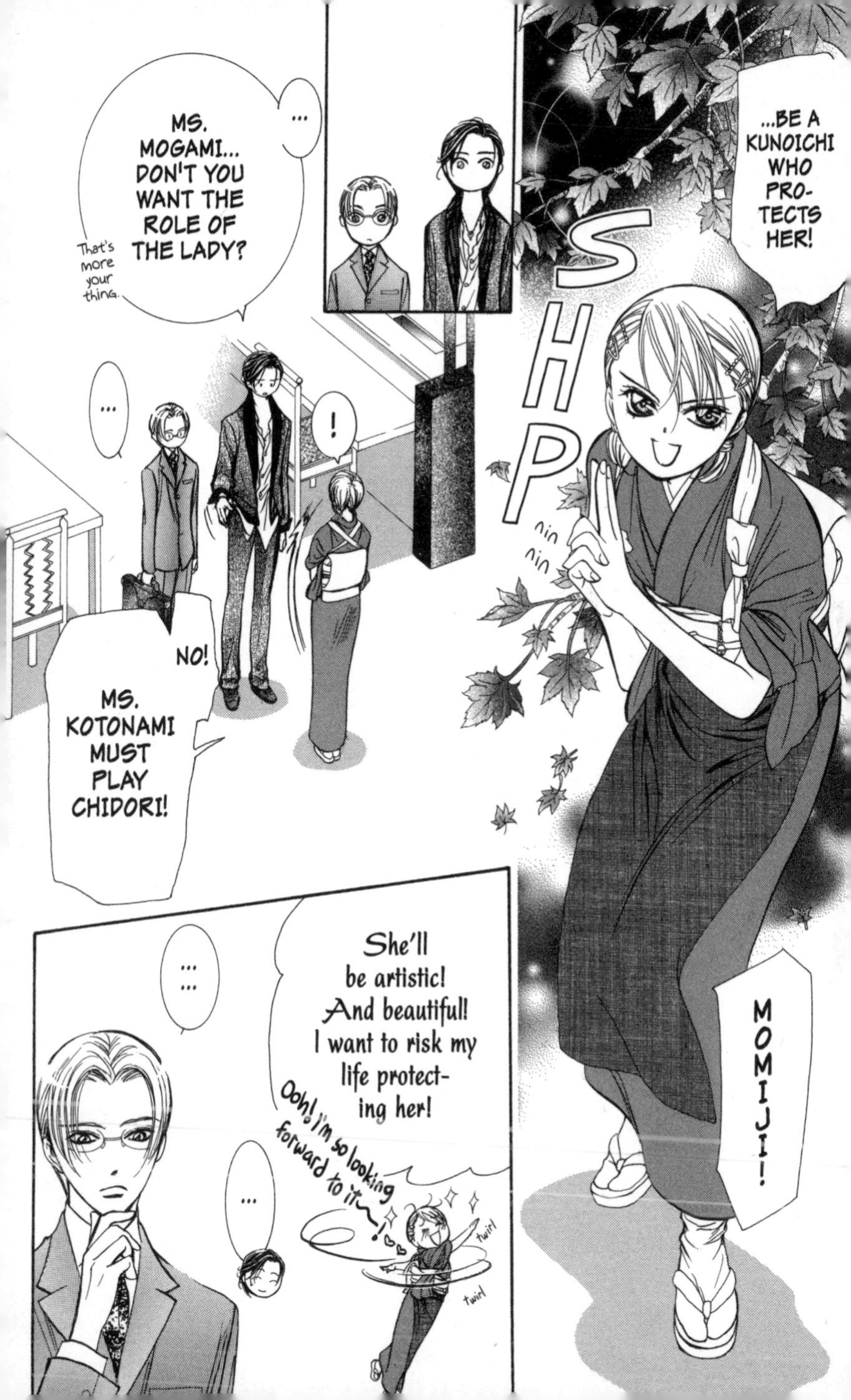
...BE A KUNOICHI WHO PROTECTS HER!
SHP
nin nin
MOMIJI!
...
MS. MOGAMI... DON'T YOU WANT THE ROLE OF THE LADY?
That's more your thing.
!
...
NO!
MS. KOTONAMI MUST PLAY CHIDORI!
She'll be artistic! And beautiful! I want to risk my life protecting her!
... ...
Ooh! I'm so looking forward to it~!
...
twirl
twirl

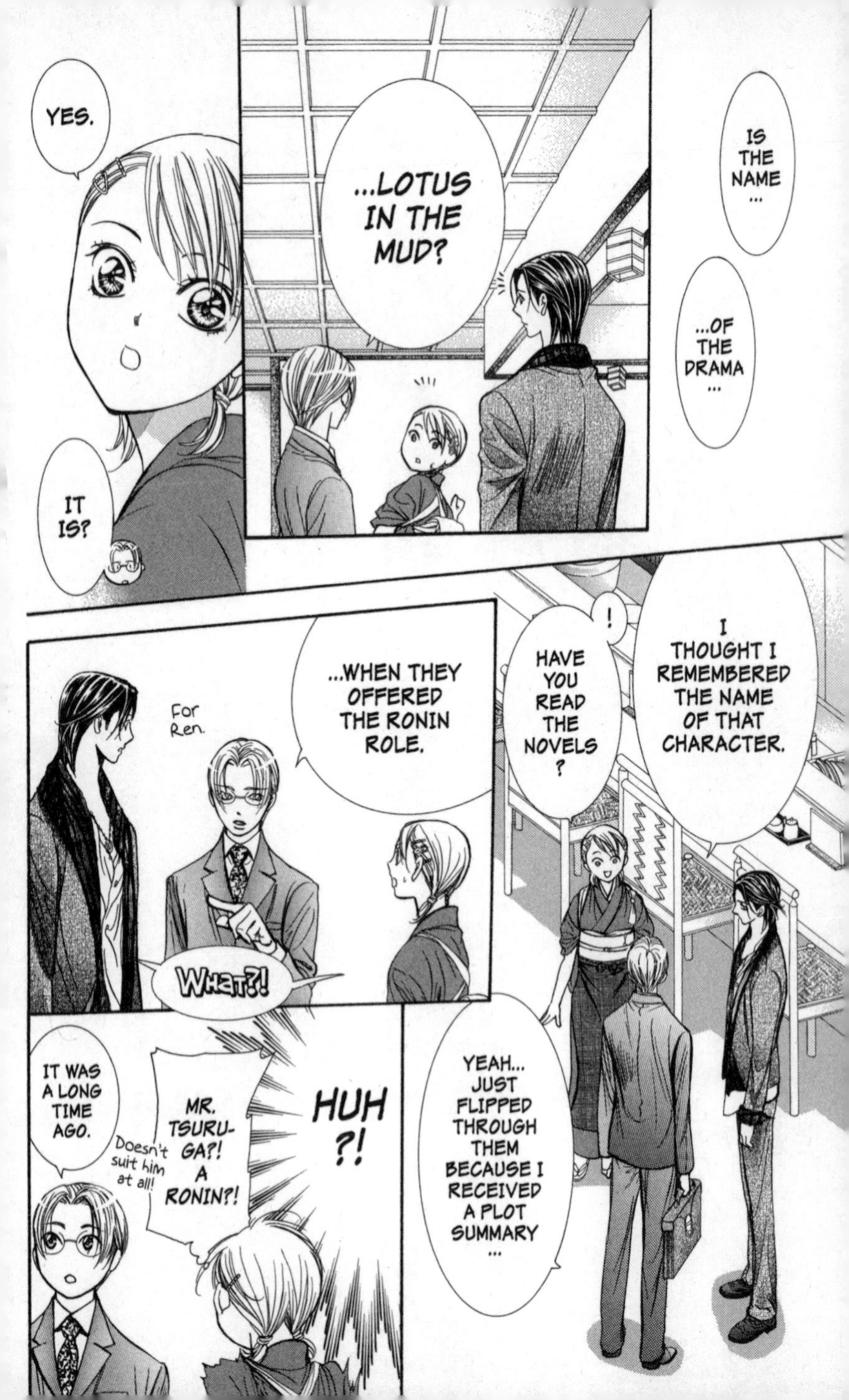
IS THE NAME...
...OF THE DRAMA...
...LOTUS IN THE MUD?
YES.
IT IS?
I THOUGHT I REMEMBERED THE NAME OF THAT CHARACTER.
!
HAVE YOU READ THE NOVELS?
YEAH... JUST FLIPPED THROUGH THEM BECAUSE I RECEIVED A PLOT SUMMARY...
...WHEN THEY OFFERED THE RONIN ROLE.
For Ren.
WHAT?!
HUH?!
MR. TSURUGA?! A RONIN?!
Doesn't suit him at all!
IT WAS A LONG TIME AGO.

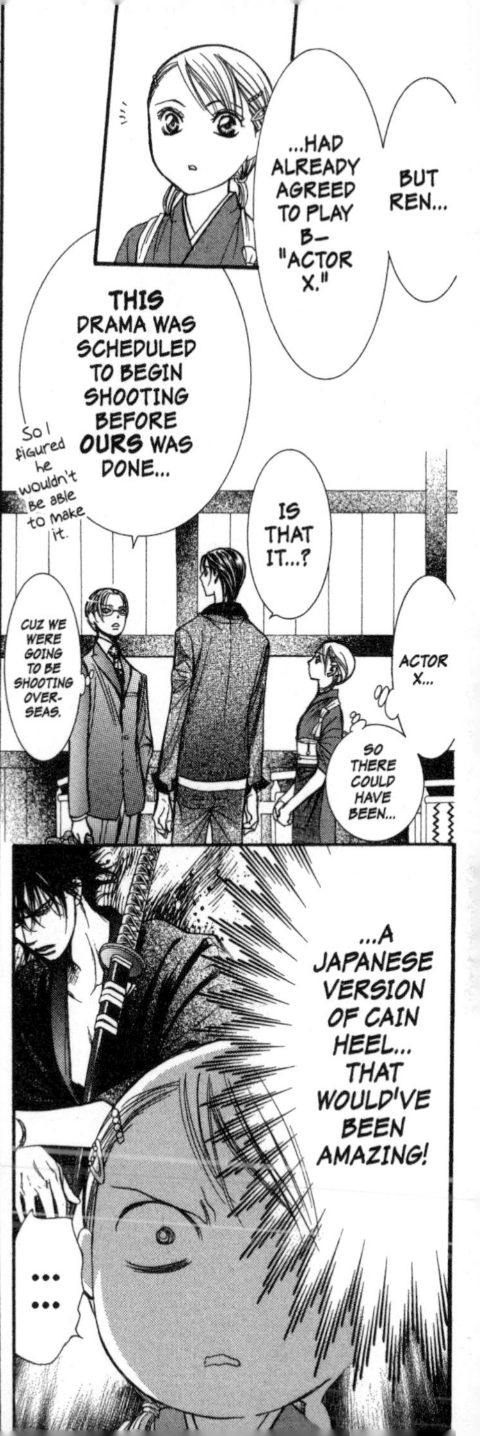
BUT REN...
...HAD ALREADY AGREED TO PLAY B— "ACTOR X."
THIS DRAMA WAS SCHEDULED TO BEGIN SHOOTING BEFORE OURS WAS DONE...
So I figured he wouldn't be able to make it.
IS THAT IT...?
ACTOR X...
SO THERE COULD HAVE BEEN...
CUZ WE WERE GOING TO BE SHOOTING OVER-SEAS.
...A JAPANESE VERSION OF CAIN HEEL... THAT WOULD'VE BEEN AMAZING!
...
...
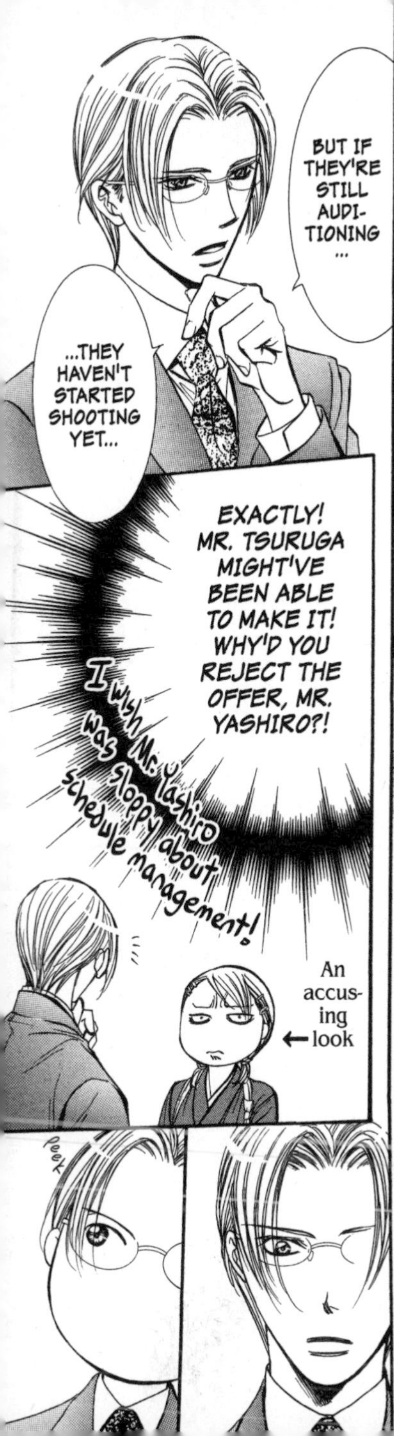
BUT IF THEY'RE STILL AUDI-TIONING...
...THEY HAVEN'T STARTED SHOOTING YET...
EXACTLY! MR. TSURUGA MIGHT'VE BEEN ABLE TO MAKE IT! WHY'D YOU REJECT THE OFFER, MR. YASHIRO?!
I wish Mr. Yashiro was sloppy about schedule management!
An accus-ing look
peek

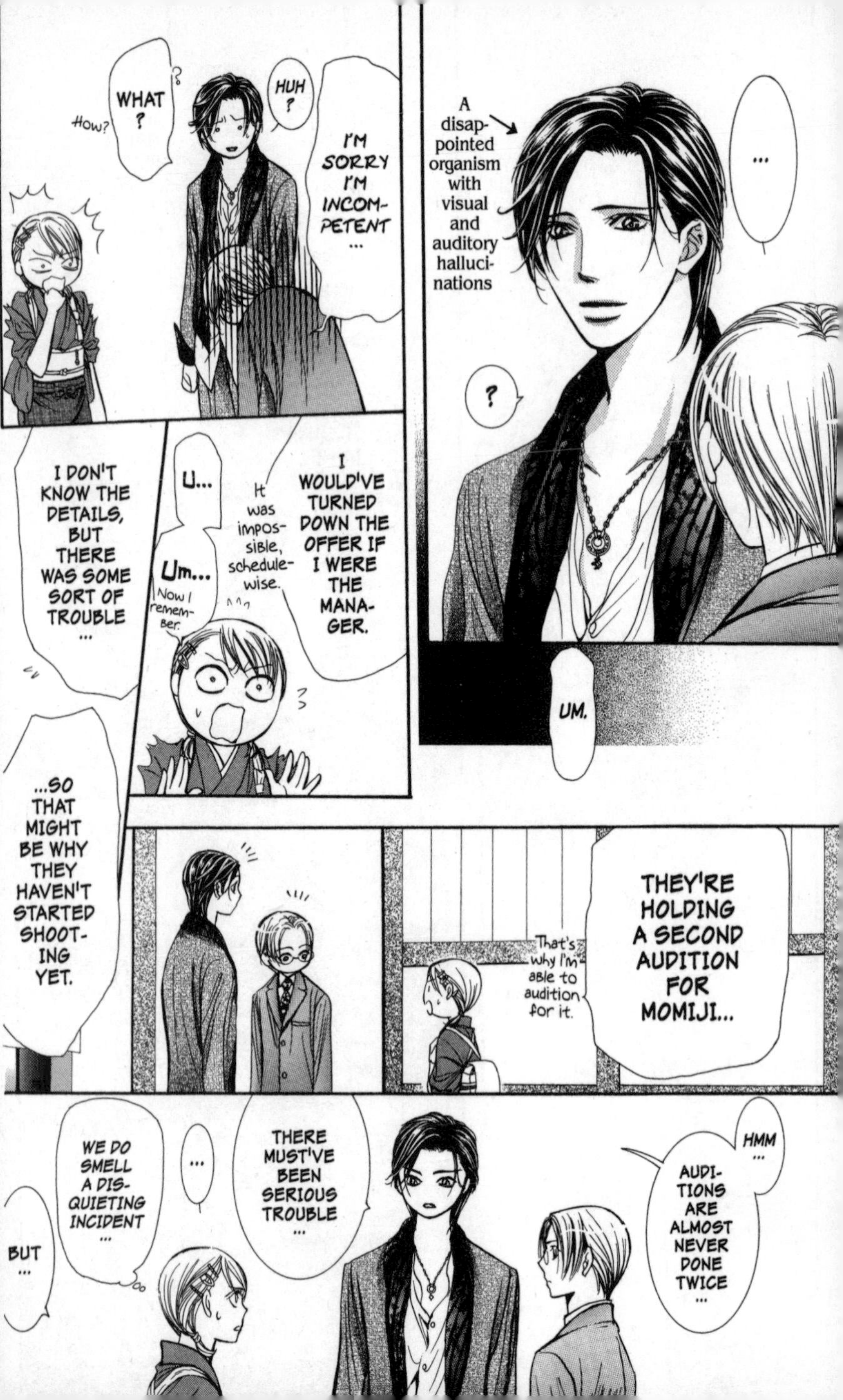
...
A disappointed organism with visual and auditory hallucinations
?
UM.
I'M SORRY I'M INCOMPETENT...
HUH?
WHAT?
How?
I WOULD'VE TURNED DOWN THE OFFER IF I WERE THE MANAGER.
It was impossible, schedule-wise.
U...
Um...
Now I remember.
I DON'T KNOW THE DETAILS, BUT THERE WAS SOME SORT OF TROUBLE...
THEY'RE HOLDING A SECOND AUDITION FOR MOMIJI...
That's why I'm able to audition for it.
...SO THAT MIGHT BE WHY THEY HAVEN'T STARTED SHOOTING YET.
HMM...
AUDITIONS ARE ALMOST NEVER DONE TWICE...
THERE MUST'VE BEEN SERIOUS TROUBLE...
...
WE DO SMELL A DISQUIETING INCIDENT...
BUT...

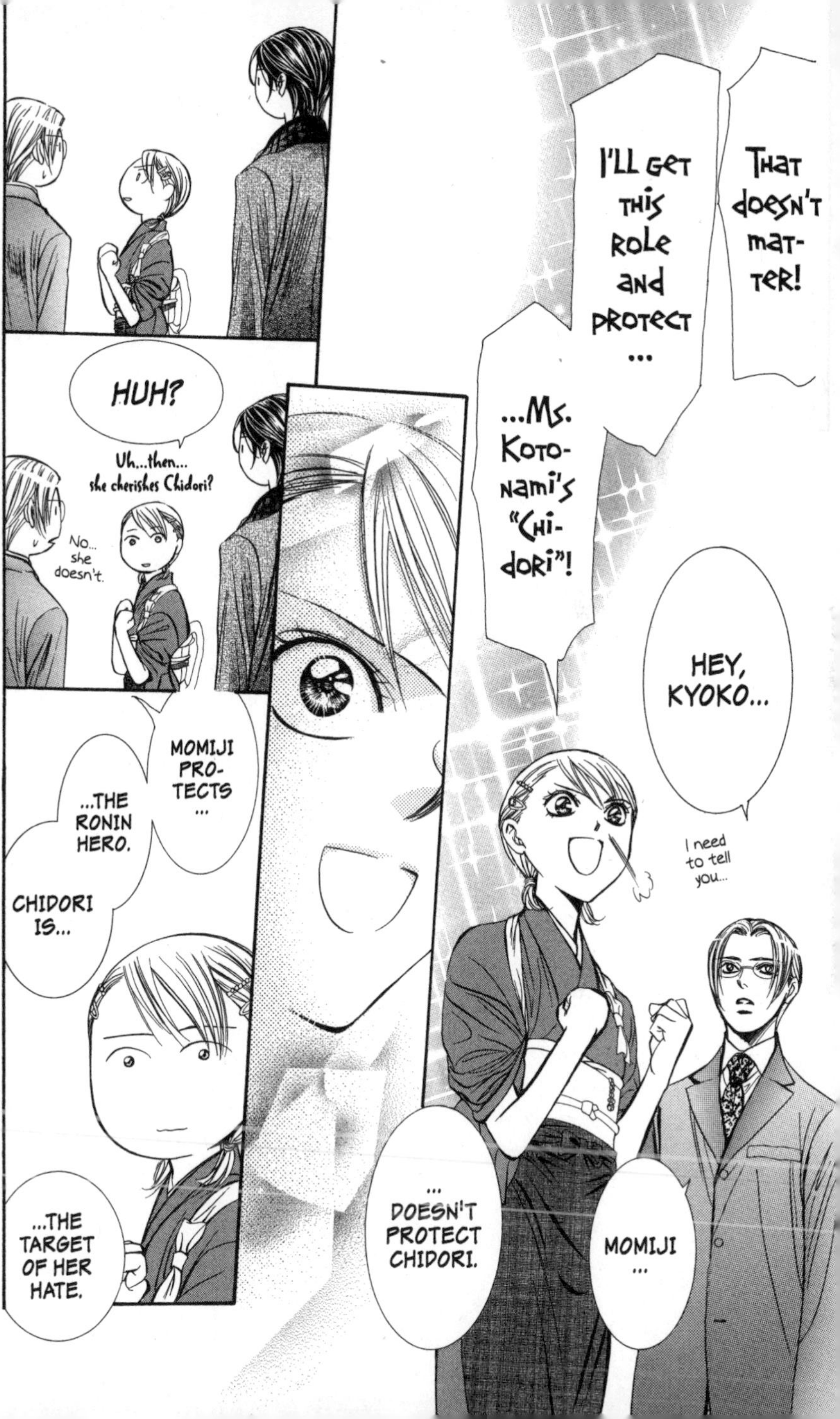
HEY, KYOKO...
I need to tell you...
MOMIJI ...
... DOESN'T PROTECT CHIDORI.
HUH?
Uh...then... she cherishes Chidori?
No... she doesn't.
MOMIJI PROTECTS ...
...THE RONIN HERO.
CHIDORI IS...
...THE TARGET OF HER HATE.
That doesn't matter!
I'LL GET THIS ROLE AND PROTECT ...
...Ms. KOTONAMI'S "CHIDORI"!

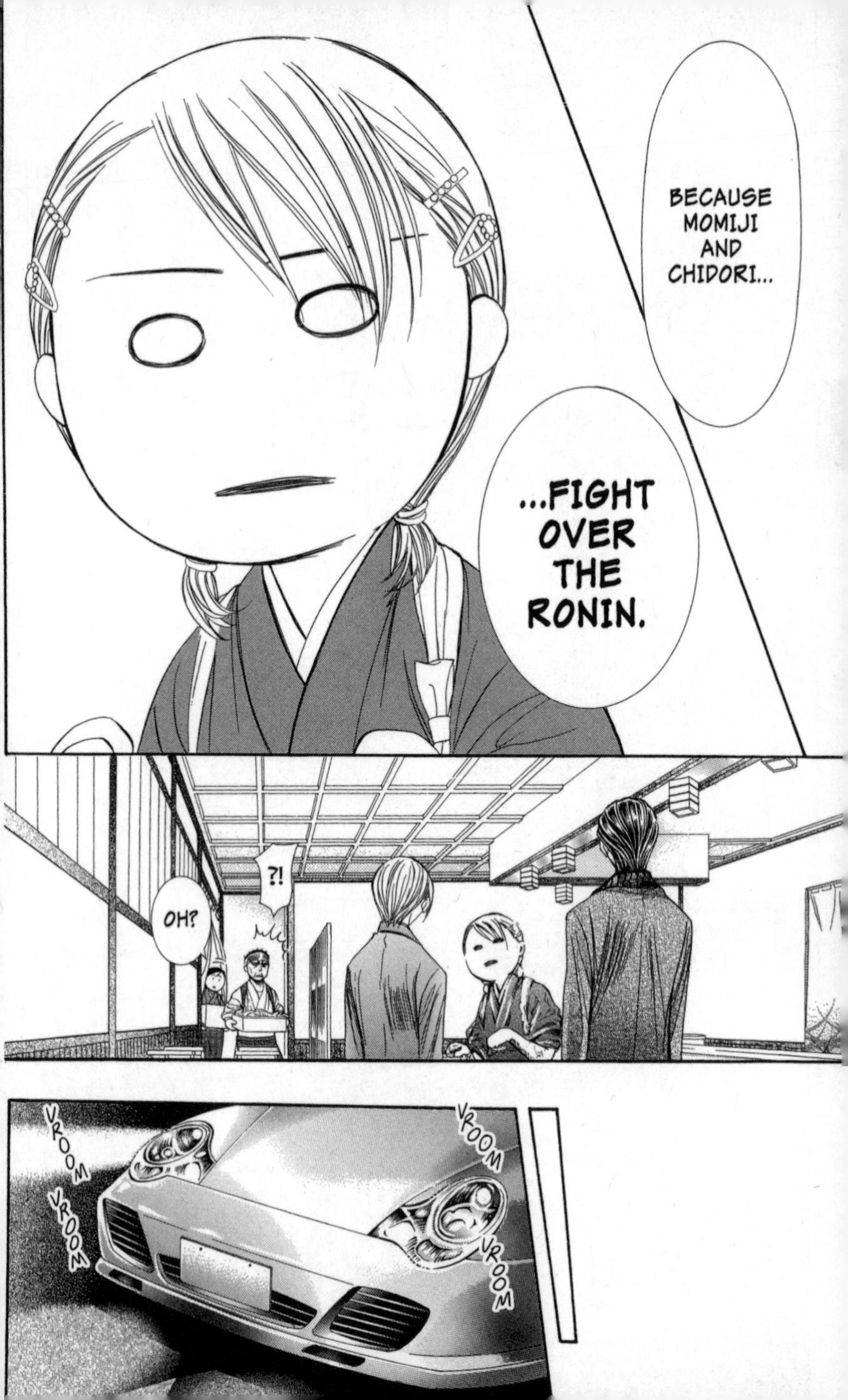
BECAUSE MOMIJI AND CHIDORI...
...FIGHT OVER THE RONIN.
?!
OH?
VROOM
VROOM
VROOM
VROOM

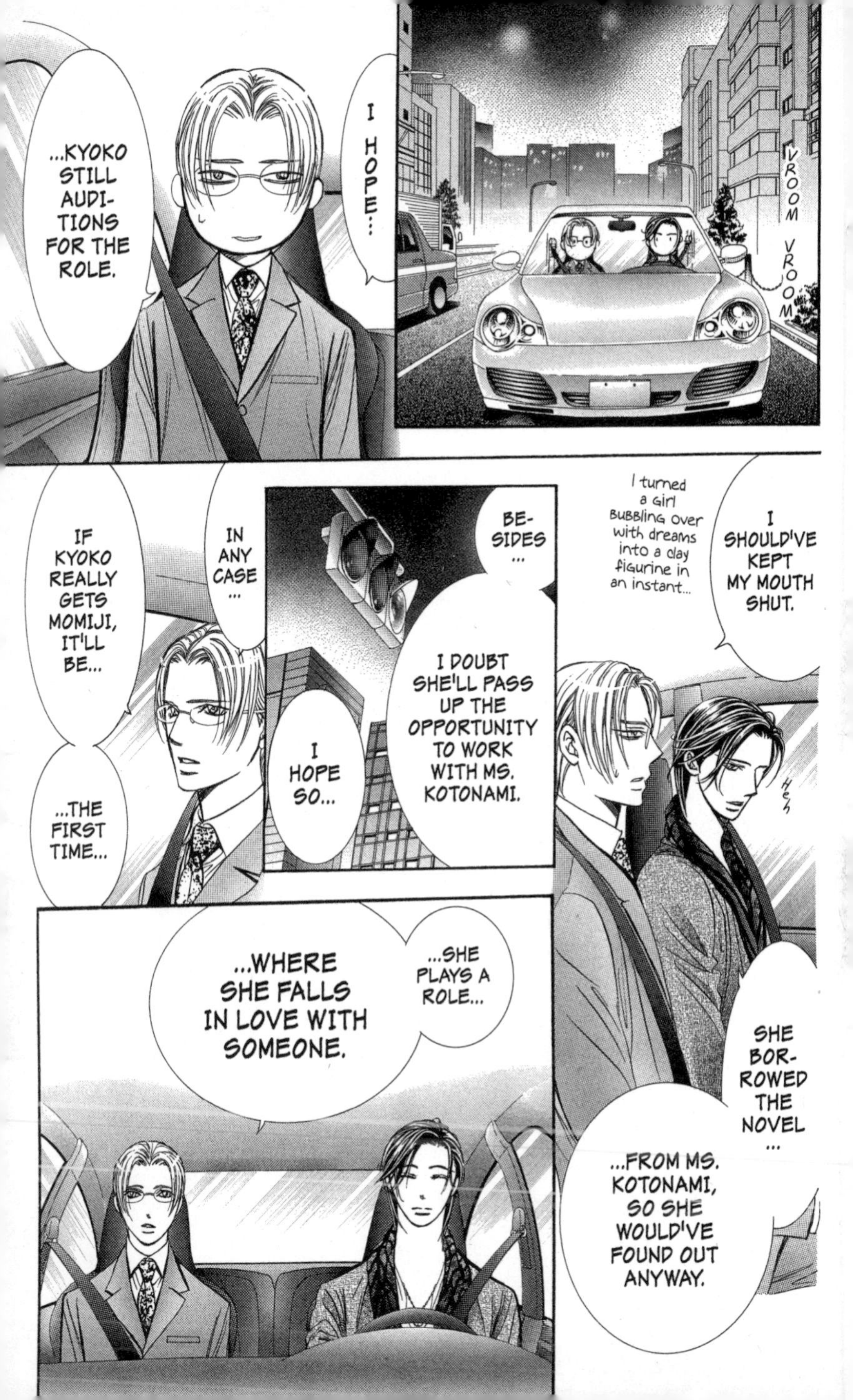
VROOM VROOM
I HOPE...
...KYOKO STILL AUDITIONS FOR THE ROLE.
I SHOULD'VE KEPT MY MOUTH SHUT.
I turned a girl bubbling over with dreams into a clay figurine in an instant...
Heh
SHE BORROWED THE NOVEL...
...FROM MS. KOTONAMI, SO SHE WOULD'VE FOUND OUT ANYWAY.
BESIDES...
I DOUBT SHE'LL PASS UP THE OPPORTUNITY TO WORK WITH MS. KOTONAMI.
I HOPE SO...
IN ANY CASE...
IF KYOKO REALLY GETS MOMIJI, IT'LL BE...
...THE FIRST TIME...
...SHE PLAYS A ROLE...
...WHERE SHE FALLS IN LOVE WITH SOMEONE.

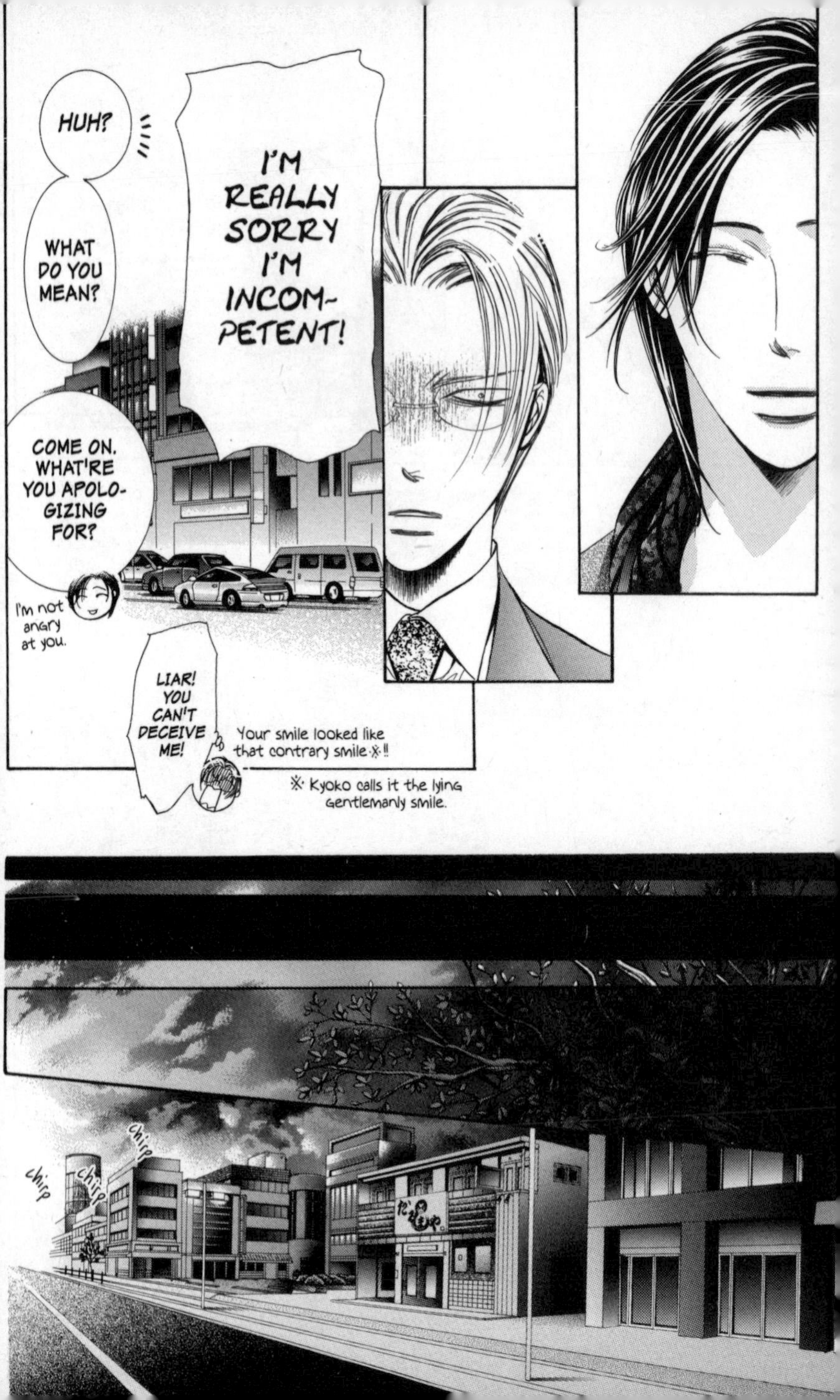
I'M REALLY SORRY I'M INCOMPETENT!
HUH?
WHAT DO YOU MEAN?
COME ON. WHAT'RE YOU APOLOGIZING FOR?
I'm not angry at you.
LIAR! YOU CAN'T DECEIVE ME!
Your smile looked like that contrary smile※!!
※: Kyoko calls it the lying gentlemanly smile.
chirp
chirp
chirp

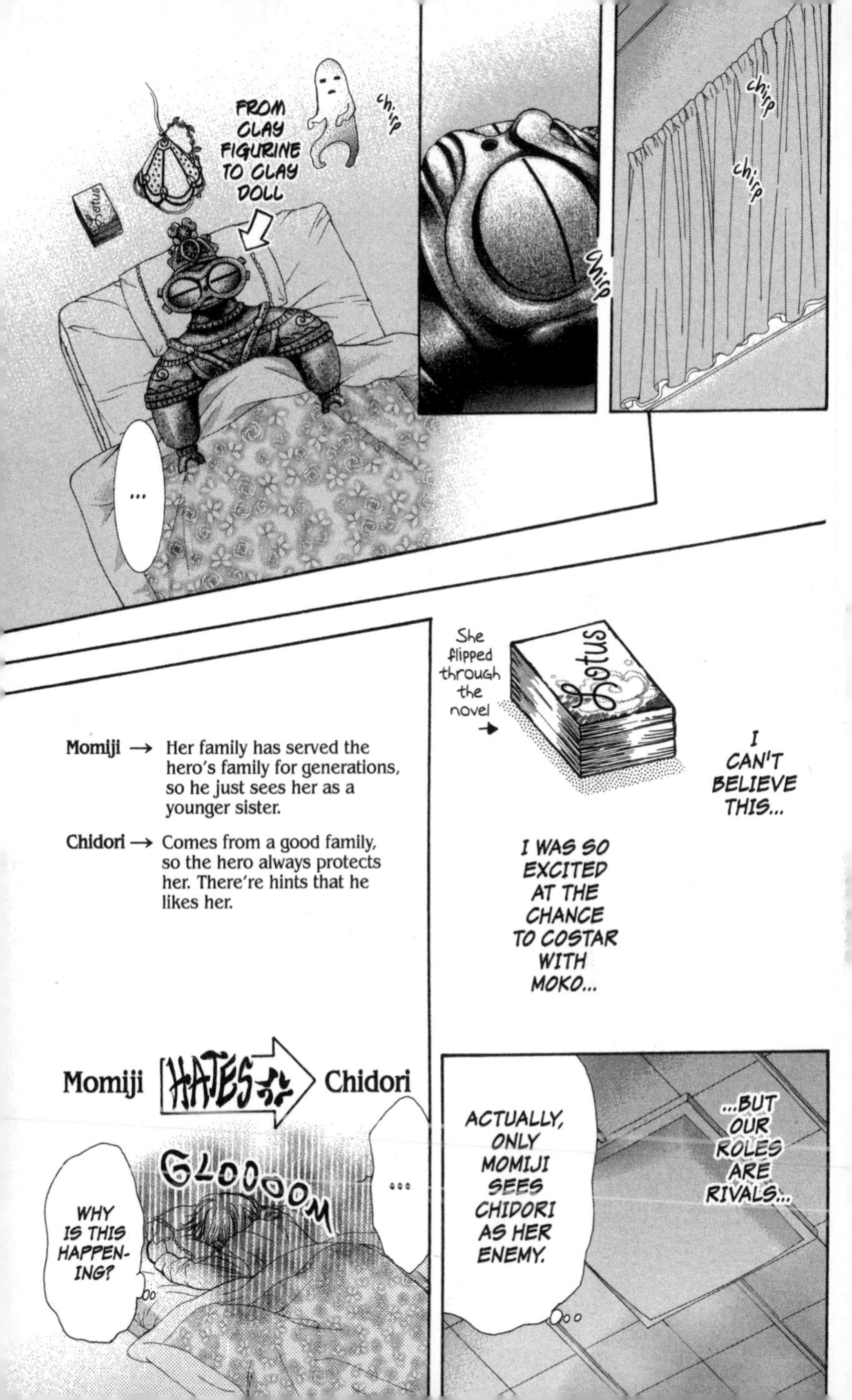
chirp
chirp
chirp
chirp
FROM CLAY FIGURINE TO CLAY DOLL
...
I CAN'T BELIEVE THIS...
She flipped through the novel
I WAS SO EXCITED AT THE CHANCE TO COSTAR WITH MOKO...
Momiji → Her family has served the hero's family for generations, so he just sees her as a younger sister.
Chidori → Comes from a good family, so the hero always protects her. There're hints that he likes her.
...BUT OUR ROLES ARE RIVALS...
ACTUALLY, ONLY MOMIJI SEES CHIDORI AS HER ENEMY.
Momiji HATES Chidori
...
GLOOOOOM
WHY IS THIS HAPPEN-ING?

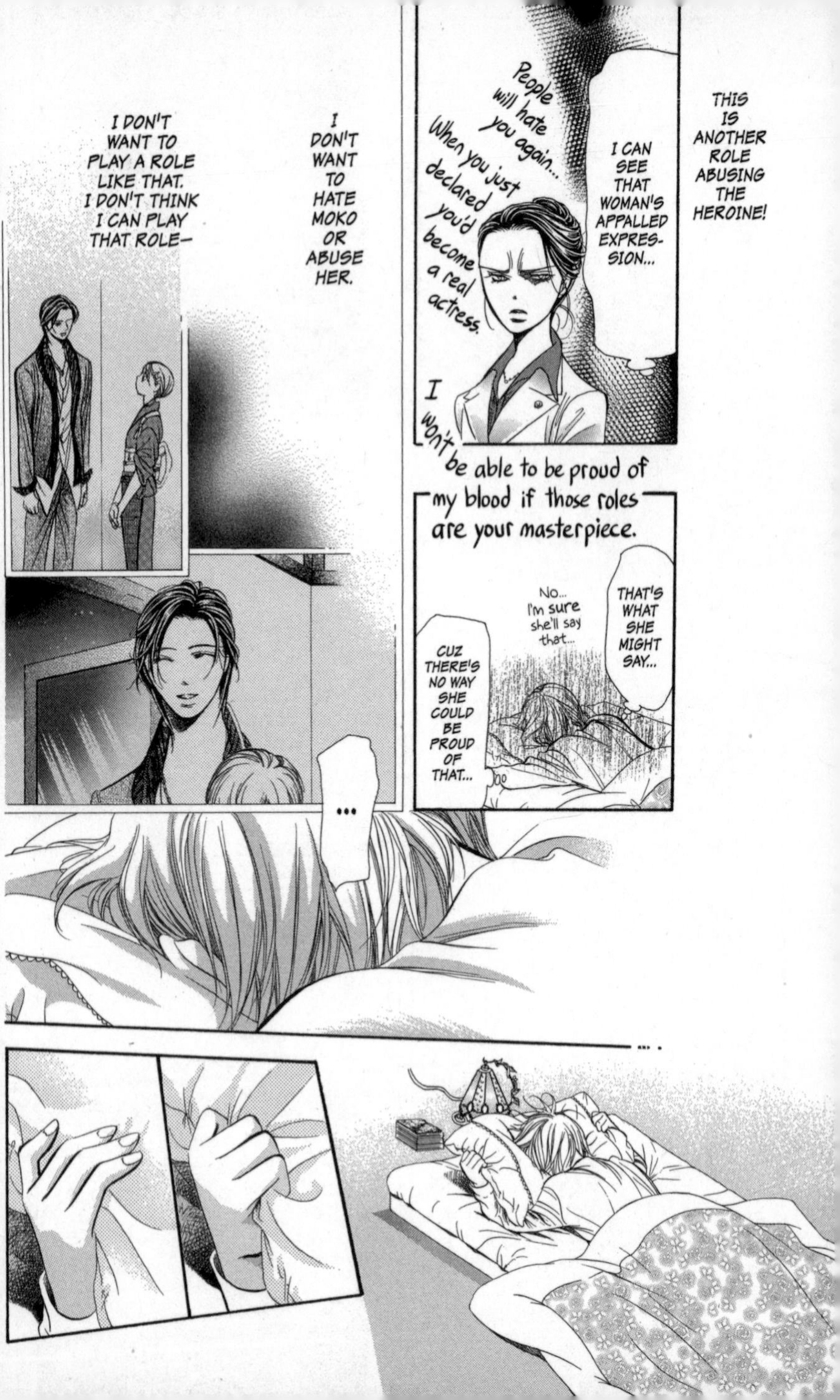
THIS IS ANOTHER ROLE ABUSING THE HEROINE!
I CAN SEE THAT WOMAN'S APPALLED EXPRESSION...
People will hate you again...
When you just declared you'd become a real actress.
I won't be able to be proud of my blood if those roles are your masterpiece.
THAT'S WHAT SHE MIGHT SAY...
No... I'm sure she'll say that...
CUZ THERE'S NO WAY SHE COULD BE PROUD OF THAT...
I DON'T WANT TO HATE MOKO OR ABUSE HER.
I DON'T WANT TO PLAY A ROLE LIKE THAT. I DON'T THINK I CAN PLAY THAT ROLE—
...
...

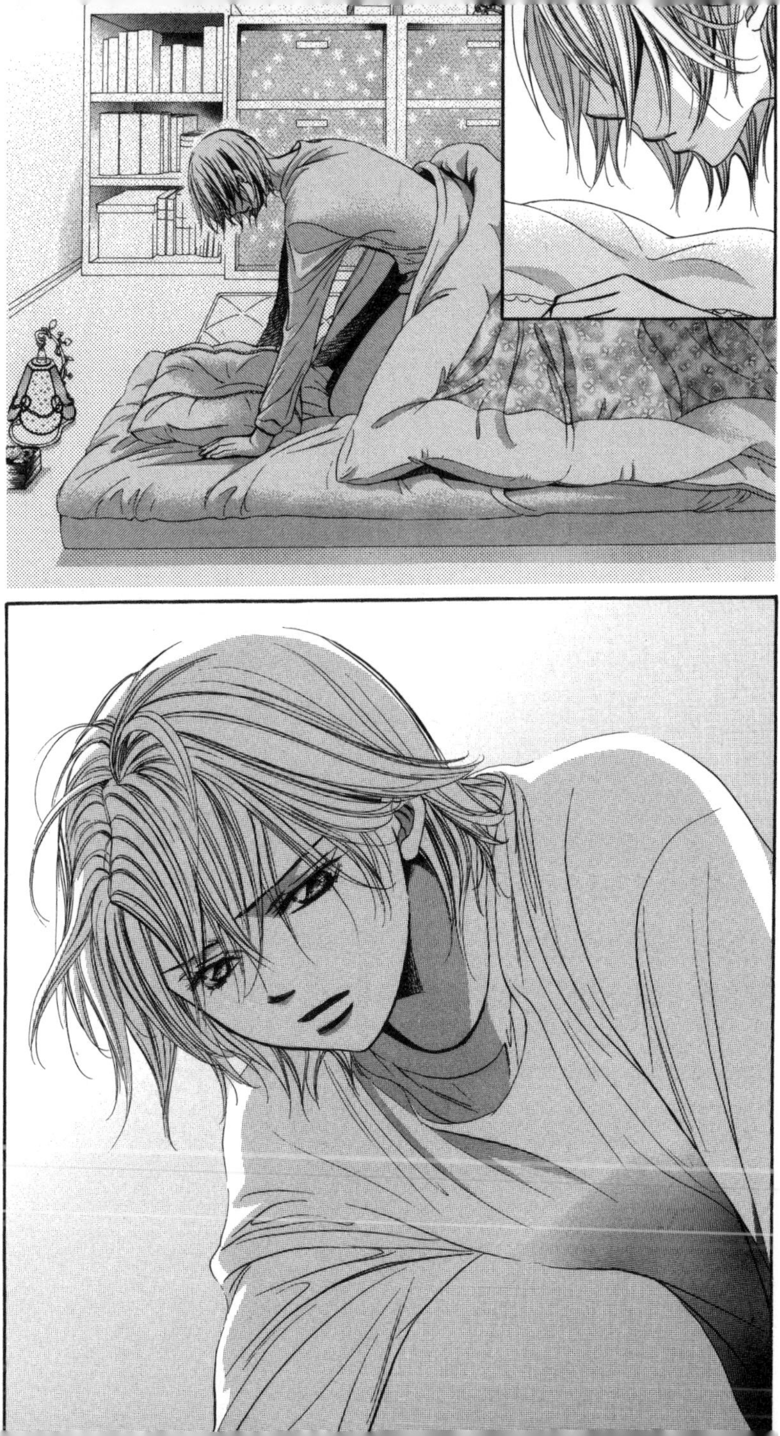

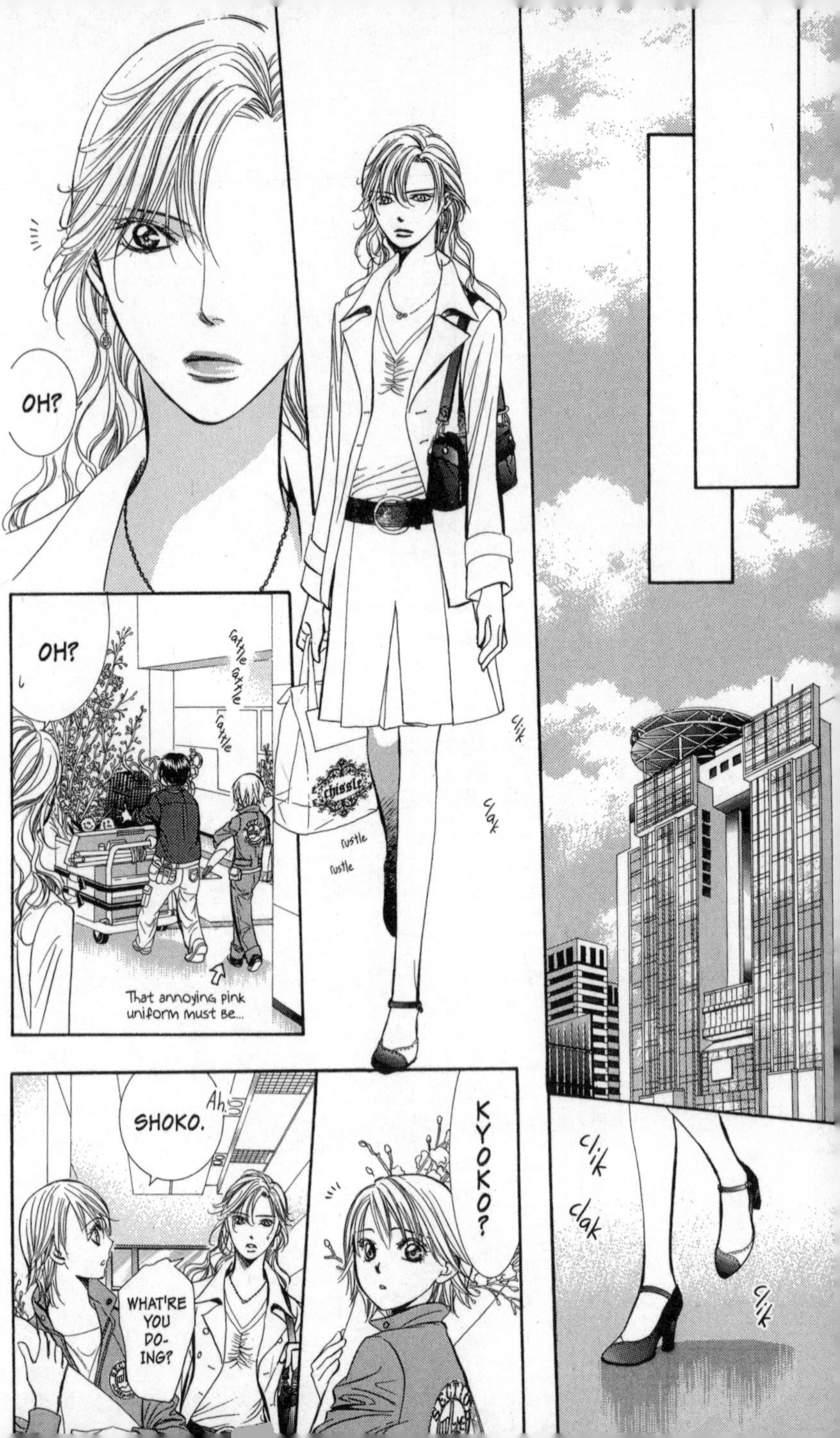
clik
clak
clik
clik
clak
rustle
rustle
OH?
OH?
rattle rattle
rattle
That annoying pink uniform must be...
KYOKO?
Ah.
SHOKO.
WHAT'RE YOU DOING?

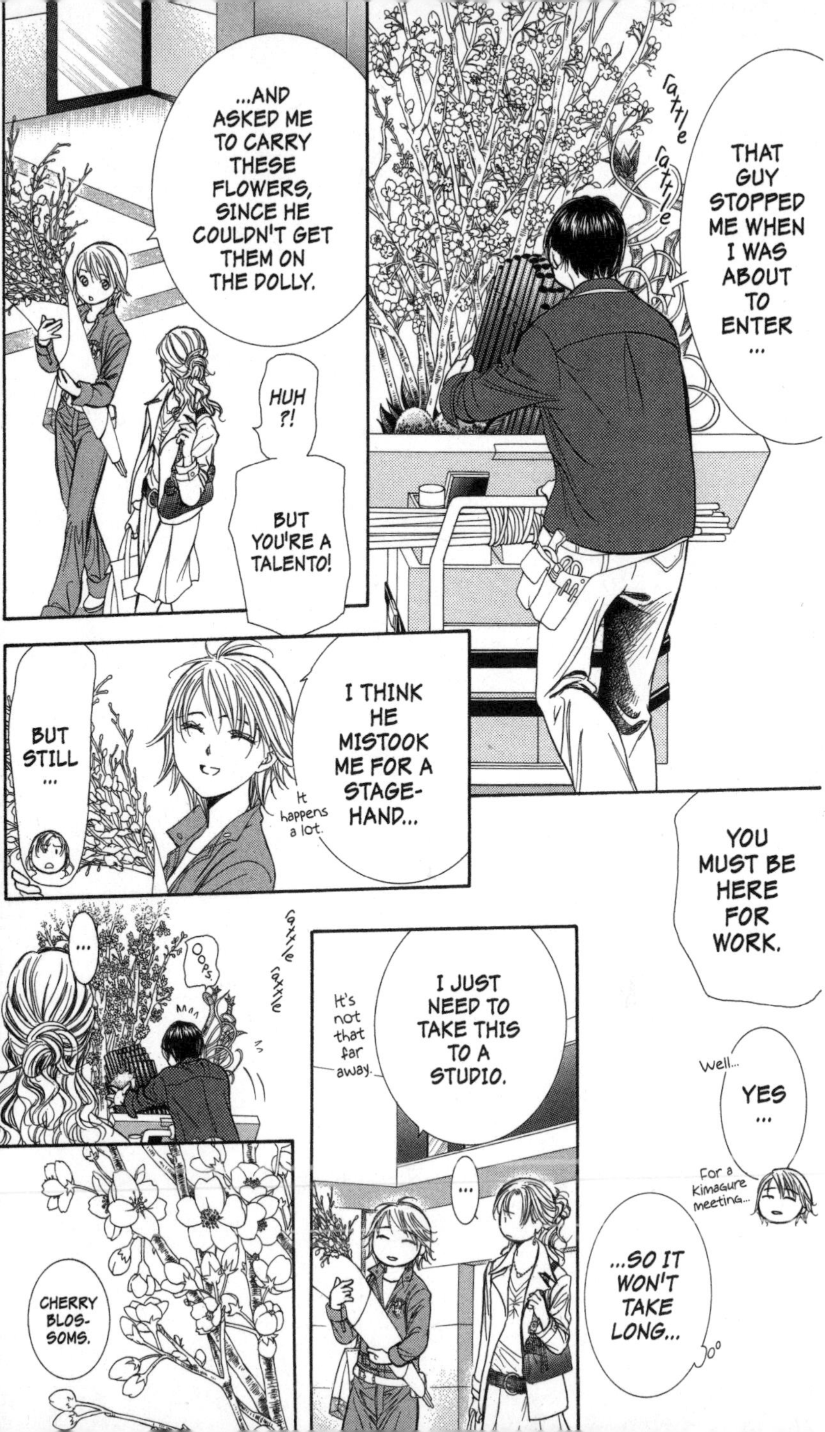
rattle rattle
THAT GUY STOPPED ME WHEN I WAS ABOUT TO ENTER...
...AND ASKED ME TO CARRY THESE FLOWERS, SINCE HE COULDN'T GET THEM ON THE DOLLY.
HUH?!
BUT YOU'RE A TALENTO!
I THINK HE MISTOOK ME FOR A STAGE-HAND...
It happens a lot.
BUT STILL...
YOU MUST BE HERE FOR WORK.
Well...
YES...
For a Kimagure meeting...
...SO IT WON'T TAKE LONG...
I JUST NEED TO TAKE THIS TO A STUDIO.
It's not that far away.
...
...
Oops.
rattle rattle
CHERRY BLOSSOMS.

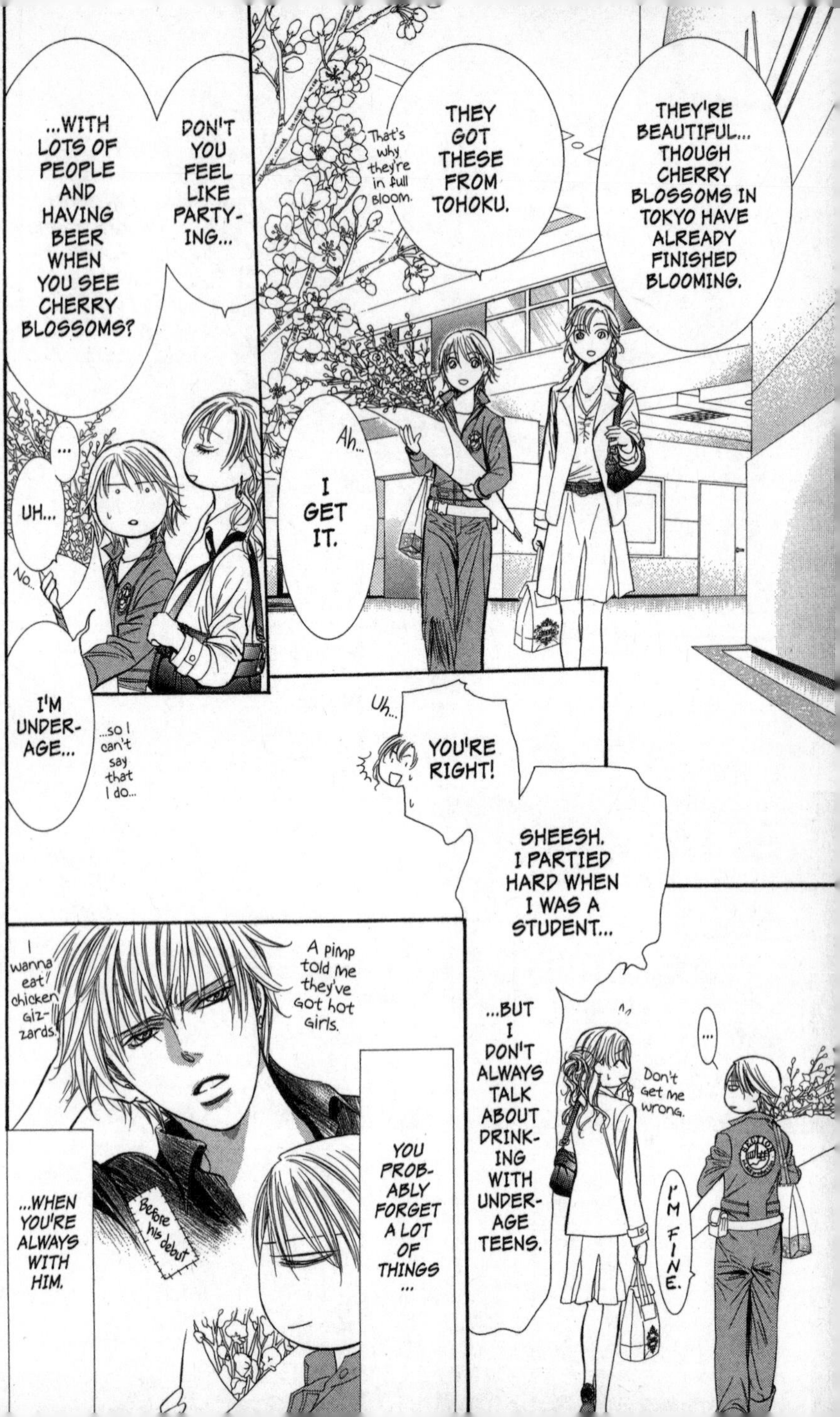
THEY'RE BEAUTIFUL... THOUGH CHERRY BLOSSOMS IN TOKYO HAVE ALREADY FINISHED BLOOMING.
THEY GOT THESE FROM TOHOKU.
That's why they're in full bloom.
Ah...
I GET IT.
DON'T YOU FEEL LIKE PARTY-ING...
...WITH LOTS OF PEOPLE AND HAVING BEER WHEN YOU SEE CHERRY BLOSSOMS?
...
UH...
No...
I'M UNDER-AGE...
...so I can't say that I do...
Uh...
YOU'RE RIGHT!
SHEESH. I PARTIED HARD WHEN I WAS A STUDENT...
...BUT I DON'T ALWAYS TALK ABOUT DRINK-ING WITH UNDER-AGE TEENS.
Don't get me wrong.
...
I'M FINE.
YOU PROB-ABLY FORGET A LOT OF THINGS ...
...WHEN YOU'RE ALWAYS WITH HIM.
A pimp told me they've got hot girls.
I wanna eat chicken giz-zards.
Before his debut

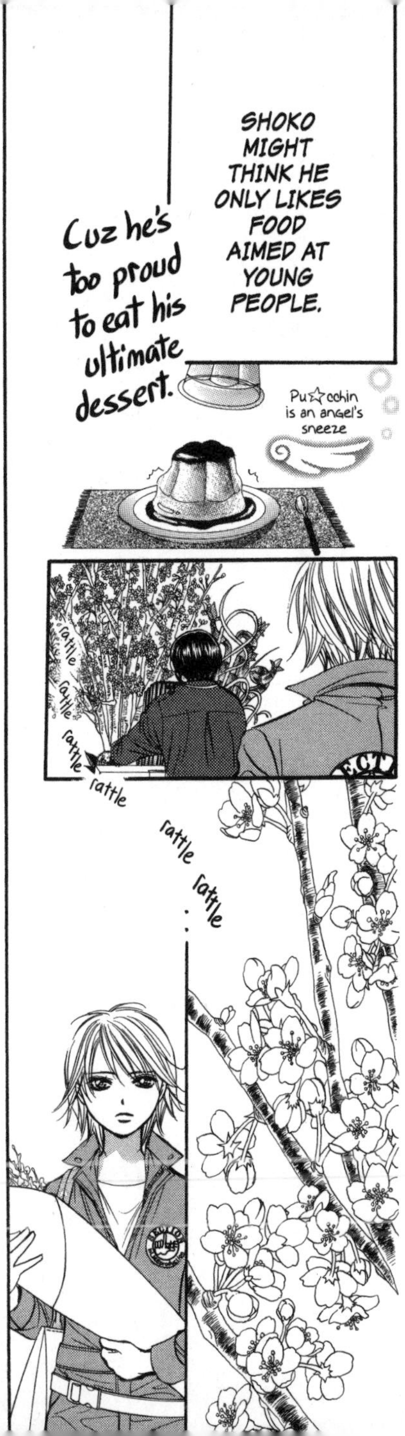
SHOKO MIGHT THINK HE ONLY LIKES FOOD AIMED AT YOUNG PEOPLE.
Cuz he's too proud to eat his ultimate dessert.
Pu☆cchin is an angel's sneeze
rattle rattle rattle rattle
rattle rattle

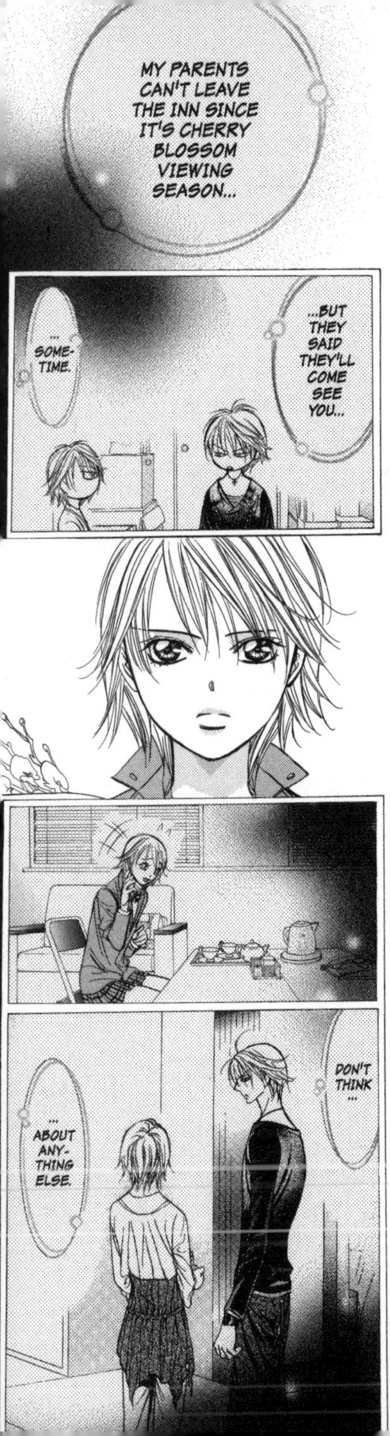
MY PARENTS CAN'T LEAVE THE INN SINCE IT'S CHERRY BLOSSOM VIEWING SEASON...
...BUT THEY SAID THEY'LL COME SEE YOU...
...SOME-TIME.
DON'T THINK...
...ABOUT ANY-THING ELSE.

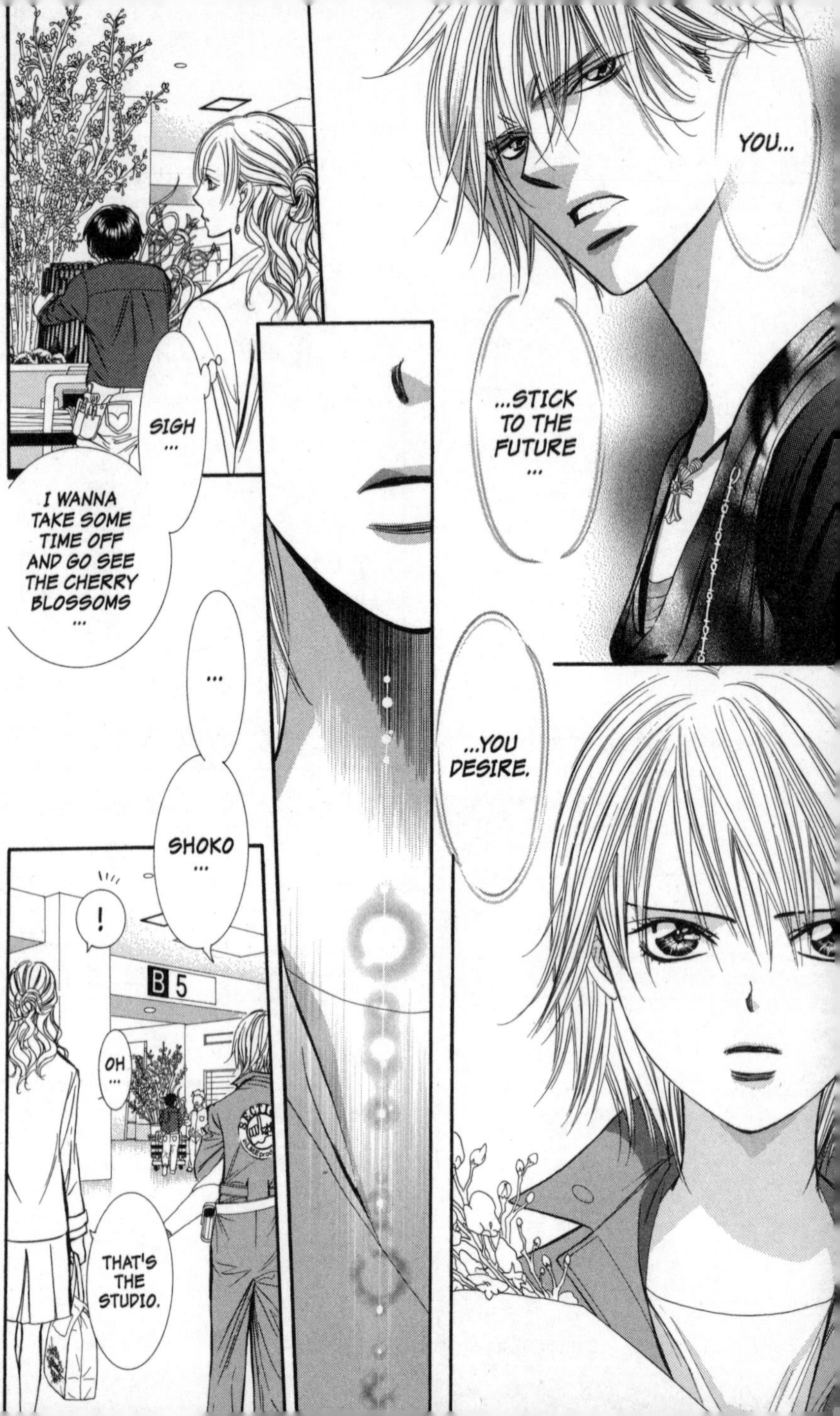
YOU...
...STICK TO THE FUTURE ...
...YOU DESIRE.
SIGH ...
I WANNA TAKE SOME TIME OFF AND GO SEE THE CHERRY BLOSSOMS ...
...
SHOKO ...
!
OH ...
THAT'S THE STUDIO.

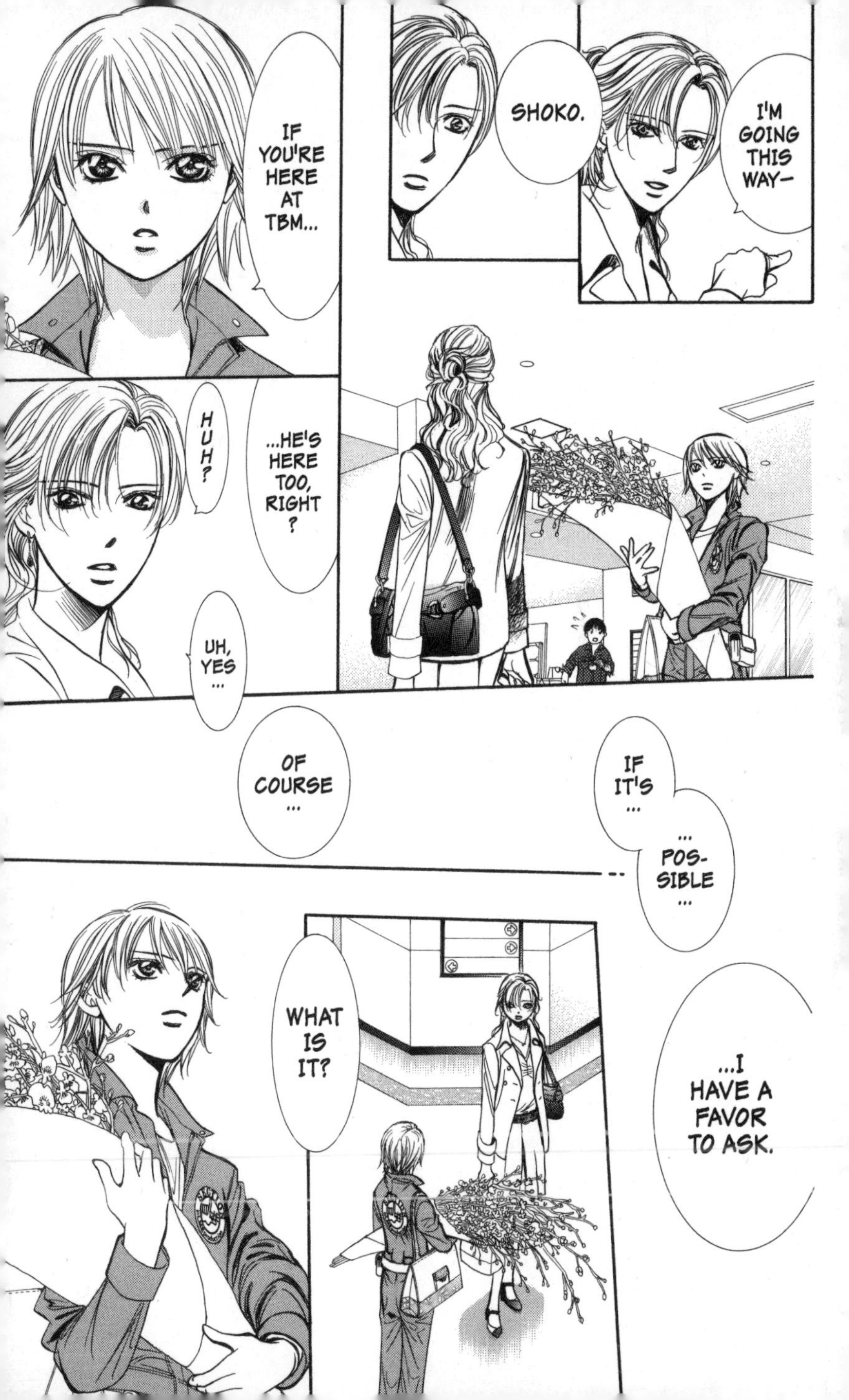
I'M GOING THIS WAY—
SHOKO.
IF YOU'RE HERE AT TBM...
...HE'S HERE TOO, RIGHT?
HUH?
UH, YES...
IF IT'S...
...POS-SIBLE...
OF COURSE...
...I HAVE A FAVOR TO ASK.
WHAT IS IT?

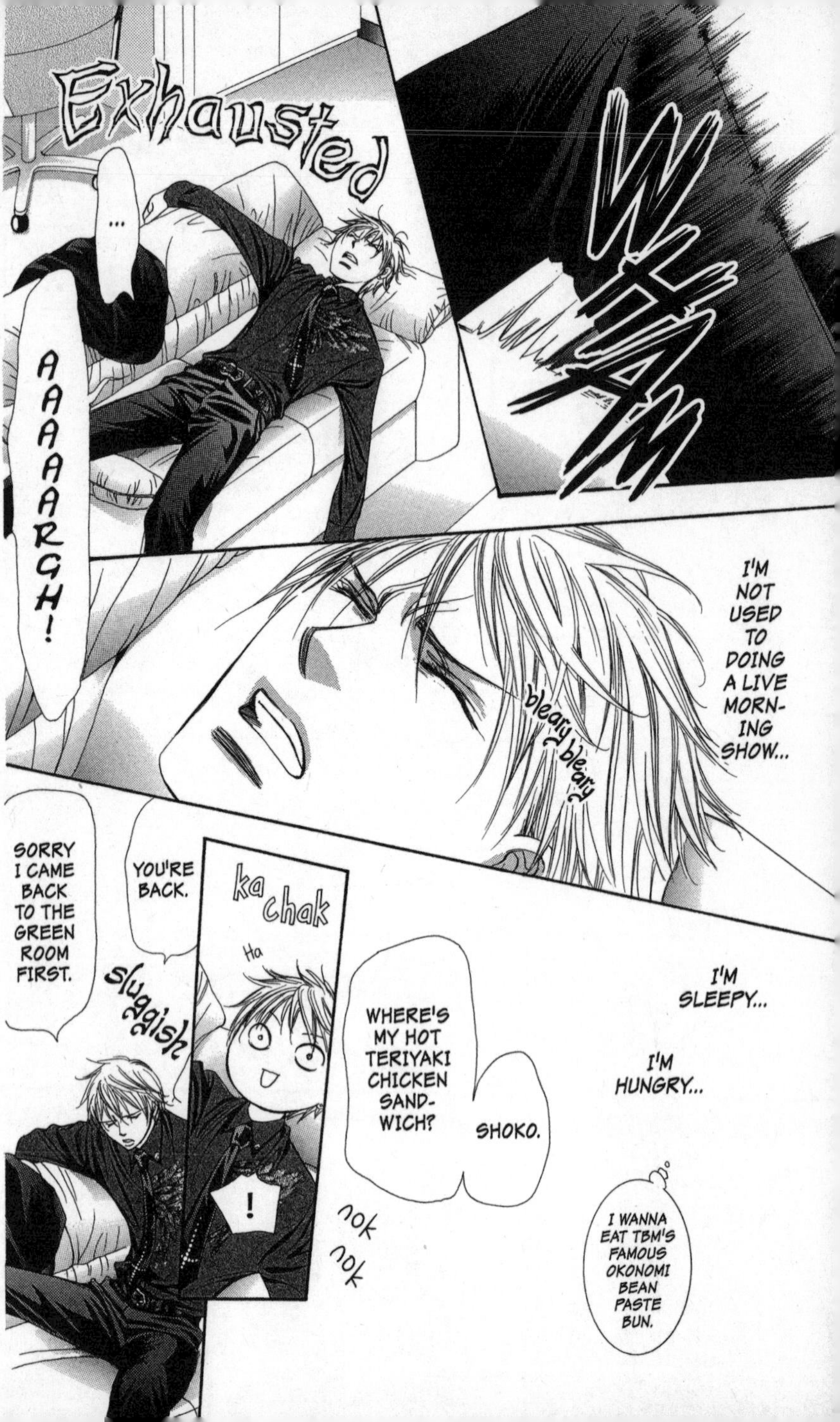
WHAM
Exhausted
...
AAAAAARGH!
bleary bleary
I'M NOT USED TO DOING A LIVE MORNING-SHOW...
I'M SLEEPY...
I'M HUNGRY...
I WANNA EAT TBM'S FAMOUS OKONOMI BEAN PASTE BUN.
ka chak
Ha
SHOKO.
WHERE'S MY HOT TERIYAKI CHICKEN SAND-WICH?
!
nok nok
YOU'RE BACK.
SORRY I CAME BACK TO THE GREEN ROOM FIRST.
sluggish

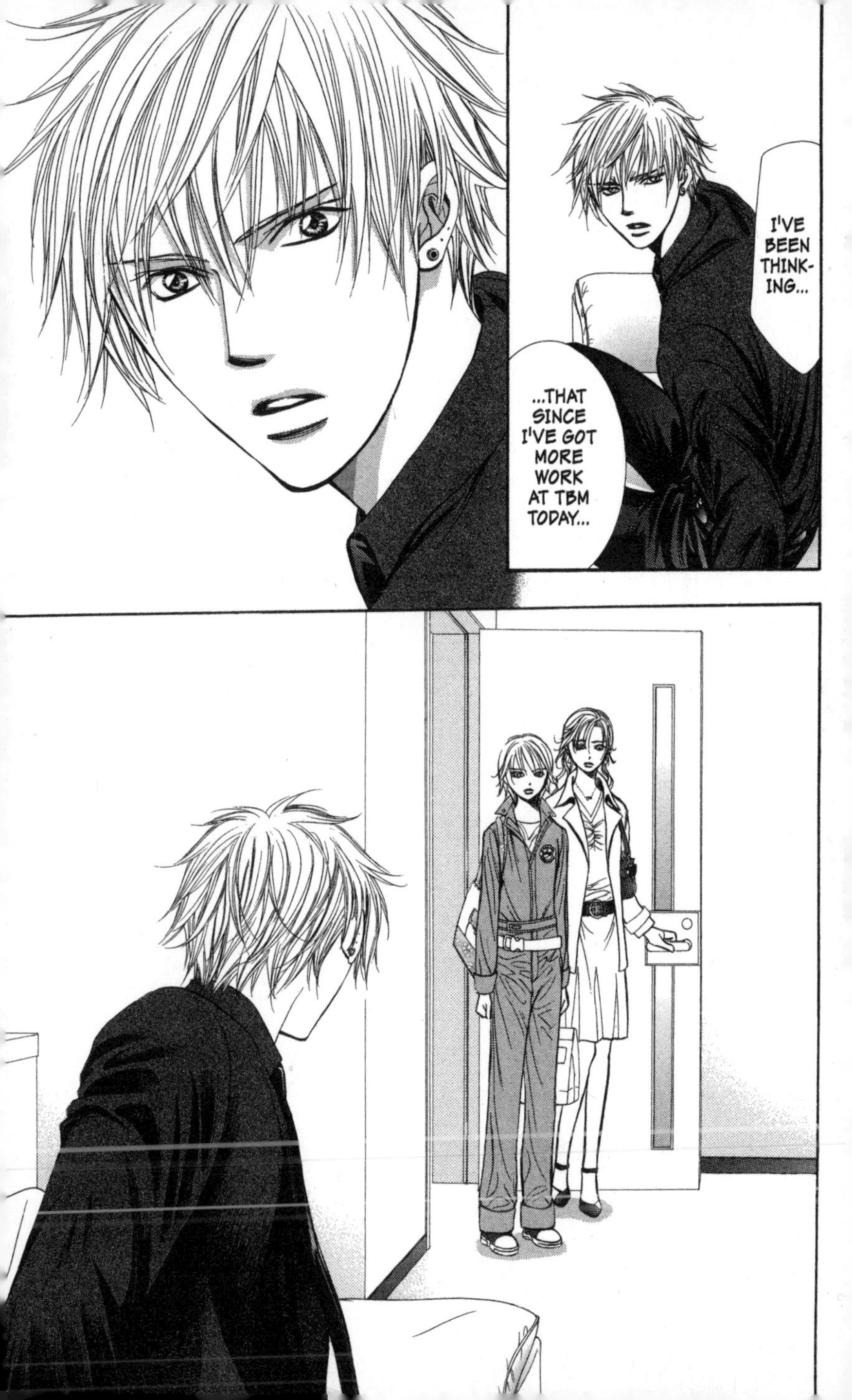
I'VE BEEN THINKING...
...THAT SINCE I'VE GOT MORE WORK AT TBM TODAY...

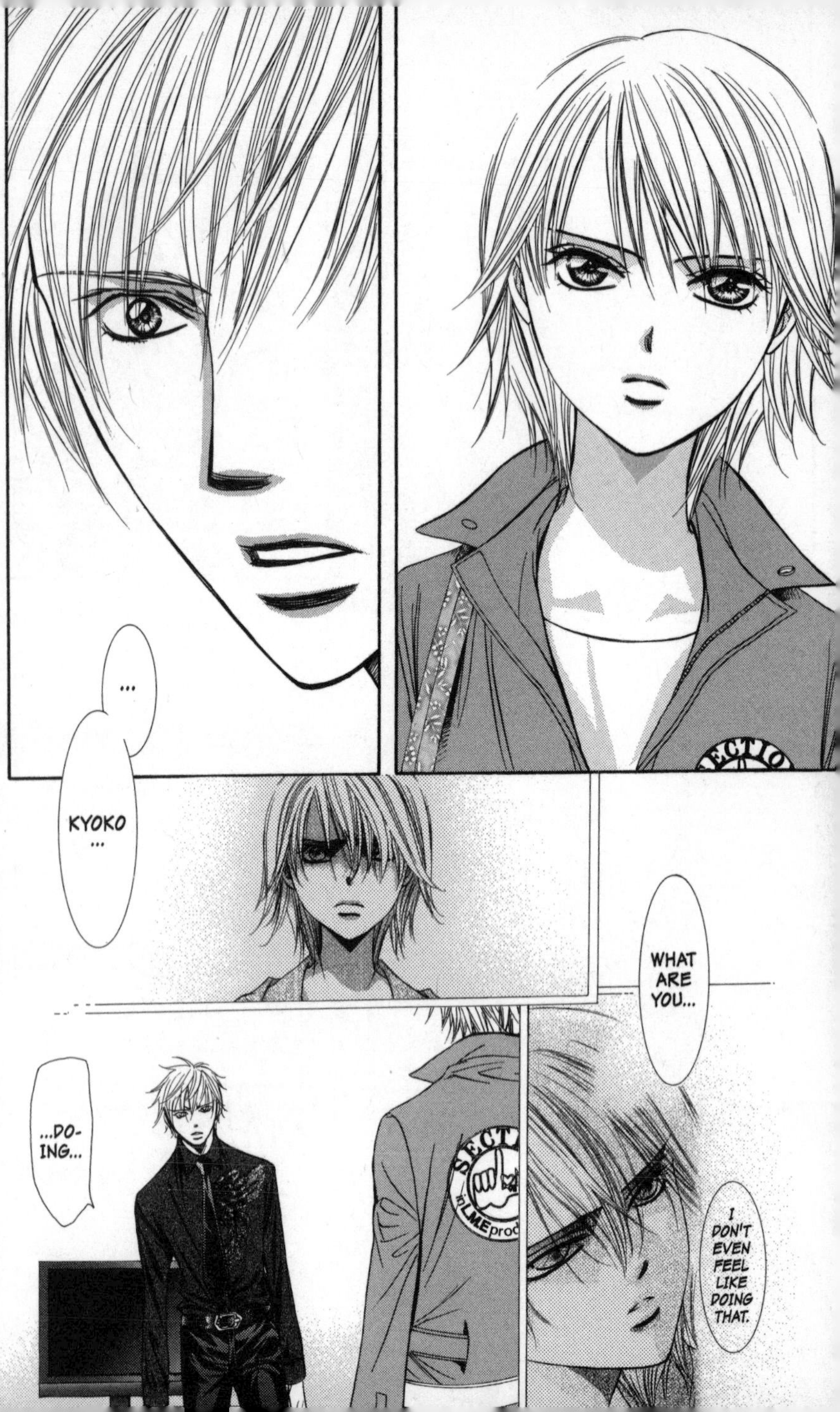
...
KYOKO ...
WHAT ARE YOU...
...DO-ING...
I DON'T EVEN FEEL LIKE DOING THAT.

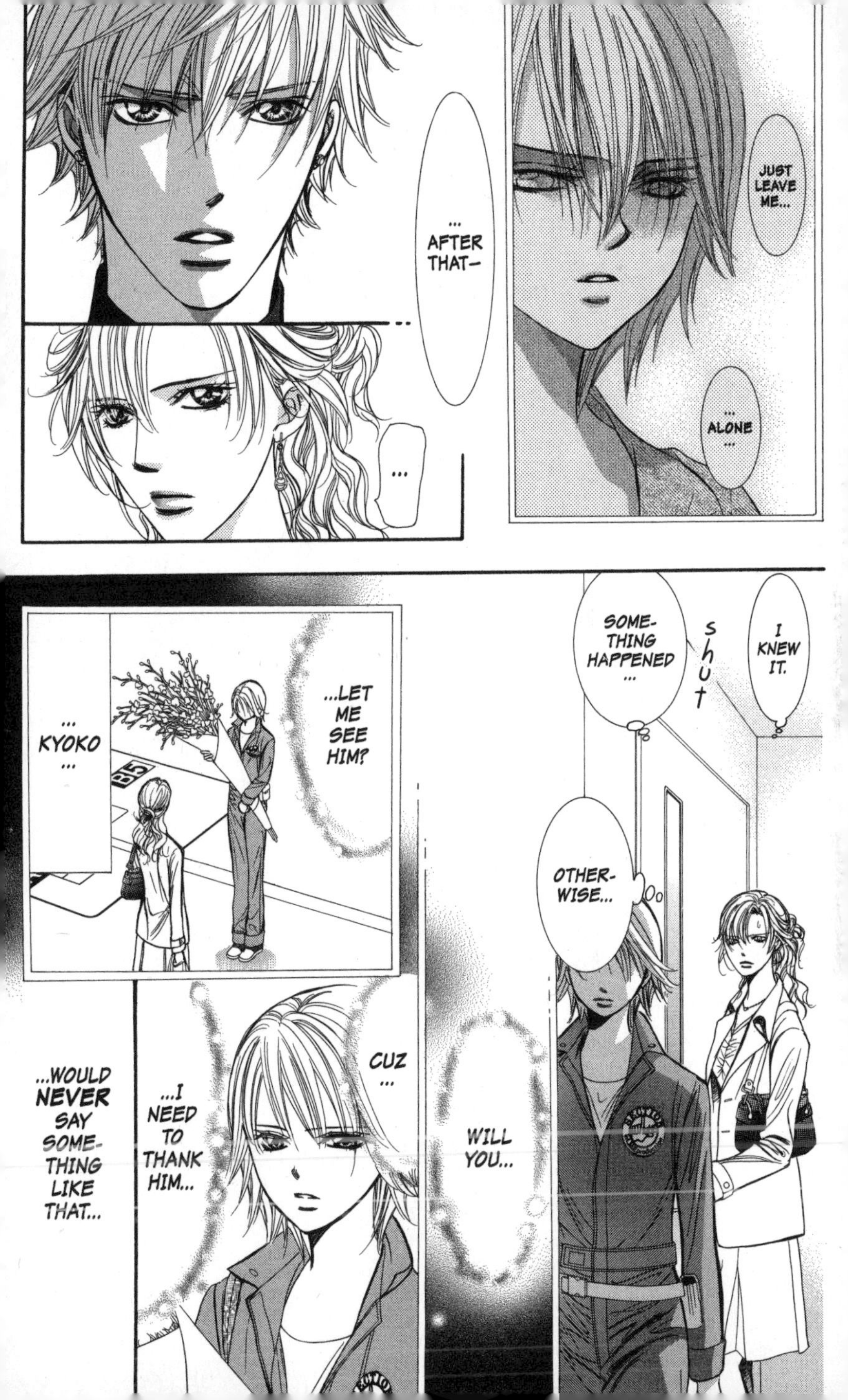
JUST LEAVE ME...
...ALONE...
...AFTER THAT—
...
I KNEW IT.
shut
SOME-THING HAPPENED...
OTHER-WISE...
WILL YOU...
...LET ME SEE HIM?
...KYOKO...
CUZ...
...I NEED TO THANK HIM...
...WOULD NEVER SAY SOME-THING LIKE THAT...

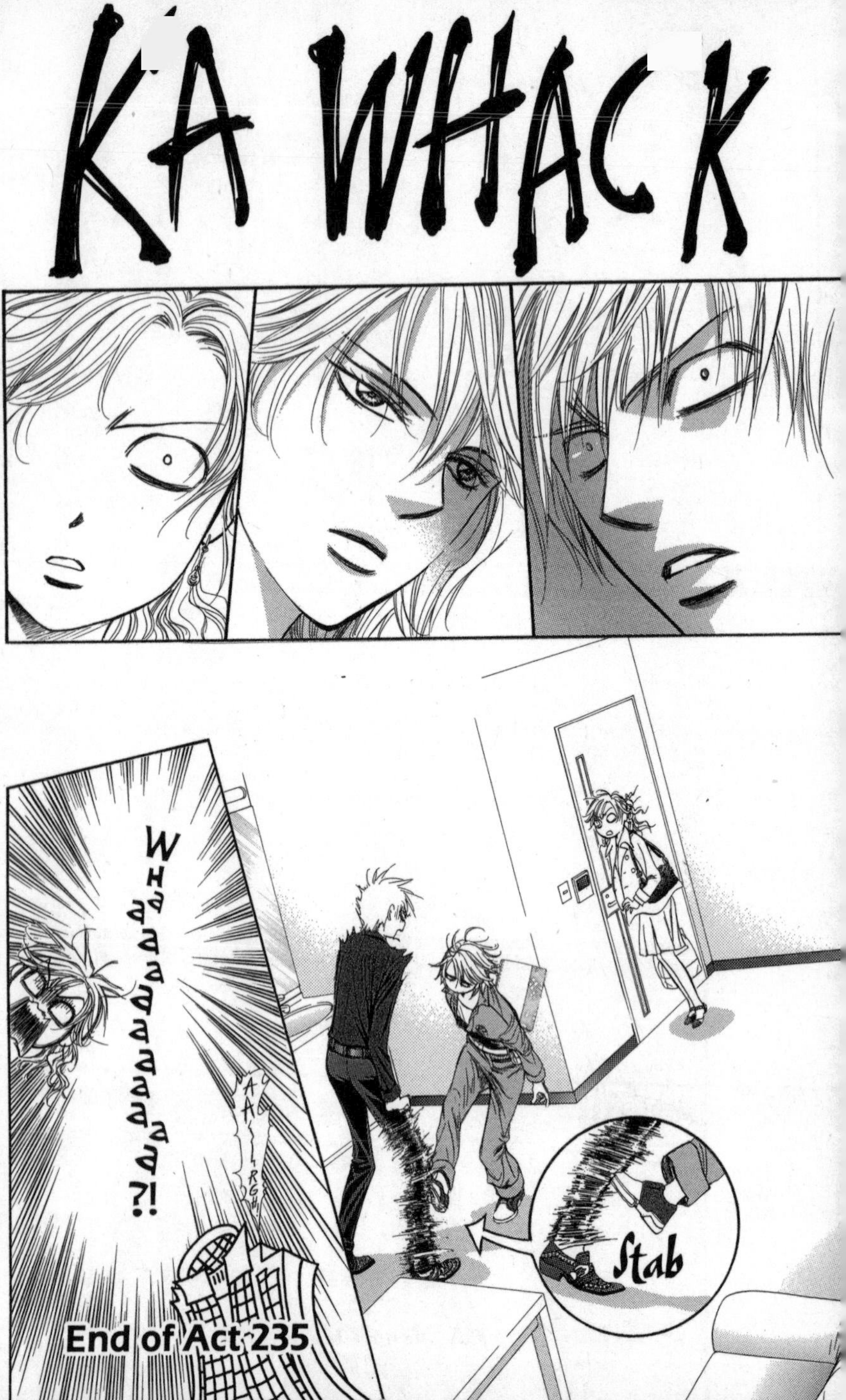
KA WHACK
Stab
AARGH!
Whaaaaaaaaaaa?!
End of Act 235

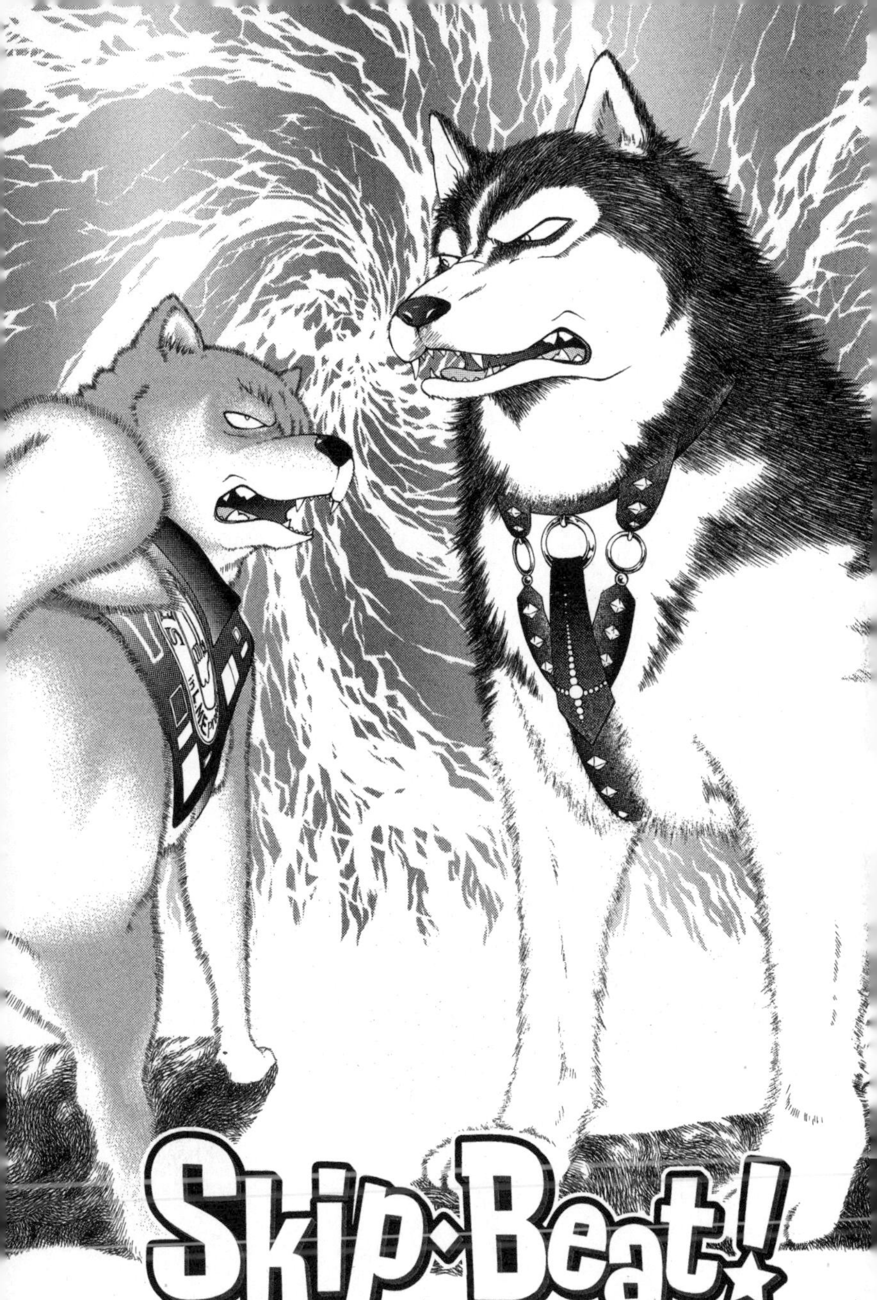
Skip·Beat!

Act 236: Howling Ambition

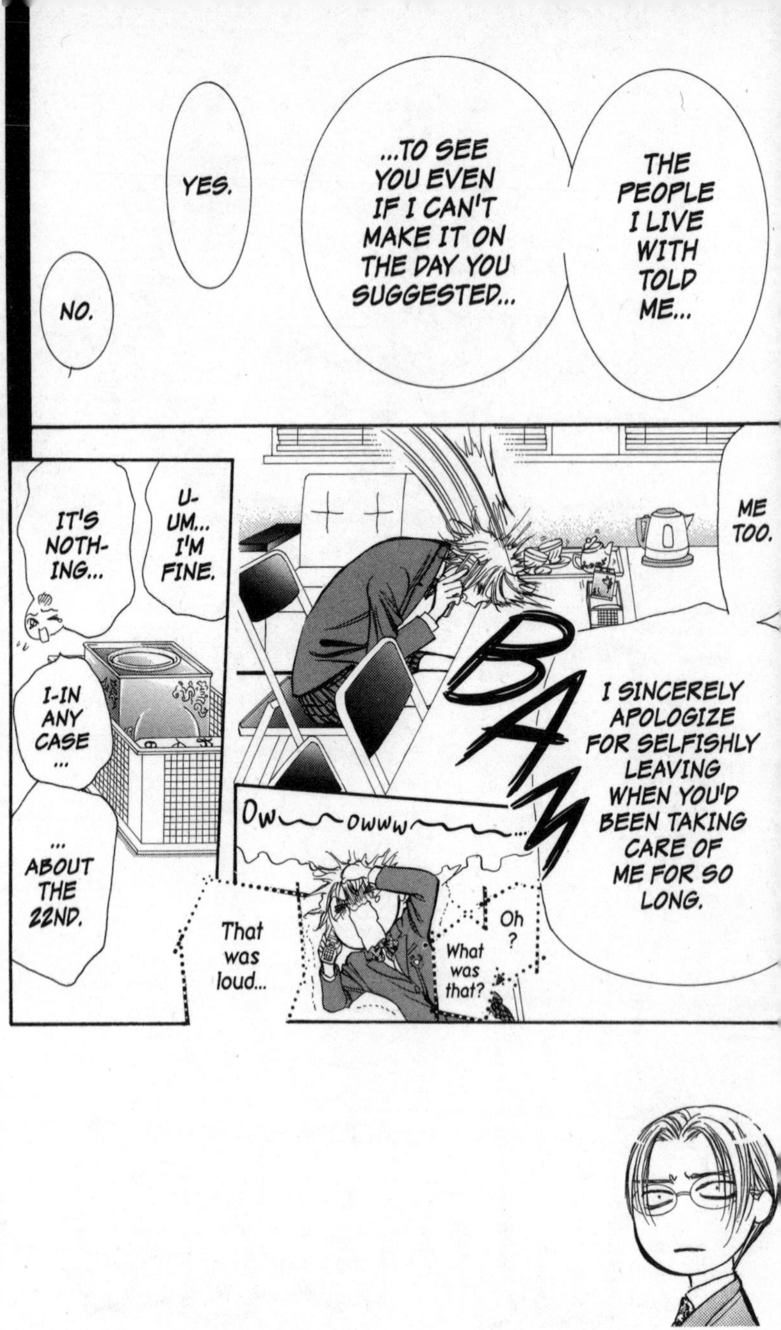
THE PEOPLE I LIVE WITH TOLD ME...
...TO SEE YOU EVEN IF I CAN'T MAKE IT ON THE DAY YOU SUGGESTED...
YES.
NO.
ME TOO.
I SINCERELY APOLOGIZE FOR SELFISHLY LEAVING WHEN YOU'D BEEN TAKING CARE OF ME FOR SO LONG.
BAM
Ow~~owww~~...
Oh?
What was that?
That was loud...
U-UM... I'M FINE.
IT'S NOTHING...
I-IN ANY CASE...
...ABOUT THE 22ND.

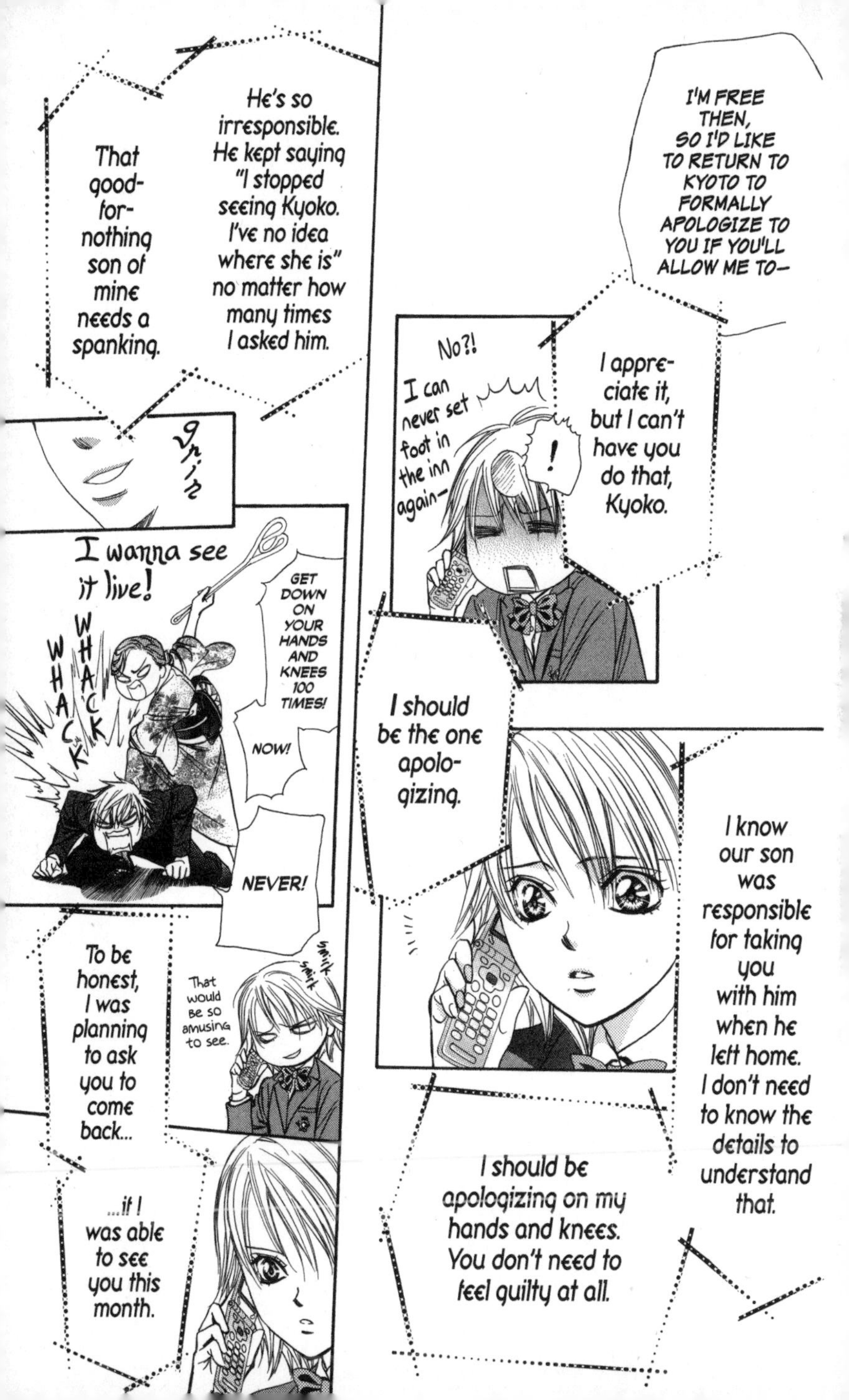
I'M FREE THEN, SO I'D LIKE TO RETURN TO KYOTO TO FORMALLY APOLOGIZE TO YOU IF YOU'LL ALLOW ME TO—
I appreciate it, but I can't have you do that, Kyoko.
!
No?!
I can never set foot in the inn again—
I should be the one apologizing.
I know our son was responsible for taking you with him when he left home. I don't need to know the details to understand that.
I should be apologizing on my hands and knees. You don't need to feel guilty at all.
He's so irresponsible. He kept saying "I stopped seeing Kyoko. I've no idea where she is" no matter how many times I asked him.
That good-for-nothing son of mine needs a spanking.
grin
GET DOWN ON YOUR HANDS AND KNEES 100 TIMES!
I wanna see it live!
WHACK
WHACK
NOW!
NEVER!
To be honest, I was planning to ask you to come back...
smirk smirk
That would be so amusing to see.
...if I was able to see you this month.

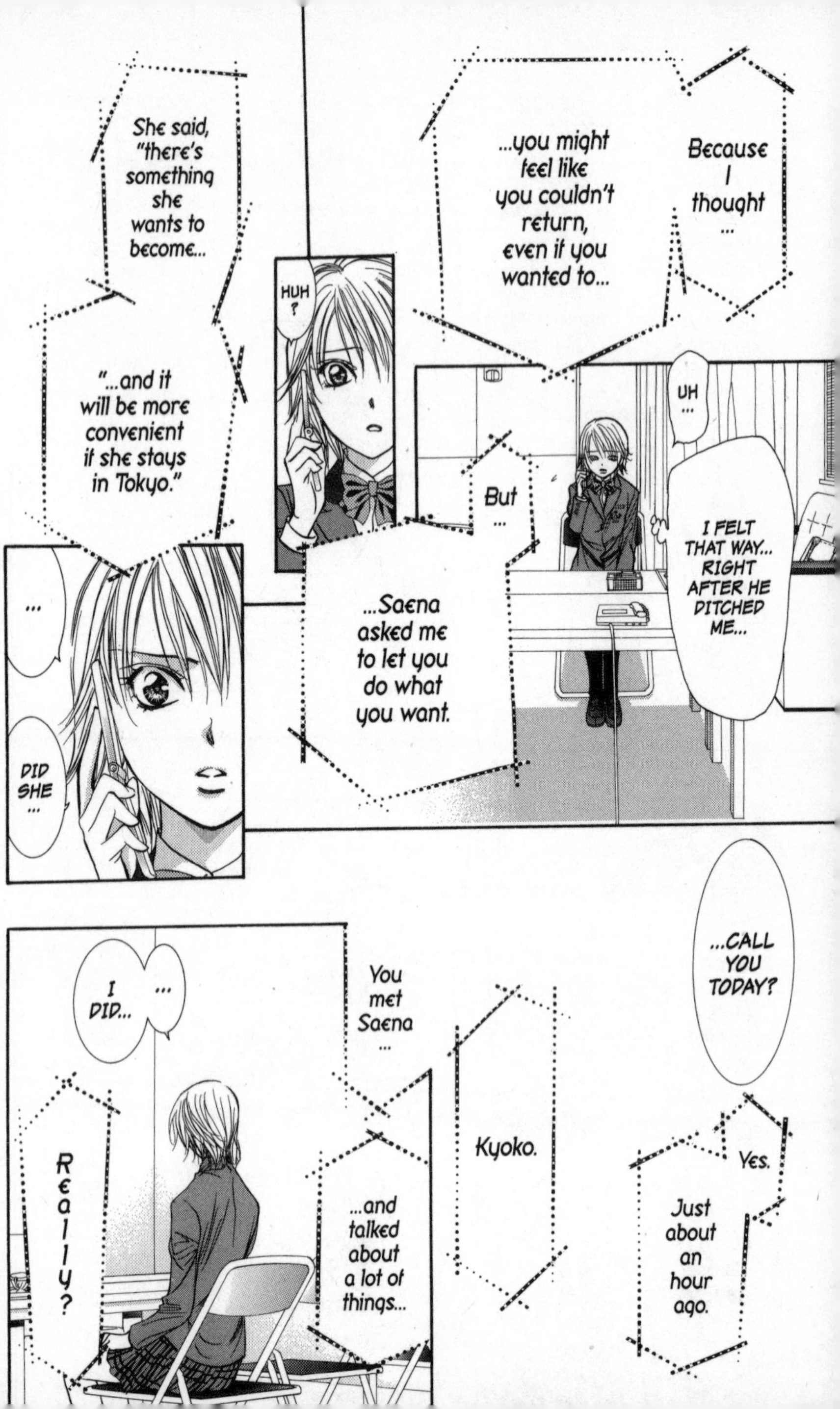

Because I thought...
...you might feel like you couldn't return, even if you wanted to...
HUH?
She said, "there's something she wants to become...
"...and it will be more convenient if she stays in Tokyo."
UH...
I FELT THAT WAY... RIGHT AFTER HE DITCHED ME...
But...
...Saena asked me to let you do what you want.
...
DID SHE...
...CALL YOU TODAY?
Yes.
Just about an hour ago.
Kyoko.
You met Saena...
...and talked about a lot of things...
I DID...
...
Really?

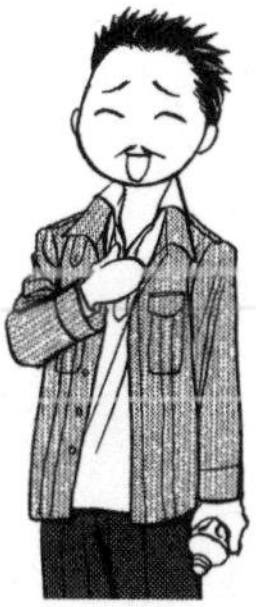

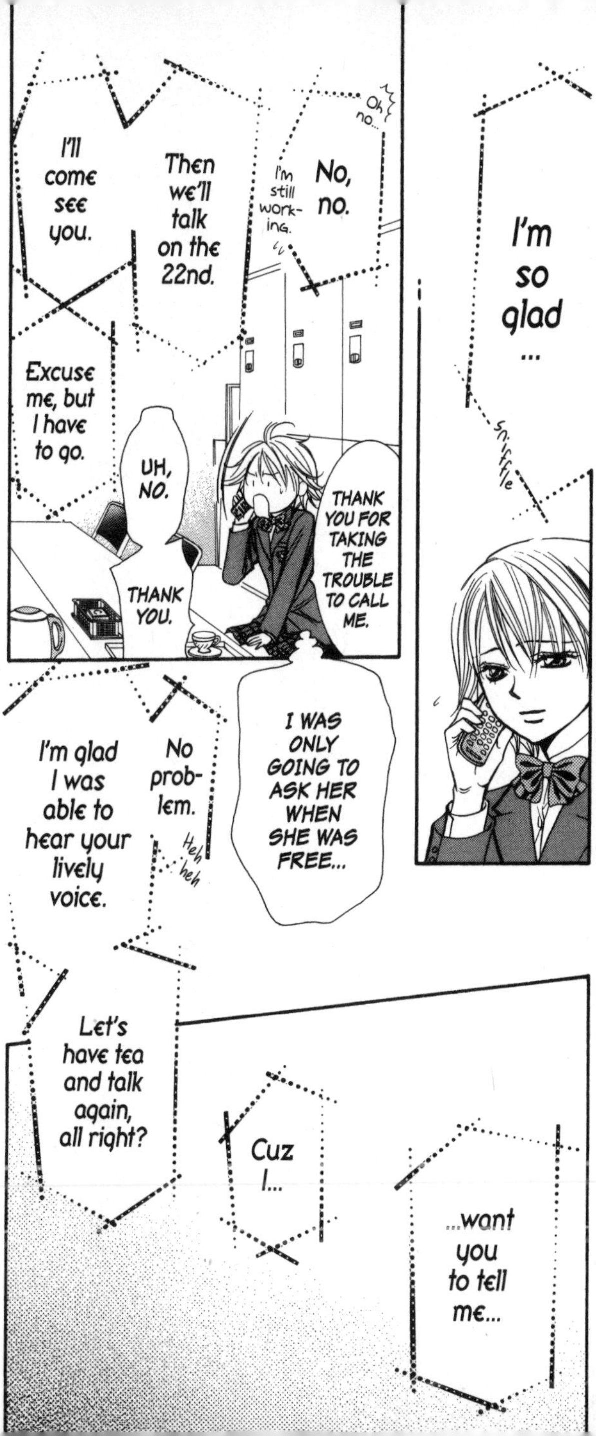

I'm so glad...
sniffle
Oh no...
No, no.
I'm still working.
Then we'll talk on the 22nd.
I'll come see you.
THANK YOU FOR TAKING THE TROUBLE TO CALL ME.
UH, NO.
THANK YOU.
Excuse me, but I have to go.
I WAS ONLY GOING TO ASK HER WHEN SHE WAS FREE...
No prob-lem.
Heh heh
I'm glad I was able to hear your lively voice.
Let's have tea and talk again, all right?
Cuz I...
...want you to tell me...

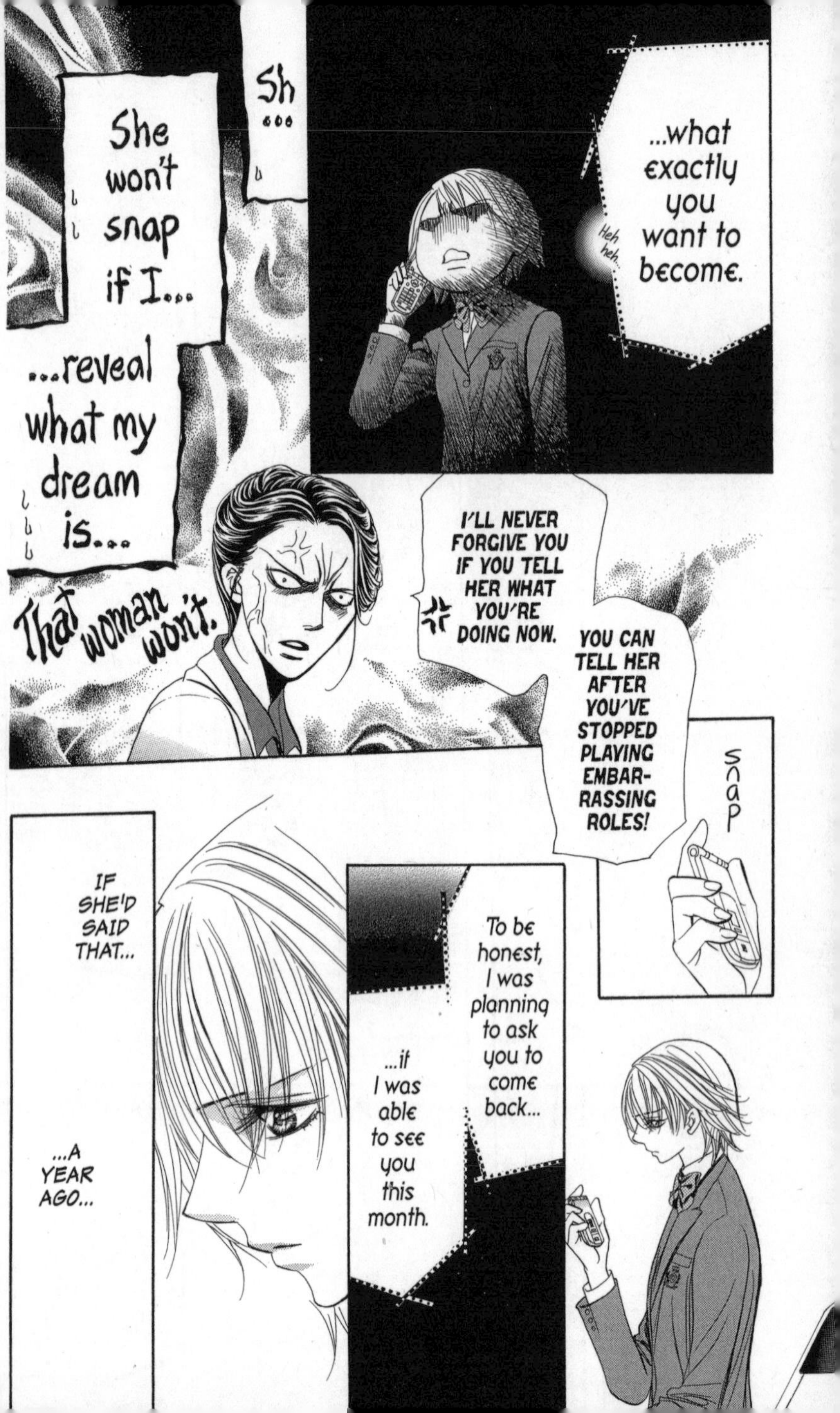
...what exactly you want to become.
Heh heh.
Sh...
She won't snap if I...
...reveal what my dream is...
That woman won't.
I'LL NEVER FORGIVE YOU IF YOU TELL HER WHAT YOU'RE DOING NOW.
YOU CAN TELL HER AFTER YOU'VE STOPPED PLAYING EMBARRASSING ROLES!
Snap
To be honest, I was planning to ask you to come back...
...if I was able to see you this month.
IF SHE'D SAID THAT...
...A YEAR AGO...

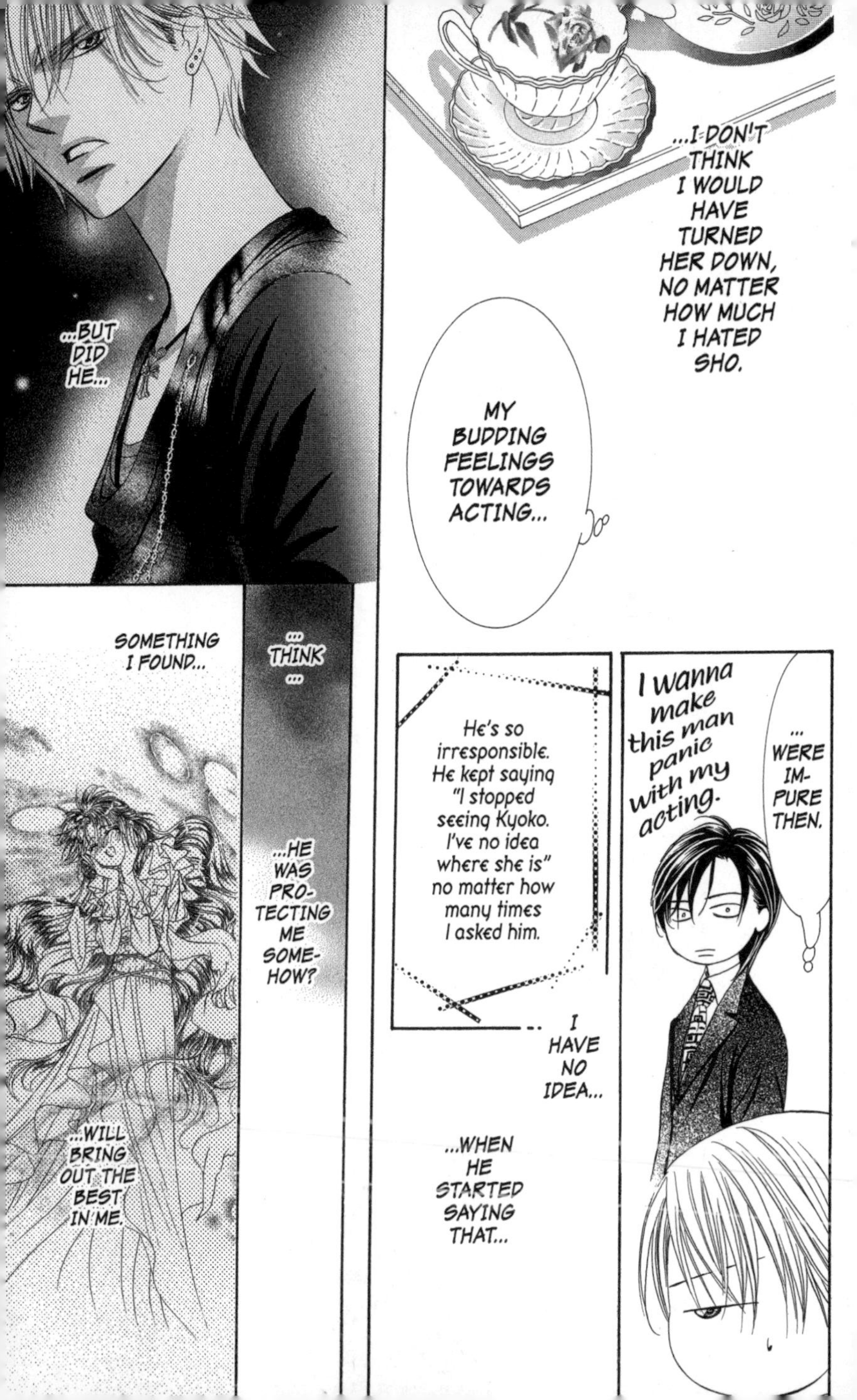

...I DON'T THINK I WOULD HAVE TURNED HER DOWN, NO MATTER HOW MUCH I HATED SHO.
MY BUDDING FEELINGS TOWARDS ACTING...
...WERE IMPURE THEN.
I wanna make this man panic with my acting.
He's so irresponsible. He kept saying "I stopped seeing Kyoko. I've no idea where she is" no matter how many times I asked him.
I HAVE NO IDEA...
...WHEN HE STARTED SAYING THAT...
...BUT DID HE...
...THINK...
...HE WAS PROTECTING ME SOMEHOW?
SOMETHING I FOUND...
...WILL BRING OUT THE BEST IN ME.

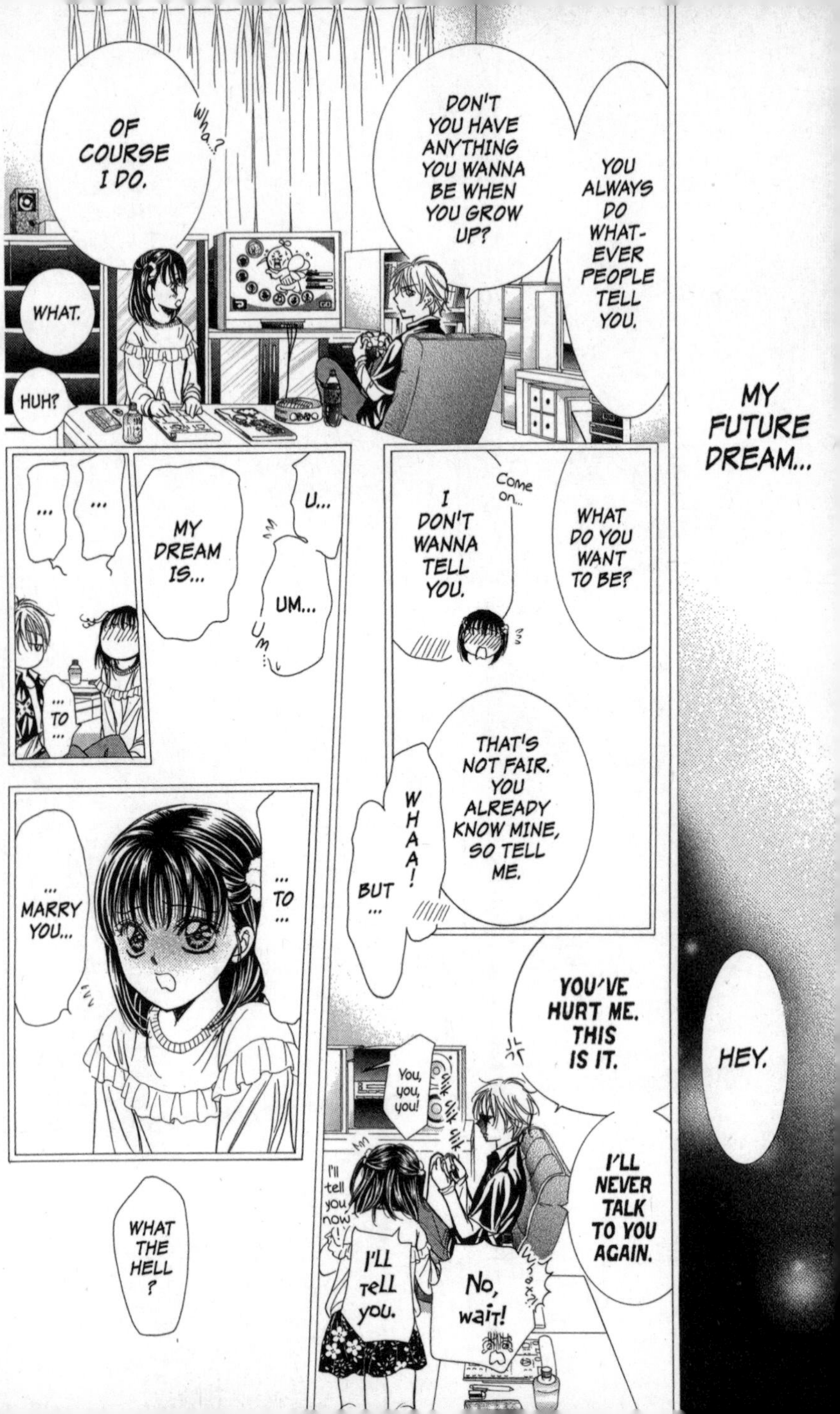
MY FUTURE DREAM...
HEY.
YOU ALWAYS DO WHATEVER PEOPLE TELL YOU.
DON'T YOU HAVE ANYTHING YOU WANNA BE WHEN YOU GROW UP?
Wha..?
OF COURSE I DO.
WHAT.
HUH?
WHAT DO YOU WANT TO BE?
Come on...
I DON'T WANNA TELL YOU.
THAT'S NOT FAIR. YOU ALREADY KNOW MINE, SO TELL ME.
WHAAA!
BUT...
U...
UM...
Um...
MY DREAM IS...
...
...
...TO...
YOU'VE HURT ME. THIS IS IT.
I'LL NEVER TALK TO YOU AGAIN.
You, you, you!
No, wait!
I'll tell you now!!
I'LL TELL YOU.
...TO...
...MARRY YOU...
WHAT THE HELL?

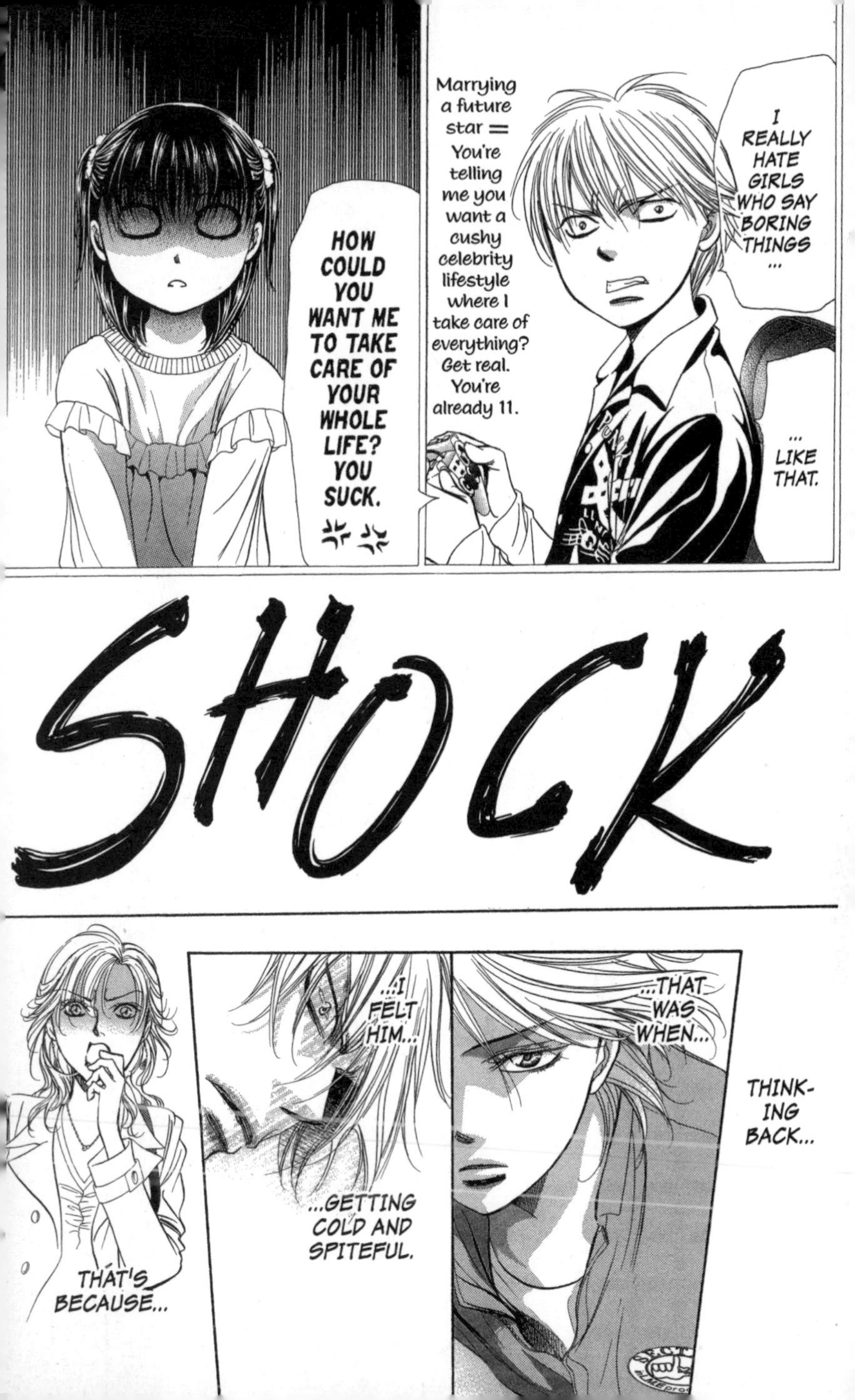
I REALLY HATE GIRLS WHO SAY BORING THINGS...
...LIKE THAT.
Marrying a future star = You're telling me you want a cushy celebrity lifestyle where I take care of everything? Get real. You're already 11.
HOW COULD YOU WANT ME TO TAKE CARE OF YOUR WHOLE LIFE? YOU SUCK.
SHOCK
THINKING BACK...
...THAT WAS WHEN...
...I FELT HIM...
...GETTING COLD AND SPITEFUL.
THAT'S BECAUSE...

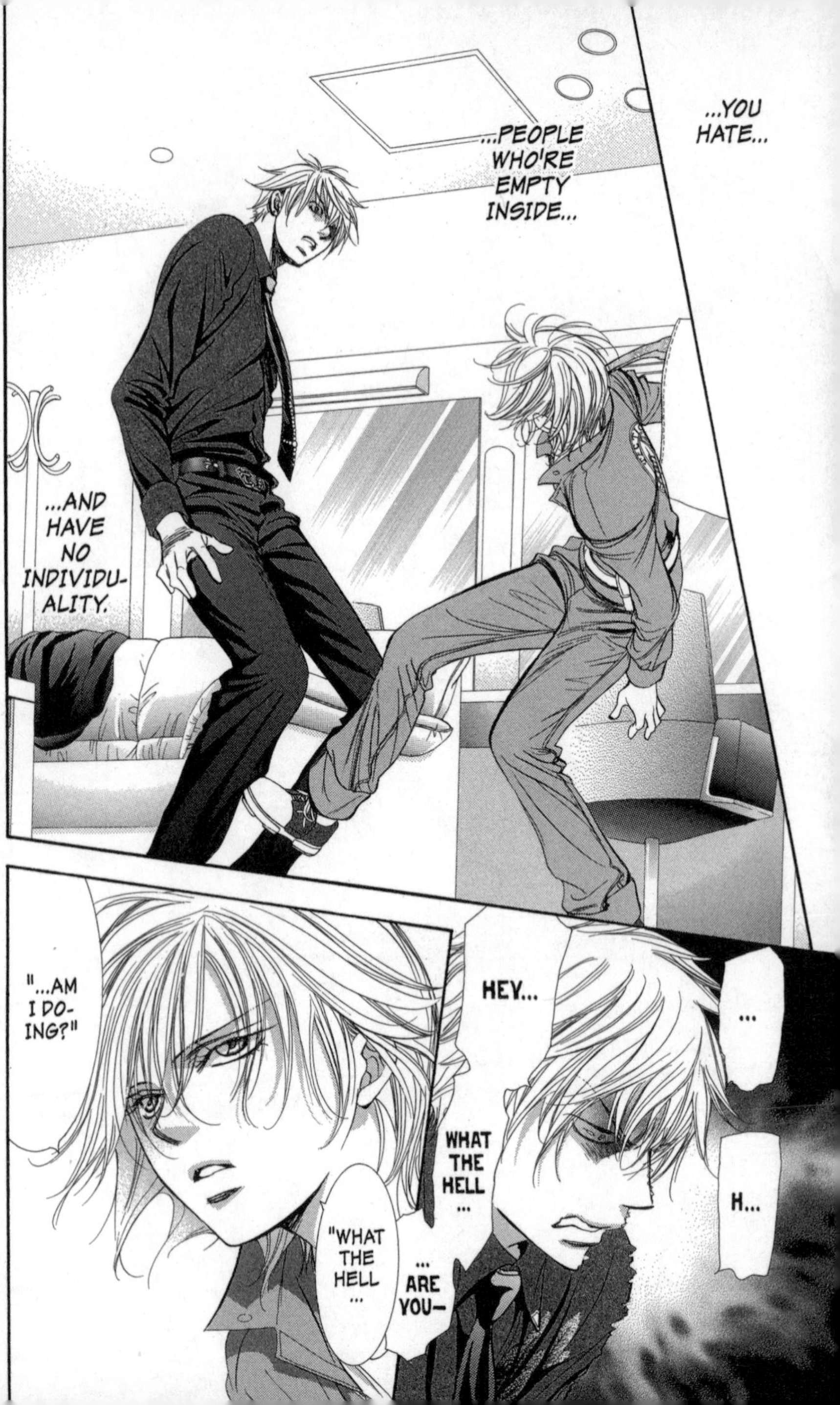
...YOU HATE...
...PEOPLE WHO'RE EMPTY INSIDE...
...AND HAVE NO INDIVIDUALITY.
...
H...
HEY...
WHAT THE HELL ...
... ARE YOU—
"WHAT THE HELL ...
"...AM I DOING?"

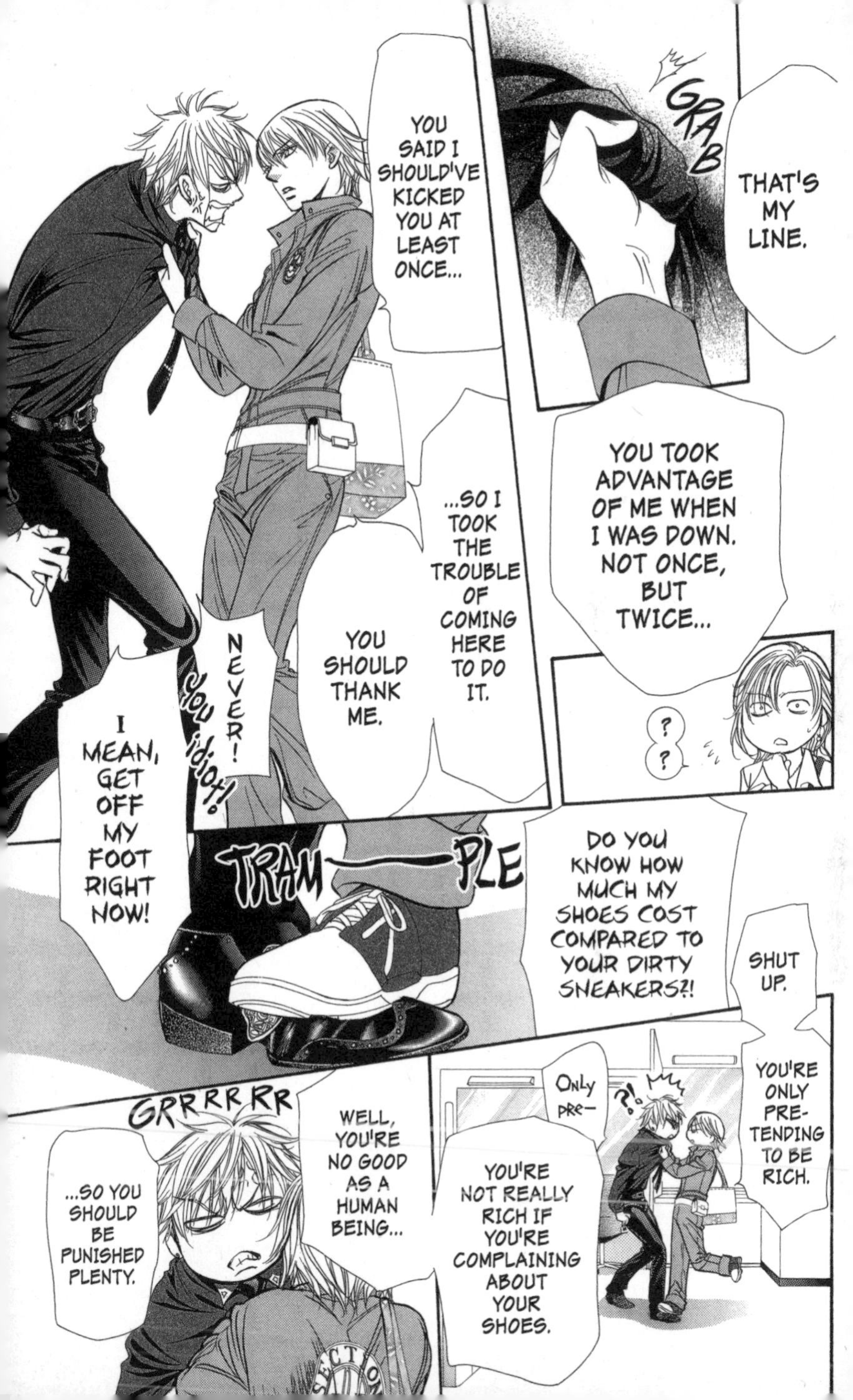
GRAB
THAT'S MY LINE.
YOU TOOK ADVANTAGE OF ME WHEN I WAS DOWN. NOT ONCE, BUT TWICE...
? ?
YOU SAID I SHOULD'VE KICKED YOU AT LEAST ONCE...
...SO I TOOK THE TROUBLE OF COMING HERE TO DO IT.
YOU SHOULD THANK ME.
NEVER!
You idiot!
I MEAN, GET OFF MY FOOT RIGHT NOW!
DO YOU KNOW HOW MUCH MY SHOES COST COMPARED TO YOUR DIRTY SNEAKERS?!
SHUT UP.
TRAM—PLE
YOU'RE ONLY PRE-TENDING TO BE RICH.
Only pre—
?!
GRRRRRR
YOU'RE NOT REALLY RICH IF YOU'RE COMPLAINING ABOUT YOUR SHOES.
WELL, YOU'RE NO GOOD AS A HUMAN BEING...
...SO YOU SHOULD BE PUNISHED PLENTY.

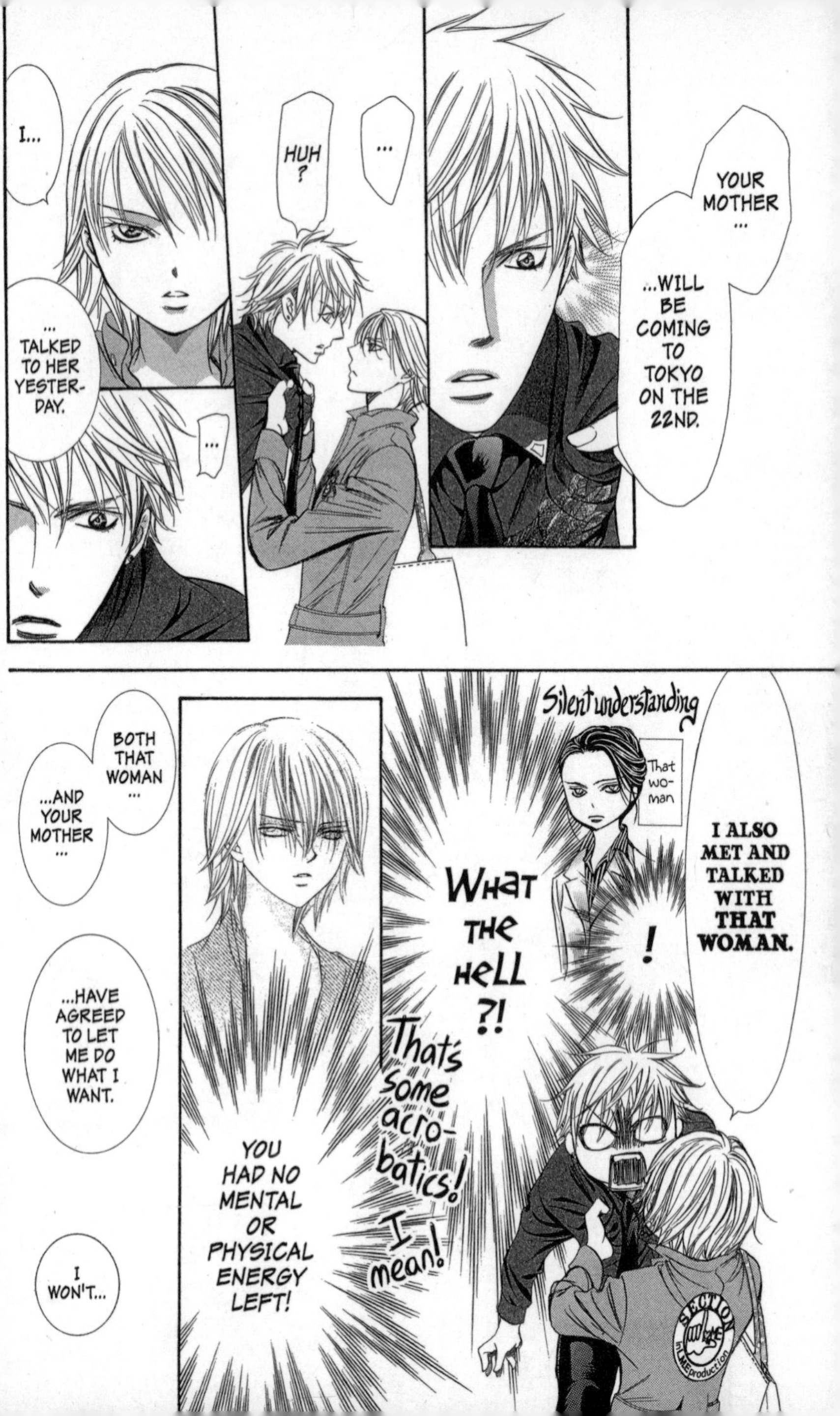
YOUR MOTHER ...
...WILL BE COMING TO TOKYO ON THE 22ND.
...
HUH?
I...
... TALKED TO HER YESTER-DAY.
...
I ALSO MET AND TALKED WITH THAT WOMAN.
Silent understanding
That wo-man
!
WHAT THE HELL?!
That's some acro-batics! I mean!
YOU HAD NO MENTAL OR PHYSICAL ENERGY LEFT!
BOTH THAT WOMAN ...
...AND YOUR MOTHER ...
...HAVE AGREED TO LET ME DO WHAT I WANT.
I WON'T...

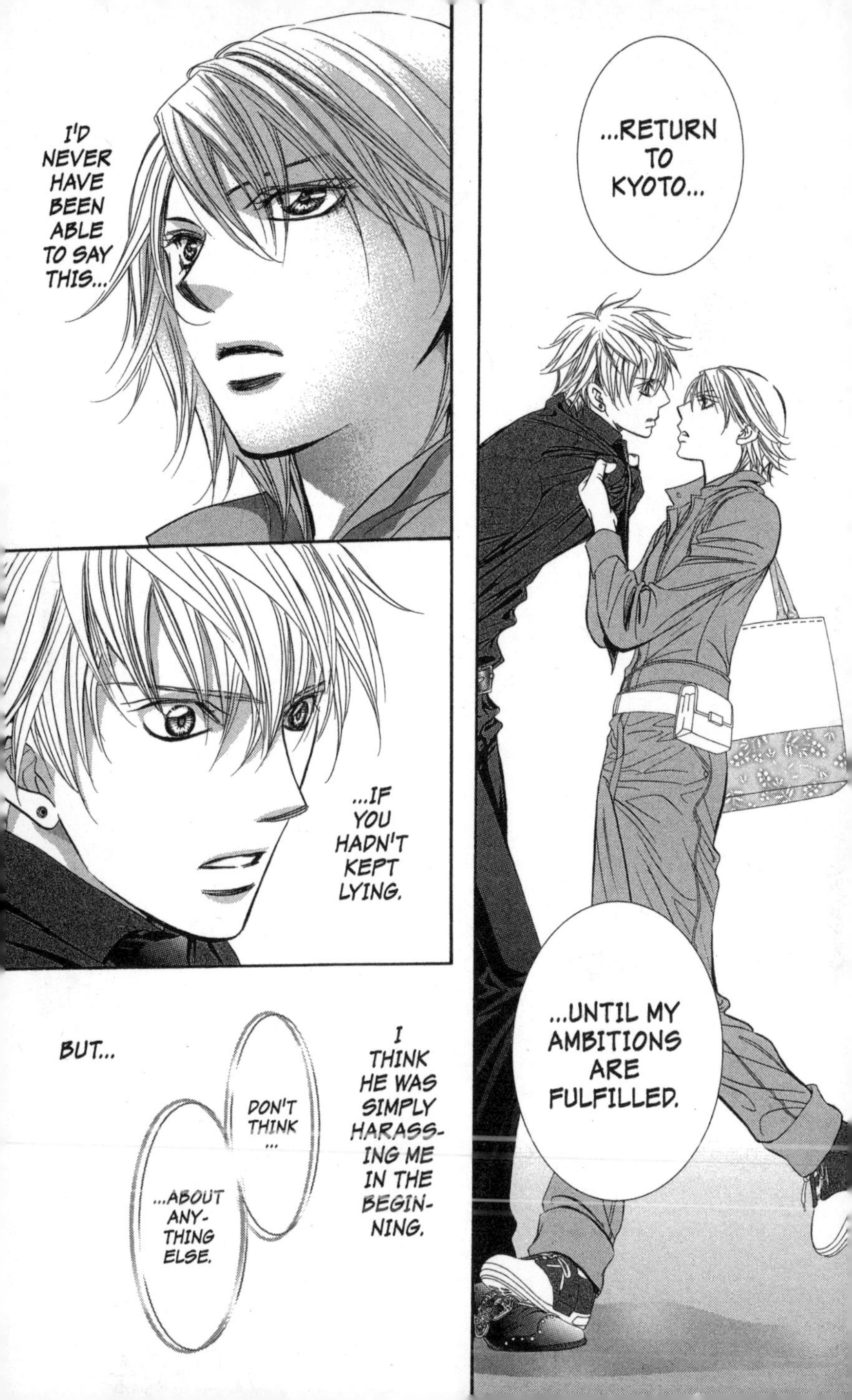
...RETURN TO KYOTO...
...UNTIL MY AMBITIONS ARE FULFILLED.
I'D NEVER HAVE BEEN ABLE TO SAY THIS...
...IF YOU HADN'T KEPT LYING.
I THINK HE WAS SIMPLY HARASS-ING ME IN THE BEGIN-NING.
DON'T THINK...
...ABOUT ANY-THING ELSE.
BUT...

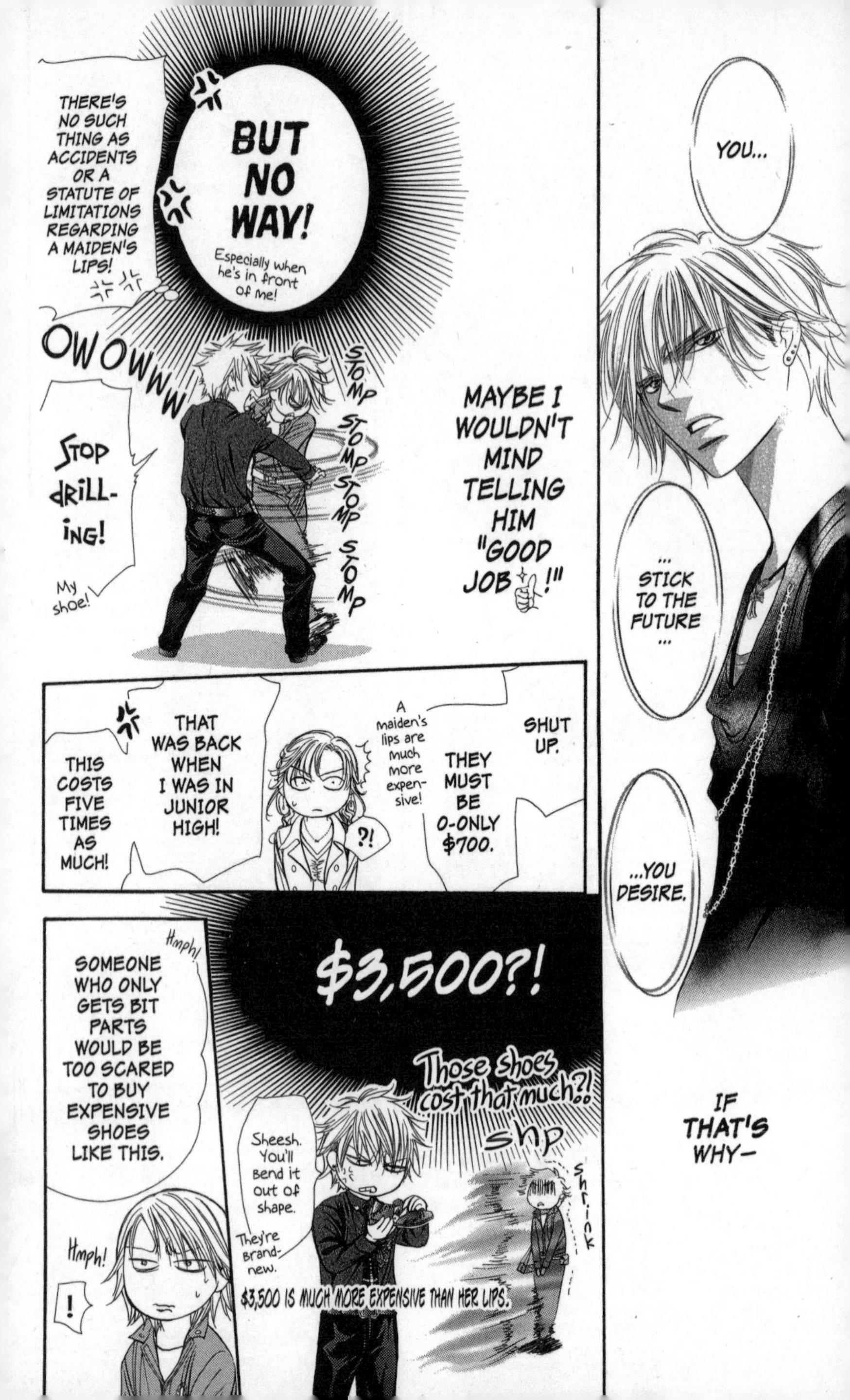
YOU...
...STICK TO THE FUTURE...
...YOU DESIRE.
IF THAT'S WHY—
MAYBE I WOULDN'T MIND TELLING HIM "GOOD JOB!"
BUT NO WAY!
Especially when he's in front of me!
THERE'S NO SUCH THING AS ACCIDENTS OR A STATUTE OF LIMITATIONS REGARDING A MAIDEN'S LIPS!
STOMP STOMP STOMP STOMP
OWOWWW
Stop drill-ing!
My shoe!
SHUT UP.
THEY MUST BE O-ONLY $700.
A maiden's lips are much more expen-sive!
?!
THAT WAS BACK WHEN I WAS IN JUNIOR HIGH!
THIS COSTS FIVE TIMES AS MUCH!
$3,500?!
Those shoes cost that much?!
shp
shrink
Sheesh. You'll bend it out of shape.
They're Brand-new.
$3,500 IS MUCH MORE EXPENSIVE THAN HER LIPS.
Hmph!
SOMEONE WHO ONLY GETS BIT PARTS WOULD BE TOO SCARED TO BUY EXPENSIVE SHOES LIKE THIS.
Hmph!
!

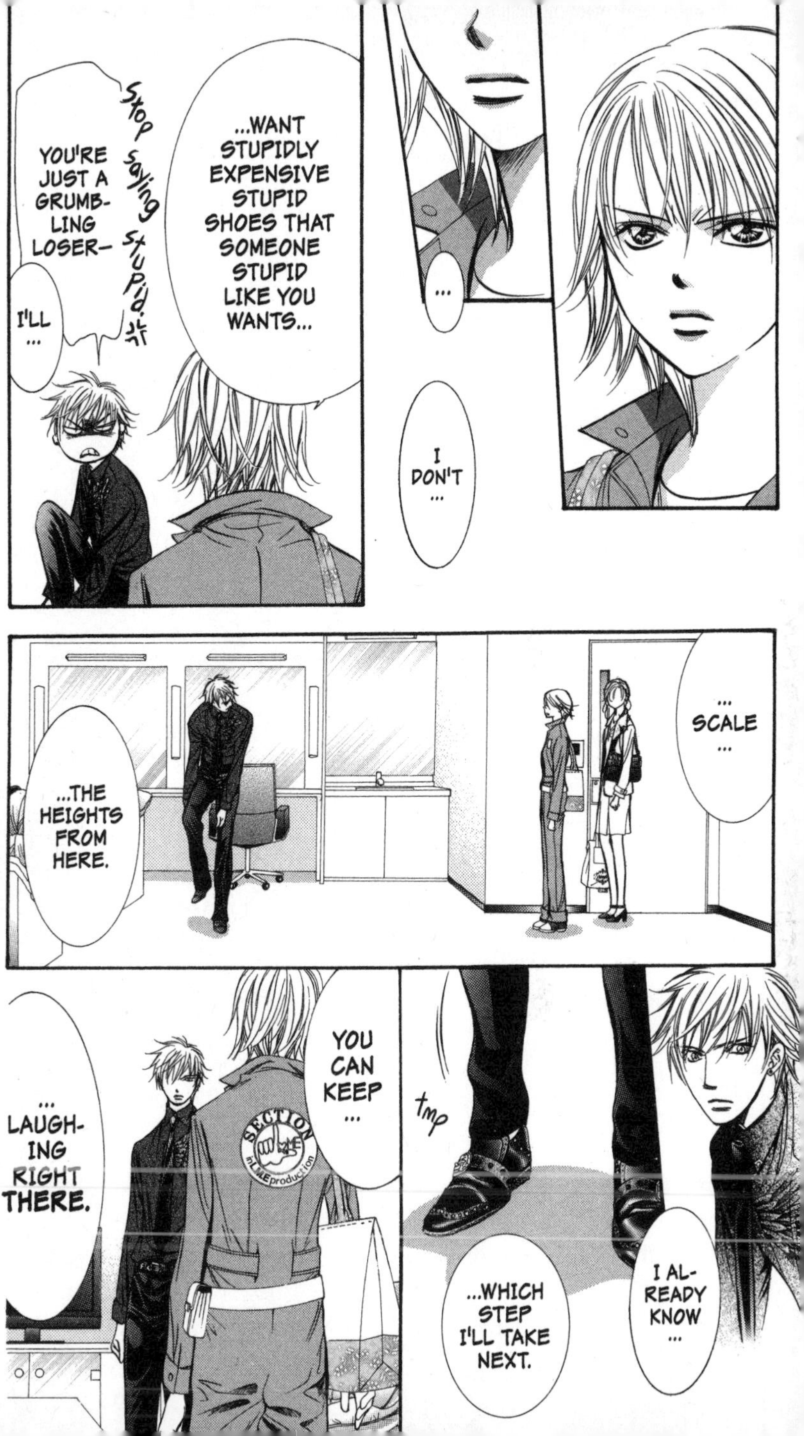
...
I DON'T ...
...WANT STUPIDLY EXPENSIVE STUPID SHOES THAT SOMEONE STUPID LIKE YOU WANTS...
YOU'RE JUST A GRUMBLING LOSER—
Stop saying stupid
I'LL ...
... SCALE ...
...THE HEIGHTS FROM HERE.
I ALREADY KNOW ...
...WHICH STEP I'LL TAKE NEXT.
tmp
YOU CAN KEEP ...
SECTION
... LAUGHING RIGHT THERE.

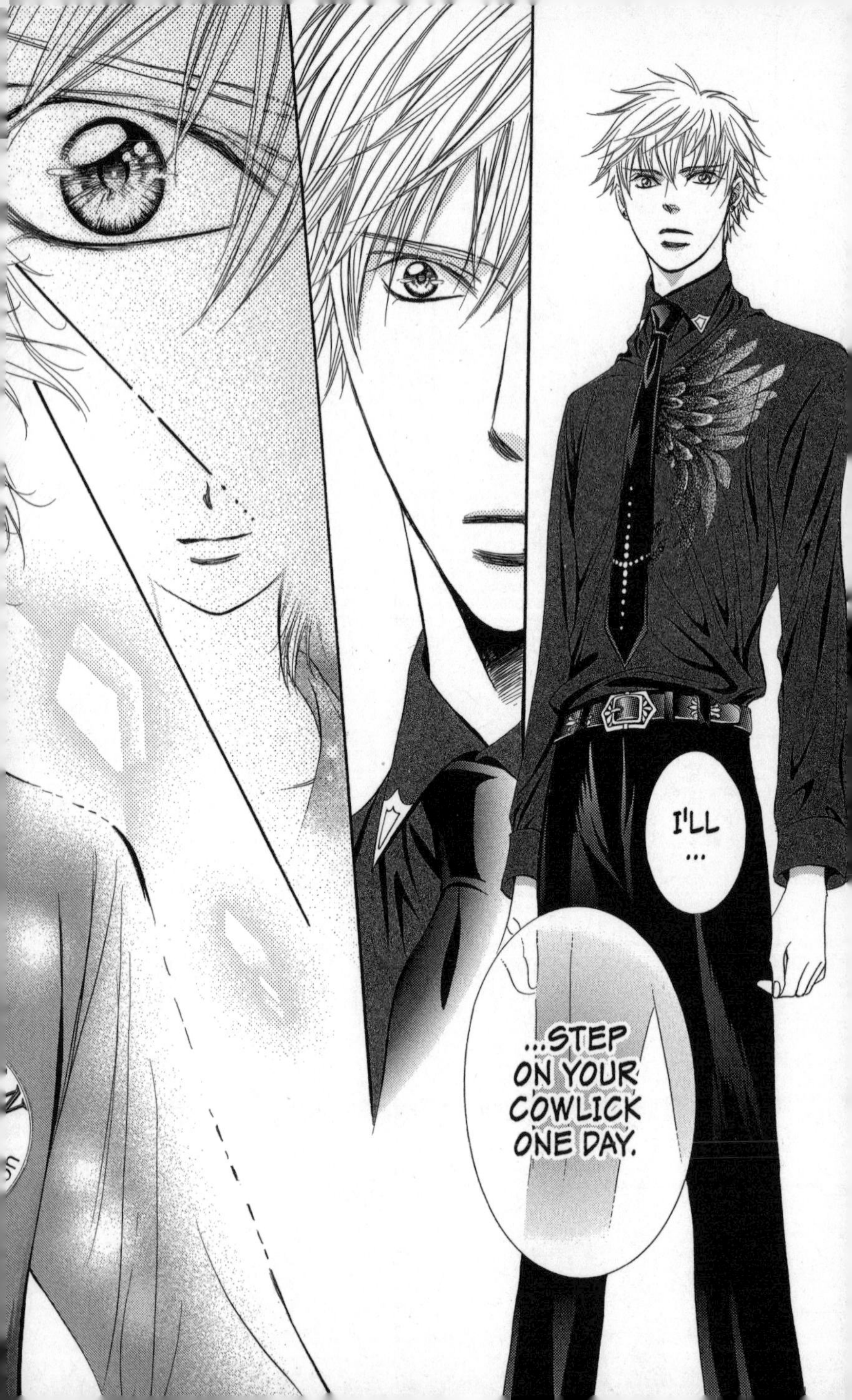
I'LL ...
...STEP ON YOUR COWLICK ONE DAY.

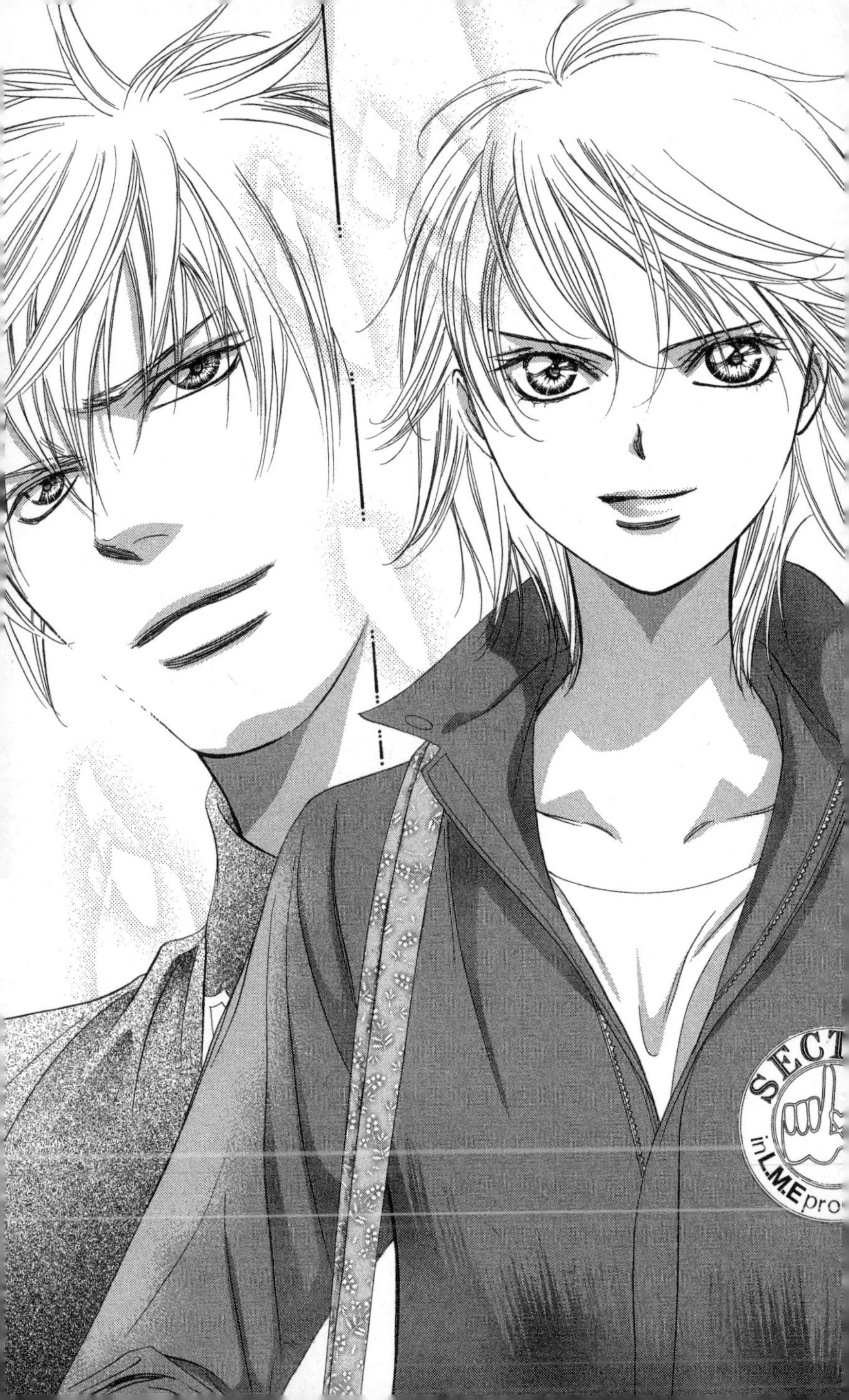
SECT
in L.M.E pro

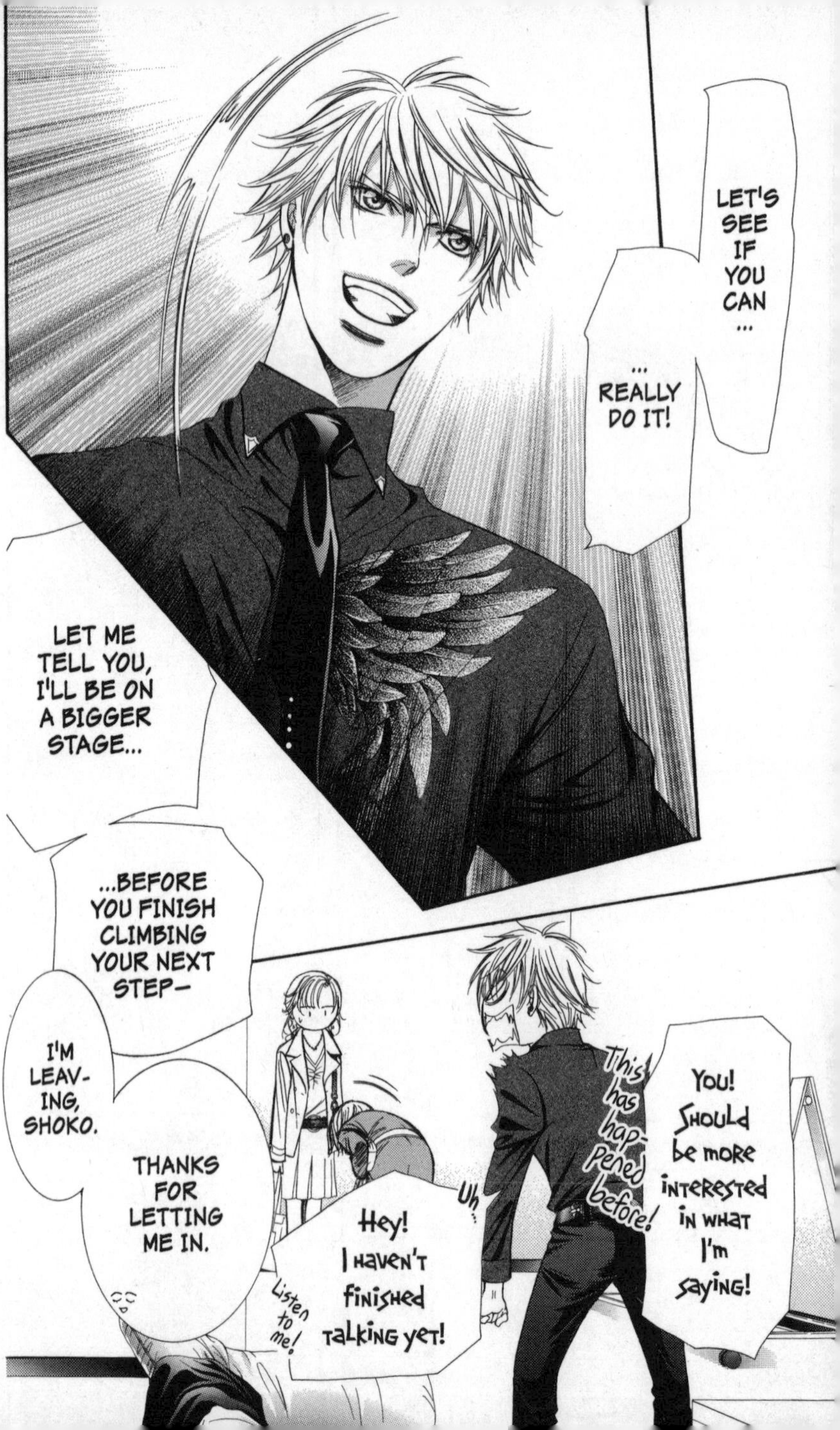
LET'S SEE IF YOU CAN...
...REALLY DO IT!
LET ME TELL YOU, I'LL BE ON A BIGGER STAGE...
...BEFORE YOU FINISH CLIMBING YOUR NEXT STEP—
You! Should be more interested in what I'm saying!
This has hap-pened before!
Uh...
Hey! I haven't finished talking yet!
Listen to me!
I'M LEAV-ING, SHOKO.
THANKS FOR LETTING ME IN.

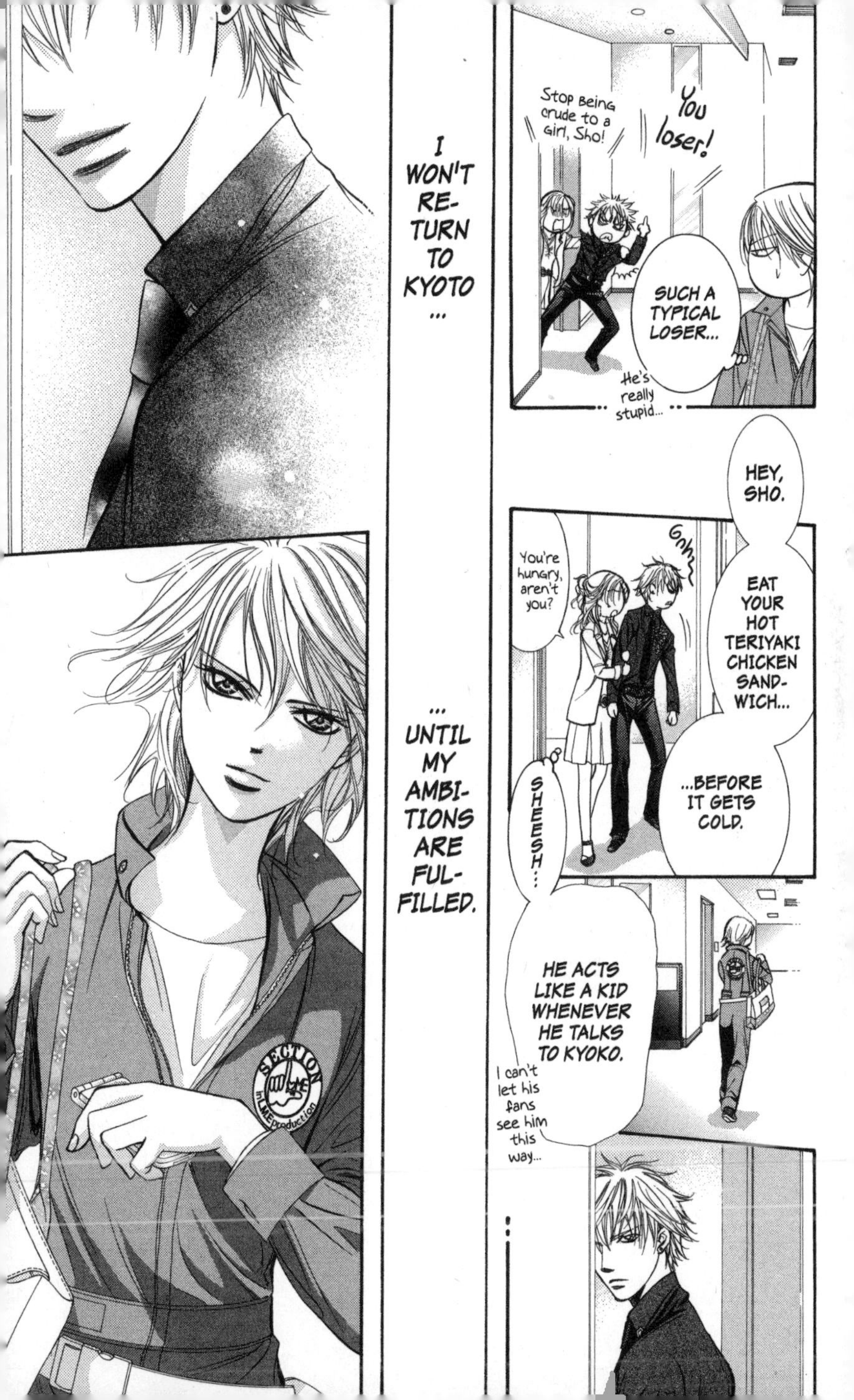
You loser!
Stop being crude to a girl, Sho!
SUCH A TYPICAL LOSER...
He's really stupid...
HEY, SHO.
EAT YOUR HOT TERIYAKI CHICKEN SANDWICH...
...BEFORE IT GETS COLD.
Gnh
You're hungry, aren't you?
SHEESH...
HE ACTS LIKE A KID WHENEVER HE TALKS TO KYOKO.
I can't let his fans see him this way...
I WON'T RETURN TO KYOTO...
...UNTIL MY AMBITIONS ARE FULFILLED.
SECTION
LME
inLMEproduction

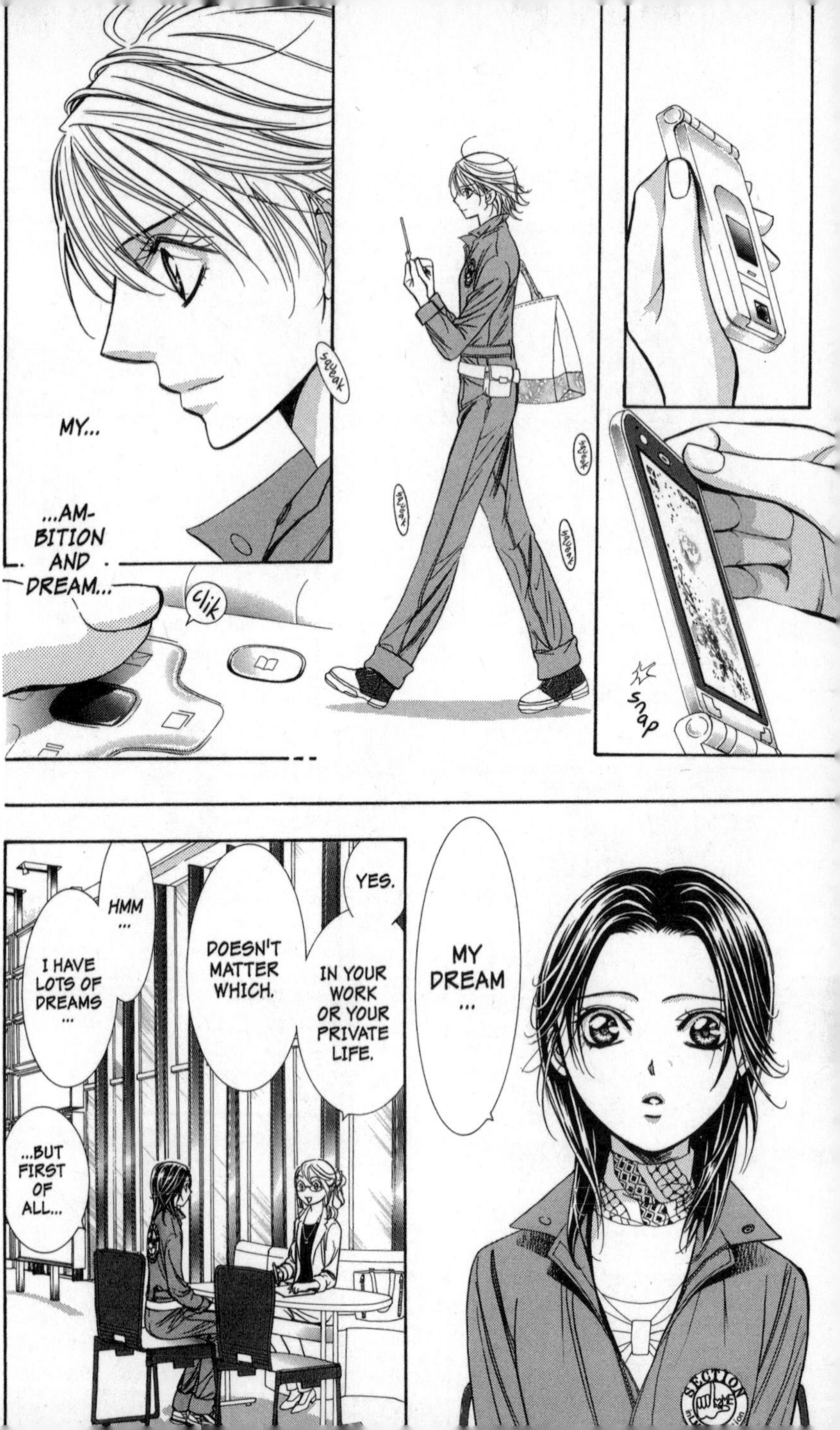
snap
squeak
squeak
squeak
squeak
MY...
...AM-BITION AND DREAM...
clik
MY DREAM ...
YES.
IN YOUR WORK OR YOUR PRIVATE LIFE.
DOESN'T MATTER WHICH.
HMM ...
I HAVE LOTS OF DREAMS ...
...BUT FIRST OF ALL...

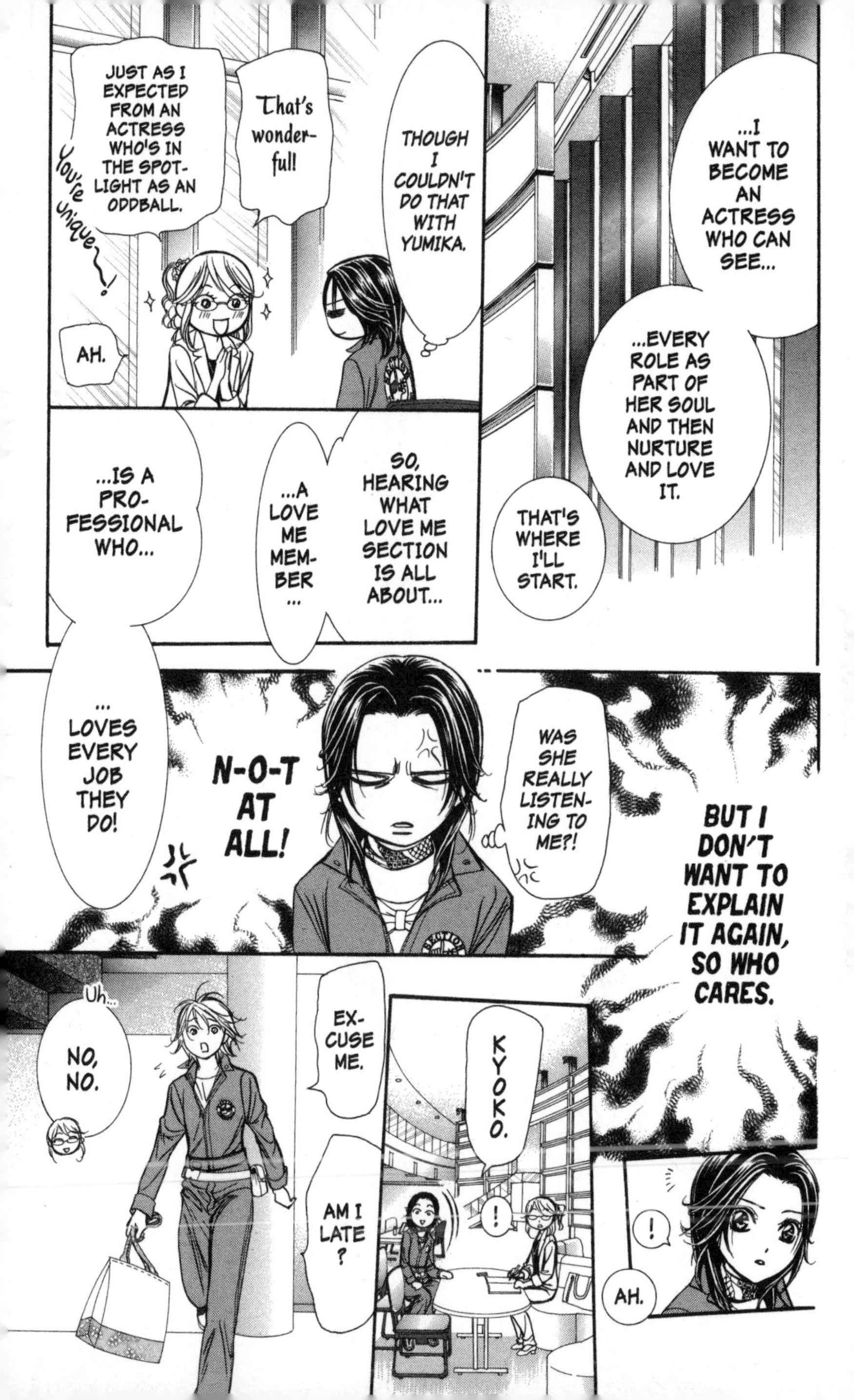
...I WANT TO BECOME AN ACTRESS WHO CAN SEE...
...EVERY ROLE AS PART OF HER SOUL AND THEN NURTURE AND LOVE IT.
THAT'S WHERE I'LL START.
THOUGH I COULDN'T DO THAT WITH YUMIKA.
That's wonderful!
JUST AS I EXPECTED FROM AN ACTRESS WHO'S IN THE SPOTLIGHT AS AN ODDBALL.
You're unique~!
AH.
SO, HEARING WHAT LOVE ME SECTION IS ALL ABOUT...
...A LOVE ME MEMBER...
...IS A PROFESSIONAL WHO...
...LOVES EVERY JOB THEY DO!
BUT I DON'T WANT TO EXPLAIN IT AGAIN, SO WHO CARES.
WAS SHE REALLY LISTENING TO ME?!
N-O-T AT ALL!
!
AH.
KYOKO.
!
EXCUSE ME.
AM I LATE?
Uh...
NO, NO.

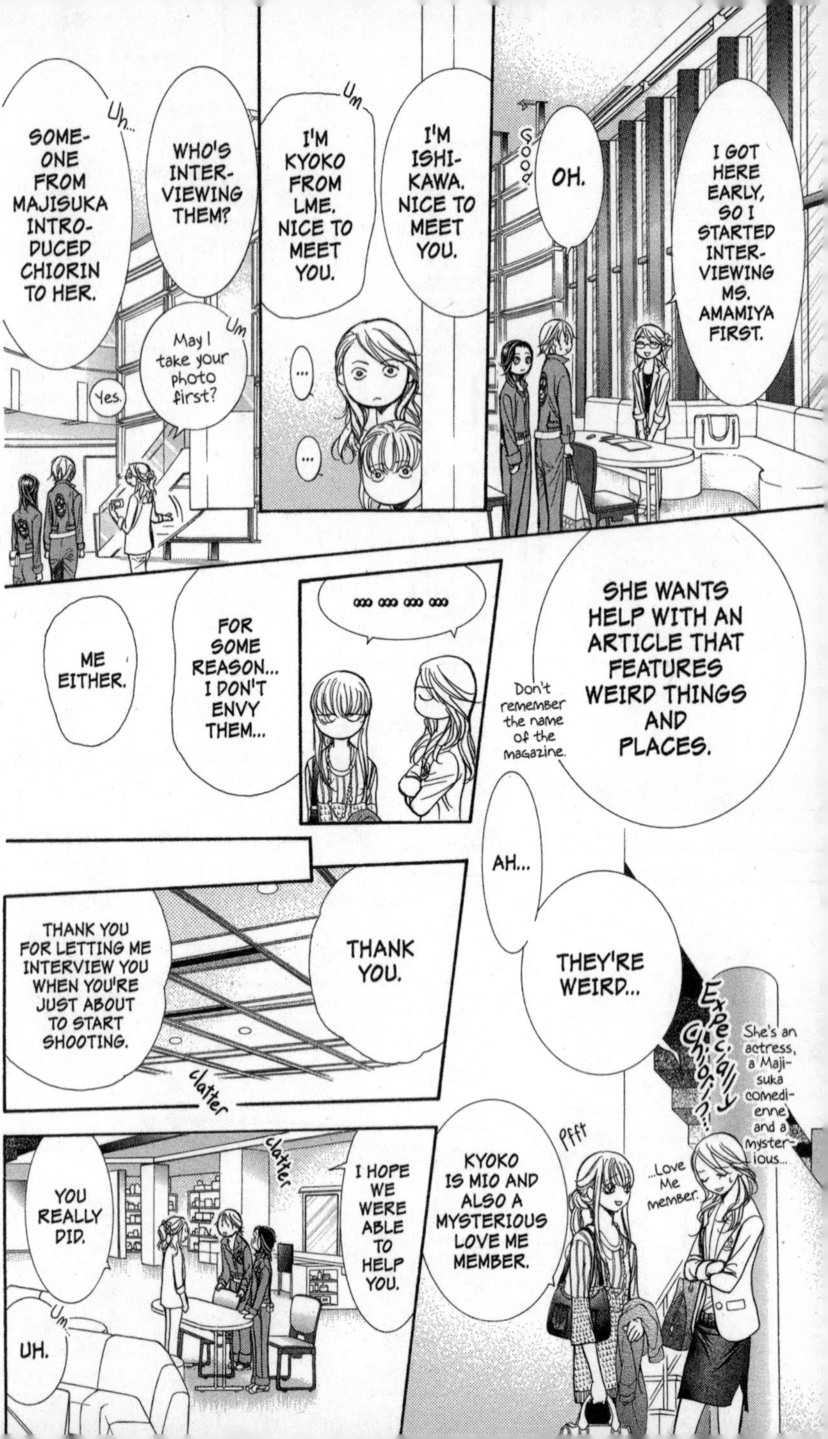
I GOT HERE EARLY, SO I STARTED INTERVIEWING MS. AMAMIYA FIRST.
Good
OH.
I'M ISHIKAWA. NICE TO MEET YOU.
Um
I'M KYOKO FROM LME. NICE TO MEET YOU.
...
...
WHO'S INTERVIEWING THEM?
Uh...
SOME-ONE FROM MAJISUKA INTRODUCED CHIORIN TO HER.
Um
May I take your photo first?
Yes.
SHE WANTS HELP WITH AN ARTICLE THAT FEATURES WEIRD THINGS AND PLACES.
Don't remember the name of the magazine.
FOR SOME REASON... I DON'T ENVY THEM...
ME EITHER.
AH...
THEY'RE WEIRD...
Especially Chiorin...
She's an actress, a Majisuka comedienne and a mysterious...
Pfft
KYOKO IS MIO AND ALSO A MYSTERIOUS LOVE ME MEMBER.
...Love Me member.
THANK YOU.
THANK YOU FOR LETTING ME INTERVIEW YOU WHEN YOU'RE JUST ABOUT TO START SHOOTING.
clatter
clatter
I HOPE WE WERE ABLE TO HELP YOU.
YOU REALLY DID.
Um...
UH.

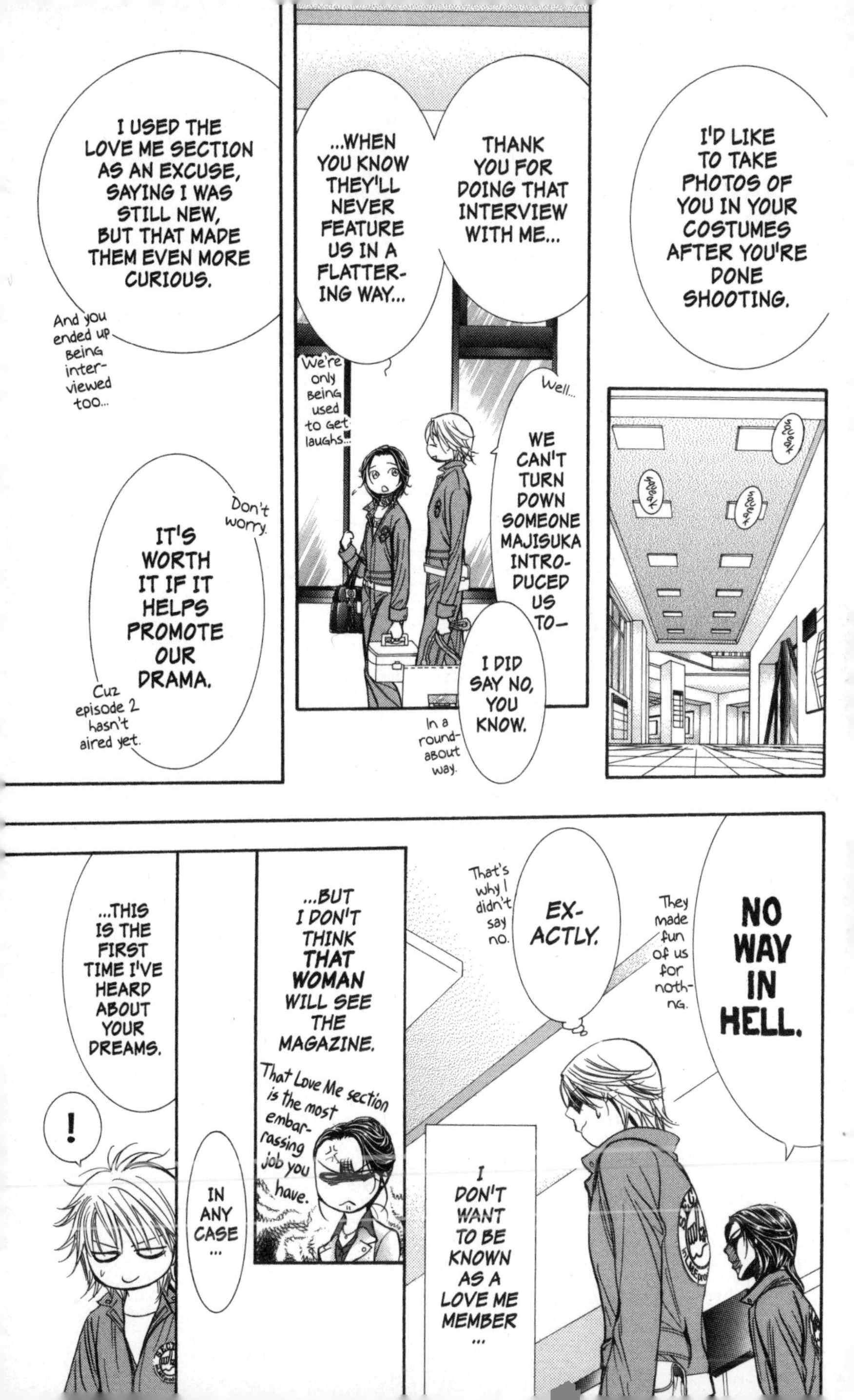
I'D LIKE TO TAKE PHOTOS OF YOU IN YOUR COSTUMES AFTER YOU'RE DONE SHOOTING.
squeak
squeak
squeak
THANK YOU FOR DOING THAT INTERVIEW WITH ME...
...WHEN YOU KNOW THEY'LL NEVER FEATURE US IN A FLATTER-ING WAY...
We're only being used to get laughs...
Well...
WE CAN'T TURN DOWN SOMEONE MAJISUKA INTRO-DUCED US TO—
I DID SAY NO, YOU KNOW.
In a round-about way.
I USED THE LOVE ME SECTION AS AN EXCUSE, SAYING I WAS STILL NEW, BUT THAT MADE THEM EVEN MORE CURIOUS.
And you ended up being inter-viewed too...
Don't worry.
IT'S WORTH IT IF IT HELPS PROMOTE OUR DRAMA.
Cuz episode 2 hasn't aired yet.
NO WAY IN HELL.
They made fun of us for noth-ng.
EX-ACTLY.
That's why I didn't say no.
I DON'T WANT TO BE KNOWN AS A LOVE ME MEMBER...
...BUT I DON'T THINK THAT WOMAN WILL SEE THE MAGAZINE.
That Love Me section is the most embar-rassing job you have.
IN ANY CASE...
...THIS IS THE FIRST TIME I'VE HEARD ABOUT YOUR DREAMS.
!

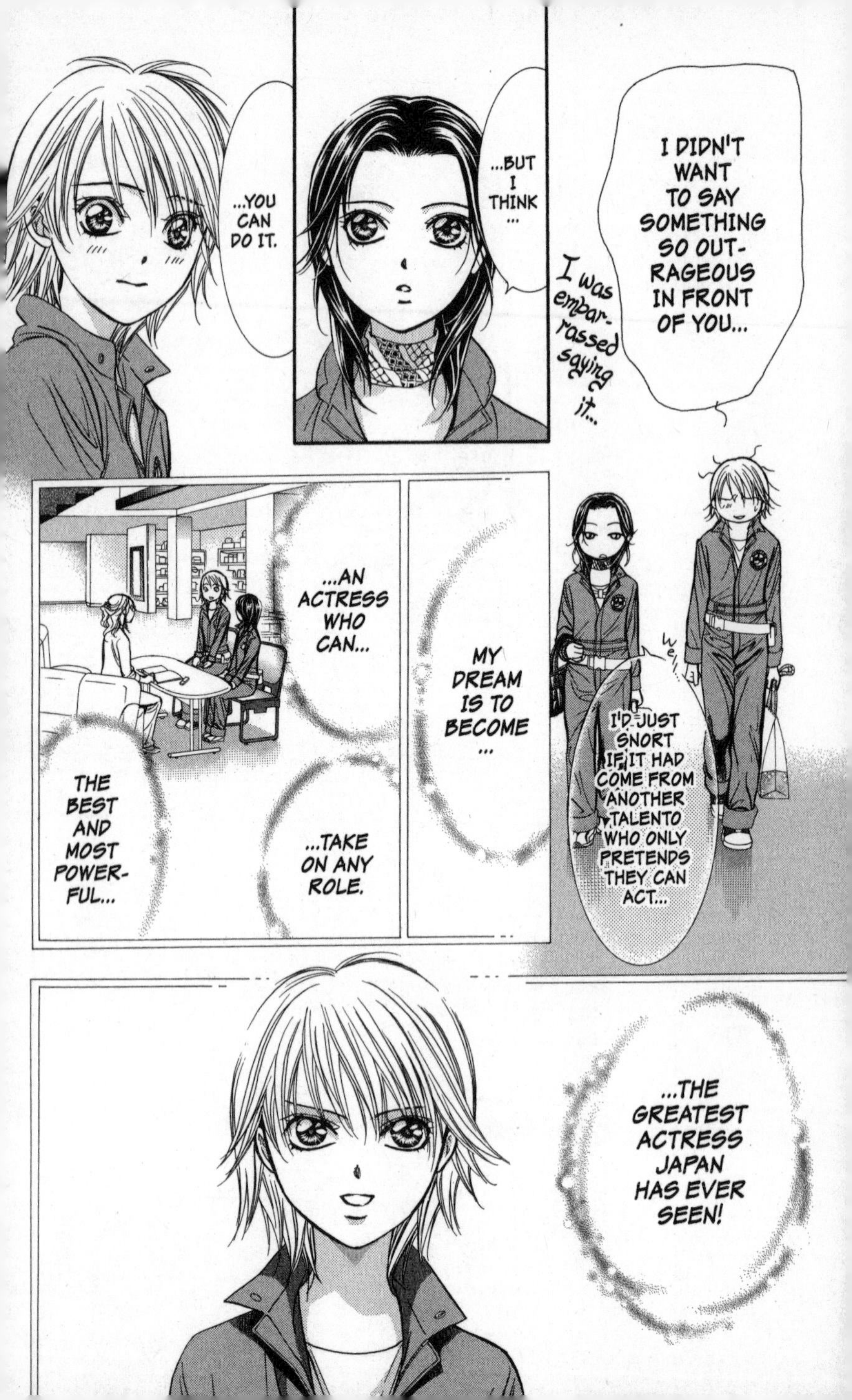

I DIDN'T WANT TO SAY SOMETHING SO OUTRAGEOUS IN FRONT OF YOU...
I was embarrassed saying it...
...BUT I THINK...
...YOU CAN DO IT.
Well...
I'D JUST SNORT IF IT HAD COME FROM ANOTHER TALENTO WHO ONLY PRETENDS THEY CAN ACT...
MY DREAM IS TO BECOME...
...AN ACTRESS WHO CAN...
...TAKE ON ANY ROLE.
THE BEST AND MOST POWERFUL...
...THE GREATEST ACTRESS JAPAN HAS EVER SEEN!

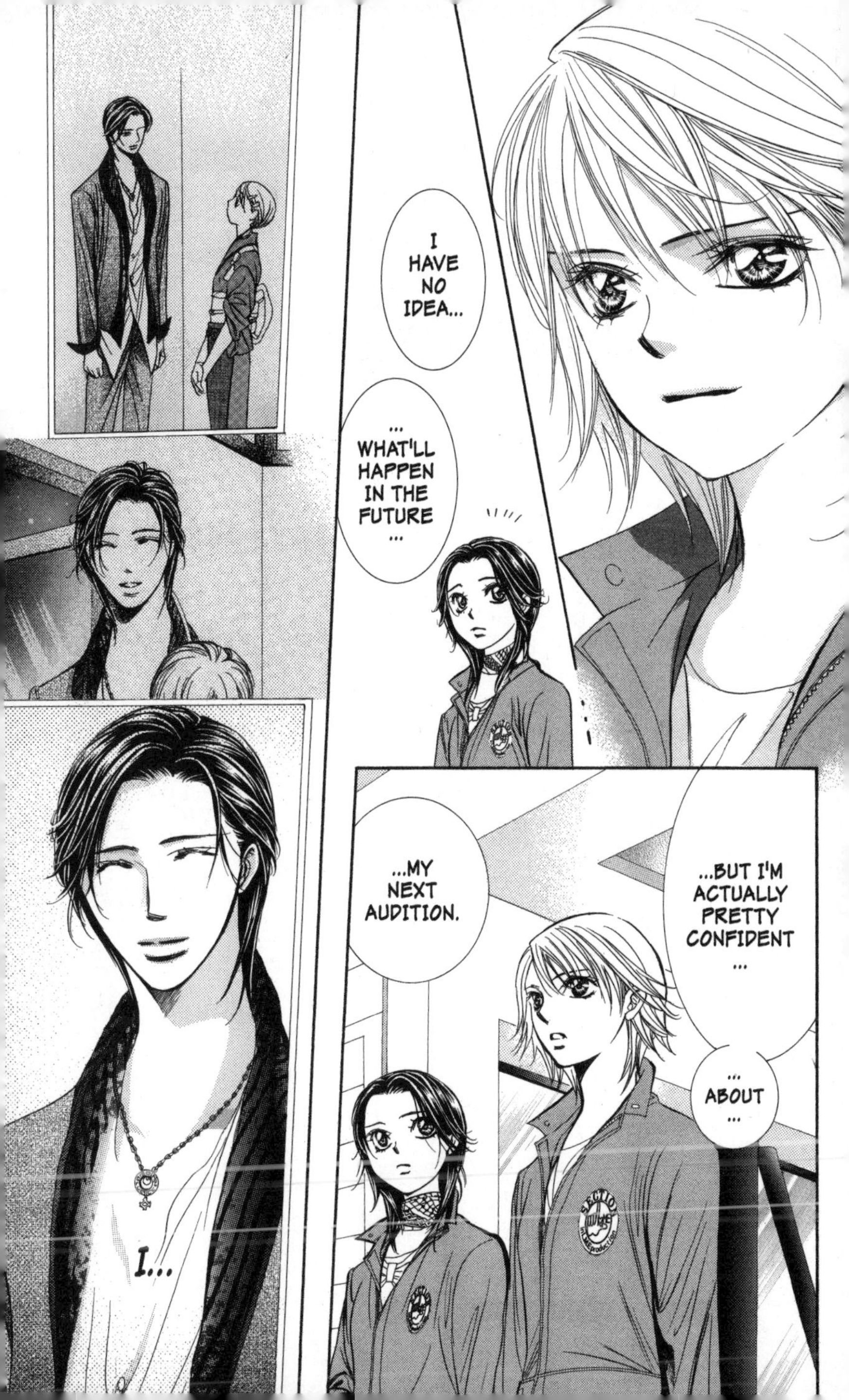
I HAVE NO IDEA...
...WHAT'LL HAPPEN IN THE FUTURE...
...BUT I'M ACTUALLY PRETTY CONFIDENT...
...ABOUT...
...MY NEXT AUDITION.
I...

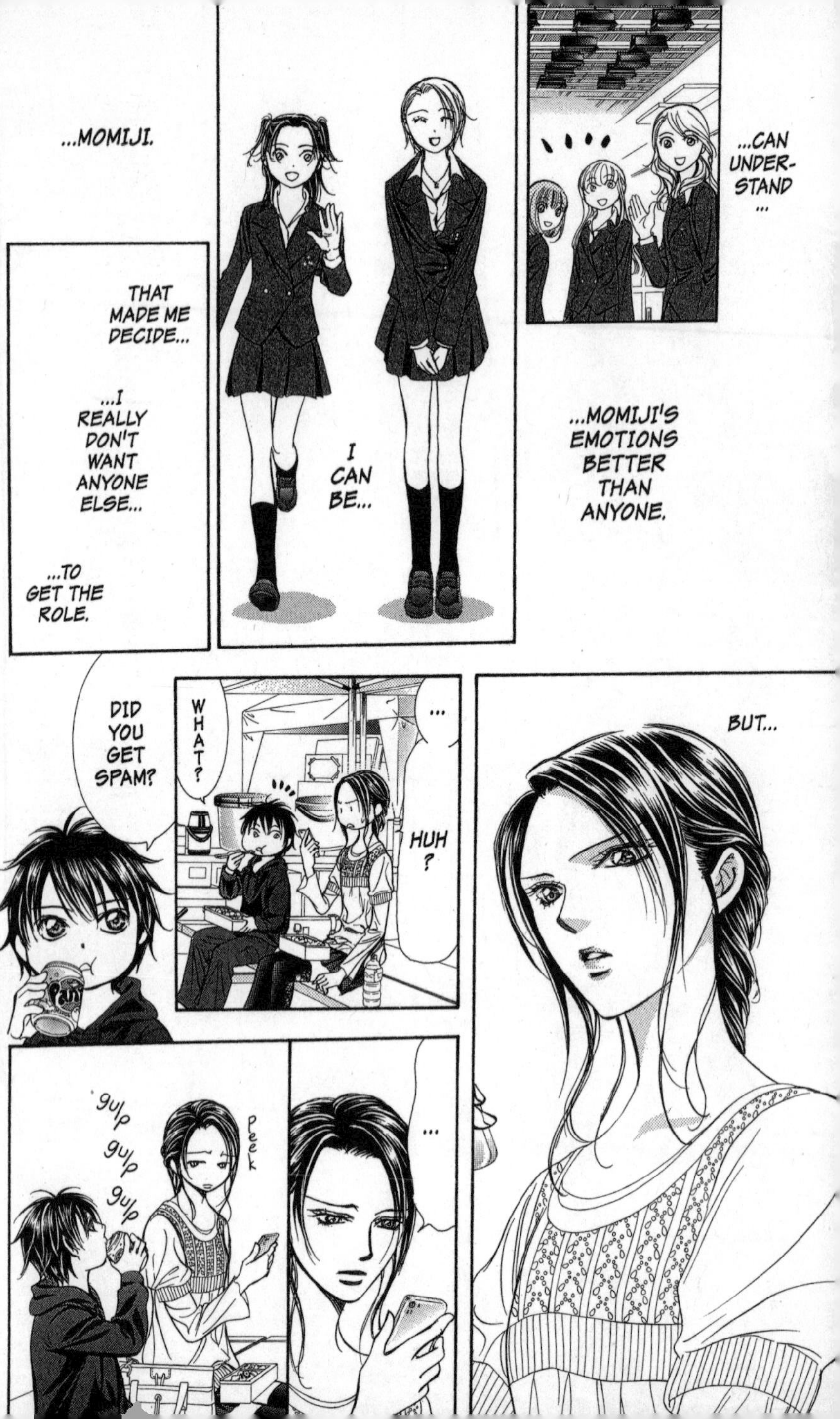
...CAN UNDERSTAND...
...MOMIJI'S EMOTIONS BETTER THAN ANYONE.
I CAN BE...
...MOMIJI.
THAT MADE ME DECIDE...
...I REALLY DON'T WANT ANYONE ELSE...
...TO GET THE ROLE.
BUT...
...
WHAT?
HUH?
DID YOU GET SPAM?
...
Peek
gulp gulp gulp

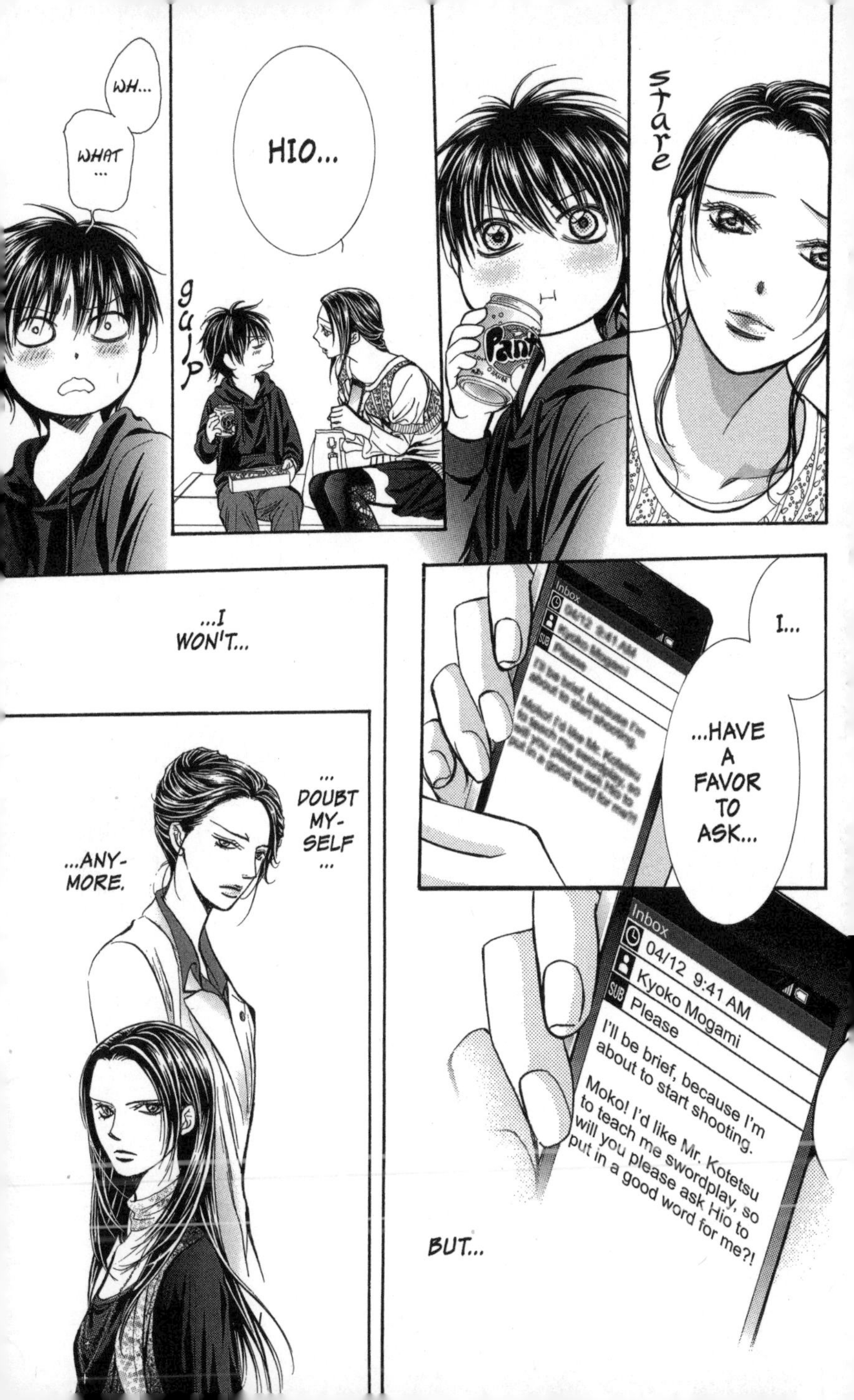
stare
HIO...
gulp
WH...
WHAT ...
I...
...HAVE A FAVOR TO ASK...
...I WON'T...
Inbox
04/12 9:41 AM
Kyoko Mogami
SUB Please
I'll be brief, because I'm about to start shooting.
Moko! I'd like Mr. Kotetsu to teach me swordplay, so will you please ask Hio to put in a good word for me?!
BUT...
... DOUBT MY-SELF ...
...ANY-MORE.

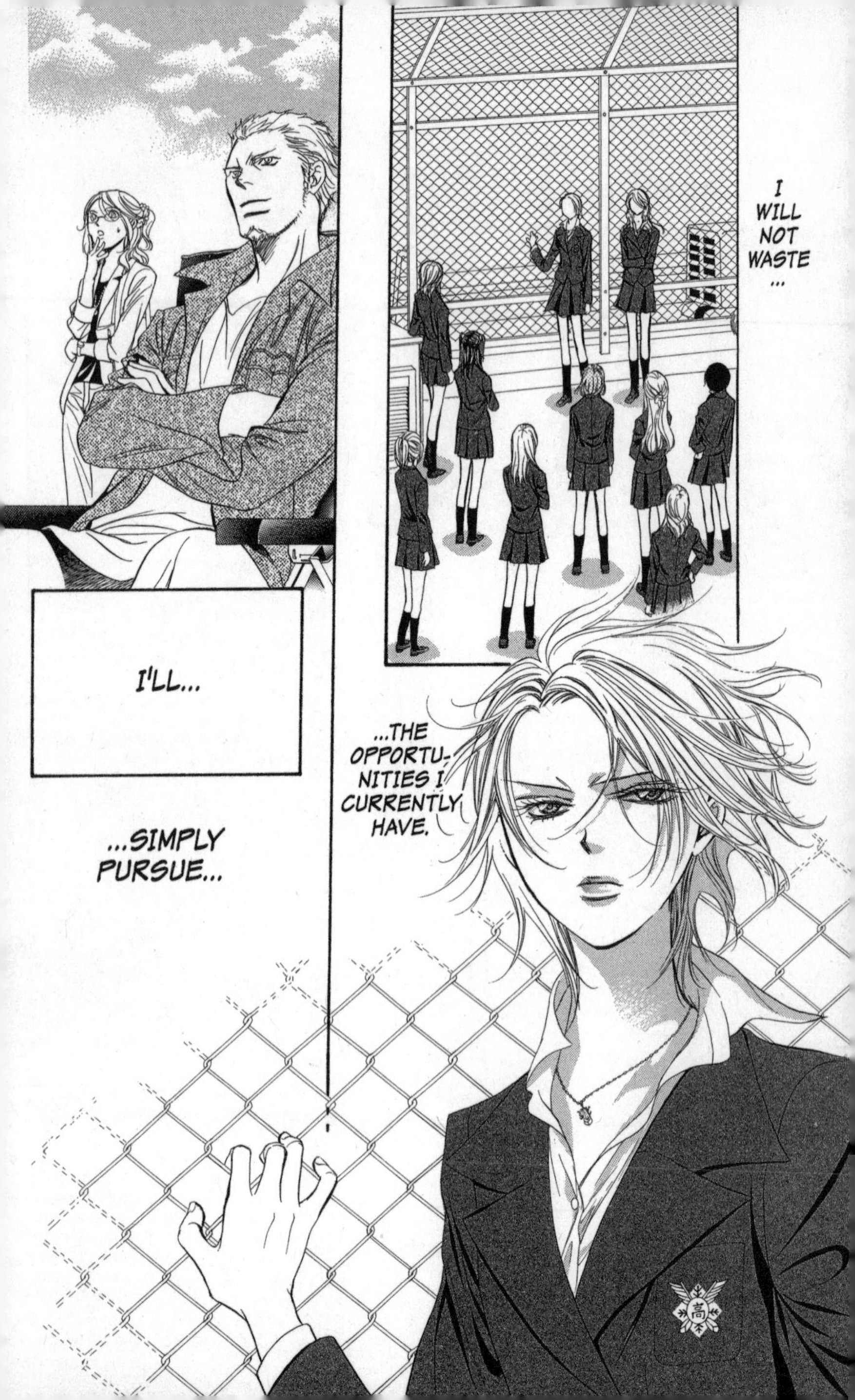
I WILL NOT WASTE...
...THE OPPORTUNITIES I CURRENTLY HAVE.
I'LL...
...SIMPLY PURSUE...

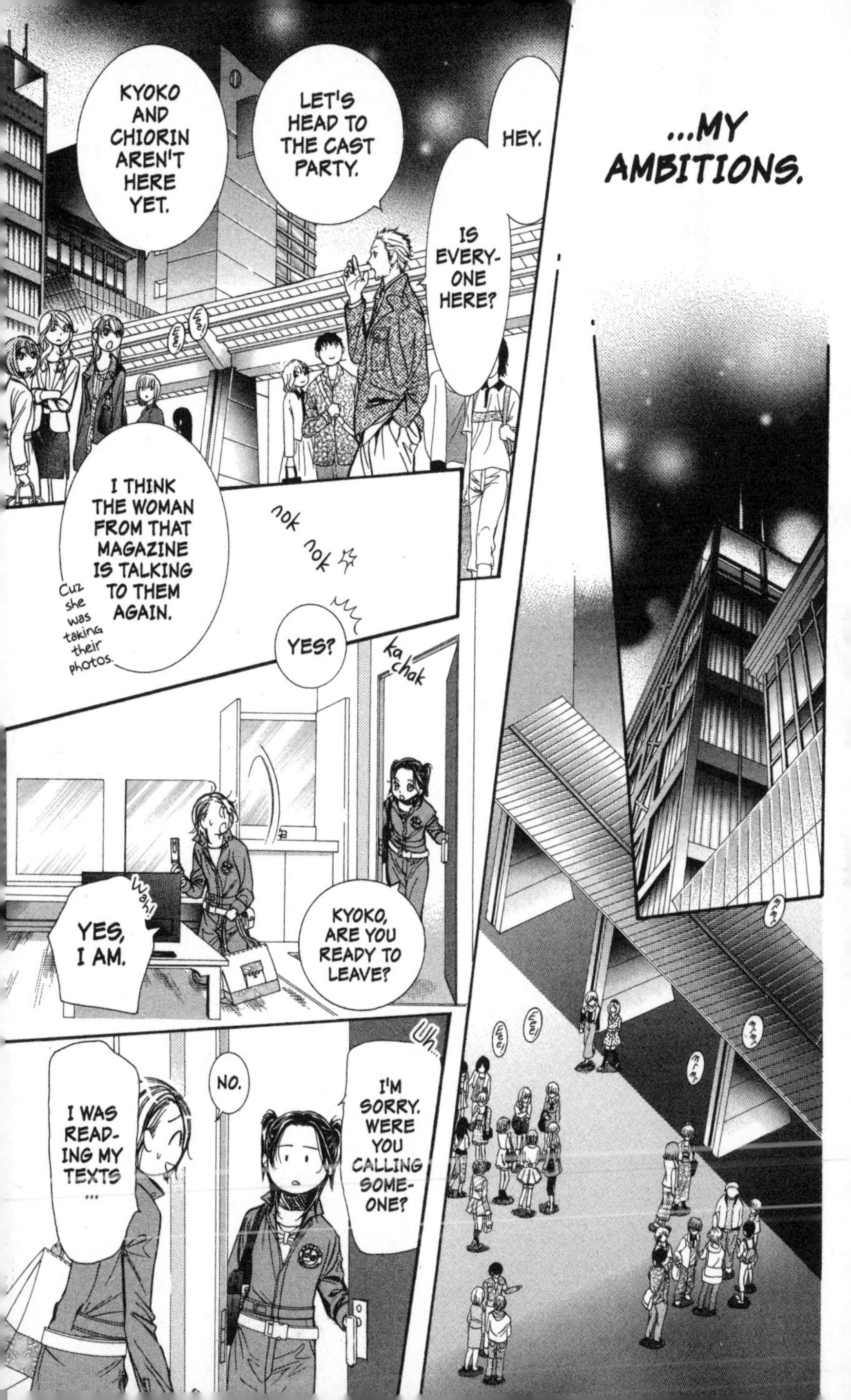
...MY AMBITIONS.
HEY.
IS EVERY-ONE HERE?
LET'S HEAD TO THE CAST PARTY.
KYOKO AND CHIORIN AREN'T HERE YET.
nok nok
I THINK THE WOMAN FROM THAT MAGAZINE IS TALKING TO THEM AGAIN.
Cuz she was taking their photos.
YES?
ka chak
KYOKO, ARE YOU READY TO LEAVE?
Wah!
YES, I AM.
Uh...
I'M SORRY. WERE YOU CALLING SOMEONE?
NO.
I WAS READ-ING MY TEXTS...

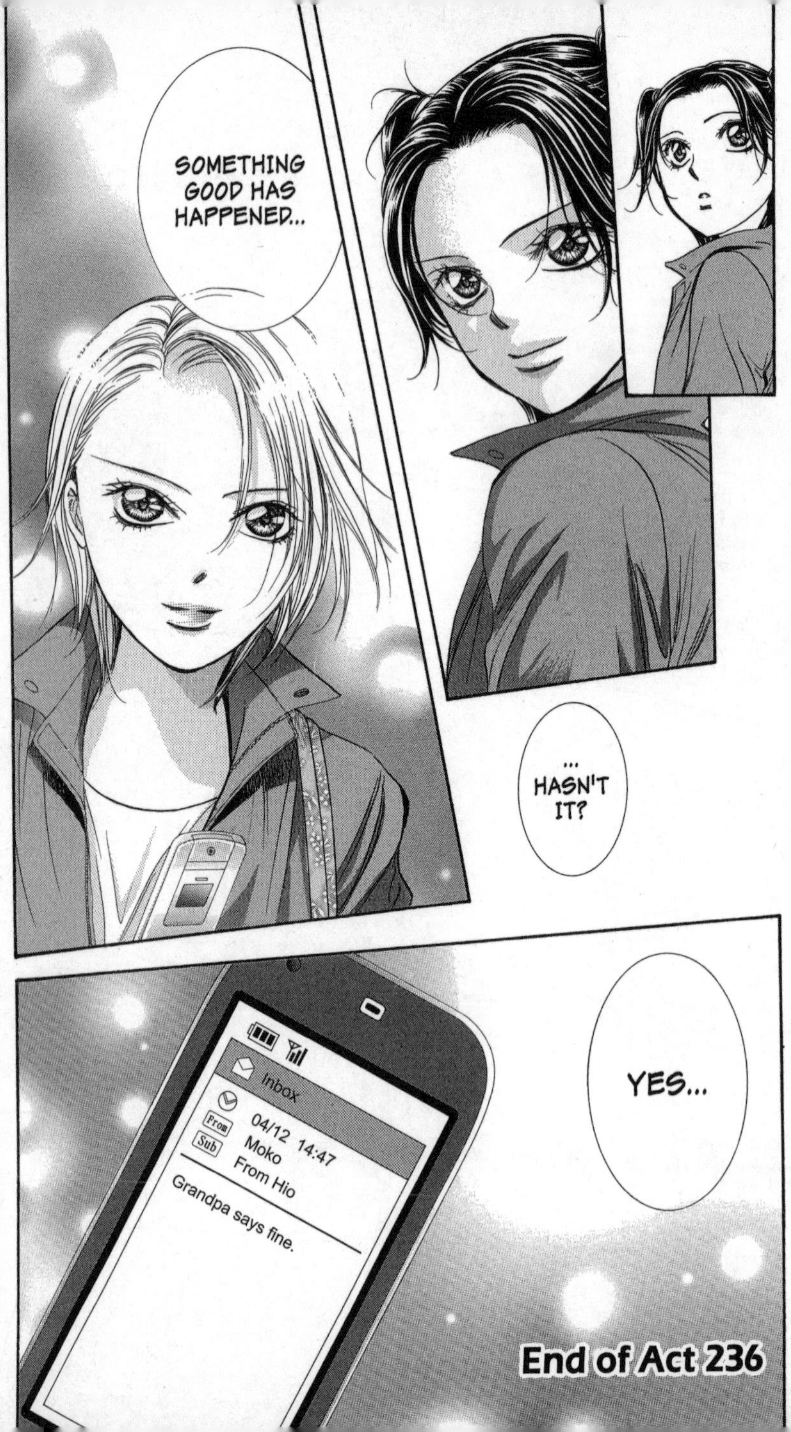
SOMETHING GOOD HAS HAPPENED...
... HASN'T IT?
YES...
Inbox
From 04/12 14:47
Moko
Sub From Hio
Grandpa says fine.
End of Act 236

How He Acted Then
MGH and the 14th Year of Fatherly Love

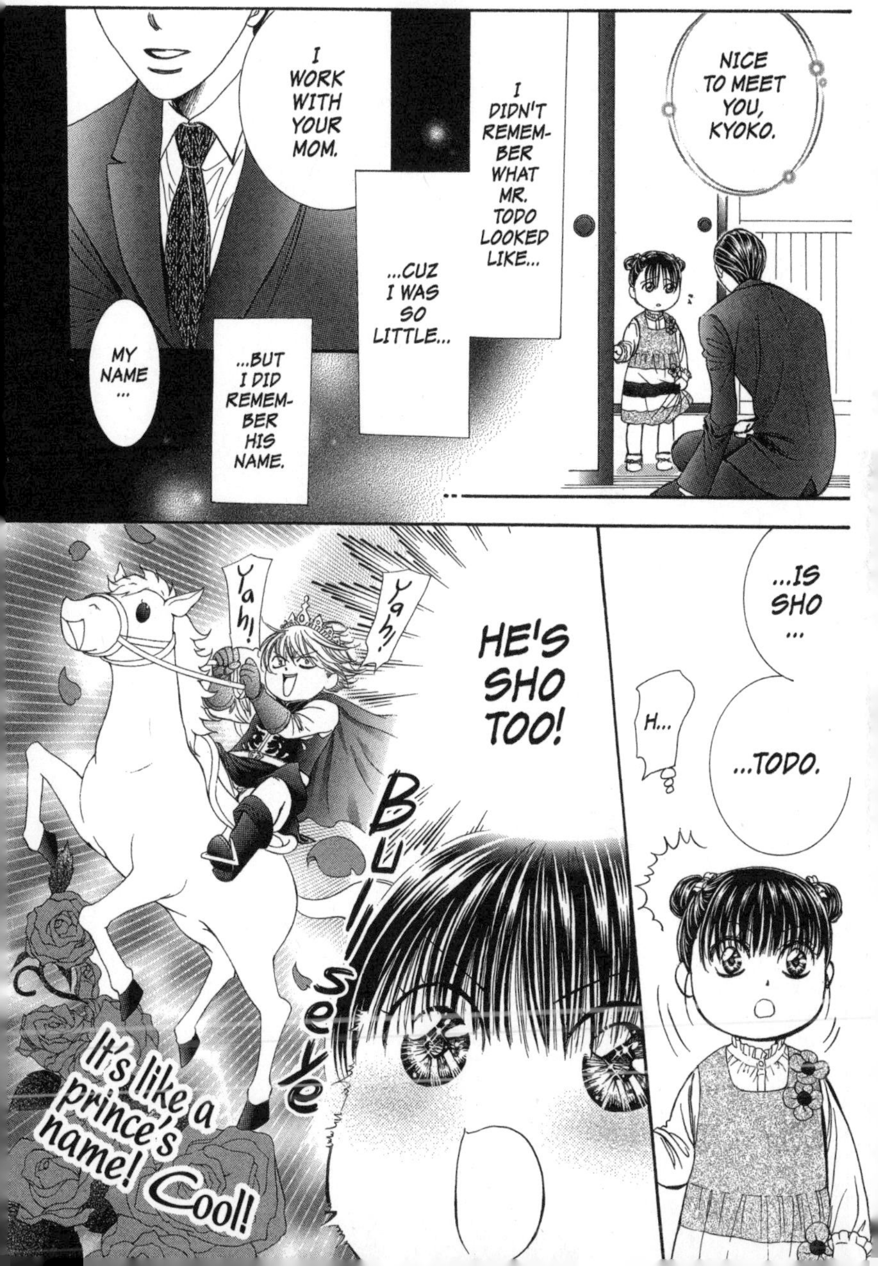
NICE TO MEET YOU, KYOKO.
I DIDN'T REMEMBER WHAT MR. TODO LOOKED LIKE...
...CUZ I WAS SO LITTLE...
I WORK WITH YOUR MOM.
MY NAME ...
...BUT I DID REMEMBER HIS NAME.
...IS SHO ...
H...
...TODO.
HE'S SHO TOO!
Yah!
Yah!
It's like a prince's name! Cool!

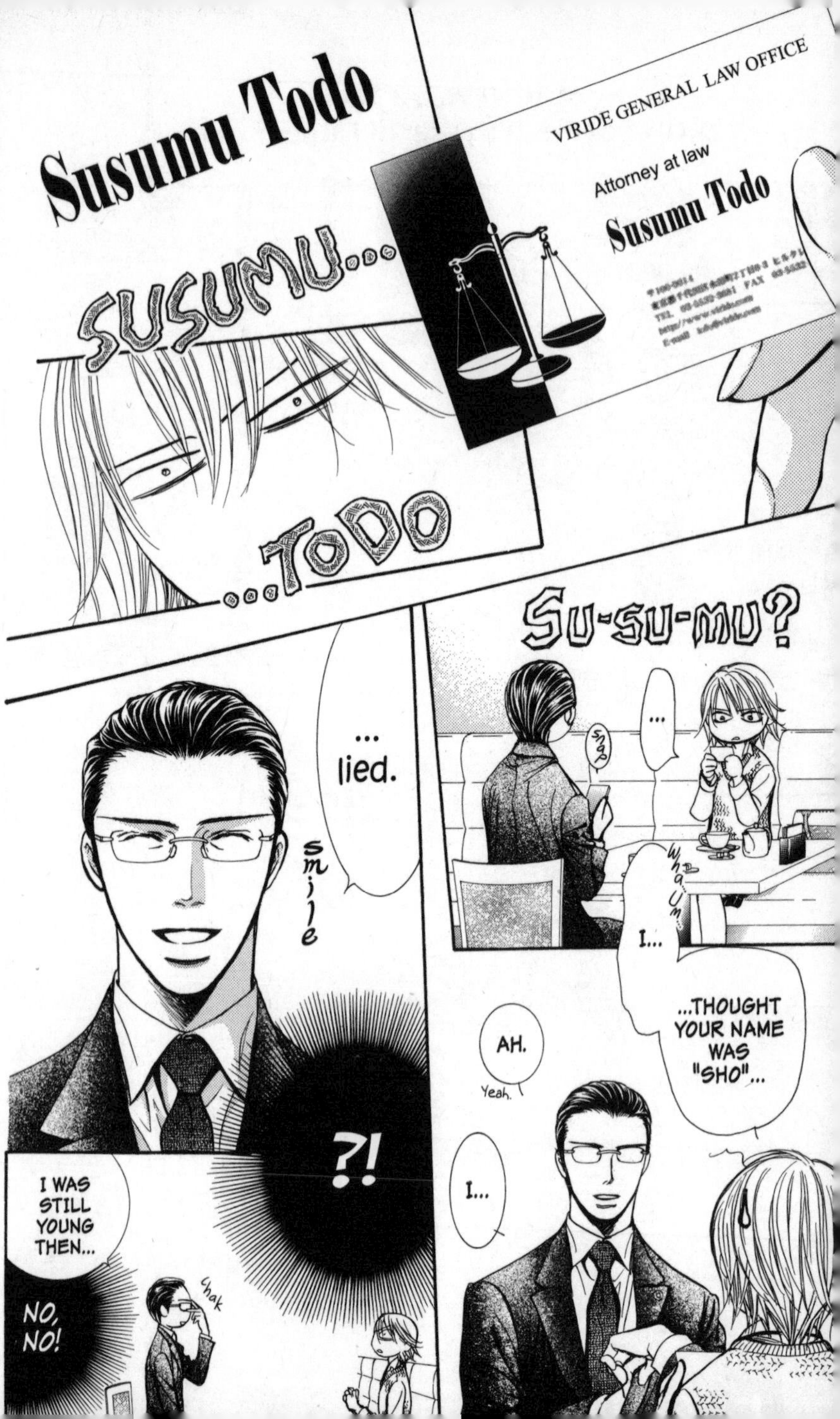

VIRIDE GENERAL LAW OFFICE
Attorney at law
Susumu Todo
Susumu Todo
SUSUMU...
...TODO
SU-SU-MU?
...
Whaa... Um...
I...
...THOUGHT YOUR NAME WAS "SHO"...
AH.
Yeah.
I...
... lied.
smile
?!
I WAS STILL YOUNG THEN...
chak
NO, NO!

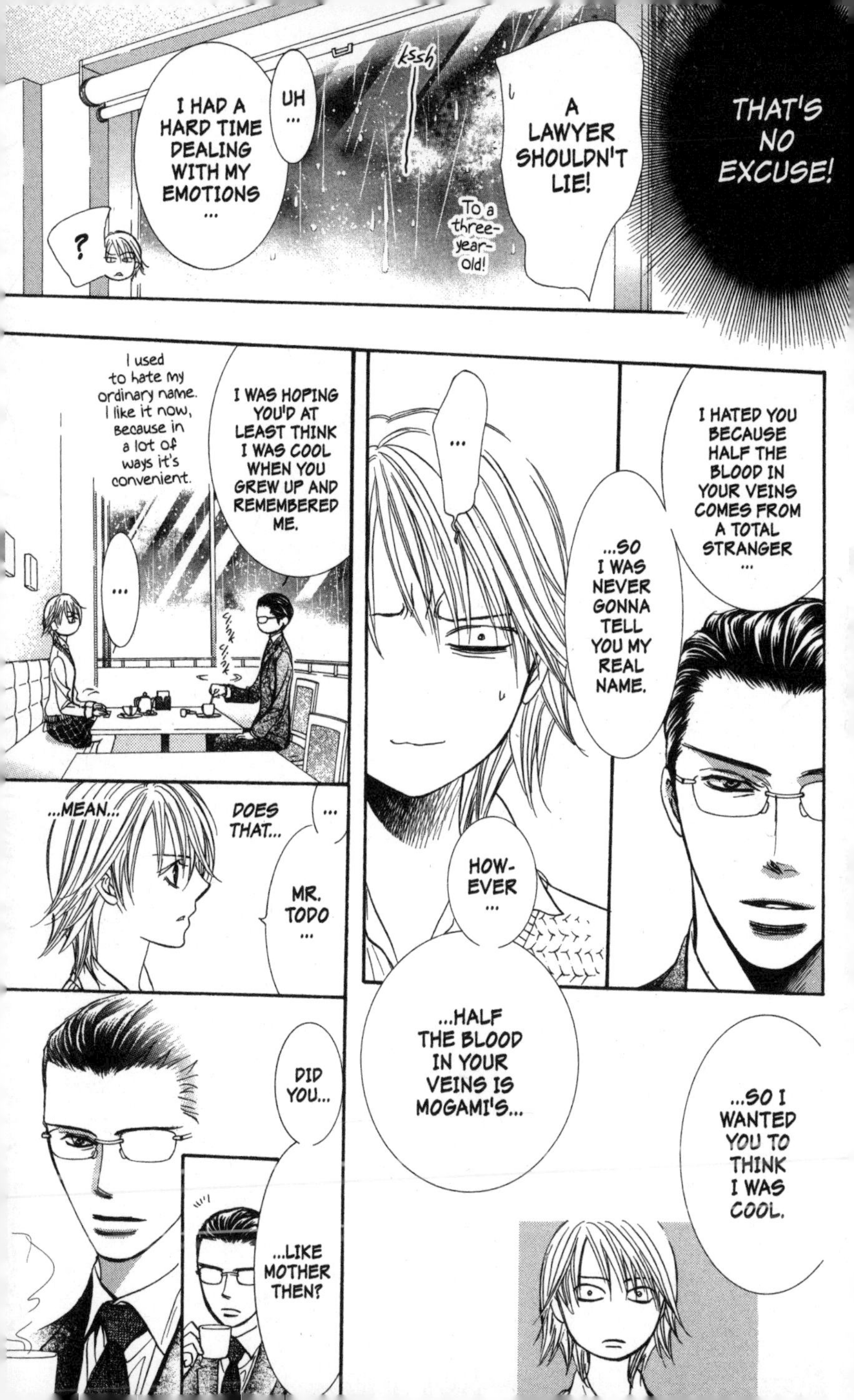
THAT'S NO EXCUSE!
A LAWYER SHOULDN'T LIE!
To a three-year-old!
kssh
UH ...
I HAD A HARD TIME DEALING WITH MY EMOTIONS ...
?
I HATED YOU BECAUSE HALF THE BLOOD IN YOUR VEINS COMES FROM A TOTAL STRANGER ...
...SO I WAS NEVER GONNA TELL YOU MY REAL NAME.
...
HOW-EVER ...
...HALF THE BLOOD IN YOUR VEINS IS MOGAMI'S...
...SO I WANTED YOU TO THINK I WAS COOL.
I WAS HOPING YOU'D AT LEAST THINK I WAS COOL WHEN YOU GREW UP AND REMEMBERED ME.
I used to hate my ordinary name. I like it now, because in a lot of ways it's convenient.
...
clink clink
...
MR. TODO ...
DOES THAT...
...MEAN...
DID YOU...
...LIKE MOTHER THEN?

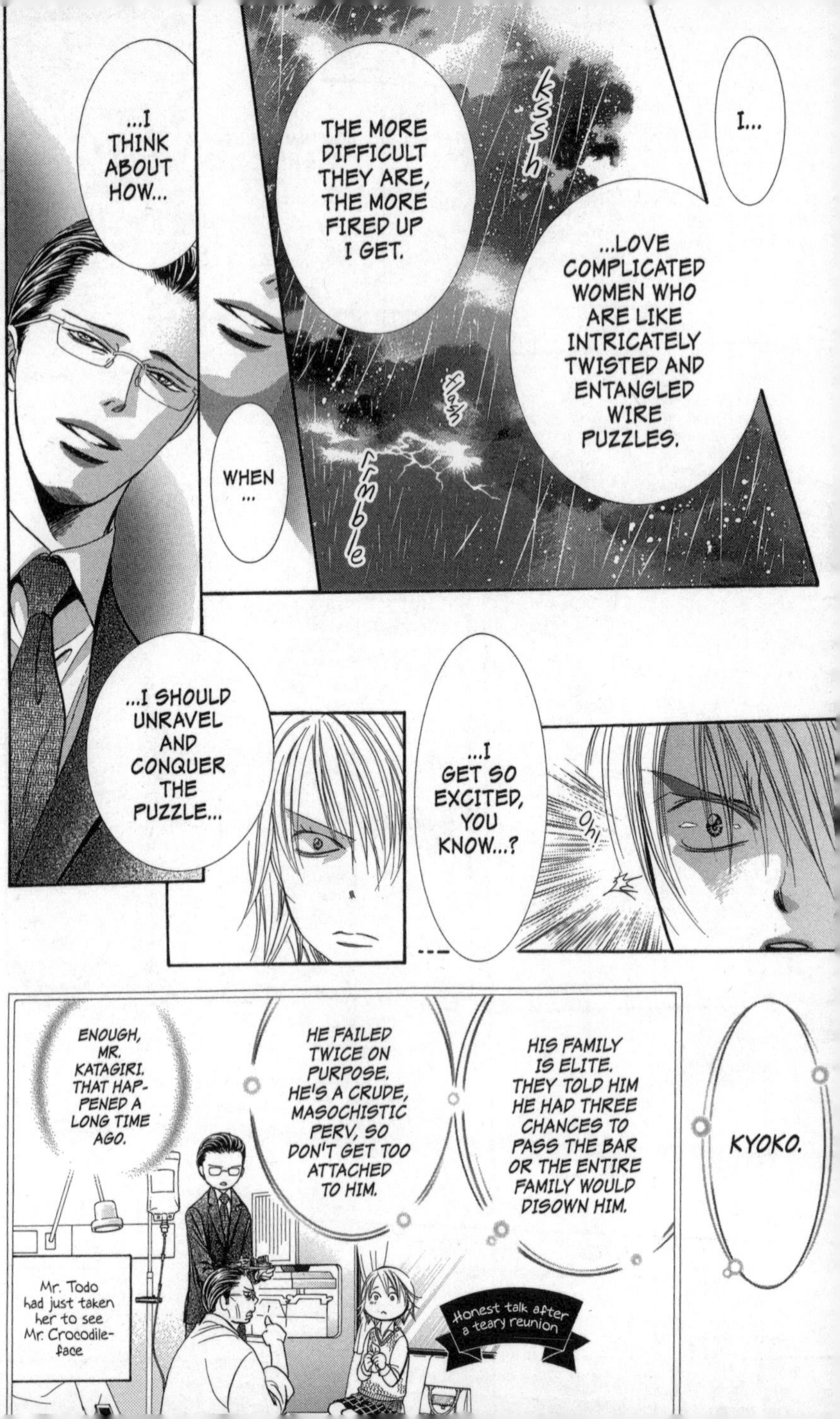
I...
...LOVE COMPLICATED WOMEN WHO ARE LIKE INTRICATELY TWISTED AND ENTANGLED WIRE PUZZLES.
kssh
THE MORE DIFFICULT THEY ARE, THE MORE FIRED UP I GET.
flash
rmble
WHEN ...
...I THINK ABOUT HOW...
...I SHOULD UNRAVEL AND CONQUER THE PUZZLE...
Oh!
...I GET SO EXCITED, YOU KNOW...?

KYOKO.
HIS FAMILY IS ELITE. THEY TOLD HIM HE HAD THREE CHANCES TO PASS THE BAR OR THE ENTIRE FAMILY WOULD DISOWN HIM.
HE FAILED TWICE ON PURPOSE. HE'S A CRUDE, MASOCHISTIC PERV, SO DON'T GET TOO ATTACHED TO HIM.
ENOUGH, MR. KATAGIRI. THAT HAP-PENED A LONG TIME AGO.
Mr. Todo had just taken her to see Mr. Crocodile-face
Honest talk after a teary reunion

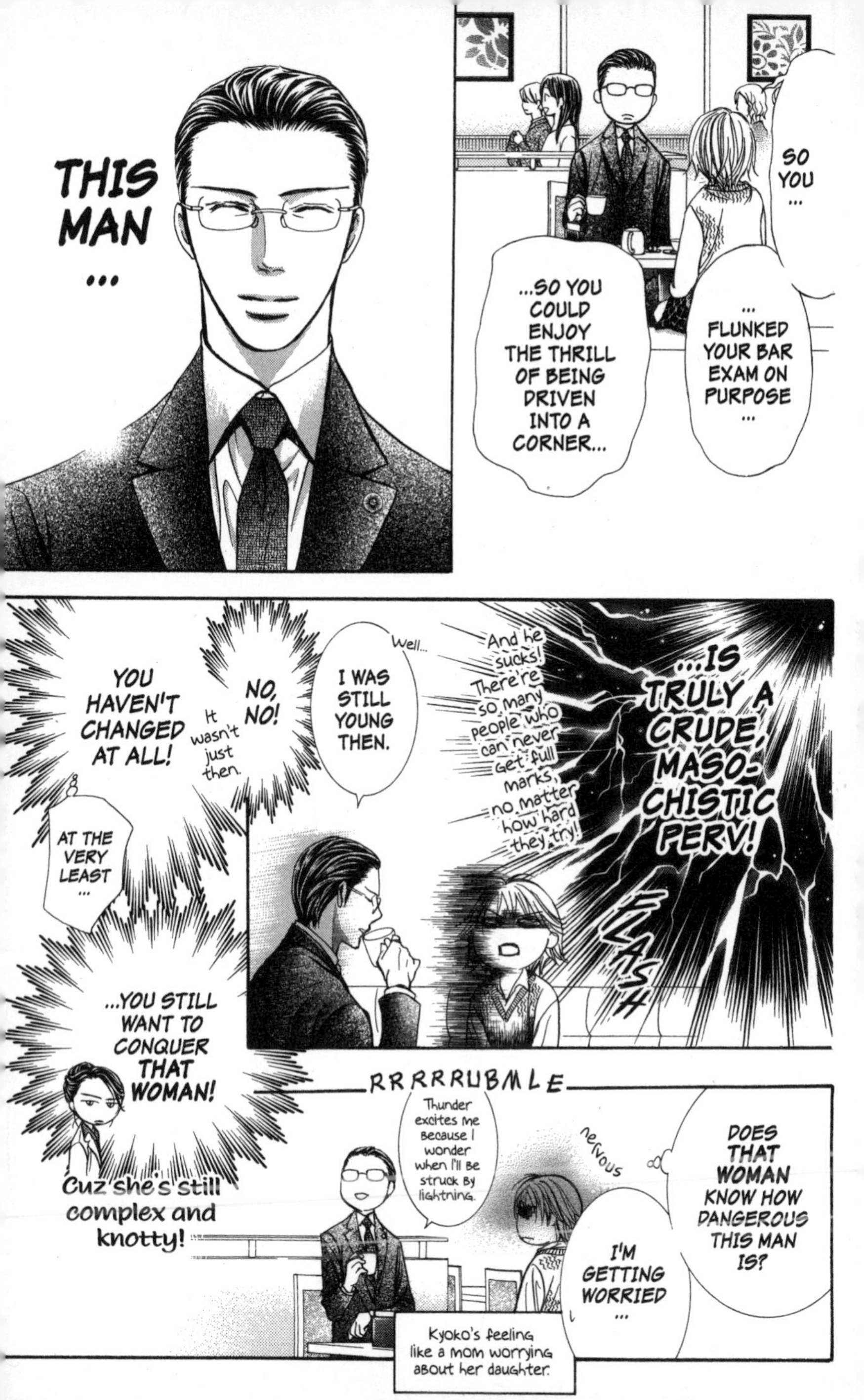
SO YOU ...
... FLUNKED YOUR BAR EXAM ON PURPOSE ...
...SO YOU COULD ENJOY THE THRILL OF BEING DRIVEN INTO A CORNER...
THIS MAN ...
...IS TRULY A CRUDE, MASOCHISTIC PERV!
FLASH
And he sucks! There're so many people who can never get full marks, no matter how hard they try!
Well...
I WAS STILL YOUNG THEN.
NO, NO!
It wasn't just then.
YOU HAVEN'T CHANGED AT ALL!
AT THE VERY LEAST ...
...YOU STILL WANT TO CONQUER THAT WOMAN!
Cuz she's still complex and knotty!
RRRRRUBMLE
DOES THAT WOMAN KNOW HOW DANGEROUS THIS MAN IS?
nervous
I'M GETTING WORRIED ...
Thunder excites me because I wonder when I'll be struck by lightning.
Kyoko's feeling like a mom worrying about her daughter.

Skip-Beat! End Notes
Everyone knows how to be a fan, but sometimes cool things from other cultures need a little help crossing the language barrier.

Page 104, panel 5: White Day
In Japan, White Day occurs exactly one month after Valentine's Day and is a chance for boys and men to give reciprocal presents to the ladies in their lives.

Page 115, panel 2: Lotus reminded me
The kanji Ren uses for his name means "lotus."

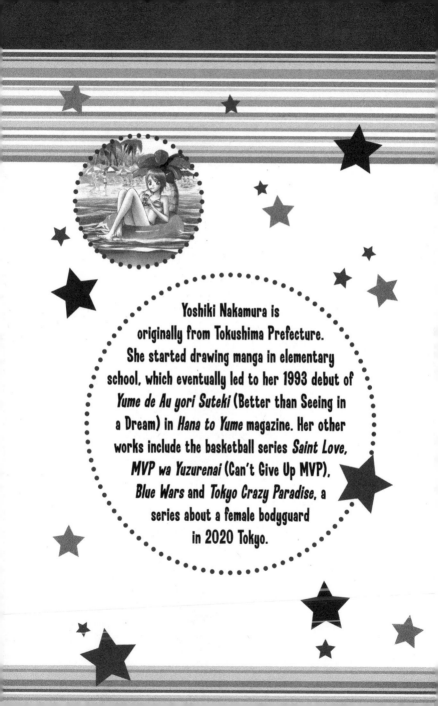

Yoshiki Nakamura is originally from Tokushima Prefecture. She started drawing manga in elementary school, which eventually led to her 1993 debut of *Yume de Au yori Suteki* (Better than Seeing in a Dream) in *Hana to Yume* magazine. Her other works include the basketball series *Saint Love*, *MVP wa Yuzurenai* (Can't Give Up MVP), *Blue Wars* and *Tokyo Crazy Paradise*, a series about a female bodyguard in 2020 Tokyo.

SKIP·BEAT!

Vol. 39

Shojo Beat Edition

STORY AND ART BY YOSHIKI NAKAMURA

English Translation & Adaptation/Tomo Kimura
Touch-up Art & Lettering/Sabrina Heep
Design/Veronica Casson
Editor/Pancha Diaz

Printed in the U.S.A.

Published by VIZ Media, LLC
P.O. Box 77010
San Francisco, CA 94107

www.viz.com

www.shojobeat.com

10 9 8 7 6 5 4 3 2 1
First printing, September 2017

PARENTAL ADVISORY
SKIP·BEAT! is rated T for Teen and is recommended for ages 13 and up. This volume contains a grudge.
ratings.viz.com

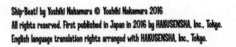

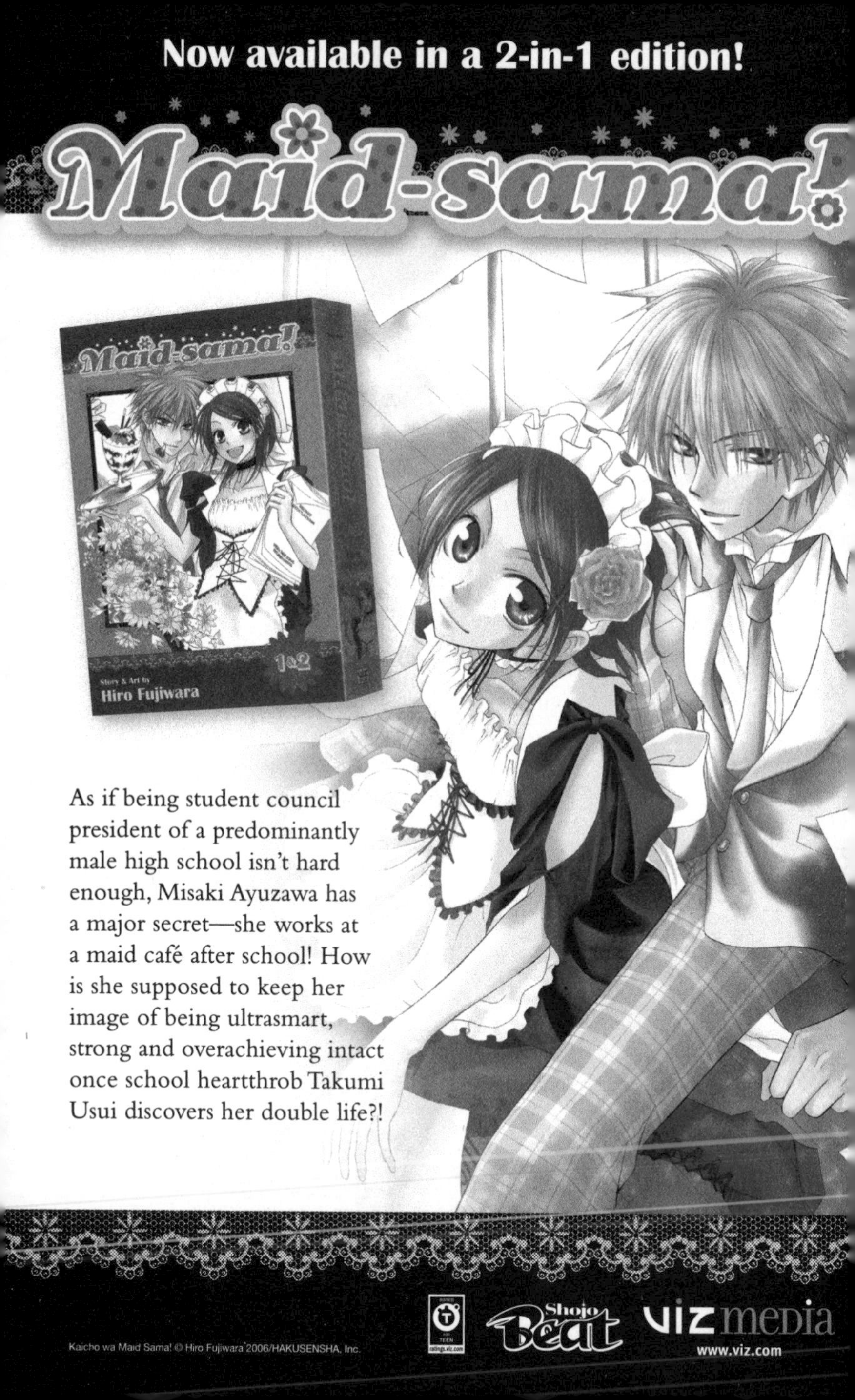
Now available in a 2-in-1 edition!
Maid-sama!
Maid-sama!
1&2
Story & Art by
Hiro Fujiwara
As if being student council president of a predominantly male high school isn't hard enough, Misaki Ayuzawa has a major secret—she works at a maid café after school! How is she supposed to keep her image of being ultrasmart, strong and overachieving intact once school heartthrob Takumi Usui discovers her double life?!
Kaicho wa Maid Sama! © Hiro Fujiwara 2006/HAKUSENSHA, Inc.
Shojo Beat
VIZ media
www.viz.com

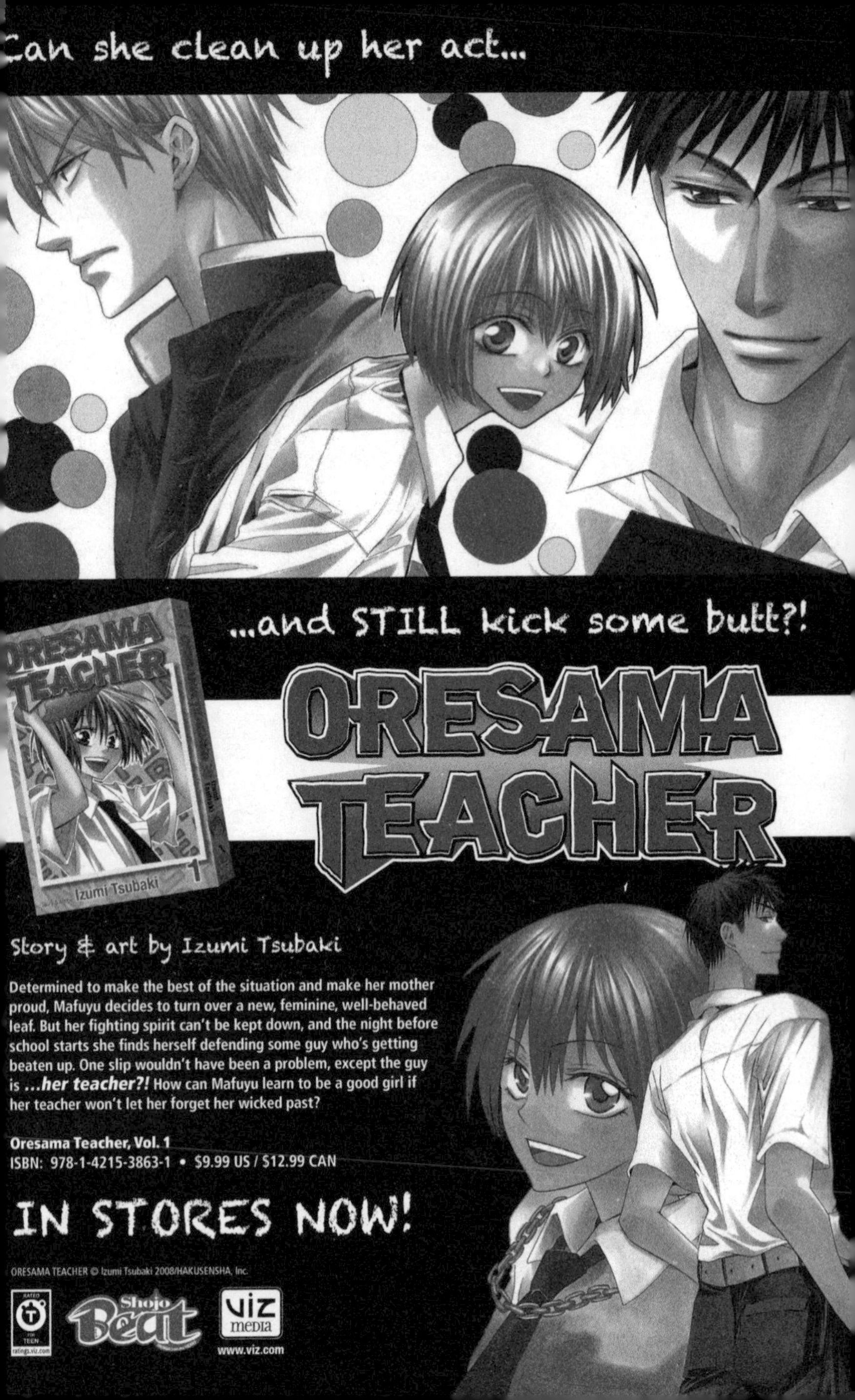
Can she clean up her act...
...and STILL kick some butt?!
ORESAMA TEACHER
ORESAMA TEACHER
Izumi Tsubaki
1
Story & art by Izumi Tsubaki
Determined to make the best of the situation and make her mother proud, Mafuyu decides to turn over a new, feminine, well-behaved leaf. But her fighting spirit can't be kept down, and the night before school starts she finds herself defending some guy who's getting beaten up. One slip wouldn't have been a problem, except the guy is ...her teacher?! How can Mafuyu learn to be a good girl if her teacher won't let her forget her wicked past?
Oresama Teacher, Vol. 1
ISBN: 978-1-4215-3863-1 • $9.99 US / $12.99 CAN
IN STORES NOW!
ORESAMA TEACHER © Izumi Tsubaki 2008/HAKUSENSHA, Inc.
RATED T FOR TEEN
ratings.viz.com
Shojo Beat
viz media
www.viz.com

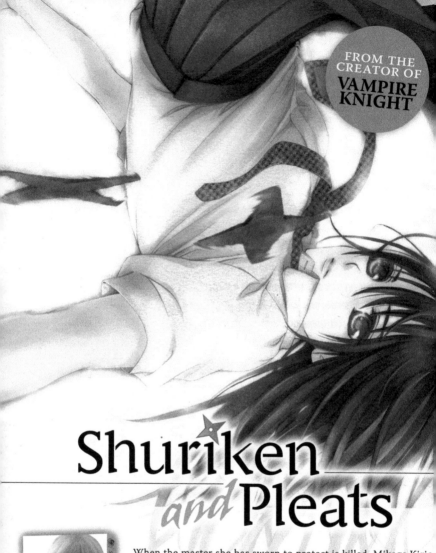

Shuriken *and* Pleats

When the master she has sworn to protect is killed, Mikage Kirio, a skilled ninja, travels to Japan to start a new, peaceful life for herself. But as soon as she arrives, she finds herself fighting to protect the life of Mahito Wakashimatsu, a man who is under attack by a band of ninja. From that time on, Mikage is drawn deeper into the machinations of his powerful family.

Kamisama Kiss

Story and art by **Julietta Suzuki**

What's a newly fledged godling to do?

Nanami Momozono is alone and homeless after her dad skips town to evade his gambling debts and the debt collectors kick her out of her apartment.

So when a m
offers her his
opportunity.
his place is a
Nanami has
taken over hi
local deity!

Now a hit anime series!

Available n

viz.com

Kamisama Hajimemashita © Julietta Suzuki 2008/HAKUSENSHA,Inc.

SURPRISE!

You may be reading the wrong way!

It's true: In keeping with the original Japanese comic format, this book reads from right to left—so action, sound effects, and word balloons are completely reversed. This preserves the orientation of the original artwork—plus, it's fun! Check out the diagram shown here to get the hang of things, and then turn to the other side of the book to get started!

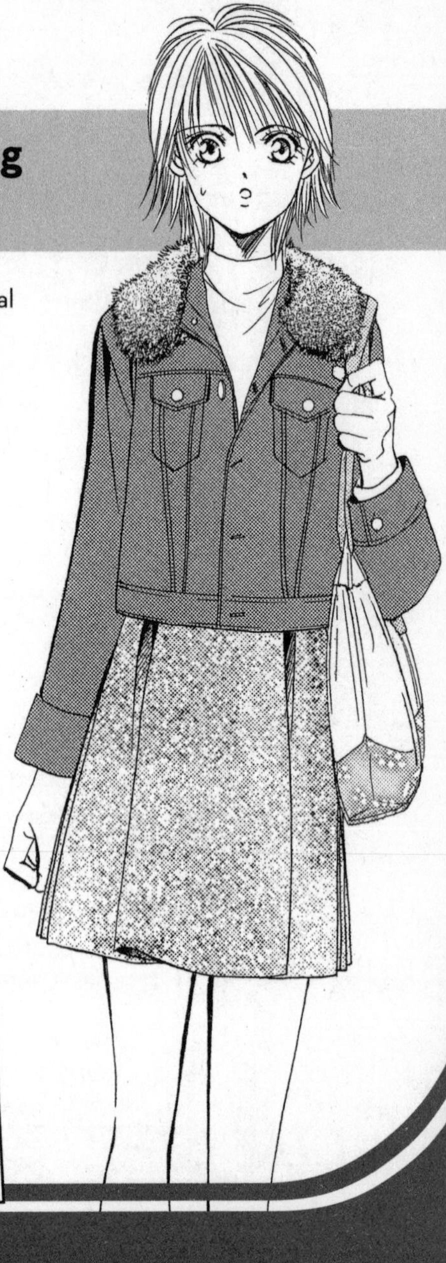

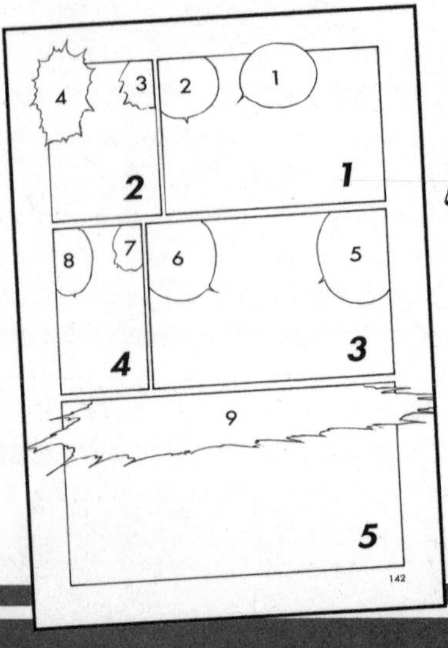
1
2
1
3
4
2
5
6
3
7
8
4
9
5
142